MW00769540

Preacher Behind the White Hoods

A Critical Examination of

William Branham and his Message

JOHN ANDREW COLLINS

Copyright © 2020
John Andrew Collins.
All rights reserved.

Dark Mystery Publications
ISBN: 9781735160900

"The great revolution in the history of man, past, present and future,
is the revolution of those determined to be free."
- *John F. Kennedy (35th President of the United States)*

Table of Contents

CHAPTER 1

JEFFERSONVILLE CHILDHOOD

"We were raised in the mountains of Kentucky[1]"

For those of us in the "Message", Jeffersonville, Indiana was a very sacred place. During Easter each year, "Message" believers from all parts of the world made their way to the city of Jeffersonville, Indiana, just north of Louisville, Kentucky. My family was no different. Like other families in the religious movement; we had immediate family, extended family, and close friends that lived in or near the Jeffersonville area. Friends and family, however, were not what brought us to the small Southern Indiana town. Our journey was a pilgrimage of religious intent, and our focus was on "heavenly things", not the things — or people — of this world. Still, we were happy to be together again.

I can still remember making the long trip before my family migrated from the Midwest back to Jeffersonville. I remember the "spiritual" thoughts that went through our minds as we looked out the window of our vehicle and watched the rolling fields pass by. We were headed to a place that felt just like home, even if "home" was hundreds of miles away and very few of my memories of Jeffersonville had my immediate family or myself in them.

My memories were similar to the memories of others who made the pilgrimage to Jeffersonville: memories of the life and times of William Marrion[2] Branham, the man we believed to be the "prophet" for our

---

[1] Branham, William. 1951, Jul 22. Life Story

"age". They were memories of a humble man with very humble beginnings as a curious child raised in a one-room log cabin in Kentucky with his siblings[3]. Vivid images of memories he shared about being a young boy trapping and fishing to feed his family in the hills of Kentucky flooded my mind at just the thought of hearing his "Life Story". At an early age, the "prophet" had migrated to Jeffersonville, IN, where he would continue his Huckleberry –Finn lifestyle long into his adulthood.

I thought about his early days as a young minister. How painful it must have been to suffer the trials that he faced! The loss of his first wife and daughter during the Great Flood of 1937 must have been more than he could bear. Yet he prevailed for the sole purpose of giving us the "Message", which we believed to be sent by God Himself to prepare us for the soon coming destruction of the United States.

It was Easter, a time most Christians celebrated the resurrection of Jesus Christ. "Message" believers from all parts of the world traveled to the "prophet's" hometown in Jeffersonville each Easter. There were events and gatherings almost every day during the week of Easter; from picnics at the local parks and singing in buildings or rooms rented for the occasion; to speeches, sermons, and testimonies in practically every place people could gather. We crowded into rented spaces and the living rooms of local "Message" families. Sure, other Christians were also celebrating the birth and resurrection of Jesus Christ, but we were celebrating much, much more. We came together in reverence for the "prophet" and his "Message". When our car crossed the bridge over the Ohio River into Jeffersonville, we could almost feel the presence of Someone greater. It was very exciting, even for us children; and not just because of the events scheduled to entertain the children and young adults. I looked eagerly through the window of our car, watching the memories came to life and thinking about the places the "prophet" described in his recorded sermons. As the buildings whizzed by, the windows of our vehicle became moving pictures of those memories; from the mighty Ohio River to the turn-of-the-century buildings and the people out walking on city sidewalks. This was the "prophet's" city!

---

[2] William *Marvin* Branham according to his draft card
[3] Branham, William. 1959, Apr 19. My Life Story

Jeffersonville was the city "chosen by God" for the "prophet" to build his Tabernacle. We were told that "angels" lined the walls of that building. It was a sacred, hallowed place. The building itself was nothing fancy to look upon, just a simple red brick building that sat on a corner of a small neighborhood city block downtown. It had two glass entry doors that opened to a tiny foyer where one of the church's deacons usually stood to smile and shake hands as the faithful entered. Above the door to the building hung an eagle, wings spread, holding an actual sword in its talons. The sword had been replaced several times, and it had drawn significant interest in the local community — especially that of the ne'er-do-wells who would steal the weapon from time to time for their own dastardly purpose.

Across the street from the church to the south and to the west sat rows of small houses, almost close enough to one another for occupants to shake hands with each other through adjacent windows. Sometimes people sitting on their front porches would smile and wave at us as we made our way down the sidewalk towards the Tabernacle. We smiled and waved back, and I often wondered if they knew the "prophet" or the reason why we gathered. People who lived closest to the Tabernacle were not so friendly, however, and did not seem to view our gathering favorably. I'm sure that it must have made their lives difficult before and after services as the crowds flowed out of the building and into the streets in front of their homes.

When my journey began, the little red brick building was just as I remembered it as a child. The small, one-story, building could barely hold all of the people that flooded into it each Easter. So many men, women, and children arrived each year that the church purchased the properties to the north and two properties to the west for additional parking. In the new lot adjacent to the Tabernacle, a large tent was sometimes setup for the overflow. Visitors sat and listened to the sermon over loudspeakers that were connected to a short-wave radio, installed in the church during the time that the "prophet" was alive. Many families, including my own, sometimes chose to sit in the comfortable seats of our vehicles with the air conditioner running while we listened to the service over the radio. The weather in the Ohio River

Valley was unpredictable, and you never knew whether it might be raining, hot and humid, or shivering cold.

Regardless of where we chose to listen, the level of excitement was always the same. All of us: men, women, and children, were eager to hear more about the "prophet". The service itself was nothing that would excite most people. It included only a simple, humble song service with a piano and an organ that transitioned into "Sunday School" and finally the sermon. The "prophet" had instructed my grandfather to avoid all instruments except for the piano and organ in the Tabernacle, and Grandpa had continued that instruction as though it were written in the stone tablets of Moses and handed down through the ages as the final decision. Slow songs were typically favored, since clapping hands during the song service was also frowned upon. Visitors from other "Message" churches did not share the same set of rules and were unaware of the format for the Branham Tabernacle's song service. Sometimes they clapped their hands during songs that their churches sang with greater enthusiasm, so it was easy to tell the visitors from the home crowd.

"Sunday School", which I often referred to as the "sermon before the sermon", consisted of my grandfather sharing his testimony of the times he spent with William Branham. He followed the format of what was typically used for sermons in other "Message" churches that I had frequently visited, so it sounded much like a sermon. The collection plates were passed, and after each person contributed, the service changed in focus from worship to teaching. Grandpa opened by reading a passage from the Bible, sometimes asking the congregation to read every other verse of a chapter in Psalms from the Old Testament, and then preached a sermon that might or might not be related to the text or psalm that introduced "Sunday School". This did not seem unusual to me at the time; it was very similar to the format used by other churches, and the majority of the "prophet's" own sermons were not based upon the opening quote from the Bible that introduced the sermon. The most important part of Sunday School, as it related to the Branham Tabernacle and other "Message" churches, were the quotes from the "prophet". Both sermons and "Sunday School" began with a quote from the Bible, but almost every "proof text" used to solidify each topic was a

10

quote from one or more of the "prophet's" sermons. To an outsider looking in, if the first ten minutes of the speech were omitted, it would seem as though the speaker were preaching from the "book of the prophet" instead of the Bible. Rightfully so, for some people refer to the "prophet's" sermons as the "Spoken Word of God".

After Sunday school, a second offering was collected. "The offering after the offering," I often thought. It always struck me funny as I watched people around me carefully divide their money into two, separate donations for the two offerings collected. Many visitors felt uncomfortable not placing money in the basket on the second collection taken. Those who did not give *twice* looked at us apologetically as they handed us the basket without putting any money in it. One person whispered, "I put money in the *other* basket!" as if we were watching them far too closely. When the second offering was collected, the sermon began.

Easter sermons were something special for those who lived in Jeffersonville. Very few guest speakers were invited to speak at the Branham Tabernacle. In fact, very few speakers *spoke* in the Tabernacle — including my grandfather. Grandpa "preached*"* "Sunday School", but then introduced the "prophet" for the main sermon. Introducing the "prophet" consisted of giving a brief testimony of his memories for that particular sermon, announcing its title, sometimes describing its audience or location, and asking his assistant in the "tape room" to press "play" on the cassette tape recording over the PA system in the building. Easter was different, though. Some Easter meetings used the same format, and visitors from around the world were given printed transcripts from the recorded sermon to read as the "prophet" preached for as long as two-and-a-half hours. On some occasions, however, guest speakers were allowed to preach. For me, these were most exciting. Our family had the entire collection of the "prophet's" recorded sermons, and I had listened to each one of the recordings several times. Hearing something new, a new insight into the "Message" and the "prophet", was something I rarely had the opportunity to experience. Even as a child, I looked forward to hearing guest speakers at Easter.

The sermons preached by "Message" church leaders were very emotional, no matter the event. The format of each sermon by each

11

speaker was very similar, matching the same format the "prophet" used for his sermons and guest speaking arrangements. They began in a very calm and reserved manner, relaxing the audience and making listeners feel at ease. Heartwarming, stories, usually stories that all listeners could relate to were used to instill a sense of comfort and familiarity. Sometimes they were stories about the "prophet" and the speaker's experiences during the "prophet's" life. Often brief stories were used, sometimes comical ones, "warming up" the audience for the burst of excitement about to come. As the service continued, the pace of words gradually increased until an explosion of rapid sentences left the speaker screaming and gasping for breath. At the beginning, microphones and loudspeakers were required to hear the speaker's very careful and articulate statements. By the end however, the volume overpowered the system so badly that if not for his voice echoing through the building, not a single word could have been understood. It was unfortunate for those of us in our vehicles or in the tent outside, for there were times when we had no idea what was being said.

Many "Message" speakers in many different countries and regions within those countries had many different styles of speaking, but their theme was always the same. The time of the "prophet's" apocalyptic predictions was upon us, and the Rapture should have already taken place. The sermons often reminded us that we were living on "borrowed time". They reminded us that the world was soon coming to a tragic and horrific end, and that we must continue living the "prophet's" specific version of the Pentecostal Holiness lifestyle in order to escape damnation. The "prophet's" name was mentioned frequently and emphatically.

As children, some of us didn't really think too much about the world ending; but when we grew into adults, we were often reminded. We believed that William Branham was sent to warn us of the events leading to the End of Days, and each speaker felt it was their sworn duty to maintain the same level of urgency in their sermons as did the "prophet" decades before.

After the service, it was as though floodgates for the Ohio River were opened at the front, sides, and back of the Branham Tabernacle. From the inside coming out, it seemed to take ten minutes to make a single step as lines flowed from each of the pews into the center aisles or to each side of the building to a tiny exit. Watching from the outside, it was like watching fireworks explode from inside; people quickly poured out into the streets to the west and south and into the parking lot adjacent to the building. Deacons attempted to corral the people out of the streets in accordance with city ordinances but with the heavy volume of people flooding into the streets, the tiny ropes they used did very little to stop the multitude.

We stood together, sometimes for hours, talking to fellow "Message" believers from all parts of the world. Looking back, these were special times. Many fond memories were made and many bonds of friendship were created that seemed strong enough never to be broken. We had special ties that bound us together, ties that the rest of the world did not have. We had the "Message". We knew the "prophet" almost personally, and we knew his words intimately.

During those times, I could have never even dreamed about the journey that would lie ahead. The thought of leaving the "Message" or its people was so foreign to me that I would have gladly faced death before ever considering it. I had no reason to leave. The "Message" was presented as absolute, verified truth that had been vindicated through time. No question had been asked that could not have been answered, and no answer had been given that could not have been unequivocally proven by the "prophet's" own words. Or so I thought, because so I had been told. *"It is more accurate and up-to-date than today's newspaper,"* my grandfather often said. *"If you have any doubt, just play a 'tape', and see whether or not it works out exactly as it should be"*.

Little did I know that the road ahead would look much different than the road left behind, or that the "unbreakable" bonds of friendship would become fragile and quickly severed with a single question. The journey in front of me would be surprising, painful, eventful, and sometimes unbelievable. When I first began to research the "prophet" and his "Message", there were many stones overturned that had not been moved for decades. What I found underneath those stones had been carefully concealed by many men and women who stood much to gain.

13

As much as it would pain me to slowly realize, some of those involved in controlling that information were very close to me.

CHAPTER 2

WHY LITTLE JEFFERSONVILLE

"Near a city called New Albany[4]"

In the "Message", our churches were a little different than other Christian churches. Other churches talked about the Bible like we did, but "Message" pastors focused on what the "prophet" said about the Bible. It was common for an entire sermon about a particular passage from the Biblical narrative to use only quotes from the "prophet" to describe that narrative — without using a single reference from any book in the Bible. This severely limited the number of Bible topics from which to base sermons. The "prophet" did not discuss many books of the Bible and many chapters from numerous books in the Bible were never mentioned in his recorded sermons. "Message" pastors did, from time to time, read or quote passages from the Bible. Usually this happened at the beginning of the sermons, with the "prophet's" statements used as references for the climax or focal point of the sermon.

In addition to Scriptural subject matter, "message" pastors included history and events of the "prophet's" life in their sermon content. Some pastors had known the "prophet" personally and had many stories to tell. Others had studied the sermons of the "prophet" and knew his words from those sermons intimately. The "prophet" often spoke about himself, his life and his history. When he did, they were often

---

[4] Branham, William. 1953, Nov 4. Deep Calleth Unto the Deep.

paralleling stories in the Bible, but not parallels that the general public would know or understand.

Growing up as children in the "Message", these stories held us captivated. When our parents played stories of the way he trapped, fished, and hunted in the Kentucky wilderness; it was like listening to stories about the Adventures of Huckleberry Finn. In fact, most of us preferred those stories *over* reading Mark Twain. The adventures of the "prophet" enriched our lives. As children, they were our favorite part of the "sermon".

One story that I remember as a child was often repeated in our church. The "prophet" told how his mother would pour "coon grease"[5] into the eyes of his seven brothers and himself while living in Kentucky[6].

In his sermons, the "prophet" had joked about the unbelievers who could not see or believe the things that we knew and believed. "They need some coon grease to open their eyes!"

In some of our homes, we had black-and-white photographs, paintings, carvings, and even embroideries of the "prophet's" log cabin in Kentucky. I often thought how the "prophet" must have loved growing up in those hills, far away from civilization. The houses in Jeffersonville, Indiana, would have seemed much different than the "humble little shack" in Kentucky as it was called.

When we thought about Jeffersonville, we thought about the Tabernacle. We never thought about it being the big city of William Branham's childhood. Most of us had never seen photos of historical Jeffersonville[7], and those of us who did never pictured William Branham in them. When the "prophet" spoke of his childhood, the scenes he described painted pictures in our minds much like the photos of the log cabin in Kentucky; clear and free for as far as the eye could see.

---

[5] Branham, William. 1958, Mar 30. Christ Knocking at the Door. "And every time we'd get sore eyes, or mattered eyes from a bad cold, mama would go get this coon grease and rub it in our eyes, so it would take the bad cold out and get the matter out of our eyes."

[6] Branham, William. 1959, Apr 19. My Life Story. "I was born in a little mountain cabin, way up in the mountains of Kentucky. They had one room that we lived in, no rug on the floor, not even wood on the floor, it was just simply a bare floor. And a stump, top of a stump cut off with three legs on it, that was our table. And all those little Branhams would pile around there, and out on the front of the little old cabin, and wallowed out, looked like where a bunch of opossums had been wallowing out there in the dust, you know, all the little brothers. There was nine of us, and one little girl"

[7] Digital Collections. Accessed Aug 17, 2018 from *https://jefflibrary.org/local-history/digital-collections*

Looking over the historic photographs, however, I realized that Jeffersonville was not a barren wilderness. It was filled with industry and entertainment. Streets were filled with automobiles, rivers with steamboats. Towering buildings lined the busy streets as people scurried down the sidewalks about their daily lives. Bicycles wove in-and-out of the traffic, careful not to run into the people crossing the streets to the local businesses, bars, and casinos.[8] Familiar as we were with his stories of backwoods life, never for a minute would we have envisioned the young "prophet" in a bustling casino town![9]

We associated the photos of his cabin that the "prophet" gave us to his childhood, just as he intended. We made paintings of the cabin, sang songs about it, and listened to stories about it in many, many sermons. Our children made wood crafts of the cabin. Some of us took trips to its location in Burkesville, KY, near the Cumberland River. We never knew that the "prophet's" cabin was used as a "prop", or that in 1948, the "prophet" said that the cabin sat beneath a housing project.[10] We were not aware that the Branham family moved to Indiana before his third birthday.[11] The images of the growing metropolis on Spring Street in Jeffersonville are not what we associated with William Branham's childhood. We gave our children coloring books, told them stories, and even acted out plays describing the "prophet's" adolescent and teenage years in the wilderness, far away from civilization.[12]

As important as the City of Jeffersonville was to the "Message", it's hard to believe that most of us never studied its history. For many who lived outside the state of Indiana and abroad, it would have been difficult to study, especially before the internet. Those who lived in Jeffersonville and the surrounding area, however, have for years had access to a wealth of historical knowledge through the local libraries and government facilities.

If this place was "chosen by God", why did He choose it? Looking back, I'm surprised that more people were not curious. Jeffersonville, Indiana, has a fascinating history. Jeffersonville was the first

[8] Historic Photos of Jeffersonville. Accessed Aug 16, 2018 *from https://www.pinterest.com/parisfrance/historic-photos-jeffersonville*

[9] Gambling Houses, Night Clubs Are Closed, Dark. 1924, July 29. Indianapolis News

[10] Branham, William. 1948, Oct. Life Story of Rev. Wm. Branham. The Voice of Healing.

[11] Fourteenth Census of the United States (Birth locations of siblings)

[12] Multimedia. Accessed Aug 13, 2018 from https://cubcorner.org/en/multimedia

Underground Railroad route crossing the Ohio River[13]. It was a strategic hub for the Union Army during the Civil War.[14] The railroad bridge enabled the Union Army to send supplies to troops in the South.[15] Jeffersonville was home to Port Fulton and the Howard Shipyards,[16] which employed thousands of people in Jeffersonville and the surrounding area. It was the largest inland shipbuilding site in America from the years 1834-1942. Ed Howard, son of Howard Shipyards owner James Howard, owned the oldest Haynes automobile in the United States.[17] The Quartermaster Depot served as a storage facility for Union supplies. During WWII, it was used to house German prisoners of war.[18] So many were held there, in fact, that they were given jobs that Jeffersonvillians wanted. It was later occupied by the "prophet's" sons for distributing the "Message"[19] and used to grow a multi-million-dollar[20] publishing company called "Voice of God" Recordings, named for a quote by William Branham *"I am God's Voice to you".*[21] Jeffersonville was home to the Indiana State Prison. It was also home to illicit gambling casinos.

Though it seems like a quiet little town today, that was not always the case. At one time, the city was booming with activity. The monkeys were a big attraction at the greyhound races[22], bringing crowds of people from multiple states to watch monkeys riding on the backs of the dogs as miniature jockeys.[23]. The city's liquor and gaming attracted famous mob bosses.[24] The criminal activity in the city was such a problem that it was frequently discussed in city council meetings.[25] City officials

---

[13] Clark County Indiana History. Accessed Aug 13, 2018 from *https://www.co.clark.in.us/index.php/about-clark-county-indiana/clark-county-indiana-history*
[14] Jeffersonville Quartermaster Intermediate Depot; History and Functions. Accessed July 18, 2018 from *https://www.qmfound.com/article/jeffersonville-quartermaster-intermediate-depot-history-and-functions*
[15] "Camp Joe Holt and Jefferson General Hospital Photographs, 1865, Collection Guide." Indiana Historical Society.
[16] Howard Steamboat Museum. Accessed Aug 16, 2018 *from http://www.howardsteamboatmuseum.org*
[17] Indiana Man to Get New Haynes for Old Timer. 1916, Oct 13. Santa Cruz Evening News
[18] Jeffersonville Quartermaster Intermediate Depot; History and Functions. Accessed July 18, 2018 from *https://www.qmfound.com/article/jeffersonville-quartermaster-intermediate-depot-history-and-functions*
[19] Quadrangle is not up for sale; preservationists disappointed. 1995, Oct 26. The Courier-Journal.
[20] Return of Organization Exempt from Income Tax. From 990. 2010, Voice of God Recordings, Inc
[21] "I am God's Voice to You". Branham, William. 1951, May 5. "My Commission"
[22] Dog Race Crowds Came to Drink Pop. 1938, Jul 9. The Courier-Journal.
[23] After Dog Racing in Jeffersonville. 1929, Aug 8. Greenfield Daily Reporter
[24] 12 Louisville Secrets You Had No Idea Existed. Accessed Aug 18, 2018 from *https://www.thrillist.com/entertainment/louisville/louisville-secrets-you-had-no-idea-existed*
[25] 'Cleanup' Is Planned for Jeffersonville. 1922, Jan 10. Courier Journal

feared Jeffersonville streets would be just as dangerous as Chicago, and, Jeffersonville became nicknamed "Little Las Vegas"[26].

...

When you look at Jeffersonville, Indiana today, it is a quiet, peaceful town. It's hard to picture it as a city that attracted visitors from all across the country in the early 1900's. Jeffboat, formerly Howard Shipyards, which once provided thousands of jobs, is no longer in business.[27] When compared to the other side of the river, Jeffersonville has always seemed insignificant.

When I was in the "Message", I used to wonder what brought the Branham family to Jeffersonville. Most "Message" believers knew William Branham and his nuclear family, but very few knew William Branham's extended family. William Branham's siblings never spent much time with the "Message".

I also wondered why "Message" believers in Jeffersonville had been told that all historical records were destroyed during the 1937 flood. I was surprised when a "Message" brother and sister told me they found that most records had survived.[28] I wondered if the Jeffersonville Library held any clues to the Branham family migration from Kentucky. They said that some of the records were stored in the Indiana Room of the Jeffersonville Public Library. When I got there, I was overwhelmed by the amount of information stored in one single room! Practically every aspect of Indiana history was contained in books on the shelves. And if the shelves didn't have something, it could easily be ordered. I was most interested in the local newspaper archives. Before modern social media, newspapers printed stories about all social events, big and small. From locals leaving town to visit relatives to new families arriving, the local newspapers would tell it all.

---

[26] Nokes, Garry J. 2002. Jeffersonville, Indiana. "Jeffersonville will always be remembered as a gambling town on account of its "decades of decadence" in the 1930s and 40s. Some have dubbed the city "Little Las Vegas"

[27] Hitting Bottom: Barge builder Jeffboat closes amid weak demand, oversupply. Accessed 2020, May 5 from *https://www.workboat.com/news/coastal-inland-waterways/barge-builder-jeffboat/*

[28] Later published findings: According To His Own Purpose And Grace. Accessed 2020, May 15 from *searchingforvindication.com/2014/01/14/According-To-His-Own-Purpose-And-Grace/*

Large cabinets with rows of long, thin drawers held hundreds, thousands of boxes containing rolls of microfiche. Each drawer held several years' worth of newspapers, all labeled and in chronological order, dating back to the 1800s. For as long as newspapers had been printed, they had been captured in the tiny little images of the microfiche rolls, like snapshots in time capturing each day of Jeffersonville history.

It took me a while to remember how to use a microfiche projector. I hadn't had to use one since my school days, and even then, I'm certain that a teacher or librarian had loaded the reel into the machine. In the age of computers and technology, this was a skill that had gotten a little rusty! The friendly staff at the library helped me, though, and I was on my way.

Getting the projector working, however, was the easy part. There were literally hundreds of thousands of newspaper articles and using this older technology, they cannot be indexed or searched. Unlike a computer query in an internet browser, each reel must be loaded, viewed, and actually read in order to find results for any search. It was a painstaking process, especially since I didn't even know what I was looking for. One thing was for certain: I became a familiar face at the library! During lunch, after work, sometimes before work, I scanned through article after article, issue after issue.

The first thing I was curious about was the actual loss of records — *if any* — because of the 1937 flood. Since we had been told that all newspapers confirming the "prophet's" stories were destroyed in the flood waters, and since I now stood before drawers dating back to the 1800s, I wanted to know *what* was missing. I was certain that the water would have had some impact, especially for any archives that were stored on the first floors of buildings. To my surprise, not a single issue was missing! The newspaper appeared to have shut down for a brief period when the flood hit, but reporters were on the scene covering the disaster *and printing it* as the disaster unfolded.

Once I had completely reversed the claim that records were destroyed, I knew that I had my work cut out for me. As I scrolled through the pages on the film, scanning each and every article on each and every page, I realized that the newspapers could hold the keys to unlocking an insight into the "prophet's" life that most of us had never seen or even heard about. I was surprised that other local "Message" believers hadn't found this treasure trove!

Using genealogy tools, other researchers had created William Branham's family tree.[29] I was also surprised that the tree didn't have very many branches! William Branham's father Charles was the son of George Branham and Mary Shaw. In 1910, nine years before William Branham's grandfather died, there was an announcement in the Jeffersonville Evening News. Benjamin Lockard and George Branham moved to Jeffersonville from Cumberland, Kentucky.[30] Could this be William Branham's grandfather? Charles Branham's father?

Sometime between 1909 and 1913, Charles and Ella Branham moved to Indiana. Melvin, Edgar, Jesse, and Charles Jr. were all born in Indiana starting at 1913. Only William and Edward (Humpy) would have been in the Kentucky cabin, according to the United States Census.[31]

There were other interesting facts found in the archives. From 1898 to 1902, Thomas E. Rader was the mayor of Jeffersonville.[32] Rader was a name that I was familiar with. Paul Rader, was a famous radio minister[33] and second president of the Christian and Missionary Alliance who wrote the hit song Elvis Presley sang, "Only Believe"[34]. It was a song we sang often in the "Message" churches. The "prophet" used it for his theme song.[35] Mayor Rader's son, Ralph Rader, was a minister involved with the Christian and Missionary Alliance Church,[36] and no doubt would have also used this song in his Jeffersonville church. Paul Rader was a relative.[37]

The Branham family was not religious, according to William Branham.[38] They would not have been interested in the Raders or other

---

[29] Duyzer, Peter. 2014. Legend of the Fall.

[30] Personals. 1910, May 10. Jeffersonville Evening News. "Benjamin Lockard and George Branham arrived yesterday from Cumberland, Ky., to locate to this city."

[31] Fourteenth Census of the United States: 1920. (lists birthplaces and ages, Edward listed by his midde name Winferd)

[32] It Is Now Mayor Rader. 1898, Sept 4. Courier Journal.

[33] The Raders. Who's Who in America. 1936-1939. Volume 20.

[34] Only Believe. Accessed 2020, May 15 from *https://www.cmalliance.org/alife/only-believe/*

[35] Branham, William. 1950, Apr 5. Expectation. "And ever since then, it's been the campaign theme song, "Only Believe."

[36] Christian Missionary Alliance. 1930, Nov 25. "revival meeting at the Christian and Missionary Alliance Church by the Rev. Ralph Rader, evangelist of Jeffersonville."

[37] Raders Start Revival Drive in Indianapolis. 1930, Oct 2. Jeffersonville Evening News.

[38] Branham, William. 1953, Jun 14. I Perceived That Thou Art A Prophet. "I was a little boy of about three

ministers. If anything, they would have been more interested in Ralph Rader's gambling. In 1900, Mayor Rader's son, Ralph Rader was shot. Sixteen-year-old Ralph went to make sure Charlie Fogarty was brutally beaten. Fogarty pulled out a .38 pistol and shot Rader in the back. [39]Ralph survived, however, and after traveling west, he returned to Jeffersonville to set up his Tabernacle[40] — about the time William Branham was ordained as a minister by Roy E. Davis[41] and started preaching.[42]

There were so many distractions! So many curious bits and pieces of information that could be found in the archives! It was like a puzzle, with a thousand tiny pieces, all scattered out on the table! Still, I was curious to find what brought the Branhams to Jeffersonville. What about Jeffersonville made the Branhams leave their family in Kentucky?

In the early 1900s, after the Big 4 Bridge was built, new factories were opened. A "considerably larger force of skilled workmen" would be needed. A transportation system was developed for workers. An inter-urban trolley ran from Louisville to Charlestown and Jeffersonville, opening the door to many, many places for men and women in the surrounding area to find work. Systems of inter-urban trolleys carried workers into other cities, like something out of the movies of old New York City! They could be seen carrying passengers all around the metro area and crossed the Ohio River using the Big Four Bridge.

The "City of Jeffersonville" ferry was another option. Workers could board the ferry at the foot of Spring Street in Jeffersonville and cross over to Louisville, KY. Louisville was filled with opportunity.

Though we may never know for sure what brought the Branhams to Jeffersonville, one single name, from one single article looked as though it might provide the answer. In the "Message", we often heard how William Branham's father Charles Branham, was a driver for Mr. Otto

---

minutes old when the Angel of the Lord come the first time. My people was not religious."

[39] Mayor Rader's Son Shot. 1900, Sept 26. Courier Journal
[40] Rader Tabernacle Opening Set May 5. 1931, Mar 30. Evening News
[41] Branham, William. 1953, Nov 10. "When Doctor Davis had ordained me into the Baptist church 53-1110 - I Will Restore Rev. William Marrion Branham"
[42] Branham, William. 1962, May 31. The Conflict Between God and Satan. "We started preaching about thirty years, something, or thirty-one years ago. About 1930, '31, somewhere along in there, I started preaching the Gospel."

H. Wathen.[43] The "prophet" described Wathen as a "multi-millionaire".[44] I had found an article describing Charles Branham's arrest, and Otto Wathen posted bail. The thought suddenly struck me: "Why was a multi-millionaire posting bail money for Charles Branham?"

I knew that the answer might be found in researching Indiana's saloon history. A battle had been brewing, long before George Branham arrived. It was a battle that employed Charles Branham and gave the family living quarters. Otto H. Wathen was Indiana's Anti-Saloon League's public enemy number one.

---

[43] Branham, William. 1959, Apr 19. My Life Story. "Mr. Wathen kept ice out there in the country. And Father was a—a chauffeur for him, a private chauffeur. 59-0419A"
[44] Branham, William. 1959, Apr 19. My Life Story. "Mr. Wathen, a rich man. He owns the Wathen Distilleries. And he owned a great shares; he's a multimillionaire 59-0419A"

TIMELINE OF SIBLING BIRTHS
Timeline. Accessed Aug 18, 2018 from
http://searchingforvindication.com/timeline.html

INSIDE THE TABERNACLE
Video clip: (Part 1) Willard Collins - Testimony on William Branham (Trophy of God's Grace) -
2005-07-10 Aug 15, 2018 from https://www.youtube.com/watch?v=tJuJQMDodbE

HISTORIC PHOTOS OF JEFFERSONVILLE, INDIANA
Historic Photos of Louisville Kentucky And Environs. Accessed Aug 16, 2018 from
https://historiclouisville.weebly.com/jeffersonville.html
Historic Photos of Jeffersonville. Accessed Aug 16, 2018 from
https://www.pinterest.com/parisfrance/historic-photos-jeffersonville
Digital Collections. Accessed Aug 17, 2018 from
https://jefflibrary.org/local-history/digital-collections/
Monumental Memories. Accessed Aug 17, 2018 from
https://www.jeffmainstreet.org/downtown-revitalization/monumental-memories/

WILLIAM BRANHAM'S CABIN
A Special Day. Accessed Aug 16, 2018 from
https://branham.org/articles/442018_ASpecialDay
Life Story of Rev. Wm. Branham. 1948, Oct. The Voice of Healing.

WILLIAM BRANHAM MOVES TO INDIANA
Fourteenth Census of the United States: 1920. (lists birthplaces and ages)
Duyzer, Peter. 2014. Legend of the Fall.

GOVERNMENT DOCUMENTS
Birth Certificate: Melvin Branham.

WILLIAM BRANHAM GENEOLOGY:
Duyzer, Peter. 2014. Legend of the Fall.
Genealogy. www.geni.com.

GEORGE BRANHAM:
Personals. 1910, May 10. Jeffersonville Evening News

CHILDREN'S COLORING OF YOUNG WILLIAM BRANHAM
Multimedia. Accessed Aug 13, 2018 from *https://cubcorner.org/en/multimedia*

MAYOR RADER:
Kind Words for Jeffersonville. 1899. The National Democrat.
It Is Now Mayor Rader. 1898, Sept 4. Courier Journal.

PAUL RADER:
Jazzset Hymns Are Winning Among Heathens. 1923, May 13. Courier Journal
Amazon Jungles Hold No Terrors for Missionaries. 1922, Sep 3. Courier Journal
The Raders. Who's Who in America. 1936-1939. Volume 20.
Only Believe. Accessed from *https://www.cmalliance.org/alife/only-believe/*

Genealogy. www.geni.com.
Only Believe by Elvis Presley on Amazon Music

RALPH RADER:
Methodists Will Have Revival. 1940, Mar 8. Angola Herald
Garner Praises Song. 1933, Oct 16. El Paso Herald Post
Warns Against Light Wine and Beer Menace. 1923, Feb 8. El Paso Herald
Rader Tabernacle Opening Set May 5. 1931, Mar 30. Evening News
Pastor Fasts 27 Days to Regain Health. 1928, Jan 8. Oakland Tribune
Pastor Flays Booze, Dances. 1923, Feb 8. Oakland Tribune
Alvarado Methodist Revival. 1939, Oct 18. Steuben Republican
Jeffersonville Pastor Ralph Rader Dies. 1951, Dec 16. Courier Journal
Misc. News. 1922, Jan 22. Courier Journal
Wire Run to Residence. 1910, Mar 8. Courier Journal
Mayor Rader's Son Shot. 1900, Sept 26. Courier Journal
Cases Are Dropped. 1930, Dec 24. Evening Republican
Faith Defenders Meet Next Week. 1929, Nov 30. Hutchinson News
Salvation Army Chaplin Passes Away. 1937, Nov 4. The Times

CHARLES BRANHAM'S ARREST:
Convicted in Liquor Case. 1924, Mar 6. Evening News, Still and Liquor Found. 1924,
	Mar 6. The Courier Journal
Asks Aid for Family. 1924, Mar 4. The Courier Journal
Serves Sentence at Night. 1924, Mar 18. The Courier Journal
Hospital Sends Township Bill. 1924, Mar 21. Evening News
Hospital Bill Rendered. 1924, Mar 21. The Courier Journal
Would Eject Branham. 1924, Jul 19. The Courier Journal

OTTO WATHEN:
American Medicinal Spirits Company. Accessed Aug 18, 2018 from
	http://www.bottlebooks.com/american%20medicinal%20spirits%20company/
	american_medicinal_spirits_compa.htm
Dry Agents Bag Booze and Three Stills in Raids. 1920, Nov 14. Chicago Daily Tribune

ANTI SALOON BILL
Anti-Saloon League Fight. 1905, Apr 21. The Call Leader

CHAPTER 3

THE JEFFERSONVILLE BRANHAMS

A driver for Mr. Otto Wathen ...

During my years in the "Message", when I thought about the "prophet's" childhood, I had mental images of the barren wilderness. There were rivers and streams and nothing else besides trees for as far as the eye could see. When the "prophet" spoke about his "Kentucky childhood", fishing and trapping to help feed his mother and brothers, it made all of us want to be just like him. Boys growing up in the "Message" had an almost unnatural fondness for western belts, boots, and shirts; and they developed a love of hunting — even boys who would have under normal circumstances gravitated toward other hobbies and modern styles similar to their peers. We all wanted to live picturesque lifestyles that, if captured by black-and-white photograph, would have fit in nicely beside portraits of the "prophet" as he posed for the camera during his many excursions out west. It was the same lifestyle he had always lived, or so we heard.

From his years as youth in the hills of Kentucky, to his time working as a "game warden"[45] just north of Louisville, the "prophet" lived most of his life secluded with nature. He often told stories about his time alone with nature, whether he had been squirrel hunting or simply meditating in seclusion.

Seeing historic photos of Jeffersonville from the early 1900s was a drastic contrast to the mental images I'd had about the "prophet" and his

---

[45] Branham, William. 1950, Jan 10. Moses. "And I was a—a game warden in Indiana."

life since my youth. Jeffersonville life was far from a life of seclusion. Learning that the "prophet" left Kentucky at age three for the busy city of Jeffersonville made me want to learn more about his *real* childhood. It also raised many questions about other memories that I'd freely accepted as fact and taken for granted, memories now starting to suddenly change as I pieced the information together.

The "prophet" had a very expensive collection of guns and rifles.[46] When I thought about this collection, I focused on the long-range rifles that he would have used for hunting. Each time he told about his time in the woods hunting squirrel and small game, my memory brought up images of his .22 rifle that could tack a squirrel square between the eyes.[47] When he spoke about bear hunting, mental images of his high-powered rifles flashed through my thoughts.

As a child, I was in awe of this collection, and I wanted one just like it. I never really thought about them as anything other than hunting gear. When I grew into an adult with poor vision, those dreams never came to fruition, but I thought about them no less, and even had a small collection of my own. It was surprising to think about the collection of weapons for a person growing up in a casino town, however. The mental images which came to mind were much different. I dug out the photographs of the "prophet's gun collection to look at them once again. Many of his weapons were not intended for hunting. Some of them were designed to carry, conceal, and kill. What did the "prophet" need with *all* these weapons?

When I learned in the newspaper articles that Jeffersonville millionaire Otto H. Wathen, a kingpin in the liquor industry, paid for Charles Branham's release from a jail sentence,[48] and that William Branham was raised in the booming city of Jeffersonville instead of the backwoods of Kentucky, I couldn't help but think about the "prophet's" collection of weapons from a new and different perspective.

During our childhood in the "Message", we had seen many photos of the "prophet" hunting; very expensive safari hunting around the world.

---

[46] Brother Branham's Den in Tucson. Accessed 2020, May 15 from *http://tucsontabernacle.org/photo-gallery/tucson-arizona/brother-branham-s-den-in-tucson/*

[47] Branham, William. 1958, Oct 5. Hear His Voice. "I turned the gun, aimed up, through the little telescope sight I seen its eye, shot it, dropped down."

[48] Asks Aid for Family. 1924, Mar 4. The Courier Journal

I never really thought about how much these images felt out of place in the life of a "Kentucky boy" raised in the hills to live off the land, obeying the laws of nature. The "prophet's" big game hunts were for sport, killing for the pleasure of the kill. It was the lifestyle of the rich and famous. This is the type of hunt someone like Otto H. Wathen would have enjoyed, not a boy raised in the wilderness and trained to respect the land. Even the "prophet" himself had said that one should never kill an animal unless they intended to eat it. Yet there were photos of zebra and other exotic animals he had as trophies that he never would have eaten.

When we thought about the "prophet's" lifestyle, we pictured scenes from Bonanza or Gunsmoke. We gave our children images of covered wagons in coloring books. We let them color pictures of a young "prophet" visiting an old "general store" to buy groceries, or a boy with a rifle alone in a big field that was miles and miles from civilization. Our mental images never included scenes from the turn-of-the-century metropolis that Jeffersonville had become by the time that the Branham family arrived. We never pictured scenes of modern machinery in the streets. In fact, we had coloring books of the "prophet" on Jeffersonville city streets depicted as dirt roads with horses and buggies.[49]

When the Branham family arrived in Jeffersonville, they came to a busy, thriving, port city to live with Jeffersonville's elite.[50] They came to be near civilization, not to avoid it. I started to notice that there were different versions of the "prophet's" life story. In some versions, he hunted and trapped to provide food for his widowed mother and siblings.[51] In other versions, they lived in the wealthy part of Utica, just outside of Jeffersonville, beside the millionaire Wathen. When the "prophet" told the Indiana versions of his childhood stories, his father Charles Branham was a driver for Mr. Wathen.

When the "prophet" described his father, it was seldom with fond memory. The Branham family was, according to the accounts, non-

[49] Multimedia. Accessed Aug 13, 2018 from *https://cubcorner.org/en/multimedia*
[50] Branham, William. 1961, Nov 5. The Testimony of a True Witness. "we lived by the side of Mr. Wathen up there on the Utica Pike 61-1105 - The Testimony of A True Witness"
[51] Branham, William. 1955, Oct 1. Expectation. "I said, "Yes, sir, that's right." I said-I said, "I know my grammar's awful." I said, "I'm sorry about that." I said, "I was raised in a family of ten, and I was the oldest. And my daddy died, and I had to take care of ten children, and my mother..." I said, "I didn't get a chance to get an education"

religious, alcoholic, partying, and of no account. There were stories of his father producing illegal moonshine, and tales of drunken women leaving their husbands for other married men in parties hosted by his father.[52] The "prophet" told of how hard he had to work to help making that liquor, carrying old cedar buckets full of water up to the still for hours of his day.[53] He described his father as a slave-driver, a task master that made the "prophet" work all day so that he could drink the night away.

I remember the bitter thoughts I had about the "prophet's" father. How could he let "drinking" get in the way of his family? From the "prophet's" stories, it almost sounded like Charles was a fugitive on the run. When he talked about his father making whiskey and throwing parties, I never really thought about it in the context of living on the rich side of town with Otto H. Wathen. I never thought about it happening during the time of prohibition in the same area as the big distilleries. I realized that it was time to learn more about Mr. Wathen and the impact that the liquor industry had on Jeffersonville.

...

Indiana and Kentucky were both impacted by anti-saloon legislation at the turn of the century. When the Moore Amendment was passed in 1905 it severely crippled the liquor industry, and the Wathen Distilleries suddenly found itself with a broken chain of sales and distribution. More than 2500 Indiana saloons were closed between 1900 and 1910.[54] Distribution quickly shifted from the distilleries to organized crime, igniting a war between the government and the mob. As the battle against liquor advanced, distribution became extremely more difficult. The transfer of liquor was very dangerous, especially during Al Capone's reign in Chicago. Federal agents arrested drivers hauling liquor to investigate the source of their supplier, and many paths of distribution led back to the Wathen Distilleries. The Wathen family quickly found themselves at the center of a criminal investigation.[55]

---

[52] Branham, William. 1953, Nov 8. Life Story.
[53] Branham, William. 1950, Aug 13. God Revealing Himself to his People. "Sorry to say, packing it to a moonshine still for my daddy, two little half-a-gallon molasses buckets."
[54] Hedeen, Jane. The Road to Prohibition in Indiana. Accessed 2020, May 15 from
https://www.indianahistory.org/wp-content/uploads/1d7d71dfbb39529a736fdba5279a5ba9.pdf

Otto H. Wathen began producing and distributing liquor under a medicinal license, making his liquor distillery one of the few that survived prohibition. By producing liquor under a medicinal license, Wathen was able to continue production of liquor and distribute for a brief time under the radar of the Prohibition officers. In 1919, when many distilleries were closing, Wathen's distillery had $750,000 worth of whiskey[56] making it one of the largest operating distilleries in the nation. With the passing of the Volstead Act in 1919, however, it became even more difficult to operate outside of the government's watchful eye.

The federal government was seizing liquor by the truckloads, and opening investigations on a massive scale in an attempt to stop the supply of whiskey to the mob. A Chicago indictment named Wathen in an illicit whiskey ring[57], bringing the government investigation to Louisville and Southern Indiana. Wathen had illegally removed 8,000 gallons of whiskey labeled for medicinal use only,[58] and distributed the liquor for drinking to the Chicago mob. Knebelkamp, secretary of the Wathen distilleries, took the fall which lifted the charges against Otto's father, R. E. Wathen.[59] But that was not the end of the Federal investigation. Shortly after his father narrowly escaped conviction, Otto H. Wathen was indicted by a Federal grand jury in Chicago. Suddenly, the Wathen Distilleries was under siege by the Federal Government. It was during the Federal investigation that Charles Branham took young William Branham out of school.[60]

I can remember weeping when I heard the "prophet's" life story, thinking how difficult it must have been for such a young boy to help feed his widowed mother and ten siblings after the death of his father, Charles Branham. It came as a great surprise when a "Message" brother and sister told me they had found Charles Branham's death certificate in the archives and that he passed away over fifteen years later.[61] I had

---

[55] Example: 1920, Jan 19. Final Step is Due Today in Wathen Whiskey Seizure. The Courier Journal.
[56] Whisky Men Face Loss. 1919, Jun 13. Kansas City Kansan
[57] Held in Whiskey Case. 1920, Jan 20. Republic
[58] Kentucky Distillers Charged with Fraud. 1920, Jan 20. Morning News
[59] Knebelkamp, Wathen Held. 1920, Jan 29. Courier Journal
[60] Branham, William. 1951, July 19. Who Hath Believed Our Report? "I got not even a grammar school education. Seventh grade was as far as I got in school. I had to go to work, take care of nine children"
[61] 1936, Nov 30. Certificate of Death: Charles Branham

never really thought about the fact that different versions of the "life story" placed the death of his father at very different points in the "prophet's" timeline.[62] In my mind, I had reconciled the different versions by unknowingly choosing the earliest point mentioned: as a child, in the log cabin, so early in his life that he quit school at seventh grade. Knowing that the "prophet's" father was working for Wathen using a whiskey still, had taken the "prophet" out of school to help run it, all during a time that Wathen was distributing illegal liquor to the mob — while passing "medicinal license" inspections made my head spin! How did he pull this off? It made me curious about the local Jeffersonville scene during that time all of this was happening.

Reading through the newspaper archives, I found that the presence of the mob had quickly changed things for the worse. All across Louisville and Southern Indiana, the local authorities were turning a blind eye to the gambling and speakeasies that were springing up on every corner.[63] Local liquor and gaming nightlife attracted all kinds of shady people from cities where liquor was unavailable, and the town of Jeffersonville was quietly being invaded by criminals. Local law enforcement could barely keep up with maintaining order as a growing mob took control. Citizens and city council noticed that the police were turning a blind eye and tried helplessly to stop it.

Louisville, Kentucky, just across the river from Jeffersonville, Indiana, was no different. The Seelbach Hotel in Louisville hosted many people that Wathen did business with, some of them now famous criminals in American history. Al Capone, the head of the Chicago mafia, frequented the Rathskeller room in the basement of the Seelbach Hotel[64], and escaped federal agents through a network of underground tunnels. Capone and others like him easily slipped in-and-out of the Louisville/Jeffersonville area conducting business and ensuring that their supply lines remained operational. As their power continued to grow, so did the demand for their product.

[62] Example: Branham, William. 1952, Aug 10. I Am the Resurrection and the Life. "I said, "Yes, sir. I know that." I said, "I just had a seventh grade education. My father had died and I had to take care of ten…""
[63] Wider Inquiry on Gambling is Forecast. 1920, Jan 25. Courier Journal
[64] Hidden Seelbach feature will be showcased on new TV Series. Accessed Aug 20, 2018 from https://www.bizjournals.com/louisville/news/2017/02/14/hidden-seelbach-feature-will-be-showcased-on-new.html

To keep up with the increasing demands of whiskey production, Wathen worked with an underground network of whiskey suppliers.[65] Local men in the counties surrounding Louisville and Jeffersonville installed whiskey stills on private property and produced large volumes of illegal liquor "off the books", leaving only the medicinal whiskey for government inspection. While the prohibition officers monitored the legal production of liquor for medicinal purposes, men working for Wathen were secretly producing whiskey and "white mule" (moonshine) for drinking, all operating in the supply chain of the mob. At one point, government agents suspected that Wathen's network had grown into a $200,000 illegal liquor ring associated with Wathen's "Grand Dad" distillery.[66]

It was during this time, shortly before the raids by federal agents, that the Branham family moved away from Wathen on Utica Pike. As Federal agents began to crack down on Wathen's operation, Charles Branham moved his family to a small house in the Brighton neighborhood of Jeffersonville, and he purchased a plot of land just outside of the city. Federal agents traced every path leading to the liquor ring, and they discovered Charles Branham's liquor still.[67]

Whiskey prices had more than doubled during prohibition in the United States. Charles could produce a gallon of whiskey for up to $25. One batch of whiskey would gain him $250 during a time in history where the average wage was under $1.50 per hour.

When Charles Branham was arrested, he was working in one of the local factories. While he was working, a prohibition officer from New Albany, Indiana and a local police officer raided the family's home. They uncovered a ten-gallon liquor still hidden under a large pile of fodder, a coil, and a barrel of mash. Officers immediately arrested Charles in the factory and took him to the local jail.

His arrest came at a very difficult time for the family. The "prophet" had been shot, allegedly while hunting. One of his brothers had a broken arm, and another brother was near death due to a neck injury. According to the newspaper reports, the family was without food, and

---

[65] Dry Agents Bag Booze and Three Stills in Raids. 1920, Nov 14. Chicago Daily Tribune
[66] Wathen Company Heads in Dry Net. 1920, Nov 25. Courier Journal
[67] Still and Liquor Found. 1924, Mar 6. The Courier Journal

their case was sent over to one of the city's official trustees for help for charity.

The property used for his participation in the whiskey ring was owned by Edwin M. Coots. Mr. Coots is a well-known name among "Message" believers; the Coots funeral home is used by many families during times of family members' deaths. Coots immediately filed an eviction notice.[68]

The court proceedings made it very evident that Charles Branham was working with Otto H. Wathen in the underground network of whiskey production. When Charles had his day in court, the judge sentenced Charles to thirty days in jail, a $100.00 fine, and court costs. Otto H. Wathen presented the money for Charles' release, but the court refused to suspend the jail sentence.

Just days after Charles Branham's arrest, The Fiery Cross, a Ku Klux Klan newspaper from Indianapolis, announced that almost all the evidence leading to liquor indictments had been secured by members of the Ku Klux Klan.

---

[68] Would Eject Branham. 1924, Jul 19. The Courier Journal

HISTORIC PHOTOS OF JEFFERSONVILLE, INDIANA

Historic Photos of Louisville Kentucky And Environs. Accessed Aug 16, 2018 from
   https://historiclouisville.weebly.com/jeffersonville.html
Historic Photos of Jeffersonville. Accessed Aug 16, 2018 from
   https://www.pinterest.com/parisfrance/historic-photos-jeffersonville
Digital Collections. Accessed Aug 17, 2018 from *https://jefflibrary.org/local-history/digital-collections/*
Monumental Memories. Accessed Aug 17, 2018 from *https://www.jeffmainstreet.org/downtown-revitalization/monumental-memories/*

LOUISVILLE HISTORICAL PHOTOS:

Historic Photos of Louisville Kentucky And Environs. Accessed Aug 17, 2018 from
   https://historiclouisville.weebly.com/center-city.html

CHARLES BRANHAM'S ARREST:

Convicted in Liquor Case. 1924, Mar 6. Evening News
Still and Liquor Found. 1924, Mar 6. The Courier Journal
Asks Aid for Family. 1924, Mar 4. The Courier Journal
Serves Sentence at Night. 1924, Mar 18. The Courier Journal
Hospital Sends Township Bill. 1924, Mar 21. Evening News
Hospital Bill Rendered. 1924, Mar 21. The Courier Journal
Would Eject Branham. 1924, Jul 19. The Courier Journal

OTTO WATHEN:

Dry Agents Bag Booze and Three Stills in Raids. 1920, Nov 14. Chicago Daily Tribune
Federal Agents Face Arrest in Rum Ring. 1920, Oct 23. Newport Mercury
Whiskey Men Indicted. 1920, Mar 17. Pittsburgh Daily Post
Chicago Banks Are Defrauded by Distiller. 1915, Jan 22. Republican Northwestern
Huge U.S. Liquor Refund Doubted. 1921, Feb 18. Courier Journal
Wathen Case is Dismissed. 1921, Feb 25. Courier Journal
Wants Story Kept Down. 1920, Jan 12. Courier Journal
Final Step is Due in Wathen Whisky Seizure. 1920, Jan 19. Courier Journal
City Linked to Chicago Rum Deal Third Time. 1920, Dec 4. Courier Journal
Collins to Decide on Wathen Charges. 1923, Dec 22. Courier Journal
Stolen Whisky Must Bear Tax. 1920, Feb 21. Courier Journal
All in Same Boat. 1919, Nov 15. Courier Journal
Wathen Meets U. S. Officials. 1920, Feb 12. Courier Journal
Wathen Company Heads in Dry Net. 1920, Nov 25. Courier Journal
Plea in Liquor Case is Denied. 1920, Nov 25. Courier Journal
Compromise is Near in Wathen Indictment. 1920, Jun 22. Courier Journal
Wathen Denies Knowledge. 1920, Nov 16. Courier Journal
Knebelkamp, Wathen Held to U.S. Court. Jan 28, 1920. Courier Journal
Knebelkamp, Wathen Held. 1920, Jan 29. Courier Journal
Whisky Firm Loses Suit for Not Filing Order. 1918, Mar 20. Courier Journal
Gem Robbers Loot Machine. 1925, Aug 5. Indianapolis Star
Whisky Men Face Loss. 1919, Jun 13. Kansas City Kansan
Kentucky Distillers Charged with Fraud. 1920, Jan 20. Morning News
Held in Whiskey Case. 1920, Jan 20. Republic

American Medicinal Spirits Company. Accessed Aug 18, 2018 from
  http://www.bottlebooks.com/american%20medicinal%20spirits%20company/.
  american_medicinal_spirits_compa.htm

JEFFERSONVILLE KKK INVOLVEMENT:
Jeffersonville Booze Ring Jolted. 1924, Apr 11. The Fiery Cross

JEFFERSONVILLE / LOUISVILLE GAMBLING
Gaming Trail Leads to Den for Women. 1920, Jan 30. Courier Journal
Wider Inquiry on Gambling is Forecast. 1920, Jan 25. Courier Journal
'Cleanup' is Planned for Jeffersonville. 1922, Jan 25. Courier Journal
Game Quiz Ends Across River. 1920, Feb 25. Courier Journal
Gambling Must Stop! 1929, Jun 27. Edinburg Daily Courier
Gambling Houses, Night Clubs are Closed, Dark. 1931, Jan 21. Indianapolis News
New Arrests in Liquor Cleanup. 1924, Jul 30. Indianapolis News

SEELBACH HOTEL / AL CAPONE INFORMATION:
Hidden Seelbach feature will be showcased on new TV Series. Accessed Aug 20, 2018 from
  https://www.bizjournals.com/louisville/news/2017/02/14/hidden-seelbach-feature-will-be-
  showcased-on-new.html
History. Accessed Aug 20, 2018 from *https://lindseyjustice.wordpress.com/history/*

CHILDREN'S COLORING:
Accessed Aug 20, 2018 from *https://cubcorner.org/en/multimedia*

CHAPTER 4

THE KANSAS OUTLAW

"Sixteenth and Henshaw[69]"

When I was a child growing up in the "Message", our family listened to cassette tapes of the "prophet". We were very devout and listened to them often. We listened to them in our home, in our car on the road — I even listened to them by myself in my Sony Walkman at school, on my walk home, and sometimes at night as I went to sleep, Sometimes I listened to them when I awakened while the family was still asleep. If I had trouble sleeping, I put on my headset and listened to them on my pillow. I still remember waking up from the uncomfortable feeling that the Walkman headset gave my ear after sleeping for a few hours on my side.

I had my own collection of favorite tapes and listened to them as often as I could. Some of them I had played so many times that the magnetic tape was wearing thin, and the voice did not sound quite right. One of my favorite stories the "prophet" told us about his childhood was about his trip out west and seeing the "Kansas Outlaw"[70]. The "Kansas Outlaw" must have been the wildest horse in all the West! The "prophet" told how he wanted to become a rodeo rider, but after watching another rider badly injured, he decided he wasn't a "rider".

---

[69] Branham, William. 1962, Jan 17. Presuming.
[70] Branham, William. 1963, Jan 27. An Absolute. "'The Kansas Outlaw.' He's a great big horse, a big black fellow about seventeen hands high. He's a real heavy, strong horse. I thought, 'Well, if that fellow can ride him, so can I.'"

When that horse shot out of the chute with a rider holding on for dear life, it only took one single buck from that horse to throw the rider into the air and send him into an ambulance. A man came to offer $500 to any man that could ride him, asked the "prophet" if he was a "rider", and the "prophet" quickly said "no!" He wasn't a rider.[71]

I used to listen to that story and wonder what made him decide to leave his log cabin in Kentucky. Before I knew that the "prophet" was raised in the booming city of Jeffersonville, I had mental images of the "prophet" running through fields and trees deep in the hills of Kentucky. Burkesville, where his Kentucky log cabin was located, sat along the Cumberland River. I often thought about what life would have been like along that river, free as a bird and without a worry or care in the world. While mistakenly thinking that Jeffersonville was an old-fashioned one-horse town, I thought that it would have made Jeffersonville, Indiana, feel just like home. "What made the 'prophet' decide to leave his family behind?" I thought. When I thought about the "prophet's" adventures out West, I never really thought about the situation he that left behind. I never thought about how difficult it must have been for them without Charles, their father — still thinking that Charles had died while the "prophet" was in grade school. The "prophet" said that he hunted and fished to feed his family, but he never really said who provided for them when he left Jeffersonville. It made me curious to learn more about his family when he left them.

I re-read the article describing Charles Branham's arrest and the desperate situation for the Branham family. I thought about the government raiding the property, with the "prophet" working all day to bring water for producing whiskey and tried to imagine how the "prophet" would have responded when the authorities arrived. The newspapers said that the "prophet" was shot while hunting. Was he?

I remembered the "prophet" describing that hunting injury. According to the "life stories", the "prophet" described another boy accidentally shooting a shotgun at him, and the shot went through both

[71] Branham, William. 1964, Apr 18. A Paradox. "Here come the caller around, you know. He said, 'I'll give any man here, five hundred dollars, that can stay on him sixty seconds.' He come right down the line. I don't know how it ever was, he picked me right out. Set there, just setting up there with all these old disfigured cowboy, you know. My legs wasn't bowed, or nothing. But I—I thought I was a real rider, I could set there with them. I was fellowshipping with them, you know, my hat setting on the back of my head. Was about seventeen years old, I guess, looking around like that. He come, said, "Are you a rider?" And I said, "'No, sir.'"

37

legs at a close range.[72] But he also said that it was a minister.[73] I remembered the "prophet" saying that the Ku Klux Klan paid his hospital bill.[74] This always struck me as a little odd, because he spoke favorably of the Klan "no matter what they did". When I thought about the Ku Klux Klan, I never had favorable thoughts.

The Ku Klux Klan was a terroristic organization, and they were responsible for the torture and death of innocent men, women, and children. When I thought about the Klan, I thought about secret meetings with burning crosses. I thought about violence, bigotry, and hatred. I thought about the fear that they caused for mothers and children. I never once thought of them with any favorable emotion. Why would the "prophet" be praising the Ku Klux Klan?

In 1920's Jeffersonville, however, the Ku Klux Klan would have seemed like heroes. They allegedly helped take down the Wathen Liquor Ring.[75] They boasted that they had secured all the evidence for officials to arrest those producing liquor, which would have included Wathen's operation and Charles Branham. All of this painted a very different image in my mind about this time of the "prophet's" life. Young William feeding the whiskey still with water during the day. Charles working with Wathen and the mob during the night. The Ku Klux Klan secretly spying on the Branham family. Charles being arrested, Wathen posting his bail and fighting for his release — it was almost overwhelming! After Charles Branham's arrest, the Ku Klux Klan published the details in the "Fiery Cross" and began a campaign to expose all of those involved in illegal activities.[76]

Still, it was the newspaper article's "age 16"[77] for the "prophet" that made me most curious. According to the life stories, the "prophet" bought a brand-new car at age 16[78]. He took his first trip out west at age

---

[72] Branham, William. 1963, Nov 11. Souls That Are in Prison Now. "We're about six months apart, in age. And Jimmy let his gun go off, and it shot me through both legs, real close to me, with a shotgun."

[73] Branham, William. 1956, Feb 29. Being Led Of The Holy Spirit. And I remember a preacher shooting at some birds and seventh shot hit me in the leg.

[74] Branham, William. 1963, Nov 10. Souls That Are in Prison Now. "Ku Klux Klan, paid the hospital bill for me"

[75] Jeffersonville Booze Ring Jolted. 1924, Apr 11. The Fiery Cross

[76] Rioters Attack Klansmen. 1924, Apr 11. The Fiery Cross

[77] Hospital Bill Rendered. 1924, Mar 21. The Courier Journal

[78] Branham, William. 1956, Jun 3. The Lamb's Book Of Life. "remember when I had that little old T-model Ford, little old '26 model? How I would polish that thing! I was just a kid, about sixteen, seventeen years old."

16. How could he afford to buy a brand-new car when the family was homeless and destitute? Was this before or after he was shot through both legs, dying in the hospital? If before, was it the liquor money that paid for the vehicle? If after, did the money come from Wathen or the Ku Klux Klan? There were so many questions.

The "prophet" often said that it was a 1926 Model T, and by his timeline claimed that it was brand-new. That would place his trip out west at age 18, according to the timeline I'd found of historical record. Curious, I dug up all the photographs that I could find of the "prophet's" early vehicles. I never really noticed it in the old photos of the "prophet's" automobiles, but the automobiles were different! All the old 1920s automobiles looked the same to me, but after examining more closely, each of the radiators were different. One radiator was thin and round at the bottom. One was wider and less round at the bottom. One was straight at the top, with an eagle ornament. One car was a two-seater with a convertible top. Another was a sedan. Quickly, I started searching for everything that the "prophet" said about his automobiles. He mentioned multiple new vehicles, both Ford and Chevy. I always thought he just didn't remember which brand of automobile that he bought. I suddenly began to realize that his memory wasn't the problem. My understanding of the "prophet's" early life was missing key facts!

The facts that I had were not making any sense at all. The "prophet" said that at age sixteen, he lived at Sixteenth and Henshaw in Phoenix.[79] Age sixteen just simply did not fit. Before the rifle "accident", he was, by all accounts, too poor to purchase any vehicle — if those accounts from the newspaper were to be believed. The "prophet" seemed to verify them when he described his hospitalization. He said that the family had no food, which matched the newspaper accounts. After the accident, based on his description of the injuries, it would have been several months before he was able to drive. If he did, in fact, purchase the 1926 vehicle and then travel out west, age 18 would make much more sense.

---

[79] Branham, William. 1960, Feb 28. Conferences. "I was about sixteen, seventeen years old. It's been around thirty years ago. And up on Sixteenth and Henshaw was a desert. That's where I stayed"

In either case, the facts uncovered raised more questions than they answered. Where did he come up with the money for the new vehicle, and why did he travel west? With each of the parties influencing the Branham family, every scenario was just as curious. Did Wathen give the "prophet" a large sum of money for fueling the whiskey still? Or as a favor to Charles for running the still? Did some rich donor offer a large charitable contribution for the Branham family, large enough to purchase vehicles for the children? Did the Ku Klux Klan give the "prophet" money for the vehicle, and if so, why?

As unlikely as it might seem, his favorable statements for the Ku Klux Klan combined with his unfavorable statements about his father and the whiskey still presented the most likely scenario. It would appear that the "prophet" had taken the anti-liquor side of the Ku Klux Klan against his father. I knew that I would never find out why the Ku Klux Klan paid his hospital bills, or how he produced the money for the new vehicle, so I decided to dig deeper into his time in Arizona.

...

I signed up for a newspapers.com subscription, which enabled me to search for articles and read newspapers in multiple cities across the United States. I was pleased with the interface; no longer was I sifting through thousands of microfiche slides to find an article; I could easily search using keywords, phrases, dates, and locations. At the time, Jeffersonville Indiana had not yet been indexed by the archives, or I would have been curious to re-examine the first eighteen years of the "prophet's" life through a more full and complete set of research data. I pulled up the historical archives of newspapers in Phoenix, Arizona to see what I could find.

I found an article in the Arizona Republican from 1928 that raised my interest. It described the school systems in Phoenix and Tempe. The phrase "Sixteenth and Henshaw" was found in an article about the Wilson School District.[80] It described the schedule of classes and activities for the school district. The schedule for "Sixteenth and Henshaw" was 7:50 AM.

---

[80] Wilson District School Will Open Tuesday Morning. 1928, Aug 31. Arizona Republic

Henshaw Road was part of a Civil Works project in 1933, which meant that photographs from the early 1930s were available. Looking towards the east, it would have seemed much like I imagined the "prophet's" lifestyle: barren. Looking away from the city towards the undeveloped land, it would have looked like wilderness. But to the west, to the city, there was quickly expanding civilization.[81] Phoenix was quite a large city with towering buildings, paved roads, automobiles moving down the streets, bicycles on the sidewalks, and busy intersections. Businessmen, dressed in fancy suits, scurried into their daily white-collar jobs in modern office complexes.

Henshaw Road was later renamed "Buckeye Rd".[82] Henshaw ran into the heart of the city, and it crossed Sixteenth Street just a couple miles from downtown. From where the "prophet" lived, the view from his windows would not have been open desert in the wild, Wild West — he would have seen the Phoenix skyline. He would have seen the large, eight-story Hotel San Carlos being erected, and watched it open in 1928.[83] He would have seen the massive Westward Ho hotel, a 16-story, 320 room hotel that towered over the city. It also opened in 1928.[84]

When I listened to the "prophet's" stories about his time out west living on the corner of Sixteenth and Henshaw, I never pictured seeing a concrete jungle filled with skyscrapers. Phoenix of the 1920s was a busy city! A busy city that was within just a few minutes walking distance for the "prophet"!

As I looked over the historic photos of Phoenix from the archives online, I started thinking about the early photos of the "prophet" from a much different point of view. Instead of picturing him rustling cattle on a dude ranch, or working as a cow hand on a ranch, I looked at them from the perspective of a city slicker going in and out of the local businesses and restaurants near his house. When I did, the old photographs of the "prophet" seemed to come alive! In the photos we

---

[81] Arizona Memory Project. Accessed Sept 5, 2018 from
http://azmemory.azlibrary.gov/digital/collection/histphotos/id/32461/rec/215
[82] Towne, Douglas. 2019, Jan 13. Drive-in Was One Wild Hayride. Accessed Sept 5, 2018 from
https://www.arizcc.com/single-post/2019/01/13/Rodeo-Drive-In-Was-One-Wild-Hayride
[83] Hotel San Carlos: A Haunted History. Accessed 2020, May 16 from https://phoenix.org/hotel-san-carlos-a-haunted-history/
[84] Historic Westward Ho in Phoenix gets $18M makeover. Accessed 2020, May 16 from
https://www.azcentral.com/story/news/local/phoenix/2017/04/20/historic-westward-ho-makeover-downtown-phoenix/100484488/

have from that era, he was well dressed, as though wearing a college uniform. The pictures appeared to be in a school setting. All the photos were professionally done — which made me think about the photographs themselves. Even the camera that took them seemed out of place in the stories of the time out west; your average ranch hand was not carrying a camera.

Some of the photographs would have made perfect yearbook photos. In the set, each photo looked to be very close in age, almost a year apart. As he aged, his facial features became more distinct. By the fourth photograph in the set, the "prophet" was a full-grown man. He often said that he quit school after seventh grade because his father died, but I'd learned that wasn't exactly true. I began to wonder: "Did the 'prophet' attend college in Arizona?"

Looking through the photos of Phoenix in the 1920's, I also realized this was a step up in life from what it would have been in the gambling town of Jeffersonville, Indiana. The "prophet's" opportunities would have been limitless! Still, I was curious: what made him decide to leave? If he did attend college in Phoenix, what made him return to Jeffersonville, Indiana, of all places?

I remembered an article that I had come across in the Louisville newspaper when I was researching downtown Jeffersonville. William Branham's brother Edward had shot and killed a man.[85] Edward was trading a firearm for an automobile, and he killed John Burse. Witnesses said that the gun was in Branham's hand when it was fired at the home of his father, Charles Branham. [86] On Jun 5, 1928, he was charged with first degree murder.[87] Only a few months later, Edward died.[88] The cause of death was listed as rheumatic heart disease.[89] In the 1929 obituary, William Branham was listed living in *Kansas!*

The more information that I found, the more the facts grew stranger and stranger. Kansas was a piece of the puzzle just that didn't fit. Why Kansas? Did the "Kansas Outlaw" have more meaning than the story intended? If he attended the school in Phoenix, he didn't immediately

[85] 16 Hoosiers Dead in Crashes, By Violence. 1928, June 4. Indianapolis News.
[86] Jeffersonville Boy Killed in Gun Trade. 1928, June 3. Courier Journal
[87] Boy Held to Circuit Court on Murder Charge. 1928, Jun 5. Jeffersonville Evening News.
[88] Boy, 19, Dies At Hospital. 1929, June 20. Evening News
[89] Certificate of Death. 1929. Edward Branham

return to Jeffersonville. Did Edward's death cause the "prophet" to return? There was an unexplained gap in the timeline. The "prophet" mysteriously fell into a sum of money, left town, stayed in Phoenix for a few years, landed in Kansas, and then re-emerged in Jeffersonville, Indiana as a preacher!

The "prophet" said that he started preaching in 1930[90], and that was one of his memories that remained consistent through all his life stories. He often told the story how Rev. Roy E. Davis ordained him as a minister.[91]

At the time, I knew very little about Roy Davis. I only knew him as "Dr. Roy E. Davis", the "Baptist" minister and that he had a church in Jeffersonville, Indiana. I returned to the local Jeffersonville Public Library and began digging through old newspapers to see what I could find about Rev. Davis. I was very surprised that his church first started in Louisville, Kentucky[92], and later moved to Jeffersonville, Indiana[93].

A couple of other researchers had found some newspaper articles of the church Davis started in Jeffersonville.[94] I was surprised as they were to learn that Roy Davis' Jeffersonville church was Pentecostal, and named the "Pentecostal Baptist Church", preaching Pentecostal Holiness doctrine.[95] The "prophet" had called it a "Baptist" church, and made it sound as though he had never been around Pentecostal people.[96] Adding to my surprise was an article, written by Roy E. Davis and published in an October, 1950 issue of The Voice of Healing, confirming the Pentecostal affiliation of the church. According to Davis, he had introduced the "prophet" to the very first Pentecostal assembly that he had ever frequented.

Another researcher found an even more disturbing document produced by the United States Government. A man by the name "Roy

---

[90] Branham, William. 1962, May 31. The Conflict Between God and Satan. "About 1930, '31, somewhere along in there, I started preaching the Gospel"

[91] Branham, William. 1953, Nov 11. I Will Restore. "Doctor Davis had ordained me into the Baptist church"

[92] Pastor Held in Mann Act Case. 1930, Oct 12. Courier Journal

[93] Three Davis Brothers Plan a Pentecostal Revival. 1931, Apr 17. Evening News

[94] Searching for Vindication. Accessed 2020, May 16 from searchingforvindication.com

[95] Davis, Roy. Wm. Branham's First Pastor. 1950. The Voice of Healing. "I am the minister who received Brother Branham into the first Pentecostal assembly he ever frequented. I baptized him, and was his pastor for some two years.

[96] Branham, William. 1952, July 20. Life Story. "They was holding it in a big tabernacle at Mishawaka. So I—I never seen the Pentecost before"

E. Davis" was mentioned in a testimony before the United States Congress during an investigation into the Ku Klux Klan after the assassination of President John F. Kennedy.[97] Was this the same Roy E. Davis?

It was time to start digging into the Pentecostal Baptist Church, and the "prophet's" conversion to Pentecostalism.

[97] The Present-Day Ku Klux Klan Movement. Report by the Committee on Un-American Activities. House of Representatives. Ninetieth Congress, First Session. 1967, Dec 11. "Prior to 1960, there had been no effective Klan activity in the State of Louisiana for several decades. The Klan was reactivated in Louisiana late in 1960 by Rev. Roy E. Davis of Dallas Texas.

WILLIAM BRANHAM'S CARS:
Branham, William. 1962, Jan 17. Presuming
Branham, William. 1960, Aug 3. Abraham

PHOENIX HISTORY:
Arizona Memory Project. Accessed Sept 5, 2018 *from http://azmemory.azlibrary.gov/*
    digital/collection/histphotos/id/32461/rec/215
History Adventuring. Accessed Sept 5, 2018 from
    http://www.historyadventuring.com/2016/09/walgreens-in-downtown-phoenix in-1933.html
Explore downtown Phoenix in the 1920's. Accessed Sept 5, 2018 from *http://phoenix.org/explore-*
    downtown-phoenix-in-the-1920s/

SIXTEENTH AND HENSHAW:
Wilson District School Will Open Tuesday Morning. 1928, Aug 31. Arizona Republic
Branham, William. 1960, Feb 28. Conferences 2
Branham, William. 1962, Jan 17. Presuming
Branham, William. 1963, Jan 19. Way of a True Prophet
Branham, William. 1963, Dec 14. Why Little Bethlehem

KU KLUX KLAN INFLUENCE:
Branham, William. 1963, Nov 10. Souls That Are in Prison
Jeffersonville Booze Ring Jolted. 1924, Apr 11. The Fiery Cross

EDWARD BRANHAM:
16 Hoosiers Dead in Crashes, By Violence. 1928, June 4. Indianapolis News.
Jeffersonville Boy Killed in Gun Trade. 1928, June 3. Courier Journal
Boy, 19, Dies at Hospital. 1929, June 20. Evening News
Certificate of Death: Edward Branham.

ROY E. DAVIS:
Wm. Branham's First Pastor. 1950, Oct. Voice of Healing.
Evangelist Draws 10-Day Jail Term. 1930, Nov 3. Statesville Record and Landmark
Davis Jailed for Contempt. 1930, Nov 1. Courier Journal
Pastor Held in Mann Act Case. 1930, Oct 12. Courier Journal
Mission Preacher Accused of Fraud. 1930, Mar 20. Courier Journal
Davis Indicted by Grand Jury. 1930, Oct 14. Courier Journal
Evangelistic Singer Jailed in Kentucky. 1930, Oct 13. Greenville News
Preacher Wins, Loses in Court. 1930, Nov 1. Greenville News
Davis' Record in Texas Aired by Ku Klux Klan. 1921, Aug 26. Wise County Messenger
Denied Use of Auditorium. 1923, Jan 12. Nebraska State Journal
Klan Refused Hall. 1923, Jan 12. Reading Times
Flaming Swordsmen Will Not Discard Arms. 1925, Jan 23. The Tennessean
Fraternity Attacked as Money Making Order. 1925, Jan 23. Lead Daily Call
Simmons' Order Growing Rapidly. 1924, Oct 6. Arkansas Gazette

CHAPTER 5

WILLIAM BRANHAM'S
FIRST CHURCH

"I Was First Ordained in the Baptist Church[98]"

During my childhood, when our family visited Jeffersonville, Indiana, crossing the bridges over the Ohio River was always one of the highlights of our trip. As a child looking out the backseat window of the car to the water below, I thought the Ohio River seemed as big as an ocean! It was always a special treat when we would look down and see a fleet of barges go under us. From the bridge above, the barges looked like toy boats floating in the water. It was even more special when the Belle of Louisville passed by. Watching the old paddlewheel riverboat was like turning a page back in time. I could picture the riverboat gamblers playing cards and smoking cigars around the tables on the lower deck; women in long, flowing gowns with skirts daintily gathered up in one hand as they ascended winding stairs with beautifully stained woodwork, and waiters dressed in dark suits carrying silver platters of drinks to guests who sat watching the banks of the river pass by.

Today, there are four bridges connecting Louisville to Jeffersonville, Indiana. So much has changed since I was a child. The oldest bridge, the Big Four Bridge, was completed in 1895. For its time, the Big Four was an architectural masterpiece. Today, however, it has little use and

---

[98] Branham, William. 1951, May 6. Believes Thou This.

has been repurposed as a walking bridge. Visitors from the Indiana side or the Kentucky side are frequently strolling up new winding ramps leading to the newly renovated bridge, and it is very common to see walkers, joggers, bicycles, and skateboards crossing the bridge on a bright, sunny day. The bridge ends in a waterfront park on both sides of the river, and these green expanses are usually filled with children at play, their parents standing near them talking to other parents or sitting on a park bench reading a book with one watchful eye toward the children.

The George Rogers Clark Memorial Bridge opened to the public in 1929[99], just weeks after the death of Edward Branham and the "prophet's" return to Jeffersonville. Construction on the bridge began in 1928 while the "prophet" would have been in Phoenix, Arizona. The opening of the bridge was big news when he started preaching in 1930. It provided quick access to the other side of the river, making travel much easier for residents and opening the door for new job opportunities in Louisville from the Indiana side. No longer did travelers need to wait for the next train to arrive or wait in line for a ferry; they could come and go as they pleased.

The George Rogers Clark Memorial Bridge was also very important to the advancement of the "Message" movement. It was the target for one of the "prophet's" "prophecies". For those of us in the "Message", the bridge itself stood as a vindication of the accuracy of the "prophet's" "prophecies".

And I looked down at the river, and there went a bridge, a big, great big bridge going across the river. And I counted sixteen men that fell off of that bridge and drowned. And I went and told mother. And I told her I seen it. And they thought I was crazy or something. They thought I was just a little nervous hysterical child. And twenty-two years from that time, on the same ground went the Municipal Bridge across, and sixteen men lost their lives on it.[100]

When I learned that the "prophet" was living in Kansas in 1929, and that he began preaching for Roy E. Davis in 1930, the pieces of the

[99] The New Bridge - Chronologically. 1929, Oct 29. Courier Journal
[100] Branham, William. 1948, Mar 2. Experiences

puzzle seemed even more disconnected. With Davis' Pentecostal Baptist church in Louisville instead of Jeffersonville at that time, what made that church more appealing than one of the many local Jeffersonville churches?

I became curious as to what it was like in Jeffersonville and Louisville when the "prophet" returned from Arizona and Kansas. Since the new bridge would have been big news at the time, the bridge seemed like a good place to start.

I remembered some research that another "Message" brother and sister published[101] which raised some concerning questions about the "prophet's" statements about the new bridge. The couple had set out to prove that his prophecies were accurate, and predictions about the new bridge and its construction also seemed like a good place for them to start. They began collecting historical documents from the time periods before, during, and after the bridge construction.

The "prophet" had "prophesied" that sixteen men fell to their deaths and drowned during the construction of the George Rogers Clark Memorial Bridge. According to the descriptions given by the "prophet" in his "life stories", he had "seen" sixteen men fall to their deaths during construction of that bridge in a "vision" as a small child. In that "vision", there was a sign that read "22". He said that twenty-two years from that day, sixteen men fell to their deaths. The biggest problem with this "vision" that I could see from the start was the *twenty-two years*. Since construction ended in 1929, and the "prophet" claimed to have been born in 1909, the prediction must have been made *two years before his birth*!

When the researchers learned that the construction was monitored by a Coast Guard Life Saving Station, they just knew they'd find records of the lives that were lost, vindicating the "prophet" and his predictions. The two traveled to the National Archives at Atlanta, where they found the collection of logbooks. Exactly two lives were lost during construction.[102]

---

[101] Posts on the Municipal Bridge. Accessed 2020, May 16 from *http://searchingforvindication.com/bridge.html*
[102] Summary of the Municipal Bridge Vision. Accessed 2020, May 16 from *http://searchingforvindication.com/2013/04/06/Summary-Of-Municipal-Bridge/*

The first death happened near the end of construction in June of 1929. It happened just one day after Edward Branham's death. The second one happened in September of 1929. Construction was monitored by the coast guard, and the logs were fully detailed.[103] From orders of food and supplies to weather conditions, the coast guard logs detailed every event — big or small — that happened during construction. The researchers who published this information were just as surprised as I was to learn that no major loss of life occurred during the construction.

Curious, I made a trip to the memorial site at the foot of the bridge on the Jeffersonville side of the river and spoke with the historian onsite. He was an older gentleman with a friendly smile and a firm handshake. When I told him the reason that I was curious about the number of deaths on the bridge, he chuckled and walked me into a meeting room on the north side of the building. On the wall were several pictures of the bridge, both during construction and after. In one of them, the much older Big Four bridge could be seen.

He pointed out the difference in construction, something I was unfamiliar with. When the older bridge was constructed, bridges were built in sections, and it was very dangerous. He informed me that there *was* a tragic event during the construction of the older bridge. In the 1800s, several men fell to their deaths when a section collapsed.[104] The construction of the new bridge, however, was so successful that the technique was used for future bridges.

Though this "prophecy" did not appear to be correct, I still wondered about the effects this bridge would have had on the "prophet's" early ministry. If this "prophecy" really occurred when he was a child, he certainly would have asked about it when he arrived. Did he return to Jeffersonville in 1930 claiming his prophecy was accurate? Or was this a claim that came years after? If he became ordained a minister, and began claiming "prophecy" for an event that the locals *knew* did not happen, what made them stay with him at his church? I began to

---

[103] Coast Guard Life Saving Station. Accessed 2020, May 16 from
http://searchingforvindication.com/2013/03/09/Coast-Guard-Life-Saving-Station/
[104] Sixteen Men Killed. 1890, Jan 29. Abbeville Press and Banner.

wonder if he introduced his "prophecy" years later after, when it was more difficult to prove.

By the 1930's, Louisville, Kentucky was a land of big opportunity. Even as the Great Depression was beginning to cripple the United States Economy, workers could find employment in Louisville manufacturing. The George Rogers Clark Memorial Bridge would have made Jeffersonville feel even more connected with Louisville, giving hope in a time of crisis. Rural Kentucky and Indiana were hit particularly hard during the Depression. It is likely that many rural families were migrating to the area to find work. Was this the reason the "prophet" returned? Or was his return during the Great Depression merely coincidence?

With opening of the new bridge, it would have been only a few minutes' drive for the "prophet" to travel to Davis's church in Louisville. Having a population of around three hundred thousand people, Louisville was much larger than Phoenix which had just a little over 48,000 people. Jeffersonville had only 12,000 people but was considered part of the Louisville metro area.[105]

The church that Roy Davis pastored in Louisville was within walking distance to the new bridge, right in the heart of busy downtown. It was located at 711 E. Jefferson, one of the busiest sections of town. With the new bridge allowing automobiles to cross the Ohio River, an influx of Indiana automobiles would have made the city seem far busier than Phoenix. Stores that Jeffersonville customers could only access by boat, train, or trolley were now just a short drive from their homes.

At 410 Jefferson Street, locals could play miniature golf. Around them were buildings towering to the sky providing jobs that were now easily accessible for citizens of Jeffersonville. Some of the buildings were so high that a person could look out of upper windows and see the tops of other tall buildings. Some could see across the Ohio River into Jeffersonville. This was certainly not what I imagined for the "prophet's" first church experience!

When I thought about his first experience as a minister, I never really pictured him driving on a busy street in downtown Louisville. Heading to church, he would have crossed the new bridge, driven past

---

[105] Statistics from United States Census

trolleys, and had to be careful not to hit pedestrians as they scurried around him. In my mind, I had pictured a humble little church in Jeffersonville, Indiana, and I had pictured Jeffersonville as a small town with just a handful of people. Since he had claimed to have been a "prophet" from a very early age[106], and some of those "prophecies" were supposed to be happening by the early 1930s, I had almost expected to find a small following of people gathered around the "prophet" to see what he would say next!

On Tuesday, October 29, 1929, the Louisville Courier Journal newspaper dedicated most of the Tuesday issue to the newly opened George Rogers Clark Memorial Bridge.[107] Ironically, this day would go down in history as "Black Tuesday", the day of the Wall Street Crash of 1929.[108] Newspapers could not have predicted the events that the day would bring, and writers filled the entire newspaper with bridge-related history, facts, and more. Articles contained everything from praise for the builders to the history of bridges themselves. Ralph Modjeski and Frank Masters received well-deserved recognition for their successful project. In fact, Modjeski received the John Fritz gold medal for his master craftsmanship. I began looking for an article — any article — that would cause the "prophet" to believe that men had died during the construction of the bridge. Since he was in town, there is no doubt that he read this issue of the Courier Journal; it was one of the biggest events in Louisville and Jeffersonville history for several years.

One article on page 5 looked promising. The Courier Journal published a detailed timeline of events in the history of the new bridge. If there was a tragedy during construction, especially as significant as sixteen deaths, surely the chronology would mention the event. Sadly, I was unable to find anything the "prophet" could use to claim any sort of "prophecy" when speaking to his church.

Using the online newspaper archive subscription that I purchased, I began searching other newspapers for a tragedy involving sixteen men. On one particular search, I forgot to enter the date range. As it turned

---

[106] Branham, William. 1953, Nov 4. Deep Calleth Unto the Deep. "At about fifteen, eighteen months old, I had my first vision"

[107] The New Bridge - Chronologically. 1929, Oct 29. Courier Journal

[108] Stock market crashes on Black Tuesday. Accessed 2020, May 16 from *https://www.history.com/this-day-in-history/stock-market-crashes*

out, sixteen men did fall to their deaths in bridge construction. To my surprise, it happened on January 29, 1890 on the Big Four Bridge,[109] almost two decades before the "prophet" was born. This must have been the event that the bridge historian had mentioned to me.

I noticed the "life-saving station" mentioned in the article from the 1800s and remembered descriptions of the "life-saving station" in the research of the new bridge. This was something that I never really thought about. As dangerous as bridge construction was and is, workers prepared for quick response to save lives. It would have been very difficult for the deaths of sixteen men to go unnoticed, regardless of the Coast Guard logs. Had the "prophet" claimed to have made this prediction as a child before his congregation, they would have had a very easy time disproving the claim. I was beginning to conclude that during his early ministry, the "prophet" would have never made this claim at all.

This made me even more curious about Davis' church in Louisville, and I wanted to know what made the "prophet" decide to choose a church in Louisville instead of Jeffersonville. If he really became ordained and started preaching in 1930 as he claimed, before Davis moved his church to Jeffersonville, something must have attracted him to Davis' church. I began digging through old Louisville Courier Journal newspapers to find something — anything — that would have had enough publicity to attract people from Jeffersonville. To my surprise, I found several articles about Roy Davis. He was gaining quite a bit of publicity, but not the type of publicity that I was looking for.

In 1930, the same year that the "prophet" started preaching, Roy Davis was denounced by Louisville ministers for using the name "Baptist" for his Pentecostal assembly.[110] Local ministers wanted to make sure that the public was aware that Davis was by no means a "Baptist" minister, and that they did not condone his actions or practices. That year, Davis was in and out of court, and in and out of jail. In March, he defrauded one Mrs. Minnie Burgin in a scheme attempting to gather enough money to purchase a larger church.[111] In

---

[109] Sixteen Men Killed. 1890, Jan 29. Abbeville Press and Banner.
[110] One Preacher on Another. 1930, Feb 8. The Courier Journal.
[111] Mission Preacher Accused of Fraud. 1930, Mar 20. Courier Journal

October, Davis was arrested for violation of the Mann Act with a seventeen-year-old child, Allie Lee Garrison.[112] Under the provisions of the Mann Act, it was illegal for a man to take an underaged girl across state lines for the purposes of sex. October 14, 1930, Davis was indicted by a Grand Jury and started serving a jail sentence. Oddly, sixty women showed up at the court trial to protest!

The thought suddenly occurred to me: If the "prophet" started preaching in 1930 as he claimed, and he was an active, ordained minister in Roy E Davis' church at the time as he claimed, and the media was publishing the illegal and immoral activities of Roy E. Davis, there was a good chance Roy E. Davis himself could provide a glimpse into his church.

I found a letter to the editor of the Courier Journal by a reader upset with Roy E. Davis. Davis had been publicly arguing with M. P. Hunt, who had apparently thoroughly investigated Roy Davis' background and criminal activities in other states. I began searching for previous communications by Roy Davis, and I came across another letter to the editor signed by Roy E. Davis himself. In the article, Davis described the environment inside his own church during sermons. To appeal to the public, Davis used common events inside the church and associated them with his position on prohibition — which would have been a hot topic in Louisville, especially with all of the distilleries that *could have* employed many people during the onset of the Great Depression. For Louisville and Southern Indiana, prohibition was costing jobs.

According to Davis, drunken men sat in the laps of women in the congregation, while drunken women disrupted service by leaving their seats for men. Young, school-age boys and girls were so drunken they could not walk, according to Davis' description of his congregation.

In my own church in this city I have had to leave the pulpit to raise drunken men out of the laps of members of my congregations. I have had to take women — drunken women — by the arm in the presence of my congregation and lead them to seats. It is not an uncommon thing to see from one to half dozen "drunks" in my audience.[113]

---

[112] Pastor Held in Mann Act Case. 1930, Oct 12. Courier Journal
[113] Davis, Roy. A Preacher on Prohibition. 1930, Feb 5.

As I read, I tried to reconcile the image it created with my memories in the "Message". The "prophet's" first ministry was far from what I had pictured. Never in a million years would I have imagined the "prophet" participating in a service with drunkards! I realized that it was time to learn more about the Reverend Roy E. Davis. Why did he leave his church in Louisville to come to Jeffersonville? How was he able to continue preaching after a criminal indictment with an underaged girl? What made William Branham decide to continue with Roy Davis after he moved to Jeffersonville?

It seemed that there was much more to Roy E. Davis than met the eye. I knew that if I would find more information about Davis, I could unlock the door that held many secrets the "prophet" had withheld about the origins of the "Message". It was time to examine the first church that Roy E. Davis started in Jeffersonville.

GEORGE ROGERS CLARK MUNICIPAL BRIDGE:
Aerial Photo of New Bridge at Louisville. 1929, Sept 23. Cincinnati Enquirer.
The New Bridge - Chronologically. 1929, Oct 29. Courier Journal
Municipal Bridge Ready to Open. 1929, Oct 29. Courier Journal
First Life Lost in Erection of Traffic Bridge. 1929, June 19. Jeffersonville Evening News
Workman Killed in 85-Foot Fall from Traffic Bridge. 1929, Sept 11. Jeffersonville
     Evening News

EXTENSIVE RESEARCH ON GEORGE ROGERS CLARK MEMORIAL BRIDGE:
Posts on the Municipal Bridge Vision. Accessed Sept 14, 2018 from
     http://searchingforvindication.com/bridge.html
Coast Guard Life Saving Station. Accessed Sept 14, 2018 from
     http://searchingforvindication.com/2013/03/09/Coast-Guard-Life-Saving-Station/
Documented Bridge Deaths. Accessed Sept 14, 2018 from
     http://searchingforvindication.com/2013/02/25/Documented-Bridge-Deaths/

NATIONAL ARCHIVES AT ATLANTA:
National Archives Catalog. Accessed Sept 14, 2018 from *https://catalog.archives.gov/id/648209*
National Archives. Accessed Sept 14, 2018 from https://www.archives.gov/atlanta

COAST GUARD LOGBOOKS:
Coast Guard Life Saving Station Conclusion. Accessed Sept 14, 2018 from
     http://searchingforvindication.com/2013/03/18/Coast-Guard-Life-Saving-Station-Conclusion/

HISTORIC PHOTOS OF LOUISVILLE, KENTUCKY:
Historic Photos of Louisville Kentucky and Environs. Accessed Sept 14, 2018 from
     https://historiclouisville.weebly.com/the-haymarket.html
Digital Collections. Accessed Sept 14, 2018 from http://digital.library.louisville.edu/
Historic Photos of Louisville, KY. Accessed Sept 14, 2018 from
     https://www.pinterest.com/lisabhines/historic-photos-of-louisville-ky

BIG FOUR BRIDGE RESEARCH:
Sixteen Men Killed. 1890, Jan 29. Abbeville Press and Banner.
Still Buried in the Caisson. 1890, Jan 11. The Times
Drowned Like Rats. 1890, Jan 10. Ottawa Journal
The Louisville Caisson Disaster. 1890, Jan 11. Brooklyn Daily Eagle
A Dreadful Fate. 1890, Jan 10. Sterling Daily Gazette

ROY DAVIS PENTECOSTAL BAPTIST TABERNACLE:
The Point of View. 1930, Feb 8. Courier Journal
The Point of View. 1930, Feb 13. Courier Journal
Wm. Branham's First Pastor. 1950, Oct. Voice of Healing

KU KLUX KLAN INFLUENCE:
Branham, William. 1963, Nov 10. Souls That Are in Prison
Jeffersonville Booze Ring Jolted. 1924, Apr 11. The Fiery Cross

EDWARD BRANHAM:
16 Hoosiers Dead in Crashes, By Violence. 1928, June 4. Indianapolis News.

Jeffersonville Boy Killed in Gun Trade. 1928, June 3. Courier Journal
Boy, 19, Dies at Hospital. 1929, June 20. Evening News
Certificate of Death: Edward Branham.

ROY E. DAVIS:
Wm. Branham's First Pastor. 1950, Oct. Voice of Healing.
Evangelist Draws 10-Day Jail Term. 1930, Nov 3. Statesville Record and Landmark
Davis Jailed for Contempt. 1930, Nov 1. Courier Journal
Pastor Held in Mann Act Case. 1930, Oct 12. Courier Journal
Mission Preacher Accused of Fraud. 1930, Mar 20. Courier Journal
Davis Indicted by Grand Jury. 1930, Oct 14. Courier Journal
Evangelistic Singer Jailed in Kentucky. 1930, Oct 13. Greenville News
Preacher Wins, Loses in Court. 1930, Nov 1. Greenville News
Davis' Record in Texas Aired by Ku Klux Klan. 1921, Aug 26. Wise County Messenger
Denied Use of Auditorium. 1923, Jan 12. Nebraska State Journal
Klan Refused Hall. 1923, Jan 12. Reading Times
Flaming Swordsmen Will Not Discard Arms. 1925, Jan 23. The Tennessean
Fraternity Attacked as Money Making Order. 1925, Jan 23. Lead Daily Call
Simmons' Order Growing Rapidly. 1924, Oct 6. Arkansas Gazette

CHAPTER 6

WILLIAM BRANHAM'S FIRST PASTOR

"I become a minister in the Missionary Baptist Church[114]"

Growing up in the "Message", there is no question that we focused on history. In the sermons we listened to, in our study, even in the conversations we had, past events had much higher value than current events. They weren't the historical events that were taught in schools, however; these were events that only a "Message" believer would know and cherish. They were the events in the life and times of the "prophet".

We all wanted to learn a little bit more about the "prophet". We wanted to know what he liked, so we could like it too. We wanted to know what he disliked, so we could dislike it as well. We especially wanted to know what he strongly opposed, because in the "Message", if the "prophet" opposed something, we could rest assured that God had told him to oppose it — no matter what it was.

I can remember how strange it was as our family migrated across the country and attended "Message" churches in different regions. Churches in the South weren't familiar with all the rules for churches in the North. Churches in the West weren't familiar with all the rules for churches in the East. Each "Message" pastor had his own idea of what the "prophet" disliked and would preach against it with the authority of the "prophet's" recorded statements. Some had known the "prophet"

---

[114] Branham, William. My Life Story. 1950, Aug 20. "I become a minister in the Missionary Baptist Church"

personally, had spoken with the "prophet", and claimed that they had inside knowledge as to what the "prophet" stood against.

One pastor out West felt it was his sworn duty to preach against ladies wearing open-toed shoes. For this pastor and his congregation, any "Message" believing woman who opened her toes to another man was nothing more than a "prostitute". You can imagine the surprise when "Message" believing women from the East visited their church wearing open-toed shoes, or when women of his congregation visited their relatives in other parts of the country. These women had no idea that they were prostituting themselves!

Personally, I grew up with a natural curiosity that went far beyond other "Message" believers. I wanted to know more than just what to like and to dislike. I wanted to know *why* I should dislike it! In my worldview, God, the "prophet", and the world around us were like intricate gears in the timepiece of eternity. The "prophet's" history was just as important as his "message". The life he lived and the choices he made were all part of a greater plan!

There were many rules that we followed as "Message" believers that other Christian churches were not aware that they needed, from avoiding television or radio, to a very specific grooming and dress code, to relationship conduct and more. Many of the rules were not found in the Bible, and we were "privileged" to have them. His reasons, if not based on the Bible, must have been part of God's greater plan! I knew that plan included a trip out west and a return to Jeffersonville, but when I learned that William Branham was preaching with Roy Davis in Louisville, I wanted to know why. How did this information fit into the plan?

I knew that I could spend years studying Louisville history, and that history would have been fascinating. Louisville, Kentucky, was a key part of many significant historical events. But after learning that William Branham followed Roy Davis from Louisville to Jeffersonville, I became curious to know more about the Rev. Roy Davis. Why did he leave Louisville to come to Jeffersonville? He had already established his church in Louisville. Compared to Jeffersonville, Louisville had more opportunity for a growing church. I decided it was time to focus my research on Mr. Davis.

I came across an interesting article in the archives of the Courier Journal. A letter to the editor claimed the writer had done a thorough investigation on Roy E. Davis. The author of the article proposed a debate with Roy Davis the same year he ordained William Branham, the same year Davis was criminally indicted by a Grand Jury. If one researcher could find information on Davis before the internet, I would surely be able to find it using the power of technology!

Since I was relying solely upon documented history, the easiest way to trace Roy Davis was backwards through time, starting with the facts that I currently knew. I knew that Davis was indicted for bringing an underaged girl to Louisville from Chattanooga, Tennessee, and that he had been accused of doing the same with other young girls in other states. Therefore, Tennessee was the best place to start digging for more information on Roy Davis. Tracing his steps backwards, I found Roy Davis arrested in 1929, in Nashville, Tennessee.[115]

In Tennessee, Davis had used the same strategy of including the word "Baptist" in the name of his Pentecostal Assembly that he used for his churches in Louisville, Kentucky and Jeffersonville, Indiana. People in Tennessee were surprised to see the pastor of the "Pentecostal Baptist Church", Roy E. Davis, threatening an opponent with a concealed weapon. That is not the way that a pastor of a church would normally behave!

In 1925, I found that Roy Davis had made national news for his after-church activities in Tennessee. The Lead Daily Call in South Dakota published an article about Roy Davis due to his unethical practices in a fraternal organization that he was attempting to establish in Tennessee.[116] Davis was a "Royal Ambassador" of the Knights of the Flaming Sword, and was holding frequent membership drives to recruit others to join this white supremacy group.

Imperial Wizard William Joseph Simmons, founder of the 1915 Ku Klux Klan, had been banished from the Georgia-based white supremacy group and was attempting to start a rival organization.[117] The formation of the Knights of the Flaming Sword was an attempt by Simmons and

---

[115] Arrested, Pastor Takes Out Warrant. 1929, Apr 20. The Tennessean.
[116] Fraternity Attacked as Money Making Order. 1925, Jan 23. Lead Daily Call.
[117] Simmons Order Growing Rapidly. 1924, Oct 6. Arkansas Gazette.

Davis to recreate the Ku Klux Klan with a different name, and attract members from his original creation as new recruits. Davis used his pastoral authority to claim religious significance for white supremacy.

According to Davis, Simmons was likened to "Moses", which was fitting for the strategy of the organization. Like the Biblical leader of the Exodus from Egypt, Simmons was attempting to start an Exodus out of the Ku Klux Klan. Davis symbolically tried to make the claim that the Knights of the Flaming Sword organization was the "Promised Land", while the Ku Klux Klan was "Egypt" and should be left behind.[118] This strategy, however, appeared to be solely motivated by personal gain, which attracted the attention of the news media. According to the Associated Press, Simmons and Davis were taking people's money while accumulating millions of dollars for themselves.

In the early 1920's, before the Indiana Klan became dominant within the different sects of the Ku Klux Klan, the original 1915 Ku Klux Klan was in complete disarray. William Joseph Simmons and "15 charter members" had started the white supremacy group in 1915 with what purported to be good intentions, but after the group was accused of being terroristic, Simmons found himself at the center of a Federal investigation. Georgia Congressman and fellow Klansman William Upshaw successfully offered up a defense in Washington, D.C. to prevent a government shutdown of the organization,[119] but for Simmons, the damage was complete. State leaders of the Ku Klux Klan decided to appoint new central leadership, and Simmons was ousted.

Even from its inception, the 1915 Ku Klux Klan was recognized for its terroristic nature. The group prided itself on its creation of vigilantes hell-bent on enforcing laws that local, state, and federal law enforcement could or would not enforce, including laws that were not widely accepted or based on the United States Justice system. These vigilantes were especially militant against Catholics, African Americans, and Jews in the South. Since members operated under the disguise of a white hood, it was difficult to know who among the citizens was one of the vigilantes and who was not. They became

---

[118] Fraternity Attacked as Money Making Order. 1925, Jan 23. Lead Daily Call. "He said that he had been led to believe Col. Simmons was one of America's greatest Christian statesmen and the Moses of the present order of things"
[119] Upshaw Explains Kuklux Attitude. 1921, October 11. The Washington Post.

known as the "invisible army". Enforcing laws that had no judicial boundaries, however, led to violence — if there were no guidelines for the laws to enforce, then there also were no guidelines as to *how* they *should* be enforced.

Some members of the Ku Klux Klan who joined the organization because they believed in white supremacy and harbored hatred of different races or religions began torturing and killing those they hated to "cleanse" the nation. Worse, since the Ku Klux Klan was established under the guise of a "Christian" organization[120], these terroristic members were performing religious "cleansing". United States Government officials and Ku Klux Klan leaders alike feared the consequences of a "holy war", and it was clear that under the leadership of Simmons, the Klan's image would be tainted in the eyes of the government.

When Simmons was banished from the Ku Klux Klan that he created, those members who *wanted* the holy war became unhappy with current leadership. Simmons, furious for having been ousted, retaliated by attempting to steal members from the organization he created to become new recruits. I knew that if Simmons chose Davis as a "Royal Ambassador" for his replacement group, the Knights of the Flaming Sword, the trail of Davis' history would likely lead to Georgia. Simmons must have known Davis personally. I began searching newspapers from 1915 to 1925 throughout the state of Georgia for anything mentioning Roy E. Davis.

The search for Davis in Georgia was more successful than I would have ever imagined! I suddenly stumbled on a goldmine of information for Davis, enough to accurately describe the character of the "prophet's" first pastor and what could possibly have been a motivation for the "prophet" to choose Davis' church over others in the area.

According to the Associated Press in 1923, Davis was an official spokesperson for the Ku Klux Klan,[121] as well as the Klan's public defender.[122] Davis started a newspaper in Georgia, the "Brickbat", to

---

[120] Constitution and Laws of the Knights of the Ku Klux Klan. 1921. "We the Order of the Knights of the Ku Klux Klan, reverentially acknowledge the majesty and supremacy of Almighty God and recognize His goodness and providence through Jesus Christ our Lord."

[121] Klan Refused Hall. 1923, Jan 12. Reading Times. "Rev. Roy E. Davis, an official spokesman of the Ku Klux Klan"

[122] Says Ku Klux Not Anti-Negro, Jewish, Catholic. 1923, Jan 13. Times Herald.

teach Klan principles. I found that he was the head of the Georgia Farmers' Union and learned that he was fired from that position for living a "dual life".[123] The Macon, Georgia newspaper ran an article about some "Texas justice" action against Davis, who was at the time going by the alias of "Lon Davis" (short for his middle name, Elonza), and pastoring a "Baptist" church. "Lon" Davis was whipped with a wet rope for abandoning his wife and child in Texas to live with another woman in Georgia.[124] The story made big news throughout the South when it was discovered that the preacher named "Lon" was the same "Roy" from the Georgia Farmers' Union and the official spokesperson for the Ku Klux Klan.

In Texas, Davis was also making headlines. Rev. "Lon" Davis of Georgia was a convicted felon from Texas.[125] When members of his Georgia church began to investigate his past, Davis used the strong, threatening arm of the Klan to retaliate. Ku Klux Klan meetings were held at Davis' church,[126] and when deacons of the church objected, Davis handed deacon H. M. Williams a threatening "anonymous" letter from the Klan.

In 1917, Rev. Roy E. Davis went to prison for bank fraud in Texas.[127] He and his brothers were involved in stealing money from the Boonesville bank in 1916, and after a series of coincidences, Roy Davis was arrested. While he was going by the alias of "Lon" in Georgia, a lady recognized him. She had met him while visiting family in Texas and attending a revival held by "Roy" Davis. When she recognized him in Georgia, she noticed that he had a different wife than the one she met recently in Texas. Davis' dual life included dual wives, multiple ministries, multiple churches[128] — and one single lady, from one single camp meeting in Georgia, brought him down!

This was not the image I had in my mind when I thought about the "prophet's" first pastor. Did Davis' Louisville and Jeffersonville churches also host secret meetings of white supremacy? Were his sermons loaded with principles of the Ku Klux Klan? Was the

---

[123] Farm Union Head Ousted by Board. 1923, Jul 1. The Index Journal.
[124] Flog Lon Davis. 1923, Aug 18. Macon Daily Telegraph
[125] Davis' Record in Texas Aired by Ku Klux Klan. 1921, Aug 26. Wise County Messenger.
[126] Pastor is Ousted by Acworth Church. 1921, Jul 15. The Atlanta Constitution.
[127] Roy Davis, Singer and Masher, Goes to Prison. 1917, Jun 29. Wise County Messenger.
[128] Rev Roy Davis Leads Dual Life. 1923, Jul 1. The Macon Daily Telegraph

"prophet", who was an active minister in Davis' church, attending these secret meetings?

These questions led me to think about some of the "prophet's" very negative statements about Civil Rights leaders such as Martin Luther King[129] and President John F. Kennedy.[130] The "prophet" said that the election of President Kennedy was *"one of the greatest mistakes the colored race ever made"*. I began to wonder how much Davis' principles influenced the "prophet". I decided it was time to focus my research back to Jeffersonville. If Davis had left a trail of criminal activity leading through several states, there was a good chance that his criminal activity continued in Jeffersonville.

I found a series of articles in the Jeffersonville Evening News newspaper from October of 1930 describing a huge gospel tent at Warner Park near Spring Street in Jeffersonville. Perhaps in an attempt to sway public opinion concerning his character, Roy Davis held several revival meetings claiming to be a converted "licensed spiritualist medium" who converted to Christianity and began to expose the tactics used by mediums and spiritualists.[131] These meetings were very successful, attracting large crowds who begged the "evangelist" Davis to continue, and pledged donations using "pledge cards."

Local Jeffersonville pastor and former mayor's son Ralph Rader joined in the tent revivals and continued working with Roy as the meetings outgrew the tent and began using the Jeffersonville Knights of Pythias Armory instead. During the meetings, it was claimed that Mrs. Belle Eaken was healed of being crippled.[132]

The next year, in 1931, newspapers described the aftermath of those meetings. Jeffersonville newspapers in 1931 described Roy Davis helping his brothers migrate from Texas to Jeffersonville to hold another revival.[133] These were the same brothers involved with the bank fraud

---

[129] Branham, William. 1963, Jul 21. He Cares, Do You Care? "I think that Martin Luther King is Communistic inspired".
[130] Branham, William. 1960, Nov 13. Condemnation by Representation. "One of the greatest mistakes that the colored race ever made, was down in Louisiana and over in there, when they voted for Kennedy, the other night, put him in."
[131] Spiritualism Is Bunk, Dr. Davis Says at Revival. 1930, Oct 9. The Evening News
[132] Gospel Healers Claim a Cure at Tent Meet. 1930, Oct 4. The Evening News.
[133] 3 Davis Brothers Plan a Pentecostal Revival. 1931, Apr 17. The Evening News.

in Texas, and they were now in Jeffersonville helping Davis and the "prophet" grow a church—one that practiced healing!

I learned that Roy Davis had also set up a publishing company in Jeffersonville, and that he was trying to force the Evening News into using descriptions he, himself created for his church services as if their reporters had written them.[134] The newspaper refused to print his stories, unwilling to let Davis embellish the truth. Suddenly, I stumbled onto the information that I was looking for in the 1931 archives.

On September 25, 1931, Governor Sampson of Kentucky ordered that Davis be extradited to face charges.[135] Davis had fled Louisville to avoid charges of defrauding members of his church, which would explain why Davis started the Jeffersonville, Indiana, church in which the "prophet" worked as assistant pastor. Governor Leslie of Indiana agreed to let Davis be remanded to the custody of Kentucky officials, and the newspaper report went on to explain how Davis managed to gain a congregation after abandoning the one he left in Louisville.

The article stated that Davis became a choir leader for Rev. Ralph Rader, and that Rader terminated Davis unexpectedly. Davis convinced several members of Rader's congregation to leave Rader's church, after which Davis started a church community in Jeffersonville. His church was on Watt Street between Chestnut and Maple.

Ralph Rader was related to Paul Rader,[136] the author of the song "Only Believe".[137] It was a song that was very special to us in the "Message"; it was the "prophet's" theme song. If the "prophet" was preaching with Rev. Roy E. Davis from 1930 while Davis was in Louisville, then followed Davis to Jeffersonville after criminal prosecution, and continued as Davis' assistant pastor while Davis stole a large portion of Ralph Rader's congregation, it is safe to assume that the "prophet" was fully aware of Davis' background. It is also likely that "Only Believe" was a popular song in Davis' church, before the "prophet" used it for his own — his congregation came from Rader's church.

[134] Church Publicity Policy Explained. 1931, Apr 18. Evening News.
[135] Governor Holds Cleric Must Face Money Charge. 1931, Sept 25. Evening News.
[136] Raders Start Revival Drive in Indianapolis. 1930, Oct 2. Jeffersonville Evening News.
[137] Only Believe. Accessed from *https://www.cmalliance.org/alife/only-believe/*

I began to wonder: what did the local religious community think about Davis and the "prophet?" Stealing another minister's congregation, criminal allegations about living with underaged women, defrauding members of the church, extradition to Kentucky — the list of reasons *anyone* should flee Davis' church was too long to count!

The "prophet" was at the center of a nationally publicized mess. It was time to dig deeper into the transition from Davis' Pentecostal church to the "prophet's" first church in Jeffersonville, Indiana. If Davis' immoral and criminal activities did not convince the "prophet" to leave Davis, then what did?

REV. ROY E. DAVIS - EARLY CRIMINAL HISTORY
Rev. Davis, Singer and Masher, Goes to Prison. 1917, June 29. Wise County Messenger.
Rev. Roy Davis Leads Dual Life. 1923, July 1. The Macon Daily Telegraph.

ROY DAVIS - DUAL LIFE
Pastor Is Ousted by Acworth Church. 1921, July 15. The Atlanta Constitution.
Dual Life, Alias, Head of Georgia Farmers Union
Head of Georgia Farmer's Union Has Been Fired. 1923, July 1. The Index Journal.
Associated Press. 1923, July 1. Farm Union Head Ousted by Board. The Houston Post.

ROY DAVIS - ATLANTA - KU KLUX KLAN
Criminal Libel Charge to Face Brickbat Editor. 1923, June 25. The Atlanta Constitution.
The K. K. K. Lecture Not Held Last Night. 1922, May 30. The Hutchinson News.
Davis' Record in Texas Aired by Ku Klux Klan. 1921, August 26. Wise County Messenger
Denied Use of Auditorium. 1923, January 12. The Nebraska State Journal.

ROY DAVIS - OFFICIAL SPOKESPERSON FOR THE KU KLUX KLAN
Denied Use of Auditorium. 1923, January 12. The Nebraska State Journal.
The K. K. K. Lecture Not Held Last Night. 1922, May 30. The Hutchinson News.
Klan Refused Hall. 1923, January 12. Reading Times.
Klan Refused Hall. 1923, January 12. Reading Times.
Associated Press. 1923, Jan 13. Says Ku Klux Not Anti-Negro, Jewish, Catholic. Times
    Herald.

ROY DAVIS - TEXAS FLOGGING
Texas Flogging, Klan Organizer of Valdosta, Meigs, and Fitzgerald Georgia
Flog Lon Davis. August 18, 1923. Macon Daily Telegraph.

ROY DAVIS - KNIGHTS OF THE FLAMING SWORD
Wade, Wyn. 1987. The Fiery Cross: The Ku Klux Klan in America. Simon and Schuster.
Associated Press. 1925, Jan 23. Fraternity Attacked as Making Money Order. Lead Daily Call.

ROY DAVIS - LOUISVILLE/JEFFERSONVILLE HISTORY
Evangelist Draws 10-Day Jail Term. 1930, November 3. Statesville Record and Landmark.
The Point of View. 1930, February 8. The Courier Journal (Louisville, KY).
Davis Is Released in Police Court. 1930, March 22. The Courier Journal (Louisville, KY).
Davis Jailed for Contempt. 1930, November 1. The Courier Journal (Louisville, KY).
Pastor Held in Mann Act Case. 1930, October 12. The Courier Journal (Louisville, KY).
The Point of View. 1930, February 13. The Courier Journal (Louisville, KY).
Mission Preacher Accused of Fraud. 1930, March 20. The Courier Journal (Louisville, KY).
Davis Indicted by Grand Jury. 1930, October 14. The Courier Journal (Louisville, KY).
A Preacher on Prohibition. 1930, February 5. The Courier Journal (Louisville, KY).
Extradition of Davis Ordered. 1931, September 25. The Courier Journal (Louisville, KY).
Wanted-To Buy. 1931, December 31. The Courier Journal (Louisville, KY).
Charge Dismissed. 1931, December 29. The Courier Journal (Louisville, KY).
Pastor Gives Up in Fraud Case. 1931, September 15. The Courier Journal (Louisville, KY).
Writ Is Issued for Evangelist. 1931, September 9. The Courier Journal (Louisville, KY).
All-Day Meeting Held. 1931, June 9. The Courier Journal (Louisville, KY).

WILLIAM BRANHAM'S DESCRIPTIONS OF ROY DAVIS' CHURCH
Branham, William. 1955, February 27. The Healing of Jairus' Daughter.
Branham, William. 1965, April 18. "It Is the Rising of the Sun."

WILLIAM BRANHAM PARIS, TEXAS CONNECTION
Branham, William. 1950, July 16. "Believest Thou This."

WILLIAM JOSEPH SIMMONS
William Joseph Simmons. 2016, March 30. Retrieved from *https://en.metapedia.org.org*.
William Joseph Simmons, American colonel and preacher. 2016, March 30. Retrieved from
    http://www.britannica.com.
Klan Wizard Is Scored as Liar. 1921, October 17. Retrieved from
    https://www.rarenewspapers.com.
The Ku Klux Klan in the 1920s. 2016, March 30. Retrieved from *https://www.pbs.org*.
Ku Klux Klan. 2016, March 30. Retrieved from *https://www.chesnutt archive.org*.
Jackson, Charles O. 1966, December William J. Simmons: A Career in Ku Kluxism. The Georgia
    Historical Quarterly Volume 50, No 4, pp. 351-365
William Joseph Simmons. 2016, March 30. Retrieved from https://www.fbi.gov.
Imperial Wizard of Ku Klux Klan to Testify Today 1921, October 12. Joplin Globe
Simmons Denies Faked Collapse. 1921, October 17. The Charlotte News
Klan Defended Vigorously by its Organizer. 1921, October 13. The Washington Herald.

WILLIAM D. UPSHAW - KU KLUX KLAN MEMBERSHIP AND DEFENSE
Associated Press 1921, October 12. Norfolk Chief of Police Said to Be Member Ku Klux. Durham
    Morning Herald.
Defends Klan in Congressional Inquiry into the Ku Klux Klan:
Associated Press. 1921, October 11. Congress Has Started Klan Investigation. The New Bern Sun
    Journal.
House Rules Committee Ready for Klan Investigation Today. 1921, October 8. The Washington
    Post.
Upshaw Explains Kuklux Attitude. 1921, October 11. The Washington Post.
Associated Press 1921, October 8. Congressman Backs Klan. The Courier Journal.
Wants Every Secret Order Investigated. 1921, October 13. The Chronicle.
Ku Klux Klan Inquiry Has Sudden, Dramatic Closing 1921, October 8. Altoona Tribune
Urge Congress to Investigate Secret Orders. 1921, October 15. Asheville Citizen.
With Mask Off, Klan Is Week, Congress Hears 1921, October 12. Chicago Daily Tribune.
Upshaw Describes Aftermath of Probe of the Ku Klux Klan. 1921, October 28. The Atlanta

Constitution.
Klan Hearing Begins by Rules of Committee of Congress Today. 1921, October 11. The Atlanta
    Constitution.
Congressional Probe of K. K. Klan Blows Up. 1921, October 18. The Charlotte Observer.
Congress Drops Inquiry into Ku Klux Klan. 1921, October 18. The Decatur Herald.
Ku Klux Klan Inquiry Ends. 1921, October 22. The Washington Post.
The Secret Orders. 1921, October 8. The New Bern Sun Journal.
Searchlight to Be Thrown on Ku Klux Klan Activities by Secret Service Officials. 1921, September
    9. Oxford Public Ledger

RALPH RADER:
Methodists Will Have Revival. 1940, Mar 8. Angola Herald

Garner Praises Song. 1933, Oct 16. El Paso Herald Post
Warns Against Light Wine and Beer Menace. 1923, Feb 8. El Paso Herald
Rader Tabernacle Opening Set May 5. 1931, Mar 30. Evening News
Pastor Fasts 27 Days to Regain Health. 1928, Jan 8. Oakland Tribune
Pastor Flays Booze, Dances. 1923, Feb 8. Oakland Tribune
Alvarado Methodist Revival. 1939, Oct 18. Steuben Republican
Jeffersonville Pastor Ralph Rader Dies. 1951, Dec 16. Courier Journal
Misc. News. 1922, Jan 22. Courier Journal
Wire Run to Residence. 1910, Mar 8. Courier Journal
Mayor Rader's Son Shot. 1900, Sept 26. Courier Journal
Cases Are Dropped. 1930, Dec 24. Evening Republican
Faith Defenders Meet Next Week. 1929, Nov 30. Hutchinson News
Salvation Army Chaplin Passes Away. 1937, Nov 4. The Times

PAUL RADER:
Jazzset Hymns Are Winning Among Heathens. 1923, May 13. Courier Journal
Amazon Jungles Hold No Terrors for Missionaries. 1922, Sep 3. Courier Journal
The Raders. Who's Who in America. 1936-1939. Volume 20.
Only Believe. Accessed from *https://www.cmalliance.org/alife/only-believe/*
Genealogy. *www.geni.com.*
Only Believe by Elvis Presley on Amazon Music
The Life History of Roy E. Davis is fully documented in the book

CHAPTER 7

WILLIAM BRANHAM'S
FIRST MISSION

"By the Company That You Keep[138]"

My grandfather was well respected within the "Message" following. From the 1960s until the fall of 2015, Grandpa was the pastor of the "prophet's" home church in Jeffersonville, Indiana, the Branham Tabernacle. He had moved to Jeffersonville from Kentucky, where he grew up not far from the "prophet's" childhood cabin in Burkesville, Kentucky. A converted Methodist preacher, Grandpa had the unique perspective of a pastor familiar with the beliefs (and problems faced by) ministers in mainstream Christianity as they compared with believers of the "Message". Many of the pastors in the "Message" either came from non-denominational or Pentecostal backgrounds, while the younger ones were born and raised in the "Message".

Grandpa's sermons weren't like anything you would hear in other churches. They were what mainstream Christianity would call "testimonies", as they often included stories about the life and times of the "prophet" and Grandpa's memories of those experiences. The congregation would listen as he described the things he witnessed in the "prophet's" ministry and explained why they were special to us, as though the "prophet" were writing extra pages in the Book of Acts from

---

[138] Branham, William. 1959, Dec 20. Identified with Christ. "The bird is knowed by his feathers, and the man is knowed by the company he keeps."

the Bible. They also included humorous stories or sayings that the "prophet" had relayed to him, either in public or in private, which had significant appeal to the younger crowd who were born after the "prophet's" lifespan. Each and every person in the audience wanted to know everything we could about those times, and Grandpa's insights were not common knowledge among the other churches in the "Message". He was one of the few remaining people who knew the "prophet" personally.

One of the "prophet's" sayings that my grandfather often repeated was, *"You can tell the type of person you are by the company that you keep"*. Of all the sayings, this one was the most insightful, as it related to members of the "Message". The "prophet" preached many sermons on the subject of *"separating yourselves from unbelievers"*[139], and *"avoiding the appearance of evil"*. If a person was affiliated with people doing things that were dreadfully wrong, and remained in association with them after discovering the wrongdoing, they were acting as part of the problem and not part of the solution. When the "prophet" made these statements, he was usually referring to "Message" believers associating with other Christians who did not believe the "prophet". It was difficult, though, not to think about this saying as it related to the "prophet" remaining with Roy E. Davis after his criminal, unethical, and immoral background was made public. Did these sayings apply to the "prophet"?

When I thought about the "prophet's" early days as a minister, I pictured a young man who was active in the local religious community, warning them about the soon-coming Judgment that would happen just before the End of Days. I thought of him as a separatist, as he was later, even during what I thought were his early days as a minister. According to the "prophet", he had been hearing "a Voice" keeping him on the straight and narrow pathway to heaven all his life, and during times he didn't listen to that "Voice", he met with tragedy. He claimed to have heard that voice since he was a toddler.[140]

---

[139] Branham, William. 1960, Mar 1. He Careth For You. "Separate yourselves from the things of the world. Come out!"

[140] Branham, William. 1953, Nov 4. Deep Calleth Unto The Deep. "At about fifteen, eighteen months old, I had my first vision. I was standing at a little branch and Something spoke to me from a bush and said, "You're going to live near a city called New Albany."

Jeffersonville, Indiana, sits right on the outskirts of the Bible Belt, which is evident by the large number of churches in the city. There is a church on almost every street corner; some of which are new, but many that already existed at the time the "prophet" started his ministry. Downtown Jeffersonville has beautiful church buildings, with wonderfully architected designs that were popular in the 1800 and early 1900s. I pictured a young "prophet" visiting each of them! I pictured him using one of his other sayings, *"Come follow me as I follow Christ!"*

When I learned about the dreadful activities of his pastor during those years, I really started to question my mental images of what the "prophet's" early ministry would have been like. Roy Davis was running from a criminal past, and he fled Louisville, Kentucky to Jeffersonville, Indiana to evade *conviction* — not because of any spiritual or religious intent. I became even more curious as to why the "prophet" stayed with him — not just during that time, but also for the decades to come!

As I collected articles about Roy Davis, I started putting them in chronological order to form a timeline. By linking the events by time, it became much easier to watch the story unfold. I knew from the few articles I'd collected so far that Davis was not a reputable person by any standards. Reading them in order chronologically, however, made me realize that the evil I sensed was far bigger than one person. This was an organized strategy. Multiple men had to be involved. No single person could have pulled it off. It was a coordinated effort, and the "prophet" was just simply a cog in a much bigger wheel.

When Roy E. Davis lost his foothold in Louisville, Kentucky after a criminal conviction, he did not abandon his objectives in the Louisville/Southern Indiana area. It was evident that Davis was a man on a mission, and though I did not yet have enough pieces of the puzzle to know *what* that mission was, it was very clear that he had gone too far to abandon it. It was also clear that other people were involved; if it were a one-man operation, he would have simply fled the area after his criminal conviction. Religious types do not generally categorize pastors with criminal records as "reputable". Yet as the story began to unfold in

Jeffersonville, his reputation was apparently unaffected by his negative publicity. I found this fact to be very strange.

In 1931, Roy's brothers Dan S. Davis and Wilbur L. Davis migrated north from Texas to help Davis rebuild his operation.[141] Like Roy, both brothers were "ministers of the Gospel", and they came to hold an old-fashioned revival in Jeffersonville. These were the same brothers who assisted Roy Davis in bank fraud, landing Roy Davis his first criminal conviction in the State of Texas and multi-state manhunt by the Texas Rangers. Like Roy, it was clear that his brothers were not reputable. Unlike Roy, however, neither appears to have been convicted in the bank fraud and they could still identify themselves as "reputable preachers" in the unsuspecting town of Jeffersonville, Indiana.

Like Roy, the Davis brothers were more than likely involved with the Ku Klux Klan. As I would later find out, his brothers were assisting Roy in his effort to raise large sums of money by defrauding unsuspecting Christians, and that money was used for a cause that would become even more evident later in my research. Regardless of their intent, his brothers' participation in the revival, combined with Roy Davis' secret meetings to recruit, was a successful combination. They were successful in helping their brother Roy back on track, even if their methods were less than honorable.

Roy and his brothers held the revival and used the publicity of the revival to build reputation. He and his brothers convinced the news media that Roy was successful in "organizing congregations in the South" — failing to mention his doing so through use of an alias or that some of those congregations ran him out of town.

His brother, Dan Davis, relocated his family from El Paso, Texas to assist in Roy's mission. Oddly, Dan did not join Roy's church; both Davis brothers had competing Pentecostal churches in Jeffersonville.[142] At first, I found this to be very strange. When one thinks of a church as having a spiritual purpose, one would assume that like-minded men of like faith could have greater impact as one church body. Their mission, however, had very little to do with the Church. While operating each of

---

[141] 3 Davis Brothers Plan a Pentecostal Revival. 1931, Apr 17. The Evening News.
[142] Dan Davis' Pentecostal Church was frequently advertised in the Jeffersonville newspaper.

their independent churches in Jeffersonville, the two men started an official "mission" in Louisville, Kentucky.[143]

...

By the early 1930's, Jeffersonville was growing by leaps and bounds. Over one million vehicles had crossed the new George Rogers Clark Municipal Bridge in 1930,[144] bringing with them a new and quickly growing business of automobile sales to Jeffersonville.[145] Even during the Great Depression, employment could be found across the river in Louisville, and those who had automobiles could find jobs.

Just north of Jeffersonville was an amusement park, "Rose Island". It was a favorite place for after-church gatherings on Sunday until the Episcopalians introduced dancing on their boat rides.[146] This caused so much controversy that the "sterner sects" segregated themselves from the more liberal Christians of the 1930's who participated in the dancing. Rose Island had an amusement park, hotel, swimming pool, wooden roller coaster named the "Devil's Backbone", and a Ferris wheel. It also had wolves in a pen, monkeys in a cage, and a black bear named "Teddy Roosevelt".

Though it would have been appealing to the youth in the "prophet's" first church, I couldn't picture this amusement park being frequented by the Davis brothers or the members of their Pentecostal assemblies. They would have sided with the fundamentalists and boycotted Rose Island due to the dancing long before it became popular among fundamentalists to do so.

Digging through the newspaper archives, I found an obituary for Roy's brother, Dan S. Davis in the June 15, 1949 issue of Courier Journal.[147] All of Dan's 5 brothers were listed, including Roy, which was the first full list of Roy's brothers that I'd identified. The obituary stated that Dan was the head of the "East Market Street Mission" in Louisville. At first, I had assumed that Dan had eventually left

---

[143] Charters Granted. 1942, Mar 6. Courier Journal.
[144] Bridge Revenue Totals $400,760. 1931, Jan 2. Jeffersonville Evening News
[145] Willcox Auto Sales Ad. 1933, Jan 4. Jeffersonville Evening News
[146] Hill, Bob. 2018, February. Chase the Ghosts of Rose Island, take a walk back in time. Leo Weekly. Accessed from https://www.leoweekly.com/2018/02/rose-island/
[147] Former Head of Mission Dies. 1949, Jul 15. Courier Journal

Jeffersonville to start a new church in Louisville, but the word "Mission" in the name caught my eye. If he was still a Pentecostal minister in 1949, what was the "mission"? By the 1940s, Pentecostalism was decreasing in popularity, and their "mission" was to survive. Why not "East Market Street Pentecostal Church" or similar to Roy had deceitfully used, "East Market Pentecostal Baptist"? Was the "prophet" involved with this "Mission"? Is this why he called Roy Davis' Pentecostal church the "Missionary Baptist"?

I found the initial charter granted for the "Mission". It was originally named "Bethel Rescue Mission". Using that name, I found several advertisements in the Louisville newspaper. Having only recently learned about the Ku Klux Klan's propaganda and negative views of the Jews, one advertisement in particular caught my eye. Rev. Dan Davis preached a sermon entitled, "The Jew's Covenant with the Anti-Christ".[148] This title sounded so similar to what I could imagine the "prophet" preaching, which he more than likely had learned from Roy Davis. The "prophet" taught that the Gospel of Jesus Christ was not for the Jews,[149] a doctrine that most Christians — including the Biblical Apostle Paul[150] — would have strongly disagreed with.

The "Bethel Rescue Mission" keyword search unlocked the door that was hiding several pieces missing from the puzzle. In 1939, Rev. Dan Davis was arrested on charges of criminal conspiracy.[151] Dan was on a "mission", like his brother Roy, a mission to quickly accumulate a large sum of money, and I wanted to know what that money was being used for.

I found another letter to the editor of the Louisville Courier Journal newspaper. Dan had opened the church with the name "Bethel Rescue Mission", and it was the same name many people used for the "Hope Rescue Mission" of the Bethel Baptist Church.[152] He and Roy could ask unsuspecting donors to contribute to the "Bethel Rescue Mission", and

---

[148] Bethel Rescue Mission. 1940, Jan 27. The Courier Journal.
[149] Branham, William. 1961, Jul 30. Gabriel's Instructions to Daniel. "But the Gospel is not even to them. There is a few renegades that's out, and so forth like that, that come in, and outside the main body of Jews, that come in and get saved."
[150] Romans 1:16. Christian Bible (ESV). "For I am not ashamed of the gospel, for it is the power of God for salvation to everyone who believes, to the Jew first and also to the Greek."
[151] Minister Arrested. 1939, Mar 13. Courier Journal
[152] The Point of View. 1939, Dec 21. Courier Journal

they would mistakenly assume that their money would be managed by trustees in the Bethel Baptist Church.

Knowing that both Dan and Roy Davis had Pentecostal churches that deceitfully misled people into thinking "Baptist", and that the "prophet" used the same strategy claiming to have been ordained in a "Baptist" church, the pieces of the puzzle were suddenly starting to fit together. What I didn't understand is why they did not simply join the Baptist Convention. Their motives and intent were clearly non-religious, one might even consider to be anti-religious. Studying the Baptist Convention, however, it became evident that the system of checks-and-balances used in mainstream churches would have hindered Roy, Dan, and the "prophet" on their "mission". Mainstream churches require accountability. If one elder noticed another hoarding large sums of money, defrauding members, and violating both the law and Christian codes of conduct, the offending party would be forced to step down. In many Pentecostal assemblies, however, pastors are accountable only to themselves. There is no official system of accountability established in these types of independent churches.[153]

This raised many questions about the "prophet" that I hadn't yet considered. Was this why he denied starting his ministry as a Pentecostal? Did the false impression of accountability increase his credibility? In his "life stories", the "prophet" always presented himself as a "Baptist minister" whose traumatic life experience in 1937 led him to Pentecostalism.

I found other articles in other states with similar arrests for Dan Davis,[154] and it was apparent that the "Bethel Rescue Mission" was the base for operations. Rev. Dan Davis and women assisting him were soliciting funds throughout the state of Kentucky. In one instance, Dan used the name "Bethel Rescue Mission Milk Fund", which I found to be comical. Other articles about Dan were very interesting. I found Dan Davis was also arrested in New Castle, Kentucky, after which, he sued Major W. O. Ulrey.[155] Somehow, Dan managed to convince Magistrate

---

[153] Hocken, Peter. 2013. The Challenges of the Pentecostal, Charismatic and Messianic Jewish Movements.
"The suspicion of the Pentecostal churches reflected the extent to which the Pentecostal movement had become 'denominationalized' with their suspicions focusing on the problems of independency, lack of accountability and of deviant teaching"
[154] Minister Arrested. 1938, Oct 11. Cincinnati Enquirer.
[155] Writ Against Ulrey Denied. 1939, Apr 29. Courier Journal

Tom Young to obtain two warrants for arrest. According to Dan Davis, Ulrey was "interfering in operation of the mission". Dan even had attorney C. R. Turner arrested, claiming "intimidation". The Circuit Judge Thomas Ballantine called the evidence against Ulrey "revolting". Charges against the Major Ulrey were immediately dropped. The judge said that he believed Davis did not have "clean hands". Shockingly, solicitors were paid *50 percent* to collect money for the Mission.

There was one aspect missing from all the articles that I had found: Roy Davis. It was very evident that Dan had moved from Texas to assist Roy in his "mission", and I'd assumed that the "Mission" started in Louisville would have been exploited to fund Roy's unknown purpose. Suddenly, I stumbled onto an article describing an accusation of Roy Davis for similar charges in connection his "Mission" in 1930. Roy was, in fact, part of Dan Davis' "Mission". Dan was raising the money, and Roy was using it.

> *Roy E. Davis, 40 years old, a preacher, at the Holy Bible Mission, 711 East Jefferson Street, was held in $300 bond on a charge of obtaining money under false pretenses when he was arraigned Wednesday in the Police Court. His case was continued until Friday in order to allow the police time for further investigation. Mrs. Minnie Burgin, 616 East Market Street, swore to the warrant. Davis denied the charge.[156]*

This suddenly reminded me of a strange description of Roy Davis' Pentecostal church that the "prophet" frequently used. In one particular instance, the "prophet" used the word "Mission" and then corrected himself to the word "Missionary". The "prophet" said he was ordained by Davis in the "Mission" ... "Missionary Baptist" church. When the "prophet' started preaching with Roy Davis, the "Mission" was to accumulate large sums of money! This *was* the *"Missionary Baptist Church"*!

When I thought about the men with whom the "prophet" was associating and discovered their illegal and unethical means to finance their operations, I began to wonder how long the "prophet" worked with them. It was time to dig deeper into the early ministry of the "prophet".

---

[156] Mission Preacher Accused of Fraud. 1930, Mar 20. Courier Journal

How long was he active with the Davis brothers? How much did they influence his doctrine? Was his evangelistic career another means to provide funding for Davis? Was the "Branham Tabernacle" just another one of many churches Roy Davis planted?

JEFFERSONVILLE HISTORY
Bridge Revenue Totals $400,760. 1931, Jan 2. Jeffersonville Evening News
Willcox Auto Sales Ad. 1933, Jan 4. Jeffersonville Evening News
Jeffersonville Photos. Digital Collection. Accessed Aug 31, 2018 from *http://jefflibrary.org/local-history/digital-collections/*

ROSE ISLAND
Playground Three Falls Cities Offers Many Opportunities for Summer Vacation Outings. 1928, June 9. Jeffersonville Evening News.
Hill, Bob. 2018, February. Chase the Ghosts of Rose Island, take a walk back in time. Leo Weekly. Accessed from *https://www.leoweekly.com/2018/02/rose-island/*

REV. DAN S. DAVIS
3 Davis Brothers Plan a Pentecostal Revival. 1931, April 17. Jeffersonville Evening News
Minister Arrested. 1938, Oct 11. Cincinnati Enquirer.
Charters Granted. 1942, Mar 6. Courier Journal
Minister Arrested. 1939, Mar 13. Courier Journal
Bethel Rescue Mission. 1940, Apr 6. Courier Journal
Bethel Rescue Mission. 1940, Apr 27. Courier Journal
Writ Against Ulrey Denied. 1939, Apr 29. Courier Journal
Bethel Rescue Mission. 1939, Aug 26. Courier Journal
Bethel Rescue Mission. 1940, Jan 27. Courier Journal
Bethel Rescue Mission. 1940, Jul 13. Courier Journal
Bethel Rescue Mission. 1940, May 18. Courier Journal
Bethel Rescue Mission. 1940, May 25. Courier Journal
Bethel Rescue Mission. 1939, Sept 9. Courier Journal
Suit Seeks to Prevent Mission Interference. 1939, Apr 16. Courier Journal
Two Warrants Obtained. 1939, Apr 23. Courier Journal
Lawyer Faces Two Charges of Intimidation. 1939, Apr 27. Courier Journal
The Point of View. 1939, Dec 21. Courier Journal
Bethel Rescue Mission. 1939, Jul 25. Courier Journal
Former Head of Mission Dies. 1949, Jul 15. Courier Journal

REV. ROY E. DAVIS
Rev. Davis, Singer and Masher, Goes to Prison. 1917, Jul 29. Wise County Messenger
Ministers Debating Church Differences. 1919, Jan 15. Columbus Ledger
Davis' Record in Texas Aired by Ku Klux Klan. 1921, Aug 26. Wise County Messenger
Klan Issues Debated. 1922, Aug 2. Arkansas Gazette
Two Burglary Complaints Are Filed in Case of Lon Davis. 1922, Sept 15. Waco News Tribune
Exponent of Principles of Klan Starts Paper. 1923, Feb 17. The Fourth Estate
Klan Refused Hall. 1923, Jan 12. Reading Times
Alleged Assailants of Klansmen Freed. 1923, May 29. Columbus Enquirer Sun
Simmons Order Growing Rapidly. 1924, Aug 6. Arkansas Gazette
Fraternity Attacked as Money-Making Order. 1925, Jan 23. Lead Daily Call
Flaming Swordsmen Will Not Discard Arms. 1925, Jan 23. The Tennessean
Arrested, Pastor Takes Out Warrant. 1929, Apr 20. The Tennessean
Minister Indicted. 1930, Oct 17. Interior Journal
Evangelist Draws 10-Day Jail Term. 1930, Nov 3. Statesville Record and Landmark
Pastor Held in Mann Act Case. 1930, Oct 12. Courier Journal

Mission Preacher Accused of Fraud. 1930, Mar 20. Courier Journal
Davis Indicted by Grand Jury. 1930, Oct 14. Courier Journal
Extradition of Davis Ordered. 1931, Sept 25. Courier Journal
Writ Issued for Evangelist. 1931, Sept 9. Courier Journal
Pastor Gives Up in Fraud Case. 1931, Sept 15. Courier Journal
Governor Holds Cleric Must Face Money Charge. 1931, Sept 9. Jeffersonville Evening News.

WILLIAM BRANHAM'S "MISSIONARY BAPTIST"
Branham, William. 1951, May 5. My Commission
Branham, William. 1951, July 18. The Angel of the Lord
Branham, William. 1951, July 22. Life Story
Branham, William. 1951, July 29. Resurrection of Lazarus
Branham, William. 1951, Sept 30. Expectation
Branham, William. 1952, July 13. Early Spiritual Experiences
Branham, William. 1953, June 4. The Angel of the Lord
Branham, William. 1953, Aug 30. Why I Am A Holy Roller

CHAPTER 8

THE BILLIE BRANHAM
PENTECOSTAL TABERNACLE

"Dedicated in 1933[157]"

For those of us in the "Message", the "prophet's" Tabernacle was a sacred place. People from all parts of the world come to visit the "prophet's" church in Jeffersonville, Indiana. The "prophet" told my grandfather that angels lined the walls of that building, and I believed it. Many brothers and sisters say they felt a "special presence" when they were inside the Branham Tabernacle. Growing up in the "Message", I felt it too.

To the locals, it's just the "church with the sword above the door". On the front of the Branham Tabernacle, just above the two glass entry doors, an eagle was attached to the outside of the building with its wings spread and a sword in its talons. This, as you can imagine, was problematic for a city which such a high rate of crime; the weapon was frequently stolen. After disappearing, however, another was always quickly put into its place. I have no doubt that many citizens of Jeffersonville looked at the building with one raised eyebrow, trying to imagine what must go on behind those closed doors. But to us, the Branham Tabernacle was much, much more than simply *"the church with a weapon above the door"*. It was the church where William Branham buried "prophecies" in the cornerstone.

---

[157] A concrete block with the inscription, "Dedicated in 1933" can be found on the right-side of the Branham Tabernacle in Jeffersonville, Indiana.

One of the most important features of the Branham Tabernacle was found on the right-hand side of the building facing South. Approaching the building from the South was a parking lot just large enough for two rows of cars parked bumper-to-bumper. Parking spaces were separated from the building by a sidewalk. After any service, the congregation poured out of the side doors and the sidewalk quickly filled with people who stood talking, sometimes for hours. Those who arrived early could not leave; their vehicles were blocked by those who arrived after them. To signal their desire to leave, the early birds stood outside their vehicles with the driver's side door open, Bible on top of the car and arms folded comfortably above the door. Beyond all of this, just at the front corner of the red-brick building, was a light gray concrete block with the inscription: *"Dedicated in 1933"*.

This block was significant. The year 1933 was important to the "Message". The block itself was nothing fancy, just a simple time marker barely high enough to be noticed as visitors walked down the sidewalk towards the front entrance of the building. To the casual observer, especially those without interest in the history of the "Message", it might have been overlooked. For us, however, this was the most important part of the building. 1933 was the year it all started! 1933 was the year that God made Himself known to the people of Jeffersonville! How could they have forgotten? It was beyond my understanding how such an incredible series of events could be lost to time.

The "prophet" said that in 1933, as he was baptizing hundreds of people in the Ohio River, as ten thousand people watched the service, a shining star came down from the heavens just over the "prophet's" head. A voice from the heavens spoke, announcing the "prophet" and the importance of his ministry. God wanted the people of Jeffersonville to hear his "prophet", and with His own voice. He told them so![158]

1933 was also the year of the "prophecies". As the "prophet" was walking to church, he had a vision of the events soon to come. He saw how the French would build a line of concrete fortification to block the

---

[158] Branham, William. 1964, Apr 27. A Trial. "Newspapers packed it all across the nation, plumb into Canada. We got the clippings. 'Mystic Light appears over local Baptist minister while preaching, or baptizing.' 186 And that Voice came down and said, 'As John the Baptist was sent forth, to forerun the first coming of Christ, so will your Message forerun the second Coming of Christ.'"

soon-to-come invasion by Germany. He saw that President Roosevelt would take the United States into the War, and how that the Fascist leader Benito Mussolini would come to an end. He saw that cars would become more and more egg-shaped while the women became more and more immoral. Eventually, the United States would elect a female President, and she would cause the destruction of the United States.[159]

According to my grandfather, the "prophet" buried this list of "prophecies" in the ground beneath the 1933 marker of the Branham Tabernacle. It was not kept there for future generations; for one of those "prophecies" described America smoldering in ashes, and the "prophet" described the hydrogen bomb that was aimed at Jeffersonville.[160] The "prophecies" were buried, never again to be seen, and he and his family were the only ones to have seen the paper before it was buried. Nevertheless, this unseen paper was "proof" that he was a "prophet"! Myself, I needed no "proof" — I believed in the unseen. Just like the "prophet" often told us, "Look to the unseen!"

When I thought about the Branham Tabernacle, I thought about the red brick building. I never really thought about what it originally looked like or the history behind its establishment. I will never forget my surprise when I saw photos of the church as it first looked in the 1930's. The red brick shell around the building was added much later, as was the concrete inset describing its 1933 dedication. One of the photographs had a *pentagram* above the door which was later replaced with the eagle!

I will also never forget my surprise when another "Message" brother and sister found the deed to the building that I knew as the "Branham Tabernacle".[161] At that time, the church carried the name "Billie Branham Pentecostal Tabernacle". Seeing the date of the document, November 9, 1936, raised many questions. The church was a fundamental part of the beginning of the "Message". We had pictures

[159] List of 'prophecies' are not consistent, but one example:
Branham, William. 1960, Dec 11. The Laodicean Church Age.
[160] Branham, William. 1957, Apr 21. And Their Eyes Were Opened And They Knew Him. "Now, friends, my home town. And I want to say this now, before closing this revival. One of these days there won't be even an ash left in Jeffersonville, there won't be one left in Charlestown, won't be one left in Louisville. This world is ripe for judgment. They have got a hydrogen bomb now that Russia can shoot from Moscow, land it on Fourth Street, and take every one of these powder plants around here, and sink it seventy-five feet under the ground, with one bomb."
[161] Warranty Deed. 1936, Nov 9. Clark County Courthouse

of the churches "1933 dedication", just as the building was dated! At first, I thought, "Maybe the 'prophet' used the church from 1933 and purchased it later", but I couldn't explain the name of the building. The "prophet" claimed that he was a "Baptist" minister and refused to heed the "Pentecostal Call" at the request of his mother-in-law[162] until after 1937[163]. The deed to the church simply did not match the background story we had all heard in many, many sermons. I knew it was time to dig deeper into the early years of the "prophet's" ministry.

...

When Roy Davis and his brothers came to Jeffersonville, they caused quite a commotion. Not only was Davis at the center of criminal and civil lawsuits, he had started a public religious war against prohibition using the Louisville Courier Journal Newspaper as his media platform. Those who would have loved to hate Davis for his immoral lifestyle with underaged women would have hesitated to say so in a community that could have been thriving during the Great Depression — Davis alleged (at that time) that he was against prohibition. To the Branham family, having been involved with the Wathen Liquor Ring, this would have been a very appealing doctrinal position.

For the "prophet" and the people of Jeffersonville, Roy Davis' highly publicized trial of sexual immorality and swindling church members was not a problem. Instead of hiding his past, Davis embraced it. He published a religious pamphlet entitled, "Ten Days in Federal Prison", and started a revival. Roy Davis began claiming to have been a "licensed spiritualist" who "converted to Christianity" and was about to expose the increasingly popular world of spiritualism. He did very well at presenting himself as a victim. So well, in fact, he attracted former Jeffersonville Mayor Thomas B. Rader's son, Ralph Rader, to join him in hosting the revival. As a "martyr", Davis was able to attract large crowds. The city of Jeffersonville quickly turned into a Pentecostal revival, and Davis transitioned from "spiritualist" to "divine healer".

---

[162] Branham, William. 1951, Apr 14. My Life Story. "And—and there, friends, is where my sorrows started. I listened to my mother-in-law in the stead of God. He was giving me the opportunity. And there this gift would've been manifested long time ago, if I'd just went ahead and done what God told me to do."
[163] Branham, William. 1951, Apr 14. My Life Story. "Just right after that, the 1937 flood come on"

This was confusing for me, since the "prophet" claimed to have never heard of Pentecostalism before a trip to Mishawaka, Indiana, years later.[164] Having joined forces with Davis, not only was the "prophet" in a Pentecostal church focused on "divine healing", he was working with Davis as a minister helping to teach it — all while Roy Davis continued to be a familiar face in the court system.

Within just two years, Rev. Roy E. Davis was filling newspapers. You could read about his criminal court cases, civil lawsuits, revival meetings, church announcements and services, and even the Pentecostal church baseball team.[165] When I thought about the "prophet's" early ministry, I never really thought about baseball! Some "Message" churches forbid children from playing baseball. The team was pretty good, too! Their victories were reported in the Louisville news.

I started digging through every archive I could find that described Roy Davis' Pentecostal church. In the early years, E. A. Seward was an elder. Eugene Seward would have worked closely with the "prophet" during this time. I learned that besides the "prophet", George DeArk and C. E. Meyers were also elders.[166] I thought to myself, "Those names sound familiar". I remembered the 1936 deed to the Billie Branham Pentecostal Tabernacle. When the "prophet's" church was established, E. A. Seward and George DeArk were trustees. The men Roy Davis had appointed were also administrators of the "prophet's" church! I began to wonder, how many other men involved with Davis were working with the "prophet"?

Hope Brumbach, the "prophet's" first wife, was also involved. [167] She led the devotional meetings for Roy Davis' church. Dan Davis, Roy Davis' brother remained involved with Roy's operations, but not in Jeffersonville. In every article I could find listing Roy's Pentecostal Tabernacle, Dan's name never appeared. Instead, Dan started his own church on Mechanic Street, just a few blocks from Roy Davis' church.

---

[164] Branham, William. 1952, Jul 20. Life Story. "They was holding it in a big tabernacle at Mishawaka. So I—I never seen the Pentecost before, so I thought, 'Well, believe I'll go and see what it looks like.'"

[165] Jeff Team Winds 1st Tilt in Indiana Loop. 1932, Jul 6. Courier Journal.

[166] First Pentecostal Baptist, Dr. Roy E. Davis Pastor. 1933, Feb 18. The Evening News. "Scripture reading by Elder Geo DeArk. Elder Wm Bronham [sic] in charge of praise service. ... C.E. Meyers Supt. Halbert Davis in charge of the Choir."

[167] First Pentecostal Baptist. 1933, Feb 4. The Evening News. "Hope Brumbach will lead the devotional meeting"

Roy's other brother, Halbert Davis, migrated to Jeffersonville and became a leader in Roy's church. I found it terribly strange that Dan remained separate in Jeffersonville, competing against his brothers for congregants while working *with* Roy to fund his operations in Louisville.

Roy Davis continued to grow and expand his operations. He started a local radio broadcast to reach listeners in Kentucky and Southern Indiana. He also created evangelists, both male and female, to spread his "gospel." On May 6, 1933, Roy Davis announced an upcoming revival. It would be held in a tent, under the direction of a "noted evangelist".[168] And just a few days later, the "prophet" started his services in a tent on Pratt street, just a few blocks away from the two Davis churches in Jeffersonville.

FOURTEEN CONVERTED
Fourteen conversions are recorded in a tent meeting conducted at Eighth and Pratt streets by Rev. William Branham.

I tried to reconcile this with the history of the "Message" that I was taught. The "prophet" said that hundreds were converted and baptized at that meeting in 1933, and that newspapers described a light shining from heaven. The way the "prophet" described the scene, he was the center of focus while crowds large enough to gain national media attention were present to listen to God speak from the heavens.[169] Yet, in the narrative presented through the weekly editions of Jeffersonville and Louisville newspapers, the Davis brothers were center of focus — and not for their "religion" so much as for their controversy. The largest crowd reported in any newspaper that I could find for the "prophet's" meetings was "fourteen converts", which was a far cry from the hundreds that he described in his "Life Story" accounts. He claimed that the associated press "packed the story", yet not a single digital archive of any newspaper in any city had any record of such a story.

---

[168] First Pentecostal Baptist. 1933, May 6. The Evening News.
[169] Branham, William. 1964, Apr 19. The Trial. "But before better than five thousand people, at two o'clock in the afternoon, in 1933, out of the skies come this Cloud coming down, speaking these Words, "As John the Baptist was commissioned to forerun the first coming of Christ, your ministry will forerun the second coming of Christ," where thousands times thousands of people heard it, and newspapers give witness of it."

Shortly after his first tent revival, the "prophet" became part of the Pentecostal lineup in Jeffersonville newspaper's church announcements. Though his church building was not yet reported, the newspapers reported that the "prophet" had a congregation.[170]   The late Mrs. Baldwin was a member when the "prophet" preached her funeral. This fact I did not find surprising, since the "prophet" described preaching in other buildings during the early days of his ministry. The name of his church, however, was surprising. The first mention of the "prophet's" church was in the newspapers in 1935, and it was listed as the "Pentecostal Tabernacle".[171]   Jeffersonville newspapers listed the "prophet's" Pentecostal church on Penn Street, just a short distance from the other Pentecostal churches.

The "prophet's" Pentecostal Church was on Penn Street, Dan Davis' Pentecostal Church was on Mechanic Street, and Roy Davis' church was on Watt Street. Ralph Rader's Pentecostal church was at the nearby armory. The newspapers did not even mention Roy Davis' brother Wilbur or his son Roy Jr., who were now also ministers in Jeffersonville. Likely, they were appointed as "evangelists." There were so many Pentecostals in such a small town!

I thought back to the 1931 article, describing the outrageous situation when Roy took a large part of Ralph Rader's congregation. I began to wonder: Was the plan to take the rest of Ralph Rader's congregation? There weren't *that* many Pentecostals converts during that era, especially in the small town of Jeffersonville. With all of these "Pentecostal" churches, there was certainly some competition. Were they trying to drive Ralph Rader out of town?

Roy Davis continued to ordain ministers and evangelists from Jeffersonville until 1934. January 24, 1934 would be the last newspaper advertisement for Roy Davis. After this, things changed at a rapid pace. Dan Davis announced that he would be leaving "indefinitely". Rev. T. Powell replaced Dan Davis as Pastor at his church on Mechanic Street. Shortly after, Roy Davis' Pentecostal church burned[172] and the

---

[170] Mrs. Baldwin Dies in Clark Hospital. 1934, May 29. Evening News
[171] Example: Pentecostal Tabernacle. 1935, Sep 7. Evening News
[172] Misc. News. 1934, Apr 3. Jeffersonville Evening News. "The church recently was burned down"

"prophet's" church was advertised on the corner of 8th and Penn Street, replacing Roy Davis' "Pentecostal Baptist Church" advertisements.

I found it odd, after all of this, that the "prophet" continued to speak highly of Davis for the rest of his life. I remembered a sermon in 1964 mentioning the fire that burnt down Davis' church. [173] The "prophet" said that he was Davis' assistant pastor at that time. If this was correct, it would mean that members of Branham's congregation described by the newspapers were also members of Roy E. Davis' church, and that the church was splitting due to growth.

I found it even more odd that the Pentecostal Baptist church was not listed again until December 1935. Rev. Joseph D. Freeman was listed as the pastor, not Davis. What happened to Roy E. Davis? Since Davis' trustees and elders were now part of the "prophet's" church, and the "prophet" said that he was Davis' assistant pastor when the church burned, did this mean that the Billie Branham Pentecostal Tabernacle was actually Davis' church instead of the "prophet's?"

I was even more curious about the "1933 prophecies". If the "prophet" was preaching for Davis as late as 1934, how much did Davis influence the perception of those "prophecies"? It was time to dig even deeper into the building of the new church. I wanted to know why Rev. Roy E. Davis, his brothers, and his son — all ministers — suddenly left town. Most of all, I wanted to know why the "prophet" changed the timeline to 1933. There was a very unexplainable transition that happened from 1935 to 1936. Not 1933. Why did the building we held with such reverence on the corner of Eighth and Penn streets in Jeffersonville have a marker on the side of the building, added years later, that stated, "Dedicated in 1933"?

It was time to examine the "1933 prophecies", and the one I was most curious to examine was William Branham's "prophecy" of the "egg-shaped automobile". It was a "prophecy" that I used as an example many times during my life when "witnessing" to other people. As an auto enthusiast, I was fully aware that the old vehicles were big and blocky. Today's cars and trucks are more aerodynamic. Though

---

[173] Branham, William. 1957, Sept 8. Hebrews Chapter Six #2. "And the Missionary Baptist Church burned down, which I was assistant pastor, at the time."

they weren't shaped *exactly* like an egg, they were more rounded than the old cars from the 1920s and 1930s!

BILLIE BRANHAM PENTECOSTAL TABERNACLE
Warranty Deed. 1936, Nov 9. Clark County Courthouse
History of Roy Davis' Church. Accessed Aug 27, 2018 from
    http://searchingforvindication.com/2013/06/29/History-Of-Roy-Davis-Church/
Branham, William. 1960, Nov 13. Condemnation by Representation
Mrs. Baldwin Dies in Clark Hospital. 1934, May 29. Evening News
Pentecostal Tabernacle. 1935, Sep 28. Evening News
Pentecostal Tabernacle. 1935, Sep 21. Evening News
Pentecostal Tabernacle. 1935, Sep 14. Evening News
Pentecostal Tabernacle. 1935, Sep 7. Evening News
Pentecostal Tabernacle. 1935, Oct 5. Evening News
Pentecostal Tabernacle. 1935, Aug 31. Evening News
Pentecostal Tabernacle. 1935, Aug 24. Evening News

WILLIAM BRANHAM - EARLY MINISTRY:
First Pentecostal Baptist. 1933, Feb 4. Evening News
First Pentecostal Baptist. 1933, Feb 18. Evening News
First Pentecostal Baptist. 1933, Feb 25. Evening News
Fourteen Converted. 1933, May 27. Evening News
Branham, William. 1955, Jan 23. The Approach to God
Branham, William. 1951, May 2. The Angel of the Lord
Branham, William. 1955, Feb 27. The Healing of Jairus' Daughter
Branham, William. 1960, Mar 10. Elijah and the Meal-Offering
Branham, William. 1960, July 16. From That Time
Branham, William. July 22. Watchman, What of the Night
Branham, William. 1962, Apr 7. The Signs of his Coming
Branham, William. 1962, Jun 23. Perseverant
Branham, William. 1963, Mar 19. The Second Seal
Branham, William. 1964, Apr 12. A Court Trial

REV. DAN S. DAVIS
3 Davis Brothers Plan a Pentecostal Revival. 1931, April 17. Jeffersonville Evening News
Minister Arrested. 1938, Oct 11. Cincinnati Enquirer.
Charters Granted. 1942, Mar 6. Courier Journal
Minister Arrested. 1939, Mar 13. Courier Journal
Bethel Rescue Mission. 1940, Apr 6. Courier Journal
Bethel Rescue Mission. 1939, Jul 25. Courier Journal
Former Head of Mission Dies. 1949, Jul 15. Courier Journal
On Revival Trip. 1934, Mar 9. Evening News

REV. ROY E. DAVIS
Rev. Davis, Singer and Masher, Goes to Prison. 1917, Jul 29. Wise County Messenger
Ministers Debating Church Differences. 1919, Jan 15. Columbus Ledger
Davis' Record in Texas Aired by Ku Klux Klan. 1921, Aug 26. Wise County Messenger
Klan Issues Debated. 1922, Aug 2. Arkansas Gazette
Two Burglary Complaints Are Filed in Case of Lon Davis. 1922, Sept 15. Waco News Tribune
Exponent of Principles of Klan Starts Paper. 1923, Feb 17. The Fourth Estate
Klan Refused Hall. 1923, Jan 12. Reading Times
Alleged Assailants of Klansmen Freed. 1923, May 29. Columbus Enquirer Sun

Simmons Order Growing Rapidly. 1924, Aug 6. Arkansas Gazette
Fraternity Attacked as Money-Making Order. 1925, Jan 23. Lead Daily Call
Flaming Swordsmen Will Not Discard Arms. 1925, Jan 23. The Tennessean
Arrested, Pastor Takes Out Warrant. 1929, Apr 20. The Tennessean
Minister Indicted. 1930, Oct 17. Interior Journal
Evangelist Draws 10-Day Jail Term. 1930, Nov 3. Statesville Record and Landmark
Pastor Held in Mann Act Case. 1930, Oct 12. Courier Journal
Mission Preacher Accused of Fraud. 1930, Mar 20. Courier Journal
Davis Indicted by Grand Jury. 1930, Oct 14. Courier Journal
Extradition of Davis Ordered. 1931, Sept 25. Courier Journal
Writ Issued for Evangelist. 1931, Sept 9. Courier Journal
Pastor Gives Up in Fraud Case. 1931, Sept 15. Courier Journal
Governor Holds Cleric Must Face Money Charge. 1931, Sept 9. Jeffersonville Evening News.
Jeff Minister Plans Attack on Prohibition. 1930, Dec 17. Evening News
Large Crowd at Pentecostal Church Revival. 1930, Dec 26. Evening News
First Pentecostal Church. 1930, Dec 27. Evening News
Jeff Team Wins 1st Tilt in Indiana Loop. 1932, Jul 6. Evening News
Church Team Plays Thursday. 1932, Aug 31. Evening News
Court Docket List. 1932, Jan 5. Evening News
Davis Broadcast from WLAP Planned Tonight. 1933, Dec 21. Evening News

CHAPTER 9

WILLIAM BRANHAM'S TRIP TO THE CHICAGO WORLD'S FAIR

"In the shape of an egg[174]"

I never will forget my first trip to California as a young man and devoted "believer" of the "Message". It was 2004, and I was nearly trembling with a flood of emotions. The company that I worked for had scheduled a meeting in San Diego, and I had to attend. I had to attend *in California.* I had to fly to *Los Angeles.*

For most people, a first trip to L.A. and Hollywood would be a fun adventure. The Walk of Fame, the Dolby Theatre, the mesmerizing acts of street performers, and the famous Rodeo Drive — all of these are sights that many Americans may never experience in person during their lifetimes. As a young man in the "Message", however, I found this trip to be bittersweet. From the moment my plane landed until the moment I left, I feared for my life! In 1965, the "prophet" "prophesied" that Los Angeles would sink beneath the ocean.[175] From the time I was small child barely old enough to understand a "Message" sermon until I became a man in my thirties, I was trained to believe that this would happen, just any day. I believed it.

I can remember the stories my grandfather told about the destruction of Los Angeles. I clearly remembered the "prophet's" voice as he

---

[174] Branham, William. 1955, May 1. The Faith That Was Once Delivered to The Saints"
[175] Branham, William. 1965, Dec 4. The Rapture. "I remember, just my last Message in California, where I thought I'd never go back again, when I predicted, 'Los Angeles will go beneath the ocean.'"

condemned the entire city for their brazen disregard for the "prophet" and his "Message". I can remember hearing the "prophet's" son, multiple times, telling each and every one of us that the "prophet" told him that Los Angeles would sink before he was an old man.[176] The "prophet's" son, by any standard, was elderly.[177] He would smile, shake his head back and forth, and tell us, "But I'm not an old man yet!"

Those words rang through my head as I looked out the window of the plane and watched the tiny squares of land turn into the outskirts of the city. As the wheels barked and the plane jolted as it struck the runway, my ribs could barely contain my heart as it tried to pound its way out of my chest. I looked down at my feet as I stepped off the plane and made my way up the exit ramp into the Los Angeles Airport. I stopped, briefly, to adjust the strap on my backpack. It felt as if I were standing on top of a million landmines! Unsurprisingly, after I experienced an exciting time touring the city, having a successful meeting, and taking hundreds of amazing pictures, I looked around to see the city of Los Angeles still standing.

Coming back to the "safety" of Indiana, I realized that I had never really thought about the purpose behind my fears. The "prophet" said that "judgment" was soon to strike Los Angeles, and I believed it. He said it would happen before his son was "old", and I believed it. Even though at that time, his son was sixty-nine years old. I believed it because he was a "prophet". I knew that he was a "prophet" because he had a series of prophecies in 1933 and those "prophecies" were predictions describing the End of Days. We were all looking forward to the End and I never had any reason to look back to the beginning.

I never thought about the dreadful tragedy that would occur should millions of people suddenly perish as Los Angeles slipped suddenly into the ocean, or about the fact that many of those dying would be believers in Jesus Christ. I never thought about the young children who had never heard the "prophet" and had never had the chance to "repent". For that matter, I never really thought about *what,* exactly, the citizens of Los Angeles were supposed to repent *for.*

---

[176] Green, Pearry. 1993. Acts of the Prophet. "'Billy' he said, 'I may not be here, but you won't be an old man until sharks will swim right where we are standing.'"
[177] Billy Paul Branham was born on September 13, 1935

The "prophet" had often condemned Hollywood actors and actresses for immoral lives and not conforming to a Pentecostal holiness dress code, but what about the rest of the people in Greater Los Angeles? What about the devout Christian mothers working day jobs in the studios to pay their children's way through school, or the poor lost soul who had never heard of Christ but one day might have that privilege? It suddenly struck me that I had never thought about the difference between believing in "Christ" and believing in the "prophet", and what it meant to be a "Message" Christian. All I had thought about was that the "prophet" said that Los Angeles would sink, and by golly, sink it would! One day I could stand proud in knowing that our little group of believers knew of this great event before it happened!

This was but one of many questions that were beginning to surface as I began to untangle the belief system that had been cultivated in my mind since birth. When I learned that the "prophet" was an assistant pastor for Roy E. Davis as his church burned in 1934, it raised many other questions. There were significant "Message" events that were supposed to have happened in 1933 as the "Message" was birthed. Yet, according to what I'd found, the "prophet" would have been baptizing converts for Davis' church in 1933. And the "1933 prophecies" — the very reason we thought him to be a prophet — would have happened during the time that the "prophet" was an assistant pastor in Davis' church.

This was difficult for me to understand and didn't match what I'd heard: *"God sent the 'prophet' for the "Message" in 1933".* I knew that it was time to dig deeper into the "1933 Prophecies".

I was surprised when I started looking over the "prophet's" statements about the "1933 Prophecies". The earliest I could find the "prophet" mentioning them was in the 1950's,[178] though he claimed they were written on a paper that none of us had ever seen.[179] I was also surprised at how the "prophet" couldn't seem to remember what year the "prophecies" came to him. These were significant, life-changing

[178] Branham, William. 1952, Aug 10. I Am the Resurrection and the Life. "And at that time, automobiles, just before the coming of the Lord, will be in the shape of an egg." Now, remember that; keep it in mind. See? That was in 1932, or something like that."
[179] Branham, William. 1955, May 1. The Faith That Was Once Delivered to the Saints. "Now, you remember that. And when Mussolini had first come in power, one morning by a vision… Now, it's written on old paper, laying at the house today, dated way back in 1933—'32 or '33"

events that happened to him, yet they didn't seem to have enough impact to create consistent memories. Sometimes he said that his series of "visions" came to him in 1933. Other times 1932. Yet other times it was 1931.[180] He did, however, leave a clue to the year of his "prophecies". He always claimed to have been a Baptist minister at the time, and I'd just learned that he was with the "Pentecostal Baptist" church until 1934.

The more I researched his "prophecies", the stranger the details seemed to become. The "prophet" said that his associates were "revising" the prophecies,[181] and in 1960, he read from a paper that was dated 1932 — describing events that did not happen until 1934.[182] I wondered, "how was he reading from that paper?" In the "Message", we had been told that the only copy of that paper was buried under the church in 1933. How was he reading from it? Where was that copy now, if it was not buried in 1933? I began to question more than just the timeline of events.

Growing up in the "Message", there was one "prophecy" that I felt that was the easiest to prove, and I used it often as I "witnessed" to other people while attempting to recruit them into the "Message". The "prophet" claimed that cars would become shaped more and more like an egg. When I compared cars today with photos of cars in the 1930's, they were much different. Both an artist and an old car fanatic, I used to sketch still pictures of old Model T Fords, Chevy 490s and the old roadsters. My favorite was the 1934 Rolls-Royce Phantom II, with its sold chrome front-end, bulging round headlights floating between the long, curved fenders and the pointed grill, and the chrome silver wraith hood ornament. When I compared the old, squared, boxy style of the vehicles of the 1930s, it was easy to see that the more aerodynamic cars of today were "shaped like an egg" compared to a rectangle. But if the

---

[180] Branham, William. 1961, Mar 19. Jezebel Religion. "I seen it, thirty…1931. Seven things happened. I got it right on paper here, with me, wrote it in 1931"

[181] Branham, William. 1960, Nov 13. Condemnation by Representation. "By the way, Mr. Mercier and many of them are going to take some of these old prophecies, and dig them out, and revise them a little, or bring them up to date, and put them in papers."

[182] Branham, William. 1960, Nov 13. Condemnation by Representation. "I'd like to read some things that I'd like for you to—to…This one, first. I'd like to read something to you. 33 "1932. Listen to this. "As I was on my way, or as I was getting ready to go on my way to church this morning, it came to pass that I fell into a vision."

first time that I could find this "prophecy" was mentioned was in the mid 1950s, could I really say that it was a "prophecy"?

This was the first "prophecy" I began to research. I knew that I could never prove that the "prophet" didn't have such a "vision" in 1933. It is impossible to prove a negative. And since his "proof" had allegedly been "buried" for no one to see, I knew that many questions would forever be unanswered. I also knew, however, that through my research I could get a better understanding of what it would have been like for a "believer" in 1933, if this "prophecy" had been announced before Roy Davis fled town. All I needed to do was search through old newspapers in the archives.

As I began to study the archives, I found that in the early 1930's, thoughts of "egg-shaped cars" were nothing unusual. In fact, you could easily read about the new and upcoming designs in newspapers local to Jeffersonville or around the world. By 1930, American and European engineers were preparing for a radical change in the automotive industry. New body shapes were tested in wind tunnels for aerodynamics. As a result of those tests, many engineers predicted that the future design of automobiles would be egg-shaped.[183] Everyone from analysts to journalists were predicting how the change would come. The Associated Press picked up the story in 1930,[184] and papers from coast to coast described egg-shaped cars. If this was "prophesied" in 1934 — or even in 1933 — wouldn't people have rejected it as simply an "informed prediction?"

In the August 17, 1930 issue of the Arizona Star, citizens of Tucson, Arizona awakened to read an article entitled "Automobiles Still Due for Many Radical Changes",[185] describing the new and upcoming designs. The photo selected for an example of the prototypes under consideration looked exactly like the curved, egg-shaped automobiles that would soon be rolling off assembly lines. The article stated, *"As a result of these tests, we may yet be riding in egg-shaped automobiles, if our esthetic senses will permit"*. That same article, put out by the Associated Press,

---

[183] Streamlining Is Looked For. 1931, Aug 9. The Courier Journal
[184] Many Changes Being Worked Out For Cars. 1930, Aug 13. El Paso Evening Post
[185] Automobiles Still Due for Many Radical Changes. 1930, Aug 17.

appeared in newspapers in multiple cities of multiple states around the United States.

Citizens of Owensboro, Kentucky, read the same article with the title, *"Days of Gasoline Engine Not Numbered, Declared"*.[186] The anticipated change of the automobile industry fueled enthusiasts for the next years, especially the egg-shaped design. Newspaper articles with titles such as *"Egg-Shaped Automobile Body Predicted for Future"*, *found in* the April 25, 1931, Ottawa Journal, spelled it out very clearly: automobiles were changing, and soon. One does not need be a "prophet" to make this prediction; all that was necessary was to read a copy of the local newspaper. It was very easy to learn more about the automotive industry and the innovators of the 1930s by simply reading the news.

I came across a magazine article describing a "prophetic book" written by designer Norman Bel Geddes. *Horizons*, written in 1932, described how the world would change as technology advanced. Newspapers, magazines, and casual readers were fascinated with Bel Geddes' automotive design. According to Bel Geddes, the egg-shaped aerodynamics were the wave of the future. "Horizons" had architectural designs for not only the egg-shaped car, but also for the egg-shaped bus, and other vehicles. These designs looked very much as if the architect had taken a pencil and traced the outline of a chicken's egg; sketching bucket seats, a dashboard, steering wheel, and outlines of windows inside the oval shape. A side view depicted the vehicle's side profile, which made the egg seem slightly larger in the front and smaller at the back. Bel Geddes' designs were so incredible that they appeared at the 1933 World's Fair.

I remembered the "prophet" talking about visiting the World's Fair in Chicago, and I was suddenly curious to know more about the "prophet's" glimpse into the future designed by Bel Geddes. The "prophet" said that he went to the Chicago World's Fair to hear Paul Rader preach in 1933. I found an article describing Paul Rader's involvement with the World's Fair.[187] Forty centuries of religion were to be depicted in a pageant on Soldier Field on July 3, 1933. The

---

[186] Days of Gasoline Engine Not Numbered, Declared. 1930, Aug 10. Owensboro Messenger
[187] Jewish Pageant to Depict 40 Centuries of Religion. 1933, Jun 9. Chicago Tribune.

pageant, entitled "The Romance of a People", was the Jewish community's contribution to the event, and it was a dazzling display of the history of the Jews from the Old Testament. The first episode of the pageant included a sacrifice to a 27-foot-tall image of the god Moloch, the Canaanite god associated with child sacrifice.

When I heard the "prophet" talk about hearing Paul Reader "preach" at the World's Fair, I never really thought about it being at a pageant about Jewish history. In fact, I never really thought about what it would have been like at the World's Fair. The 1933 "*A Century of Progress Exposition*" World's Fair was massive. Entire villages were created representing histories, nationalities, technologies, and significant world events. Visitors could walk the "streets of Paris", or attend a carnival. They could even visit a casino, hang out in the "Hollywood Club", or visit the "Hall of Religion" where they could learn more about different denominations of faith. Chrysler, Ford, Chevrolet, and other motor companies had exhibits to display prototypes of the automotive future, and with the new shift towards aerodynamics, the "prophet" would have seen the "prophecy" before the "prediction" was made.[188] One of the vehicles on display was made almost entirely of glass; only nine working parts were necessary in the prototype.

The most extreme "egg-shaped" design was the Dynamaxion designed by American inventor Buckminster Fuller. It had three wheels, a rudder steering mechanism, and was shaped entirely like an egg. The vehicle looked very much like its designer stretched an egg slightly longer and set it upon a set of wheels, like the front-end of an airplane without wings or a tail. It was also top-heavy. Until it overturned and caught fire,[189] some visitors travelled from their parking spaces onto the fairgrounds aboard the Dynamaxion.

I began to wonder if anyone in Jeffersonville, Indiana traveled with the "prophet" to visit the Chicago World's Fair. I also wondered if Rev. Roy Davis visited, and what sermons would have been like when the "prophet" returned to Roy Davis' Pentecostal church. If the "prophet" returned and began claiming to have seen a "vision" of automobiles

[188] CHICAGO, UNITED STATES 1933-1934 Century of Progress International Exposition. Accessed Oct 9, 2018 from https://americasbesthistory.com/wfchicago1933.html
[189] Experimental Three Wheeled Automobile Overturns. 1933, Oct 28. Chicago Tribune.

soon to change in design to an egg-like shape, how would they have responded? I certainly never knew that the "prophet" would have seen the design before the "prophecy", or that the egg-shaped design was a hot topic of the early 1930s.

It made me curious about what life would have been like in the "prophet's" early church after Roy Davis left Jeffersonville, Indiana. Now that I knew about his shady background, I could easily picture Roy Davis returning to Jeffersonville and claiming to have had a "spiritual vision" while describing exhibits in the Chicago's World Fair. I could not picture the "prophet" doing this, however. Were the "prophet's" early years as the pastor of his own congregation focused on his "1933 Prophecies" and the impending "destruction of America"? Or did this notion actually originate with Roy Davis?

BILLIE BRANHAM PENTECOSTAL TABERNACLE TIMELINE
Warranty Deed. 1936, Nov 9. Clark County Courthouse
History of Roy Davis' Church. Accessed Aug 27, 2018 from
 http://searchingforvindication.com/2013/06/29/History-Of-Roy-Davis-Church/
Branham, William. 1960, Nov 13. Condemnation by Representation
Mrs. Baldwin Dies in Clark Hospital. 1934, May 29. Evening News
Pentecostal Tabernacle. 1935, Sep 28. Evening News
Pentecostal Tabernacle. 1935, Sep 21. Evening News
Pentecostal Tabernacle. 1935, Sep 14. Evening News
Pentecostal Tabernacle. 1935, Sep 7. Evening News
Pentecostal Tabernacle. 1935, Oct 5. Evening News
Pentecostal Tabernacle. 1935, Aug 31. Evening News
Pentecostal Tabernacle. 1935, Aug 24. Evening News

LOS ANGELES PROPHECY:
Green, Perry. Acts of the Prophet.
Branham, William. 1965, July 11. Ashamed

1931, 1932, 1933 PROPHECIES:

1931:
Branham, William. 1961, March 19. Jezebel Religion
Branham, William. 1963, July 31. There Is Only One Way Provided by God For Anything

1932:
Branham, William. 1955, May 1. The Faith That Was Once Delivered
Branham, William. 1960, Nov 13. Condemnation by Representation

1933:
Branham, William. 1955, May 1. The Faith That Was Once Delivered by the Saints
Branham, William. 1956, Apr 28. God's Covenant w/ Abraham.
Branham, William. 1956, May 13. Teaching on Moses
Branham, William. 1957, Apr 7. God Keeps His Word
Branham, William. 1957, Jun 2. Life

EGG-SHAPED CAR:
Streamlining Is Looked For. 1931, Aug 9. The Courier Journal
Automobile at Nice Breaks All Records. 1902, Apr 14. The Brooklyn Daily Eagle
Sensation Created by Egg-Shaped Car with Rear Motor. 1921, Nov 13. The Brooklyn Daily Eagle
Many Changes Being Worked Out for Cars. 1930, Aug 13. El Paso Evening Post
New Silver Arrow. 1933, Feb 18. El Paso Herald Post
Airplane Type Car Stressed. 1934, Jan 15. Oakland Tribune
Sidelights. 1933, Nov 20. The Galveston Daily News
Bel Geddes, Norman. 1932. Horizons.
Norman Bel Geddes Fixes a World. 1933, Jan 8. Brooklyn Daily Eagle Sun
Century of Progress is Basis of Many New Books. 1933, Jul 20. Casper Star.
First Glass Car to be Shown at Fair. 1933, Jan 25. Harrisburg Telegraph
Dynamaxion Car Unlike Anything Ever Produced in Vehicle Lane. 1933, Jul 30. Los Angeles
 Times.

Dan Neil: Dymaxion Car-Cool, How Does It Drive? Accessed Oct 7, 2018 from
  https://www.youtube.com/watch?v=N1yxFDvqALI
Patton, Phil. 2008, June 15. A 3-Wheel Dream That Died at Takeoff. New York Times. Kolbert,
  Elizabeth. 2008, Jun 9. Dymaxion Man

1933 CHICAGO WORLD'S FAIR
Branham, William. 1962, Jun 12. Behold, A Greater than Solomon is Here.
Russell V. Zahn Collection. Accessed Oct 7, 2018 from
  *http://www.chicagofilmarchives.org/collections/index.php/Detail/Object/Show/object_id/1517
  7*
Chicago, United States 1933-1934 Century of Progress International Exposition. Accessed Oct 9,
  2018 from *https://americasbesthistory.com/wfchicago1933.html*
A Century of Progress - 1833-1933. Accessed Oct 7, 2018 from
  https://chicagology.com/centuryprogress/
Jewish Pageant to Depict 40 Centuries of Religion. 1933, Jun 9. Chicago Daily Tribune (Paul Rader
  Article)
Parade Today Opens Fair. 1933, May 27. Chicago Tribune
Experimental Three Wheeled Automobile Overturns. 1933, Oct 28. Chicago Tribune.
Ahoy, Children! This is your Day at World's Fair! 1933, Jun 19. Chicago Tribune

CHAPTER 10

WILLIAM BRANHAM'S AWARD-WINNING MUSIC BAND

"This, their modern stripteases, are their choirs[190]"

As children growing up in the "Message", we always considered it a treat when we got to visit downtown Jeffersonville. Our family was migratory, moving from one "Message" church in one state to another "Message" church in another state for most of my younger life. We lived in cities from Arizona to South Carolina and everywhere between, always longing to move back to the hometown of our "prophet". Visits to Jeffersonville usually included a brief visit with family, Sunday morning and evening services at the Branham Tabernacle, and occasionally a Wednesday evening service.

One of the favorite experiences for "Message" believers was a visit to Schimpff's Candy Store. Schimpff's cinnamon red hots were the "prophet's" favorite candies, and they were our favorite candies as well. Grandma always had a can of them on her kitchen counter, as did my aunts and uncles. If the "prophet" liked red hots, we were sure to like them! Many families in the "Message" also had a white can of those red hots on their kitchen counters and offered them to "Message" guests who came to visit. Even "Message" families from out-of-state ordered cans of the red hots and had them shipped to their homes. Some

---

[190] Branham, William. 1963, Jul 7. The Indictment.

families, those who visited Jeffersonville, purchased them in person at the little store inside the row of old-fashioned brick buildings in downtown Jeffersonville. Even as an adult, I found that visiting the candy store brought fond memories. We'd park along Spring Street, often under an awning that said, "Le Rose" and stand in line to purchase a can of those red hots.

As a child with candy on my mind, I never thought much about "Le Rose", or any of the other storefronts in the heart of old Jeffersonville. At one time, "Le Rose" was a big attraction; it was the first theater in Jeffersonville to have a "talkee", or a motion picture with sound. The "prophet" wasn't the only child to enjoy those red hots. Back in the early 1900s, children would line up outside Le Rose to see the latest films. The "in" thing to do at the time was to visit Schimpff's for peanuts and red hots before watching the latest "talkee".[191] Inside the theater, three sections of seating were available, and the theater was filled with people. It was also open for an afternoon matinee, packed with children, peanuts, and red hots.

Entertainment in the "Message" was taboo, and movies were no exception. The "prophet" harshly condemned the entertainment industry, especially movies and television.[192] For decades after his death, many families who followed the "Message" abstained from various forms of entertainment. This was a touchy subject for many; not every family had the same level of abstinence from entertainment, and not every "Message" church abided by the same rules. In the prophet's hometown of Jeffersonville, for instance, my grandfather was very rigid in his preaching against entertainment. Grandpa forbade televisions in the homes, visiting movie theaters, specific musical instruments, and even certain genres of Gospel music in the church.

The "prophet's" children, who also attended the Branham Tabernacle, did *not* follow the same set of rules Grandpa taught, which caused a division in codes of conduct for people in the church. Watching television, for instance, had been a part of the Branham

---

[191] Monumental Memories. Accessed 2020, May 22 from *https://www.jeffmainstreet.org/wp-content/uploads/2016/06/2015-monumental-memories.pdf.*
[192] Branham, William. 1963, Apr 12. The World Falling Apart. "And used to be, you was ashamed. Oh, it was a disgrace for the Christian to go to a movie. They shouldn't do that, at all. The devil put one over on you. He stuck a television right in your house, and brought the movie to you, all kinds of corruption, everything else, and you permit it"

family life even while the "prophet" was alive,[193] and they viewed the "prophet's" statements condemning television and those who watched it much differently than my grandfather. Some churches in the "Message" had large bands, and choirs. There were "Message" churches that condemned their counterparts, reminding them that the "prophet" condemned a church with a choir. The "prophet" would make statements like, *"This, their modern stripteases, are their choirs"*, and certain sects of the "Message" would frown upon the "striptease" "Message" churches with choirs or musical bands.

I had a natural desire for music, and really didn't miss watching video. Like many of the migrant families in the "Message", my family would have a television for a few years, feel condemned by preaching from one of the more rigid sects, destroy their television, and get another after attending a church with a much less strict set of rules. When my family decided to rid their house of the television during my teenage years, I buried myself in music. This, too, was taboo.

The "prophet" had told my grandfather that Christians shouldn't play guitars. According to my grandfather, my grandma, aunts, and uncles had at one time been talented musicians. Before meeting the "prophet"; the family traveled the country evangelizing, playing, and singing a variety of instruments — from an accordion to a piano, organ, and guitars. Grandpa often told the story about the "prophet" telling him that his family must quit playing those instruments, and that they shouldn't be played in church. Only a piano and an organ were allowed in the Branham Tabernacle under Grandpa's authority.

When I found a photograph of the "prophet" playing a guitar, I hung it on my wall and enjoyed my guitar. My maternal grandfather, who lived in a different region of the country and belonged to a much different sect of the "Message", rejected the notion that the "prophet" spoke against musical instruments. He had given me the photo of the "prophet" and his guitar during my early teens, and much to the dismay of my father, had given me my first guitar. This, as you can imagine, caused quite a bit of friction. I sided with my maternal grandpa and my new guitar, however, and did my best to ignore the insulting comments that came from my father's side of the family. At the time, I formed the

---

[193] According to family members, Branham's house had multiple televisions inside.

opinion that if the "prophet" said two things that we thought were contradictory to each other, we must not understand what he said about them. I always wondered about the history behind that photo, though, because it somehow didn't seem to fit the image of the "prophet" that we had grown accustomed to seeing.

Learning that the "prophet" was active in the church led by Roy E. Davis in 1933 was a surprise, but learning what that the early church was like inside was an even greater surprise. Besides having an immoral and criminal background, Roy Davis himself was an entertainer. According to the newspapers, he was known throughout Texas as a "singer and masher",[194] a person who entices others through music and religion. It was easy to see that from his leading the choir for Rev. Ralph Rader and stealing his congregation, not much had changed from the time of his prison sentence in the early 1900s to his transition to Jeffersonville, Indiana in the role of a Pentecostal minister. As the official spokesperson for the Ku Klux Klan during the 1920s, Davis held public debates to both entertain and recruit. His letters to the editors of the local newspapers in Louisville and Southern Indiana served the same purposes. Even his meetings with the advertised claim to have been "converted" from a "spiritualist" was nothing more than entertainment for the purpose of recruiting. Roy Davis knew the business, and he knew it well — whether it was applied to the Ku Klux Klan, the Knights of the Flaming Sword, or his local Jeffersonville, Indiana Pentecostal church. I knew that if the newspapers described him using phrases like *"singer and masher"*, he was using his style of religious meetings to seduce. Entertainment brought the crowds, and the crowds brought money and power.

Davis's brothers were also musically inclined, playing multiple musical instruments and attracting the crowds through their music. When Davis was released from prison in 1931; and Roy's brothers migrated to Jeffersonville, Indiana to help him recover, they held a Pentecostal revival with singing. When they left town, no doubt on secret missions for the white supremacy groups they participated in, Roy Davis would return "with his party" and introduce new songs to his congregation. I couldn't help but compare this to the current Branham

---

[194] Rev. Davis, Singer and Masher, Goes to Prison. 1917, Jun 29. Wise County Messenger.

Tabernacle and its unusual stance against music. When did the musical church stop?

A "Message" brother and sister told me that the Jeffersonville courthouse still had records for both the "prophet" and Roy Davis. They also informed me that the records were freely available — a person could simply walk into the building, grab a book of records off the many shelves, open it, and read. In this day and age, that was both highly unusual and fortunate for my inescapable curiosity. I made a quick trip, and found records dating all the way back to the 1800's!

It took me some time to learn how the system worked. There were rows and rows of books stacked from floor to ceiling, in multiple rooms, some of which had tables that allowed me to lay them down, open them, and read. They were heavy books, and brittle. Not only did I have to handle each book with extreme care to keep them intact, I had to make sure that they were placed back in the correct order. Under the tables were even more rows of books, often in unusual or disorganized sequences. One rack on the left-hand side of the room might stop at one set of years, continue under the table with another set of years, and finish on another wall with the remaining years.

There were several different rooms filled with books, schematics, and other documents. One room contained all the property records, including maps with the layouts of each neighborhood in the city, archived by year. Those maps were numbered, and each number was used in another room to access the purchase, tax, and other history of the properties. Yet another room contained the deed to each property. One room contained records of civil and criminal court records. It was almost overwhelming!

The couple had found the deed for the church when it was transferred from Roy E. Davis, Sr. to his son Roy E. Davis, Jr. Roy Davis' Pentecostal church was officially sold May 10, 1934.[195] They had given me a copy of the document, which I was also able to find at the courthouse. With those documents, specifically with the dates of each document, I could then travel to the nearby public library and search through the rolls of microfiche containing the newspaper archives. By looking at the roll containing the first few months of 1934,

---

[195] Warranty Deed. 1934, May 10.

I was able to link a newspaper article to a court record. With the court record and the newspaper article, I was able to search the transcripts of the "prophet's" sermons and establish a timeline. The "prophet's" timelines were not always accurate, but by matching his descriptions, I could link a story in the timeline to the actual recorded history.

A few days after Roy E. Davis, Sr. sold the church property to his son, on May 29, 1934, the newspapers contained the first mention of the "prophet" in the newspapers having a "congregation". Roy Davis' church had closed (according to both the "prophet" and the newspapers had burned down), the land had been given to his son. From all appearances, Davis had handed his congregation over to the "prophet". The "prophet" said that he was Davis' assistant pastor until Davis' Pentecostal church burned. According to the permit, this happened in April of 1934. After the church burned, all traces of Roy Davis seemed to disappear and did not reappear until the mid 1940's when the "prophet" first started his "healing" ministry. This made me even more curious. What would make Davis decide to abandon his congregation and leave town?"

In the books of records found at the courthouse, I found an entry in the circuit courts record for Roy Davis in 1934. He had filed a lawsuit to claim the estate of Ms. Laura Belle Eaken, and sued several people, churches, and organizations, including the Walnut Ridge cemetery and the local Methodist church. "Belle" Eaken was one previously "healed" in Davis' revival meetings. Searching this date in the newspaper archives, I found that on March 30, 1934, the story appeared in detail in the Jeffersonville Evening News. When the wealthy Ms. Eaken died, her fortune was supposed to be disbursed according to a last will and testament she had signed a few years earlier. According to Davis, however, Ms. Eaken created a *second* last will and testament, and he was the beneficiary of her estate!

This no doubt angered many people in the town of Jeffersonville, shortly before his church burned to the ground, and Davis moved back across the river to Louisville, Kentucky where he started preaching at the "Bethel Rescue Mission" with his brother Dan. At about the same time, both Roy and Dan Davis used the Mission as a base of operations and closed their Jeffersonville churches. Roy's time there was short-lived, however. Roy Davis was soon extradited to Arkansas on charges of grand theft auto,[196] and elders from his church transitioned to the Billie Branham Pentecostal Tabernacle. From that time, his immoral lifestyle caught up with him, and he eventually landed in the Huntsville Prison in Walker County, Texas. In a record dating July 9, 1940, the prison log listed Roy Davis as a "sex pervert".[197]

There were so many entrances to trails of research that I found it difficult to focus. I shifted my attention back to the early days of musical talent in the Billie Branham Pentecostal Tabernacle. If there were any details about the entertainment in the "prophet's" early church, I wanted to find it. The best place to start was in the newspaper archive, so I started sifting through the rolls and rolls of microfiche at the Jeffersonville Public Library.

After the deed to the Tabernacle was signed in 1936, the church was advertised in the newspapers as the "Pentecostal Tabernacle". Continuing Davis' strategy, the church was deeply involved with music. The "prophet's" first church had a stringed band,[198] a choir,[199] an orchestra, [200]and advertised a song service with recognized local singers.[201] Some of those singers were frequently involved with the music of other churches, which sounded very much like the "prophet" invited popular local singers to attract bigger crowds.

One family in the "prophet's" first church, the Broy family, had a band. This musical family is where the "prophet" would meet his second wife, Meda Broy. Though the "prophet" would later condemn churches with choirs, the Billie Branham Pentecostal Tabernacle had a choir that was advertised in the local newspaper. This choir was not only active in the church, it was active in competition settings. In fact, the choir was a prize-winning musical group. They were so good that

---

[196] Extradition of Preacher is Signed. 1939, Jan 14. The Cincinnati Enquirer.
[197] Saltarella, Jim Magus. 2017. Acworth; Heritage History Hauntings. "A record dating July 9, 1940 showed him in Huntsville Prison, in Walker County, Texas. The note 'sex pervert' was handwritten on the log beneath his name"
[198] Pentecostal Tabernacle. 1939, Jun 3. Jeffersonville Evening News. "Evening worship and sermon in charge of pastor, assisted by choir and stringed band"
[199] Pentecostal Tabernacle. 1938, Mar 23. Jeffersonville Evening News. "Special music by the choir in appreciation of contributions received to purchase new chairs and floor covering".
[200] Pentecostal Tabernacle. 1936, Nov 21. Jeffersonville Evening News. "Music by Orchestra and Choir"
[201] Pentecostal Tabernacle. 1936, Jun 13. Jeffersonville Evening News. "Anthem by the Choir. Accordion solo, Mrs. Alice Worrell. Song by the audience. Baritone Solo, 'Jerusalem' by Sante Davidson"

they competed in contests and won.[202]   The Pentecostal Tabernacle invited other musical groups to perform with them — at the church — such as the Henryville Orchestra.   And the Pentecostal Tabernacle musicians performed at other churches, sharing their musical talent with other Christians.   When Ralph Rader opened his new "Holiness Tabernacle", the "prophet" preached, and his musical band performed to celebrate.

I began to wonder, when and why did it stop? The "prophet" came from a musical family. From the early photos of his ministry that I had in my collection it was evident that music was a part of his early life. When did the Billie Branham Pentecostal Tabernacle lose its love for music? When did the "prophet" start condemning other churches instead of participating with them?   When did he stop using stringed instruments in his church? It was time to focus my research on Hope Brumbach, the "prophet's" first wife.   From the "prophet's" own account, it was her death that signified a turning point in his life. Who was Hope Brumbach? How did she meet the "prophet"? What was she doing in Roy E. Davis' Pentecostal church? Most importantly, why did her mother not want the "prophet" to take her around "those Pentecostals?" Was it because of the religion? Or something else?

---

[202] Pentecostal Tabernacle. 1936, Jul 10. Jeffersonville Evening News. "Old time singing. Our choir will sing one of the songs they won the Contest at Carwood Tuesday evening, the 7th. We have plenty of fans, so come and spend an evening with the Lord"

LE ROSE AND SCHIMPFS CANDIES
Le Rose Theatre. Accessed Oct 10, 2018 from http://cinematreasures.org/theaters/20219
Le Rose Theatre after flood. Accessed Oct 13, 2018 from
    https://digital.library.in.gov/Record/PPO_NAFCHistoricArchive-35192E29-EB38-409A-
    9E86-425089506021
Le Rose Theatre. Accessed Oct 13, 2018 from *http://wikimapia.org/30108645/Le-Rose-Theatre*
Nokes, Garry. 2002. Jeffersonville.
Jeffersonville Historic Signs, Downtown Jeffersonville

PENTECOSTAL TABERNACLE MUSIC PROGRAM:
Pentecostal Tabernacle. 1936, Sept 12. Jeffersonville Evening News
Rev. Ralph Rader to Open New Tabernacle. 1936, Sept 12. Jeffersonville Evening News
Pentecostal Tabernacle. 1936, Sept 19. Jeffersonville Evening News
Pentecostal Tabernacle. 1936, Oct 24. Jeffersonville Evening News
Pentecostal Tabernacle. 1936, Nov 7. Jeffersonville Evening News
Pentecostal Tabernacle. 1936, Nov 21. Jeffersonville Evening News
Pentecostal Tabernacle. 1936, Jun 13. Jeffersonville Evening News
Pentecostal Tabernacle. 1936, Jul 10. Jeffersonville Evening News
Pentecostal Tabernacle. 1936, Jul 3. Jeffersonville Evening News
Rev. Branham Given Anniversary Party. 1936, Apr 15. Jeffersonville Evening News

REV. ROY E. DAVIS
Wade, Wyn. (1987). The Fiery Cross: The Ku Klux Klan in America. Simon and Schuster.
Associated Press. (1925, January 23). Fraternity Attacked as Making Money Order. Lead Daily
    Call.
Mission Preacher Accused of Fraud. (1930, March 20). The Courier Journal (Louisville, KY).
Davis Indicted by Grand Jury. (1930, October 14). The Courier Journal (Louisville, KY).
A Preacher on Prohibition. (1930, February 5). The Courier Journal (Louisville, KY).
Extradition of Davis Ordered. (1931, September 25). The Courier Journal (Louisville, KY).
Wanted-To Buy. (1931, December 31). The Courier Journal (Louisville, KY).
Charge Dismissed. (1931, December 29). The Courier Journal (Louisville, KY).
Pastor Gives Up in Fraud Case. (1931, September 15). The Courier Journal (Louisville, KY).
Writ Is Issued for Evangelist. (1931, September 9). The Courier Journal (Louisville, KY).
All-Day Meeting Held. (1931, June 9). The Courier Journal (Louisville, KY).

CHAPTER 11

WILLIAM BRANHAM'S
FIRST MARRIAGE

"Bunco, bingo, parties, teenagers rock-and-roll, twists, all these stuff![203]*"*

No matter how many times my family returned to Jeffersonville, Indiana, it always seemed that a flood of emotions overwhelmed my senses when I saw the mighty waters of the Ohio River. The mile-wide river seemed wild and untamed, not much different than it would have been when the "prophet" powered his motorboat up and down past the muddy banks. Each time we crossed the bridge from Kentucky to Indiana, I leaned towards the window to catch a glimpse of the water's edge on the Jeffersonville side to picture scenes of the "prophet" baptizing hundreds of people in front of "thousands" watching.[204]

Where must they have stood to see the service? How were hundreds of people lined up? Were they all baptized in their clothes, or were men and women assisting the people in the line? How long would it have taken to baptize hundreds of people? I tried to do the math in my head, trying to imagine the time it would have taken for a quick prayer and a dunk into the water. If there were five hundred people,[205] and they were

---

[203] Branham, William. 1965, Sept 19. Thirst.

[204] Branham, William. 1964, Apr 12. A Court Trial. "About ten thousand people standing on the bank, when one afternoon…My first great revival, somewhat around a thousand converts, and I was baptizing them out there in the water."

[205] Branham, William. 1960, Jul 22. Watchman, What of the Night? "I can remember 1933, August the 16th at two o'clock in the afternoon—I mean June the 16th at two o'clock in the afternoon. I'd just recently been

able to get in and out of the water in a minute's time per person, the "prophet" would have been in the water for over eight hours. Yet he said that almost one thousand were baptized![206] That must have been a long service! It must have taken between eight and sixteen hours, at least! I was surprised that I could find nothing even resembling that kind of revival in the newspapers — a service like that would have made *international* news.[207]

Traveling to Jeffersonville from out of town, the mighty river made me feel homesick. Homesick for the city of my birth, though I wouldn't live there until much later during my adult years. In a strange sort of way, it made me homesick for the world to come. This river had special meaning in the "Message". Not just for the "prophecy" of the deaths of "sixteen men", or the massive baptismal service — this river was instrumental in the creation of the "Message", according to the "prophet". This was the river that "God" would use to enact his vengeance against the "prophet's" wife for his refusing to heed the Pentecostal call. It was a living, breathing, bringer of both life and death through the power of God Himself. The Ohio River was a fundamental part of the "prophet's" "Life Stories", a turning point in both his life and each and every one of our lives.

He told the story often, and it was handed down to us on cassette tape. I listened to each and every one of his sermons, often. I couldn't even count the times I wept with the "prophet" as he told about his first wife and how "God" brought his wrath upon her because the "prophet" wouldn't go around "those Pentecostals".[208] I was surprised when I learned that both he and she were already Pentecostal before their marriage. The more I researched, the more I began to wonder, *"how*

---

ordained a Missionary Baptist minister, and holding my first revival where three thousand something people attended. And then, that afternoon, I was baptizing five hundred converts at the—the river's bank at the foot of Spring Street at Jeffersonville, Indiana, where I lived. And the newspaper photographers was out, and many of the church people; there was around seven or eight thousand people on the bank."

[206] Branham, William. 1964, Apr 12. A Court Trial. "I was a young Baptist preacher, and was baptizing there. About ten thousand people standing on the bank, when one afternoon...My first great revival, somewhat around a thousand converts, and I was baptizing them out there in the water. The seventeenth person, I was leading out into the water. I heard a noise, and I looked around. It was hot. It was on June, 1933, at the foot of Spring Street at Jeffersonville, Indiana."

[207] Branham claimed that it did make international news, implying Associated Press. Example: 1960, Mar 10. Elijah and the Meal-Offering. "And the newspapers put a great article, "Mystic light appears over—over a local Baptist minister while baptizing." Went all the way into Canada, got on the Canada press."

[208] Branham, William. 1950, Feb. Here We Have No Continuing City. "I don't want my daughter drug out among that bunch of trash."

many of the details in the 'life story' accounts were real?" Oddly, it was a small house by the grave of the "prophet's" first wife where the real story began. It was at this cemetery where the "prophet's" first wife Hope Brumbach's family began, and at the same cemetery where her body was laid to rest after her life tragically ended.

...

The "prophet's" first wife, Hope, was born Hope Amelia Brumbach in 1913.[209] Her grandfather was Elza (Ellsworth) Brumbach, and he lived in a small house next to the cemetery that is now her final resting place. Elza was the superintendent of the cemetery[210] and tended the grounds where his granddaughter's tombstone would be planted, and where his son, Hope's father, would nearly die at a young age. When Hope's father, Charles Brumbach, was 13, he was assaulted near the Brumbach home by attackers who mistook him for an adult. The newspaper accounts did not explain why, but Charles' attackers brutally beat him.

Tuberculosis, which claimed the life of Hope Branham, claimed other lives in the Brumbach family. During the 19th and twentieth centuries, tuberculosis was the leading cause of death in the United States.[211] It was rightfully named "the consumption", because the disease consumed a victim's body until it wasted away to nothing. Hope's uncle George died of Tuberculosis in 1910,[212] though the family tried desperately to seek a cure — both from medical experts and religious. The family had taken George to Franklin, Louisiana, for healing, but were unsuccessful in their attempts to save him.

Hope's father, Charles Brumbach, was a locomotive fireman. In 1912, Charles married her mother, Hazel Scott, and the newlywed couple moved to Logansport, Indiana, where Hazel's health would suddenly decline. Hazel became critically ill. When Charles' mother came to visit, however, Hazel started to improve. It was later learned

[209] Marriage License: William Branham and Hope Brumbach. 1934, June 22.
[210] Mystery. 1902, Nov 26. The Courier Journal
[211] Early Research and Treatment of Tuberculosis in the 19th Century. Accessed 2020, May 16 from *exhibits.hsl.virginia.edu/alav/tuberculosis/*
[212] Succumbs to Tuberculosis. 1910, Mar 20. The Courier Journal

that Charles had been abusive to Hazel,[213] and their marriage would end in divorce for the first time. When Hope was one year old, Hazel made it known that Charles had been abusive, had abandoned the mother and child, and was no longer providing for them.

By 1919, Charles had returned to Jeffersonville, Indiana, and risen to limited fame for his achievements on the railroad. During a meeting of the Order of Firemen and Enginemen, Charles was recognized for his work with the lodge. It was announced that his daughter had returned to stay with him for a brief time, and it seemed that Charles was turning his life back around. In the early 1920s, Charles entered politics. At the end of 1923, Charles accepted the nomination for Democratic trustee when control of the local government passed from the Republican Party to the Democrats. In January 1924, Charles won election in the fourth district.

Suddenly, I remembered that this was the same year that Charles Branham, the "prophet's" father, was arrested for his involvement in the production of illegal liquor for the R. E. Wathen Distilleries and Otto H. Wathen. There was an article in The Fiery Cross, the Ku Klux Klan's Indiana newsletter, describing the Ku Klux Klan headquarters in Jeffersonville after it burned. It was during this time that Jeffersonville newspapers were exposing names of the Ku Klux Klan, which was under scrutiny throughout the State of Indiana during the reign of Ku Klux Klan leader D. C. Stephenson and his control of Indiana government. Jeffersonville had become a hotspot of activity against the Klan, and during the heat of the battle, the headquarters and all records burned.

The Jeffersonville Ku Klux Klan headquarters was on the second floor of the Spieth Building on the corner of Spring Street and Chestnut (the same building where Shimpff's first started his candy store).[214] Jeffersonville had multiple branches of the Ku Klux Klan, both male and female, and the building was used as a headquarters for both branches. One part of the building was used for the women, while the other part was used for the men. According to the newspapers, Mr. Brumbach had the key to the Klan headquarters.[215]

---

[213] Young Wife Alleges Cruelty. 1914, Dec 24. The Courier Journal
[214] Charles A. Shimpff. 1916, Feb 11. Jeffersonville Evening News.

It was about this time that the "prophet" made his first trip west to live on the corner of 16th Street and Henshaw Road in Phoenix, Arizona. During his absence, Hope was finishing her schooling. She was an honor roll student[216] during the years William Branham was in Phoenix and became close friends with many schoolmates that would later become part of William Branham's life off-stage.

Parties were often held at the Brumbach house,[217] according to the local newspapers, and details of their attendees and events were newsworthy with Mr. Brumbach's position in the government. From all appearances, the Brumbach home had changed for the better. Charles and Hazel were temporarily together and holding "beach parties".[218] The second attempt at a successful marriage would not last, however. Three years before the "prophet" married Hope Brumbach, her father divorced Hazel[219] for the final time and four months later, married Grace Creigh.

His remarriage did not seem to slow Hope Brumbach, who continued partying. She was so active that her name was mentioned often in the newspapers. Hope was involved with many local clubs. She was often enjoying Bunco,[220] games, swimming, dancing, and enjoying life. The Jeffersonville newspaper, which reported everything, captured each story.

All of this was difficult for me to reconcile. In the many accounts of "prophet's" life story, he often described the happy home of Hope Brumbach's mother and father when he asked Charles for her hand in marriage. Hope's mother was not only present[221] in those accounts — at

---

[215] Organization, Control, and Membership of the Local Ku Klux Klan. 1924, Aug 26. Jeffersonville Evening News. "At the present time a man by the name of Brumbach has the key to the men's dept.

[216] Honor Roll of Howard Park School for Last Six Weeks. 1926, Feb 4. Jeffersonville Evening News

[217] Example: Surprise Party. 1921, Aug 21. Jeffersonville Evening News

[218] Misc. news. 1927, Aug 1. Jeffersonville Evening News. "Miss Hope Brumbach entertained with a beach party Sunday afternoon. Swimming and boating were the diversions"

[219] Divorce Granted. 1928, May 21. Jeffersonville Evening News.

[220] Misc. News. 1927, Apr 15. Jeffersonville Evening News.

[221] Branham, William. 1951, Apr 15. Life Story. "So that night, I remember I had to ask. I sat there and I... My, I wasn't having me a good time at all. He was playing the victrola, you know. And I went outside. I got to the door, and she looked at me. You know, I was going to go without asking him, you know. And I said... And Charlie was setting there typing on the typewriter, you know, and it was nine-thirty. Time I had to go...?... He said... I walked to the door, and I said, "Hmmph, Charlie?" He said, "Yes, Bill." I said, "Uh—uh... Could I speak to you out here just a minute?" He said, "Yes?" He looked over at Mrs. Brumbach, and she looked at me, you know. Oh, oh, oh, oh. And I said, "Here's where it all ends is right here." We went outside. Then I thought maybe that Hope had already told her mother, and her mother had done told him to say "No," you know. So I had it all fixed out how it was going to be."

the Brumbach home — but continued to be a part of the "Life Story" long after the "prophet" and Hope had married. And the "prophet" spoke harshly against women who played "bunco". It was difficult for me to picture the young "prophet" marrying someone who was featured in the newspapers for her partying.

By the time she became active in Roy E. Davis' Pentecostal Church, Hope was a familiar name in the community. Though Hope led devotional meetings at the Pentecostal Church, it was unclear whether she started attending before or after the "prophet" also joined Davis' church. The first mention of Hope in advertisements for Roy Davis' church was in February of 1933, years after the "prophet" received ordination by Davis. According to the timeline, the "prophet" would have attended Davis' church in Louisville before he fled criminal charges to Indiana, and there was no mention of Hope in the Louisville church.

Both Hope's death and Hope's mother were fundamental parts of the "prophet's" "Life Story". In almost every version of his stage persona, he claimed that this was his reason for avoiding his "calling" to the Pentecostal faith which caused her death.   According to the "prophet", it was Hope's mother who was to blame. She wouldn't let him take Hope around Pentecostals,[222] and as a result "God" took her life during the 1937 Flood of the Ohio River. Yet according to the advertisements in Roy Davis' Pentecostal church, both Hope and the "prophet" were Pentecostal before their marriage.

William Branham and Hope Brumbach married on June 22, 1934. Their marriage came just weeks after Roy and Dan Davis fled town and Branham's first "Pentecostal Tabernacle" advertisement appeared. A little over a year later, in 1935, Branham's first son, Billy Paul Branham, was born. But their happy home would not last. Hope was deathly ill. In January of 1936, Hope received a diagnosis of tuberculosis, and so began a fight for her life that she would not win. According to her death certificate, Dr. Sam Adair listed tuberculosis as the cause of death. This matched what the "prophet" said in his "Life

---

[222] Branham, William. 1950, Aug 20. My Life Story. "I knew what was up. She said, 'You cannot take my daughter.' I said, 'Look, a... Look, them's the nicest bunch of people.' She said, 'I've heard of that bunch of people; they're holy rollers.' And she said, 'You're not pulling my girl out across this world. Today she's got something to eat and tomorrow she's starving amongst that bunch of trash.'

Story", but the "prophet" did not mention that Hope had been deathly ill for over a year before she died. The date of onset for Hope's tuberculosis, according to hear death certificate, was January of 1936.

In April, Hope threw one last party, this time for William Branham.[223] It was a big one. She surprised her husband with a birthday party, and invited many, many people. In the article, Hope Branham listed William Branham's age placing his birth year at 1908 instead of 1909. This contradicted the versions of Branham's stage persona in which Branham claimed to have been "born under a sign" in 1909.[224] It did, however, match the year and age William Branham himself used in his marriage certificate to Hope.

1936 would have been a very traumatic year for the "prophet". While Hope was dying from tuberculosis, she and the "prophet" conceived a daughter, Sharon Rose.[225] Hope would have been suffering with tuberculosis while pregnant, and from the look of her photographs from the last years of her life, her life was quickly fading. The photographs were a clear representation of why the illness was called "the consumption". Sharon Rose, who died five days after her mother, likely contracted tuberculosis in the womb.

I wanted to learn more about her final years. If the "Life Story" misrepresented the truth about her final days, I wanted to know what really happened. It was time to dig deeper into the "prophet's" famous "Mishawaka Trip".

---

[223] Rev. Branham Given Anniversary Party. 1936, Apr 15. Jeffersonville Evening News
[224] Branham, William. 1952, July 13. Early Spiritual Experiences. "And she said, 'Did you know you were borned under a sign?' ... 'five o'clock in the morning in 1909'"
[225] Infant Follows Mother to Grave. 1937, Jul 26. Jeffersonville Evening News. "Sharon Rose Branham, 8 months old daughter of the Rev. William Branham"

BRUMBACH FAMILY HISTORY:
Nominate Candidates. 1923, Sep 7. Jeffersonville Bulletin
List of Court Trials. 1933, Apr 4. Jeffersonville Evening News
Funeral of J. A. Sewart. 1924, Aug 4. Jeffersonville Evening News
Meeting of Democratic Committee. 1924, Aug 16. Jeffersonville Evening News
Preparing the Program for Defense Day. 1924, Aug 28. Jeffersonville Evening News
Tramps. 1902, Dec 8. Jeffersonville Evening News
Misc. News. 1927, Jul 16. Jeffersonville Evening News
Society and Personal. 1924, Jun 28. Jeffersonville Evening News
Personals. 1914, Mar 25. Jeffersonville Evening News
Railroaders Surprise One of Members. 1919, May 21. Jeffersonville Evening News
Divorce Granted. 1928, May 21. Jeffersonville Evening News
Charlie Brumbach. 1902, Nov 26. Jeffersonville Evening News
List of Court Trials. 1931, Oct 26. Jeffersonville Evening News
Sudden Rain Follows Burial of Mr. Sparks. 1924, Sep 2. Jeffersonville Evening News
Judge Marsh. 1902, Dec 5. Jeffersonville National Democrat
The Baby Fell Two Stories. 1921, Jul 5. Jeffersonville Star
Personals. 1914, Mar 16. Jeffersonville Star
Misc. News. 1914, Mar 18. Jeffersonville Star
13 Plead Guilty to Breaking Dry Laws. 1921, Mar 16. Messenger Inquirer
Misc. News. 1916, Jun 9. The Courier Journal
Misc. News. 1902, Nov 28. The Courier Journal
Democrats Nominate. 1923, Sept 7. The Courier Journal
Misc. News. 1902, Dec 1. The Courier Journal
Misc. News. 1912, Jun 17. The Courier Journal
Five Towns to Elect Officers. 1923, Nov 5. The Courier Journal
Misc. News. 1902, Nov 29. The Courier Journal
Misc. News. 1909, Aug 8. The Courier Journal
Succumbs to Tuberculosis. 1910, Mar 20. The Courier Journal
Misc. News. 1914, Mar 22. The Courier Journal
Clark Co. Bodies are Organized. 1924, May 11. The Courier Journal
Young Wife Alleges Cruelty. 1914, Dec 24. The Courier Journal
Misc. News. 1902, Dec 2. The Courier Journal
Town Officers Change Today. 1924, Jan 1. The Courier Journal
Scott to Resign Committee Post. 1924, Dec 31. The Courier Journal
Mystery. 1902, Nov 26. The Courier Journal

KU KLUX KLAN:
Organization, Control, and Membership of the Local Ku Klux Klan. 1924, Aug 26. Klan
    Headquarters
Mysterious Fire Ruins Klan Hall. 1924, Dec 12. The Fiery Cross

HOPE BRUMBACH
Misc. News. 1927, Apr 15. Jeffersonville Evening News
Rev. Branham Given Anniversary Party. 1936, Apr 15. Jeffersonville Evening News
Misc. News. 1927, Aug 1. Jeffersonville Evening News (3 articles)
Surprise Party. 1921, Aug 21. Jeffersonville Evening News
Misc. News. 1927, Aug 27. Jeffersonville Evening News
Birthday Party. 1924, Feb 1. Jeffersonville Evening News

Honor Roll of Howard Park School for Last Six Weeks. 1926, Feb 4. Jeffersonville Evening News
Misc. News. 1928, Feb 11. Jeffersonville Evening News
Howard Park. 1927, Feb 12. Jeffersonville Evening News
Misc. News. 1927, Feb 14. Jeffersonville Evening News
Misc. News. 1927, Jul 16. Jeffersonville Evening News
Society and Personal. 1928, Jul 25. Jeffersonville Evening News
Howard Park. 1929, Mar 15. Jeffersonville Evening News
Howard Park. 1929, Mar 23. Jeffersonville Evening News
Misc. News. 1927, May 17. Jeffersonville Evening News
Entertained Pupils. 1926, May 25. Jeffersonville Evening News
Misc. News. 1927, Nov 7. Jeffersonville Evening News
Howard Park Honor Roll. 1926, Nov 12. Jeffersonville Evening News
Misc. News. 1928, Nov 29. Jeffersonville Evening News
Howard Park. 1922, Oct 16. Jeffersonville Evening News
Howard Park. 1926, Oct 19. Jeffersonville Evening News
Miss Brumbach Entertains Friends. 1928, Sep 25. Jeffersonville Evening News
First Pentecostal Baptist. 1933, Feb 4. Jeffersonville Evening News
First Pentecostal Baptist. 1933, Feb 25. Jeffersonville Evening News

CHAPTER 12

WILLIAM BRANHAM AND
THE MISHAWAKA TRIP

*I had saved up my money and I was going to take a little vacation,
going up to a place, the Paw Paw Lake[226]"*

In Nashville, Tennessee, just three hours south of Jeffersonville, stands a full-scale replica of the ancient Parthenon of Athens Greece. It towers over the sea of grass in Centennial Park just west of downtown Nashville just as you might expect a temple to the gods to do, dominating everything in its view. Like the ancient structure, its rows of round columns line the 228-foot-long sides of the building and are visible from a long distance. Facing the replica, visitors are awestruck by the 101-foot width temple in the style of the ancients surrounded by modern buildings and technology. Unlike its ancient counterpart, however, the Nashville Parthenon is fully in-tact, and gives visitors a glimpse of what the ancient Parthenon would have looked like before it was nearly destroyed during the siege of the Acropolis in 1687.

One of our family vacations was a trip to Nashville, and I had an opportunity to visit the Nashville Parthenon. Driving down the long road next to the open field, the massive structure and its surroundings were like a framed painting coming to life. In fact, we stopped multiple times along the way to capture the scene with our cameras. The

---

[226] Branham, William. 1959, Apr 19. My Life Story.

Nashville Parthenon sits alone in an open field near Vanderbilt University, where families have picnics, children and adults play sports, and stroll along the paths around Lake Watauga. Inside the temple, the building serves as an art museum. A massive statue of the Greek goddess Athena towers over guests as they admire the artwork. Confederate veteran William Crawford Smith designed the Nashville Parthenon, and its construction lasted from 1897 to the opening of the interior in 1931.

During his early ministry, the "prophet" held Pentecostal Revivals with Roy E. Davis. One of their joint campaigns took place on the grounds of the Nashville Parthenon. They must have toured together a lot, because the "prophet" couldn't remember which city had this massive structure. In his sermon, the "prophet" thought it was at their revival at Memphis, but when he described the location, he described the Nashville Parthenon.[227]

Roy Davis' Pentecostal revivals in Memphis were even more interesting, according to the "prophet's' description of the events that took place. Pentecostals of Kentucky and Tennessee of that era were well-known for their "snake handling churches". Ministers in the "snake handling" sect of Pentecostalism often quoted the last chapter of the Gospel of Mark. It was one I knew well; the "prophet" mentioned it often in his sermons. The passage reads: *"They shall take up serpents" "and if they drink any deadly thing, it shall not hurt them" "they shall lay hands on the sick, and they shall recover".*[228] It was the foundational text for the "prophet's" version of "Divine Healing", which should have come as no surprise.[229] The "Divine Healing" movement within in Pentecostalism had many similarities to the "snake handling" sect, and likely had shared some of the same historical branches — at least from the limited research I had done to this point. Some who practiced "Divine Healing" also handled snakes in the churches. They also drank

---

[227] Branham, William. 1962, Sept 9. In His Presence. "One day down in Memphis, Tennessee, or one...I don't think it was in Memphis. It was one of the places there. I was with Brother Davis and was having a—a revival. It might have been Memphis. And we was, went to a coliseum, and they had in there, not a coliseum, it was kind of an art gallery, and they had the—the great statues that they had got from different parts of the earth, of different, Hercules and so forth, and great artists had painted."

[228] Mark 16:18. Christian Bible (KJV)

[229] Branham, William. 1957, Aug 4. The Great Commission. "They shall take up serpents; and if they drink any deadly thing, it shall not hurt them; they shall lay their hands on the sick, and they shall recover."

poison, testing their "faith" in front of members as a display of "God's healing power". I often wondered: "Why did the 'prophet' focus so much on the 'snake-handling' verses"? I also wondered why he and Roy Davis were together drinking poison in their meetings.[230] Hearing the "prophet" praise Davis for drinking poison made me very uncomfortable. Even during my time in the "Message" I was aware of the dangers that this type of religion could bring.

When I learned that the "prophet" was a Pentecostal minister when he married his first wife Hope Brumbach and that the timeline the "prophet" described in his "Life Stories" was not accurate, I began to wonder about his first years in the ministry as a Pentecostal evangelist. I wondered especially about the year before Hope's death, when the "prophet" claimed to have rejected Pentecostalism.

I was also curious about the "Message" doctrines that we believed had originated with the "prophet". From the advertisements for the Pentecostal churches in Jeffersonville that the "prophet" participated in, there were too many similarities to ignore. How many of the "prophet's" doctrines were influenced by Pentecostal minister Roy Davis and his brothers? Was the "prophet's" frequent reference to the snake-handling passages a result of Roy Davis' training?

The center of focus for the "prophet's" alleged "rejection" of Pentecostalism in his "Life Story" accounts was the famous "Mishawaka Trip", which happened shortly before the death of his wife, Hope. It was during this leisure trip that the "prophet" said that he "accidentally" stumbled onto his "first experience" with Pentecostalism. According to the "prophet", he left his wife[231] at home while he took a vacation to Lake Paw Paw in Michigan.[232] I always wondered why he would leave her at home, but with Hope dying of tuberculosis (or so I thought at the time), she likely would have refused had he asked.

Lake Paw Paw was a popular resort area[233] in Berrien County, Michigan, just west of Kalamazoo near Lake Michigan. Thousands of

---

[230] Branham, William. 1953, Sept 7. Lord, Show Us the Father and it Sufficeth Us. "So Roy when he made that challenge said, 'Why not some of you guys out there believe that God's so real,' said, 'try this sulfuric acid test.'"
[231] Branham, William. 1950, Aug 20. My Life Story. "When I went home, I'll never forget. Running in... My wife always met me with her arms stretched out; I can see her yet today, bless her heart. She come running to the door; I said, "Oh, honey, I got something to tell you. I met the best bunch of people in the world."
[232] Branham, William. 1958, Feb 8. The Queen of the South. "And I remember one day I had saved up my money and I was going to take a little vacation, going up to a place, the Paw Paw Lake, to fish."

people from multiple states came to the resort lake, many of which come from just across Lake Michigan in Chicago, Illinois. It was known as "Berrien's Playground for Thousands" and "The Playground of Chicago" according to the News-Palladium.

Mishawaka, Indiana, sits about 10 miles outside of the large city of South Bend, Indiana about an hour south of Lake Paw Paw. Both cities are just a few miles south of the University of Notre Dame. Coming up Indiana State Highway 31, the "prophet" would have come directly through South Bend on his way to and from Lake Paw Paw. Just before South Bend, however, he would have saved a few miles by getting onto United States Highway 12, going through Mishawaka and heading north.

At the time the "prophet" said he "stumbled upon" the Pentecostals, both South Bend and Mishawaka had grown in population. Like downtown Louisville, Kentucky or Phoenix, Arizona, the streets were filled with automobiles, towering buildings, and businessmen scurrying up and down the sidewalks to coffee shops, restaurants, and office buildings. I never pictured this when he spoke about Mishawaka; by the way he described his "first encounter", it sounded as if he stumbled onto a backwoods revival near a lake in the middle of nowhere — but then, I also never pictured this trip as one to a thickly-populated lake resort.

The details that the "prophet" gave about the Pentecostal meeting were helpful in learning more about the revival. He described a large convention, with many Pentecostal ministers, and many people in the audience. I had always pictured a tent revival but learning the landscape of Mishawaka and the surrounding area, I realized that the revival would have been more likely in one of the city's convention centers. If so, this would have made news in the local newspapers, or at least within the Pentecostal community. Pentecostalism was in decline, and such a gathering of Pentecostals would have been significant.

I found an article in *The Old Landmark*[234] describing noteworthy, significant gatherings of Pentecostals, and I began looking for those held in Mishawaka. Two General Assemblies of Pentecostals occurred

---

[233] For Nearly Half Century Paw Paw Beckons to Resorters. 1934, Jan 1. News Palladium.
[234] This Month in Pentecostal History. Accessed Apr 6 2014 from *http://oldlandmark.wordpress.com/this-month-in-pentecostal-history/*

in the city of Mishawaka. One was in September of 1941, much later than the "prophet" would have visited. By 1941, his wife had already died. The other gathering took place in September 17-23, 1934, shortly after the "prophet" married Hope.

This made me even more confused. 1934 was *before* Hope contracted tuberculosis, so her illness was not the reason that he did not bring her along. Less than 90 days after his wedding, the "prophet" went on "vacation" without his newlywed wife! He described it as a vacation — not as an evangelistic trip or religious trip of any sort. Why did he need a "vacation" so soon?

I read, and re-read, and read his "Life Stories" again. I'd always thought that the trip happened close to the time of Hope's death, and for good reason. When the "prophet" spoke about his "Mishawaka trip", it sounded much different than the historical timeline suggests. He certainly made it sound like it was much later than a few weeks post-wedding!

He talked about how hard he and Hope had scrimped and saved for him to go on the trip, how little they could afford. How they could not scrape two pennies together, renting a small two-room apartment for four dollars a month furnished with purchases from a junk dealer.[235] How he never took an offering, and she worked at a shirt factory to make ends meet, but somehow saved a "few dollars" for a trip. It sounded like a cheap fishing trip — not a trip to a lake resort

After learning that he was still holding Pentecostal revivals with Roy Davis at this time, and that he was a Pentecostal evangelist when he "stumbled" onto the General Assembly of Pentecostals in Mishawaka, I also began to wonder: why did he claim to be a Baptist minister at the time? Was this "Mishawaka Trip" actually an evangelism tour with Roy Davis? Did he leave Hope behind because she was not involved with his already established evangelistic ministry? Whatever the reason,

---

[235] Branham, William. 1950, Feb. Here We Have No Continuing City. "I rented; my rent cost me four dollars a month. And I went into a little old place there, and somebody give us an old fashioned folding bed. You remember that old folding bed? Straw mattress, straw tick on it... And then... And we had a little old table we bought from Sears and Roebuck, and chairs; we had to—to paint it ourselves. And—and so I painted it. And we had two linoleum rugs, got from Johnny Jobbers. That was just a second hand place down into the, Jeffersonville. I said that John Jobbers so they could catch get the benefit of it. And so we got... I think they cost a dollar and a quarter apiece. And I went over to Mr. Weber's; he was a junk dealer and bought a—a cooking stove. And I give him a dollar and something for it, and I had to pay a dollar and seventy-five cents for grates to put in. I got an icebox from Public Service Company for fifty cents, one they took in on swap."

the "prophet's" "Life Story" was much different than the facts I'd collected about the historical timeline were beginning to suggest.

I began searching for other revivalists who would have been there with the "prophet" and Roy Davis. I remembered the "prophet" talking about the African American preaching, and how unusual his sermon was. The more I researched, the more surprised I became at how unusual the Pentecostal revivalists were at the time. The General Assembly at Mishawaka would have featured all sorts of unusual speakers and doctrine. They were meeting to discuss merging the different Pentecostal sects into one Pentecostal faith.[236] Suddenly, I remembered the "prophet" mentioning the merger.[237] I found that other Pentecostal conferences were held in cities the "prophet" often referred to in his sermons. I began to wonder how many of them the "prophet" attended, and why he claimed that his evangelism started in 1947 instead of 1934. According to the timeline I had pieced together from the newspapers and government documents, combined with his statements of meetings with Roy Davis, I was certain that he was fully active in the Pentecostal ministry in the early 1930s. To what end, however, I could not yet determine.

I became curious about the merger of the different sects of Pentecostalism. In the "Message", we heard that "God" sent the "prophet" to prepare the way for the Second Coming of Christ. We were taught that he opened the "hidden mysteries" of Christianity. The most important hidden mystery he taught was how to "properly" baptize converts. Without the "prophet", we'd have never known to baptize in the Name of the Lord Jesus Christ! Yet the "PAJC", or Pentecostal Assemblies of Jesus Christ, was an entire sect of Pentecostals who rejected the Trinitarian baptism! An entire demographic had spread around the globe, who already baptized like the "prophet"! This seemed very confusing.

The "prophet" was a Pentecostal, trained under Rev. Roy E. Davis. Did that mean that "God" also sent Davis to prepare the "prophet" so

---

[236] Pentecostal History. Accessed Oct 20, 2018 from *http://www.apostolicfriendsforum.com/archive/index.php/t-26307.html*

[237] Branham, William. 1957, Sept 8. Hebrews Chapter Six #2. "They had to have it in the North, on account of segregation. The colored and white were together. The P.A. of W. and the P.A. of J.C. had really merged and become the United Pentecostal. But what a revival they were having, there at Brother Rowe's tabernacle at Mishawaka."

that *he* could prepare the way? What about the hundreds of other ministers also baptizing in the Name of Jesus Christ? Were they "messengers of God"? The more I researched, the more I questioned the "prophet's" statements about his past. I continued to find more questions than answers.

I knew that one part of his story was still true: The death of his first wife had a huge impact on his life. He said that it was enough to lead him into Pentecostalism, though I now knew this was not the case. He and Roy Davis were already holding Pentecostal revivals together, and one of them was at the Nashville Parthenon. I began to wonder: "What changed?". If he did not experience a conversion to Pentecostalism, what about the "prophet" changed? What about his 1930 through 1937 Pentecostal preaching was different than his 1938 through 1965 Pentecostal preaching? Was he trying to hide the fact that Roy E. Davis introduced him to it?

Since he was working so closely with Roy E. Davis, an outspoken leader for the Ku Klux Klan and other white supremacy groups; while married to the daughter of Mr. Brumbach, who rose to sudden political fame during the Ku Klux Klan's rise to political power in Indiana (who also held the keys to the Ku Klux Klan's headquarters in the Speith Building) I knew that the "prophet" would have been influenced by the things that he heard. He might even have been involved with those groups, though I knew that I would never find membership records to the clandestine organization. Which of the doctrines that I grew up believing — that I was *trained* to believe — came from these men?

It was time to look at the most controversial doctrine of the "prophet's" ministry. I knew that it was controversial for a reason; if it were simply a doctrine found in the Bible, others who read the Bible would have eventually discovered it. His most controversial doctrine was one that he called "Serpent's Seed". It was the notion that the Original Sin in the Garden of Eden was not a result of eating fruit as the Bible narrative describes. According to the "prophet", Eve, the mother of all living, had opened her legs to the Serpent, and had sex. The result of this sexual encounter, according to the "prophet", had brought forth two bloodlines: good and evil. This doctrine was controversial because of its common usage by notorious leaders and hate groups. Adolf Hitler

125

believed in two bloodlines, and attempted to enact genocide of the Jews. The Ku Klux Klan also used it for their hate speech against both Jews and people with black skin. If the "prophet" was, in fact, touring with Roy Davis during his early years as a minister, and was actively participating in services conducted by Davis and his brothers in Jeffersonville, I had no doubt that this doctrine would have been a topic of discussion many, many times.

NASHVILLE PARTHENON:
The Parthenon. Accessed Oct 20, 2018 from *https://www.nashville.gov/Parks-and-Recreation/Parthenon.aspx*
The Parthenon. Accessed Oct 20, 2018 from https://www.trolleytours.com/nashville/parthenon
Tennessee Centennial and International Exposition Collection. 1966. Tennessee State Library and
    Archives. Accessed Oct 20, 2018 from *https://sos-tn-gov-files.tnsosfiles.com/forms/tennessee_centennial_and_international_exposition_1895-1900.pdf*
Branham, William. 1962, Sept 9. In His Presence. p48

SNAKE HANDLING AND POISON SECT OF PENTECOSTALISM:
Arsenic-Drinking Cult Must Get Rid of Snakes. 1946, December 30. Pittsburgh Post-Gazette.
Sect Defies Snakes Demonstrate Faith Healing. 1945, July 3. Great Falls Tribune.
Arsenic-Drinking Cult Must Get Rid of Snakes. 1946, December 30. Pittsburgh Post-Gazette.
Branham, William. 1953, Sept 7. Lord, Show Us the Father and It Sufficeth Us. (Davis drinking
    poison)
Branham, William. 1950, July 16. Believest Thou This. (Example Mark 16)

HOPE BRUMBACH/BRANHAM:
Misc. News. 1928, Feb 11. Jeffersonville Evening News
Howard Park. 1927, Feb 12. Jeffersonville Evening News
Misc. News. 1927, Feb 14. Jeffersonville Evening News
Misc. News. 1927, Jul 16. Jeffersonville Evening News
Society and Personal. 1928, Jul 25. Jeffersonville Evening News
Howard Park. 1929, Mar 15. Jeffersonville Evening News
Howard Park. 1929, Mar 23. Jeffersonville Evening News
Misc. News. 1927, May 17. Jeffersonville Evening News
Entertained Pupils. 1926, May 25. Jeffersonville Evening News
Misc. News. 1927, Nov 7. Jeffersonville Evening News
Howard Park Honor Roll. 1926, Nov 12. Jeffersonville Evening News
Misc. News. 1928, Nov 29. Jeffersonville Evening News
Howard Park. 1922, Oct 16. Jeffersonville Evening News
Howard Park. 1926, Oct 19. Jeffersonville Evening News
Miss Brumbach Entertains Friends. 1928, Sep 25. Jeffersonville Evening News
First Pentecostal Baptist. 1933, Feb 4. Jeffersonville Evening News
First Pentecostal Baptist. 1933, Feb 25. Jeffersonville Evening News

PAW PAW LAKE:
For Nearly Half Century Paw Paw Beckons to Resorters. 1934, Jan 1. News Palladium.
Paw Paw Lake Area Enjoyed Big Season. 1941, Dec 31. News Palladium
Best Season Ends Monday Paw Paw Lake. 1941, September 2. News Palladium.
Paw Paw Lake is Mecca for Many Vacationers. 1948, Sept 1. News Palladium.
Berrien is Ready for Big 1929 Resort Season Opening. 1929, Jun 29. News Palladium.
Paw Paw Lake. 1906, Jun 24. Chicago Tribune
Branham, William. 1959, Apr 19. My Life Story.

MISHAWAKA, IN:
About Mishawaka. Accessed Oct 20, 2018 from *http://mishawaka.in.gov/aboutmishawaka*
This Month in Pentecostal History. Accessed Apr 6, 2014 from
    http://oldlandmark.wordpress.com/this-month-in-pentecostal-history/

Pentecostal History. Accessed Oct 20, 2018 from
    http://www.apostolicfriendsforum.com/archive/index.php/t-26307.html
Branham, William. 1950, Feb. Here We Have No Continuing City.
Branham, William. 1950, Aug 20. My Life Story
Branham, William. 1951, Apr 15. Life Story
Branham, William. 1951, July 22. Life Story.
Branham, William. 1952, July 20. Life Story.
Branham, William. 1952, Aug 10. I Am the Resurrection and the Life
Branham, William. 1953, Jun 9. Demonology, Religious Realm.
Branham, William. 1953, Nov 8. Life Story.
Branham, William. 1955, Jan 17. How the Angel Came to Me and His Commission.
Branham, William. 1955, Oct 8. The Results of Decision
Branham, William. 1957, Apr 14. Corinthians, Book of Correction
Branham, William. 1957, Sep 9. Hebrews Chapter 6.
Branham, William. Feb 7. Jesus Christ the same Yesterday, Today, and Forever.
Branham, William. 1958, May. The Eagle Stirring Her Nest.
Branham, William. 1959, Aug 15. As the Eagle Stirreth Her Nest.
Branham, William. 1959, Dec 19. Questions and Answers on the Holy Spirit
Branham, William. 1960. Mar 4. Thirsting for Life
Branham, William. 1960, Aug 4. As the Eagle Stirreth Her Nest.
Branham, William. 1960, Aug 7. Debate on Tongues
Branham, William. 1961, Jan 22. As the Eagle Stirs her Nest
Branham, William. July 23. God Being Misunderstood.
Branham, William. 1962, Mar 18. The Spoken Word is the Original Seed
Branham, William. Jun 21. The Path of Life.
Branham, William. 1963, Jan 21. Zacchaeus, the Businessman.
Branham, William. 1965, Jan 18. The Seed of Discrepancy.

PENTECOSTALISM:
History of the Pentecostal Assemblies of Jesus Christ. Truth Liberty and Freedom Press (TLFP).
    Dr. Bernie L. Wade, Copyright 2001
Pentecostal Assemblies of Jesus Christ. Accessed Oct 20, 2018 from *https://www.pajci.org/*
Branham, William. 1959, Apr 19. My Life Story.
Church Groups Take Action Towards Merger. 1931, Oct 24. Winnipeg Tribune.
Pentecostal Church Holds Conference in Vandalia. 1939, Nov 24. Decatur Daily Review.
Negro Who Claims He Is 105 And Who Saw Planet Fall Here For A Revival. 1927, Mar 23. The
    Bee, Danville.
The New International Dictionary of Pentecostal and Charismatic Movements, "Charismatic
    Movement: B. The Emergence of the Movement (1960–1967)
Bernard, David (1993). "The Lord God and His Spirit". The Oneness of God. Word Aflame Press.
    ISBN 978-0-912315-12-6. Archived from the original on February 16, 2008
Constitution of the Pentecostal Assemblies of Jesus Christ. Preamble. 1955

CHAPTER 13

WILLIAM BRANHAM AND
THE SERPENT'S SEED

"Nothing designed, in all creation, that can stoop as low as a woman can[238]"

Throughout Indiana and Kentucky, there are many, massive cave systems. Some of the caves are quite large, and nationally recognized as tourist attractions. Mammoth Cave in Kentucky has over 400 miles explored and much yet unexplored. There are over 4,000 known caves in Indiana. The longest cave system in Indiana is the Brinkley Cave System, about 30 miles west of Jeffersonville. As a tourist, I never really thought much about how convenient this was for clandestine operations, such as the secret meetings of the Ku Klux Klan. During the 1920s, the years in which Indiana boasted as having the largest membership of the Ku Klux Klan,[239] these caves could have been used for meeting and planning strategy. Unlike other parts of the country where it was difficult to hide except after dark, Indiana had a natural system of hiding places. Meetings held in secret did not have to take place in the shadows at night in Indiana. Even under the noonday sunlight, the caves are so dark that you cannot see your hand in front of your face.

---

[238] Branham, William. 1965, Feb 21. Marriage and Divorce.
[239] Example: Pulaski's Grand Knights of the Ku Klux Klan. 1999. The Sociological Quarterly. Vol 40 No 1. "At the unveiling, a local pastor honored the men 'who came from dens and caves in the weird mystery of nightfall to the defense of our rights and homes. The Klan was an army of defense, a safeguard of virtue, and a victory for the right.'"

After learning the background history of Roy E. Davis and why he and his brothers came to Jeffersonville, Indiana to set up their base of operations, I began to wonder how many secret meetings took place inside these caves. Davis arriving during the height of Klan activity, at a time when the Indiana Klan lacked leadership due to Grand Dragon D. C. Stephenson's conviction for murder, all of which seemed *too* coincidental. It appears as if Roy Davis and those working with him were attempting to seize the opportunity of stepping into the leadership void, and his brothers had migrated from Texas to assist him.

I had no doubt what went on behind closed doors in the "prophet's" first church, whether the "prophet" was involved or not. But I suspected the "prophet's" involvement, because even after the long trail of criminal and immoral acts committed by Roy Davis was exposed to the public, the "prophet" continued to support Davis and praise him throughout the remainder of his ministry as a "faith healer". The real question for me was whether the "prophet" used these cave systems for private meetings of his own after Davis was extradited to Arkansas on charges of Grand Theft and was eventually locked up in a Texas prison for his immorality.

The "prophet" spoke often about spending time in caves. He even claimed that an "angel" first met him in a cave.[240] His cave played a significant part of his "Life Story". Though in other sermons he also claimed that the "angelic" meeting place was in his room,[241] or in a cabin,[242] I knew that the "prophet" spent a great deal of time in a cave because he mentioned caves frequently in his sermons. Suddenly, I thought about the leading members of Roy Davis' Pentecostal church that transitioned themselves to elders in the Billie Branham Pentecostal Tabernacle. They would have been in the clandestine meetings held by Roy Davis. Did they continue these meetings with the "prophet"?

---

[240] Branham, William. 1953, May 9. The Pillar of Fire. "Well, one night up yonder in Green's Mill, Indiana, to a cave where I was at in a place, the Angel of the Lord appeared and said, "You're to go pray for sick people."
[241] William Branham, 1947, Nov 2. The Angel of God. "I was sitting in the room. I was reading my little Scofield Bible, and I heard something. First, I saw a Light. And I thought it was an automobile that turned the corner. ... And He said, "Fear not. I'm sent from the Presence of God to tell you that this peculiar life of yours, peculiar birth"
[242] Branham, William. 1951, Sept 23. The Principles of Divine Healing. "But when the Angel of the Lord appeared to me out there on Green's Mill bank, out there in that little cabin that night"

I remembered some articles I found during the early years of the Ku Klux Klan in Georgia. At that time, Roy Davis was an official spokesman for the Klan, and held meetings with Col. William Joseph Simmons, the leader of the Ku Klux Klan during its 1915 rebirth. I had never heard of Mr. Simmons and was quite surprised when I began to study who he was and what he stood for. A member of several secret societies, Simmons re-birthed the Ku Klux Klan in 1915 as a fraternal organization. I was also surprised to learn that the Ku Klux Klan began as a "Christian" organization, and that in their lectures, Roy Davis and William Simmons promoted it as being "Christian". I was most surprised that both Simmons and Davis were traveling "preachers", or "evangelists",[243] who were experienced promoters of "fraternal orders" or "secret societies". Understanding that these movements were operating under the auspices of being "Christian" would become helpful in untangling the web of deceit as facts critical to the "Message" started to accumulate. Was the "Message" movement also serving another purpose under the guise of Christianity?

...

Learning *how* the Billie Branham Pentecostal Tabernacle was formed was a critical milestone in my journey. It was something that I had always pictured to be a story tale fable, with choirs of angels surrounding a meek and humble man as God Himself began molding a willing servant into a leader of many nations. Mostly I had pictured scenes from the early church planted in my mind by the "prophet" himself in his sermons. Still, there was always a part of me that wanted to imagine other scenes surrounding the ones the "prophet" had suggested. The facts I had uncovered this far looked nothing like those scenes Branham described, and the men who surrounded the "prophet" as the congregation transitioned to his own were far from angelic.

Learning that these men, some of them criminal, had formed religious alliances in the town of Jeffersonville and surrounding cities, I also realized that there would be a set of core doctrines used to grow

---

[243] Lee, Tom. 2005. The Tennessee-Virginia Tri-Cities. "by insurance man and part-time evangelist William Joseph Simmons"

those alliances. In the Christian religion — especially in the fundamentalist, Pentecostal sect of the Christian religion, incompatible core doctrine formed walls of division rather than open arms of unity. The religious connections who were aware of Roy Davis' (now public) history would have agreed on certain doctrines, some of which would have aligned with the central focus of white supremacy. Those in his congregation would have also agreed on certain doctrines. If not, they would have either ousted him as did a congregation in Acworth, Georgia, [244] or simply left. There was no shortage of churches in Jeffersonville and the surrounding area.

Many elders in Davis' church, including the "prophet", would have not only agreed with those core doctrines, but would also have supported, promoted, and even taught them.[245] When the congregation, elders, and religious affiliations transitioned from Davis to the "prophet" after Davis' sudden flight, the "prophet" would have naturally continued to promote those core doctrines in order to continue what Davis had started. From the looks of the articles in the newspaper, it was easy to see that those connections and those doctrines continued to exist well into the "prophet's" early career as an evangelist.

One of the elders that transitioned from Roy E. Davis' Pentecostal Church was a man by the name of George DeArk.[246] This was a name that the "prophet" mentioned in his sermons, and one that many of the locals in the Jeffersonville sect of the "Message" remembered. According to documents found in the Clark County Courthouse, E. A. Seward, George DeArk, and Frank Weber were the "prophet's" trustees when the Billie Branham Pentecostal Tabernacle's business entity began. These men, part of Roy E. Davis' inner circle, were now part of the "prophet's" inner circle. With Davis' lifelong focus on white supremacy, these men likely were involved.

---

[244] When Roy Davis was ousted from the Acworth Church in 1921, he had been holding Klan discussions. Example: Pastor is Ousted by Acworth Church. 1921, Jul 15. The Atlanta Constitution. "a meeting of the Ku Klux was held on the steps of the church."

[245] Example: George DeArk teaching Christian Identity: Branham, William. 1953, Jul 29. Questions and Answers on Genesis. "he said, "I tell you where Cain got his wife," said, "Cain went over and married a great big female ape." And said, "Out of that ape come forth the colored race."

[246] Branham, William. 1959, May 25. Images of Christ. "Yesterday, I picked up the old ledger of the church. It's been…I haven't seen it. Well, frankly, it's the first time I ever looked into it. I had to use it when the church was first founded. And there was Brother Seward's name on there, and there was Brother George DeArk, and Brother Weber, all them names on there."

I was surprised when I began to research the core values of white supremacy — especially the core values of the historical version of white supremacy groups in the United States such as the Second Ku Klux Klan. There were several research documents available on the subject of the "Christian Identity Doctrine" and its relation to white supremacy.[247] As a "Christian" organization, the Ku Klux Klan had one fundamental doctrine, the notion that members were "identified" with the supreme race, which the Klan promoted as "Christian". Supporters of the Christian Identity Doctrine believe that there were two bloodlines that resulted from the Original Sin in the Garden of Eden. In the Ku Klux Klan's version of Christian Identity, one bloodline (white) was "supreme" (white supremacy). The other bloodline, according to this theology, is inferior. Many white supremacists believe the inferior race was a result of a sexual union between Eve and the Serpent, while the other, the "supreme race", was a result of the sexual union between Adam and Eve. In fact, this strange notion of "sex in the Garden" was the basis for white supremacy campaigns against "mixing races", interracial marriage.

Stumbling onto this information both surprised me and made me ill. Surprised, because as a "Message" believer, I was trained to believe this doctrine was one that was unique to the "Message". Ill, because I was only now learning its connection to white supremacy and suddenly realizing the many implications.

In the "Message" movement, Christian Identity was one of the "secret truths" brought to us by the "prophet".[248] Because of the way that it had been presented to us, I had always thought that the "prophet" was the first to teach about "Eve having sex"[249] with the Serpent from Genesis, and that only a "chosen few" believed it. Yet the more I researched, the more I found different sects with the same belief. Each sect had their own variation of what race was produced by Eve and the Serpent.

---

[247] Christian Identity. Southern Poverty Law. Accessed Oct 24, 2018 from https://www.splcenter.org/fighting-hate/extremist-files/ideology/christian-identity

[248] Branham, William. 1962, Dec 30. Is This The Sign of the End, Sir? "The serpent's seed, that's been a hidden mystery, all through the years."

[249] Branham, William. 1965, Oct 31. Power of Transformation. "Now remember that Eve become pregnant by Satan"

The "prophet" said that he first heard about Christian Identity (two bloodlines) from George DeArk.[250] According to DeArk, it was the son of Adam and Eve who created the two bloodlines, when *"Cain went over and married a great big female ape"* and *"Out of that ape come forth the colored race".*[251] In 1957, the "prophet" said that he rejected the "two bloodlines" doctrine,[252] which I had always found to be odd since later sermons used the two bloodlines as themes for sermon content. I wanted to learn more about George DeArk, and to my surprise, finding information about Mr. DeArk was as easy as reading through the newspapers of Louisville, Kentucky, New Albany, Indiana, Charlestown, Indiana, and Jeffersonville, Indiana. In fact, there were so many articles that I began collecting them to read later so that I could organize them chronologically by date.

George DeArk was a member of the Masons.[253] He met at New Albany Lodge #1, Independent Order of Odd Fellows Masonic gathering. He also attended meetings in Indianapolis as a delegate for the New Albany masonic lodge.

George moved to Jeffersonville to work as a packer at the Quartermasters Depot in 1895, a building that would later be leased by "Spoken Word Publications" (later transitioning to Voice of God Recordings) and used to distribute the "prophet's" sermons around the world. As a government employee, George DeArk made $45 per month[254] — which was almost double the average wage at that time. He was the guardian of William and Herbert McGregor, and was able to travel with them internationally, which suggested that he lived comfortably on his earning.[255] William and Herbert were not his children, yet he cared for them and put them through college at the University of Louisville, Kentucky. George DeArk managed the estate of their late father, James

---

[250] Branham, William. 1957, Oct 6. Questions and Answers on Genesis. "Brother George DeArk and them down there. And I was walked, and the Lord led me to a little place. And they was discussing where the colored man came from. And they were trying to say that the colored man…That Cain married an animal like an ape, and through there come forth the colored race."

[251] Branham, William. 1957, Oct 6. Questions and Answers on Genesis.

[252] Branham, William. 1957, Oct 6. Questions and Answers on Hebrews #3. Now, that's wrong! Absolutely, that's wrong! And don't never stand for that. Cause there was no colored or white, or any other different, it's just one race of people unto the flood."

[253] Officers of Three Secret Societies are Chosen. 1911, Dec 24. Courier Journal

[254] Blue Book Figures on Government Employees. 1902, Jan 14. The Evening News

[255] Misc. News. 1921, Aug 9. Jeffersonville Star.

McGregor, which led me to believe that George DeArk had access to their inheritance, something that would have appealed to Roy Davis.[256]

During the time that Roy Davis began making headlines in the local newspapers for his civil and criminal trials, and during the time that the "prophet" was an elder in Davis' church, George DeArk was also an elder.[257] At the same time the "prophet" would have been defending Davis for his actions to members of the congregation, DeArk would have been doing the same. Because both men continued to work with Davis until his departure and that they worked together in the new church, it is safe to assume that the "prophet" and George DeArk were aligned with Davis in his doctrinal positions. It is also safe to assume, based on Davis' history, that these doctrinal positions would have included Christian Identity Doctrine. With Roy E. Davis' rank in white supremacy groups such as the Ku Klux Klan (Official Spokesperson[258]) and the Knights of the Flaming Sword (Ambassador[259]), Christian Identity doctrine would have been a focal point in his meetings. Yet the "prophet" claimed to have rejected this doctrine in the early years of his ministry. As late as 1957, the "prophet" rejected the notion of two bloodlines. Why?

> *Now, it's been said...And I hope that my colored friends that's in*
>
> *here will excuse this remark, because it's absolutely not right.*
>
> *The first time I ever met anyone in my life, after I had been*
>
> *converted...I was...met Brother George DeArk and them down*
>
> *there. And I was walked, and the Lord led me to a little place.*
>
> *And they was discussing where the colored man came from. And*
>
> *they were trying to say that the colored man...That Cain*
>
> *married an animal like an ape, and through there come forth*
>
> *the colored race. Now, that's wrong! Absolutely, that's wrong!*
>
> *And don't never stand for that. Cause there was no colored or*

---

[256] Misc. News. 1925, Sep 17. Jeffersonville Evening News.
[257] First Pentecostal Church. 1933, Feb 18. Evening News
[258] Klan Refused Hall. 1923, Jan 12. Reading Times. "Rev. Roy E. Davis, an official spokesperson for the Ku Klux Klan"
[259] Fraternity Attacked as Money Making Order. 1925, Lead Daily Call. "Dr. Roy E. Davis, royal ambassador of the Knights of the Flaming Sword"

white, or any other different, it's just one race of people unto the
flood. Then after the flood and the tower of Babel, when they
began to scatter out, that's when they taken their colors and so
forth. They're all come from the same tree. That's exactly right.
Adam and Eve was the father and mother, earthly, of every
living creature of human beings that's ever been on the earth.

That's right. Black, white, pale, brown, yellow, whatever color
you might be[260]

I began to wonder what changed between 1957 and 1958 that made the "prophet" change his doctrinal position. Before 1958, he taught that Adam was the father of the human race. After 1958, he taught that Adam was only father of the "elect seed", and that the Serpent (which he taught to be Satan) fathered the "Serpent's Seed", or inferior race.

In 1958,[261] the country was strongly divided on the issue of Integration of black and white children into schools. Nine African Americans had enrolled in Little Rock Central High School at the end of 1957.[262] During the course of 1958, the issue of Integration went all the way to the Supreme Court. The Ku Klux Klan and other white supremacy groups were actively recruiting in Little Rock, Arkansas to block integration,[263] and had successfully convinced the public to keep the schools segregated.

This became a key battle for Civil Rights in the United States, an event in the Civil Rights timeline known as the "Little Rock Nine". The Federal Bureau of Investigation was working undercover in Little Rock, Arkansas at that time, and found Rev. Roy E. Davis at the center of the integration protests. The very same day of the vote, the "prophet" introduced his Christian Identity doctrine to the public.[264] It came only

[260] Branham, William. 1957, Oct 6. Questions and Answers on Genesis
[261] Timeline of the Civil Rights Movement. Accessed Oct 20, 2018 from
https://en.wikipedia.org/wiki/Timeline_of_the_civil_rights_movement
[262] Little Rock Nine. Accessed Oct 20, 2018 from https://www.history.com/topics/black-history/central-high-school-integration
[263] Office Memorandum. 1958, Oct 2. F.B.I. Vault
[264] Branham, William. 1958, Sept 28. The Serpent's Seed. "All right, we'll just find out whether it's wrong or

a few months after he denied the sexual union between the Serpent and Eve. The "prophet" re-branded Christian Identity with his own title, "The Serpent's Seed".

> *Just like it was on The Serpent's Seed, but it's absolutely proven to be right. I got papers right here, out of the paper, where women right now...and even in—in the great...Some of the great dioceses has got the pictures of the original, a snake crawling on a woman's leg, and just in how it goes around her; she has all kinds of sensations and things, something a man could never touch her with, with this huge snake wrapping around her, and so forth. That's exactly the truth. And it's going worse and worse[265]*

---

not. "And I will put enmity between thy Seed and the serpent's seed." What? The serpent seed! She had a Seed, and he had a seed."

[265] Branham, William. 1965, Feb 21. Marriage and Divorce.

INDIANA AND KENTUCKY CAVES:

Indiana Caverns. Accessed Oct 26, 2018 from http://indianacaverns.com
Indiana Cave Trail. Accessed Oct 26, 2018 from https://www.indianacavetrail.com
Marengo Cave, US Landmark. Accessed Oct 26, 2018 from http://www.marengocave.com
Mammoth Cave National Park. Accessed Oct 26, 2018 from https://www.nps.gov/maca/index.htm
Mammoth Cave Online. Accessed Oct 26, 2018 from https://mammothcave.com

GEORGE DEARK

Officers of Three Secret Societies are Chosen. 1911, Dec 24. Courier Journal
First Pentecostal Church. 1933, Feb 18. Evening News
Galena. 1898, May 13. New Albany Weekly Tribune.
Blue Book Figures. 1902, Jan 14. Evening News
Man and Woman are Injured in Crashes; Mayor Escapes Hurt. 1926, Jul 13. Evening News
Misc. News. 1925, Sept 17. Evening News
Utica. 1895, Dec 20. Jeffersonville National Democrat
Misc. News. 1916, Feb 25. Jeffersonville National Democrat
Misc. News. 1921, Aug 9. Jeffersonville Star
Personals. 1895, Nov 21. New Albany Evening Tribune
I.O.O.F. Notes. 1896, Jan 13. New Albany Evening Tribune
Misc. News. 1895, Nov 21. New Albany Evening Tribune

WILLIAM JOSEPH SIMMONS

William Joseph Simmons. (2016, March 30). Retrieved from https://en.metapedia.org.org.
William Joseph Simmons, American colonel and preacher. (2016, March 30). Retrieved from
    http://www.britannica.com.
Klan Wizard Is Scored as Liar. (1921, October 17). Retrieved from
    https://www.rarenewspapers.com.
The Ku Klux Klan in the 1920s. (2016, March 30). Retrieved from https://www.pbs.org.
Ku Klux Klan. (2016, March 30). Retrieved from https://www.chesnutt archive.org.
Jackson, Charles O. (1966, December) William J. Simmons: A Career in Ku Kluxism. The Georgia
    Historical Quarterly Volume 50, No 4, pp. 351-365
William Joseph Simmons. (2016, March 30). Retrieved from https://www.fbi.gov.
Imperial Wizard of Ku Klux Klan to Testify Today (1921, October 12). Joplin Globe
Simmons Denies Faked Collapse. (1921, October 17). The Charlotte News
Klan Defended Vigorously by its Organizer. (1921, October 13). The Washington Herald.
Ku Klux Klan Ritual Parodies Christian Baptism. 1921, Sept 13. Evening Public Ledger
Will the Ku Klux Klan Come Back? 1946, Jun 16. Star Tribune.

1957-1958 INTEGRATION BATTLE

Court Orders Integration Now; Little Rock Schools are Closed. 1958, Sept 13. Democratic
    Chronicle
Voters Defeat Integration. 1958, Sept 28. Arizona Republic
Cooper v. Aaron. 1958, Sept 12. 358 U.S.1. 78 S. Ct. 1401; 3 L. Ed. 2nd 5; 1958 U.S. Lexis 657; 79
    Ohio L. Abs 452
Freyer, Tony A. 2007. Little Rock on Trial: Cooper v. Aaron and School Desegregation.

Bomboy, Scott. 2018, Sept 12. On this day, Supreme Court orders Little Rock desegregation.
    Accessed Oct 20, 2018 from https://constitutioncenter.org/blog/on-this-day-supreme-court-
    orders-little-rock-desegregation

Cooper v. Aaron. Accessed Oct 24, 2018 from https://www.oyez.org/cases/1957/1_misc

LITTLE ROCK NINE
Tony A. Freyer, "Politics and Law in the Little Rock Crisis, 1954–1957," The Arkansas Historical
    Quarterly, 60/2, (Summer 2007): 148
Little Rock Nine. Accessed Oct 20, 2018 from https://www.history.com/topics/black-history/central-
    high-school-integration
Little Rock School Desegregation. Accessed Oct 20, 2018 from
    https://kinginstitute.stanford.edu/encyclopedia/little-rock-school-desegregation
Little Rock Nine: 60th Anniversary of Central High School Integration. Accessed Oct 24, 2018 from
    https://www.biography.com/news/little-rock-nine-60th-anniversary
Timeline of the Civil Rights Movement. Accessed Oct 20, 2018 from
    https://en.wikipedia.org/wiki/Timeline_of_the_civil_rights_movement

ROY E. DAVIS
Office Memorandum. 1958, Oct 2. F.B.I. Vault
United States v. Original Knights of Ku Klux Klan, 250 F. Supp. 330 (E.D. La. 1965). 1965, Dec 1.
    F.B.I. Vault
Present-Day Ku Klux Klan Movement. 1967, Dec 11. 90th Congress 2d Session.
The K. K. K. Lecture Not Held Last Night. 1922, May 30. Hutchinson News
Klan Refused Hall. 1923, Jan 12. Reading Times

CHRISTIAN IDENTITY AND SERPENT'S SEED
Cornering the Hate Market. 1998, Apr 19. Anniston Star
Branham, William. 1957, Oct 6. Questions and Answers on Hebrews #3, p602. (Branham rejecting
    two bloodlines)
Branham, William. 1958, Sept 28. The Serpent's Seed
Christian Identity. Southern Poverty Law. Accessed Oct 24, 2018 from
    https://www.splcenter.org/fighting-hate/extremist-files/ideology/christian-identity
Barkun, Michael. 1996. Religion and the Racist Right: The Origins of the Christian Identity
    Movement.
How the Christian Identity Movement Began. Southern Poverty Law. Accessed Oct 24, 2018 from
    https://www.splcenter.org/fighting-hate/intelligence-report/1998/how-christian-identity-movement-
    began
Christian Identity: A "Christian" Religion for White Racists. Accessed Oct 24, 2018 from
    https://www.equip.org/article/christian-identity-a-christian-religion-for-white-racists/
Quarles, Chester L. (2004). Christian Identity: The Aryan American Bloodline Religion.

CHAPTER 14

THE 1930 ODD FELLOWS
MASONIC REVIVAL

"The Ku Klux Klan paid the hospital bill for me, Masons[266]"

Most churches in the "Message", no matter which sect, are decorated with relics associated with the "prophet", some of which are considered "holy". The most common relic among churches in the "message" is an enlarged photograph of the "prophet" captured with what appears to be a "halo" above his head. "Message" believers are told that the bright light above the "prophet's" head is the only supernatural photograph ever captured,[267] and that God Himself allowed his image to captured by the camera onto the film.

In the Branham Tabernacle in Jeffersonville, Indiana, the "halo" relic hung on the wall directly behind the pulpit facing the congregation. During services, the "prophet" stared at the people on the left side of the room, for the photograph captured the right side of the "prophet's" face. For as long as I could remember, visitors and members of the Branham Tabernacle sat in pews silently while listening to a 1947-1965 recorded sermon of the "prophet". As they listened, they sat facing the "prophet's" image with "God" hanging above his head in the blurred image of light. For me, sitting through sermons while looking at the

---

[266] Branham, William. 1963, Nov 10. Souls That Are In Prison Now.
[267] Branham, William. 1951, July 18. The Angel of the Lord. "And one of them hangs in the Religious Hall of Art, in Washington, DC, as the first photograph that was ever taken of a supernatural Being."

"halo" relic made the sermon feel more "alive". It felt as though there were a "spiritual" bond between the "listener" (me) and the "prophet".

I was surprised the first time I saw old photographs of the "prophet's" early church. It was one thing to use the "halo" photo as a frame of reference for an image of the speaker that we listened to every Wednesday evening and two times on Sunday. It was entirely different, however, to think about the "prophet" standing in front of a photo of the "prophet". Yet as I looked at the early photographs of the "prophet" in his church, this was exactly what happened. That same image of the "halo" hung on the wall near the pulpit while the "prophet" was alive, and the "prophet" could turn and look at himself hanging on the wall! I began to think about how strange it would be for a preacher in this position. What if every preacher had a picture of themselves behind the pulpit? It would not take long before the congregation began to wonder if the focal point of the sermon was supposed to be on God or the preacher whose portrait hung on the wall staring at them!

Above the pulpit hung a familiar Bible verse, and under normal circumstances it would have seemed less eerie. In bold, thick black letters, just above the "prophet's" enlarged photograph read the verse from Psalm 46:10 in the Bible: *"Be still and know that I am God"*. As a child, I can remember looking up at the words, *"I am God"*, looking down at the "prophet's" halo, then looking back at the words on multiple occasions. Even in my youth I wondered if anyone else saw the irony in those words and their location, not yet realizing that this was likely the intent. In his later years, the "prophet" made it clear that it was not his voice that we were listening to, but that it was God speaking through him to us.[268] He told us that Jesus Christ was returning to earth in the form of a "prophet",[269] and I just knew that our "prophet" was *THE* "prophet". I was being still, but I was confused as to *who* was God — I never knew that I was supposed to believe the "prophet" was God, and always found it odd that some sects within the "Message" did believe just that.

---

[268] Branham, William. 1951, May 5. My Commission. "Now see, I can say nothing in myself. But what He shows me, I say it."

[269] Branham, William. 1965, Nov 27. "the Elijah of this day is the Lord Jesus Christ. He is to come according to Matthew the seventeen-...Luke 17:30, is, the Son of man is to reveal Himself among His people. Not a man, God! But it'll come through a prophet"

I began to wonder what it was like in the "prophet's" church before that Psalm quotation plaque was hung above the pulpit. In the early photographs of the church, it was not there. Specifically, I was curious to learn more about the church before the "prophet" was the center of focus. Looking over the old photographs of the church, I found that there were very few relics hanging on the wall. Most of the ones that we had in our churches came much later, but it was odd seeing the walls without the relics I had always seen in the "Message" churches.

Suddenly, while looking at the old photographs of the Branham Tabernacle, I noticed something even more unusual than the "I am God" sign above the pulpit. The early photographs of the church depicted a building that was much taller than the building in the newer photographs. I knew the building in the new photographs well; not only was it my grandfather's church, it was a sacred building that many of us knew inside and out. The early photographs were not the same building!

The 1936 tabernacle on Eighth and Penn Streets was only slightly taller than the side windows, but the photographs we had of the early congregation were taken inside a building that was at least fifteen feet taller. There was no way that "the prophet's early church" (as we were told) would fit inside the Branham Tabernacle. Two large beams, clearly taller than the church building I attended for several years of my life, stretched from the floor to the lower ceiling of the building in the older photograph. Above those beams, a much higher ceiling stretched above the visible part of the photograph. On the beam to the right, it looked as though a plaque was positioned just above the heads of the adults as they passed by, but it could not be read due to the reflection of light from the camera. When the "prophet" talked about the verses painted on the church beams, he mentioned "*Sammy* Davidson" painting them.[270]

I remembered an article that I had found in the Jeffersonville local newspaper which described the music program at the "prophet's" early church. The special program, according to the newspaper, was directed by "*Sante*" Davidson.[271] I wondered, "was '*Sante*' the same person as

---

[270] Branham, William. 1962, July 20. A Testimony on the Sea. "I remember Sammy Davidson painted that on there about twenty-five years ago"

'*Sammy*'?" And who, exactly, was this man directing music at the "prophet's" church? Why was he chosen by the "prophet, and why was he never mentioned?

The answer came while I was studying the connections of the men involved with the "prophet" that were associated with Freemasonry. I found that some groups within the Masonic order published names of their higher-ranking members, a practice that seemed unusual today. Today, freemasonry is notorious for their secretive practices and lack of public membership listing. Surprisingly, this was not the case in the early 1930s. Sante Davidson, the "prophet's" first music minister, was a ranking member of the Independent Order of Odd Fellows.[272]

According to the newspapers, Sante Davidson led the devotional services at the Billie Branham Pentecostal Tabernacle. In the "prophet's" accounts of his early church, he mentioned temporarily using the Masonic Hall for services.[273] Sante was likely involved with opening the Masonic Doors to the Pentecostal church as it transitioned from Roy E. Davis to the "prophet". He was a skilled painter,[274] so it was not surprising that he also painted the signs that hung in the early church.

Sante was deeply involved with the Independent Order of Odd Fellows Masonic order and featured in photographs published in the Louisville Courier Journal describing members of rank.[275] In 1925, Sante Davidson's photo was featured as rank of "guardsman", or bodyguard. Having a rank of "bodyguard" would imply that he had been involved with the secret meetings for quite some time and trusted enough to keep others out. According to the Jeffersonville and New Albany, IN newspapers, Sante had been participating in Odd Fellows activities since as early as 1902.[276] At that time, Sante was listed as an officer in the Tabor Lodge.

Sante was involved with more than one fraternal organization. He was also a Deputy Grand Chancellor of the Knights of Pythias. In 1915,

[271] Pentecostal Tabernacle. 1937, Jun 12. Jeffersonville Evening News.
[272] Odd Fellows. 1902, Jun 9. Jeffersonville Evening News
[273] Branham, William. 1960, Dec 8. The Thyatirean Church Age. "And now, and as I started the Sunday school I fell into a trance. We was having it over here at the old Masonic home"
[274] House of Sign Painting. 1910, Oct 19. Salem Democrat.
[275] Officers and Members of Tabor Lodge I.O.O.F. 1925, Sept 13. Courier Journal.
[276] Misc. News. (Tabor Lodge). 1902, Jun 26. Courier Journal

Sante was president of the "Order of the Owls".[277] This group helped fund orphans and widows.

Though a member of the Jeffersonville lodge and participating in the "prophet's" (and likely Roy E. Davis's Jeffersonville church), Sante lived in Salem, IN. His role as "choir master" did not begin with the Billie Branham Pentecostal Tabernacle. In 1901, he was appointed choirmaster of Wall Street Sunday School. His painting of signs did not begin with Bible verses on church beams; Sante had a business as a painter and was part of the "masonic painting union." In 1909, Sante attempted to focus solely upon painting, which apparently was a dangerous trade. At one point, Sante poisoned his eye in an accident and lost a middle finger.

In the evenings, Sante managed the Etzler Opera House.[278] The Opera House provided vaudeville entertainment to Southern Indiana and attracted visitors from all around the country. Sante was also involved with band concerts and directed the band accompaniment for local events. He was a writer who published humorous, thought-provoking articles in the local newspapers. His "The Ten Commandments" was aimed at local business owners, which would have been humorous to many. He also wrote poetry to encourage those out of work, and articles to focus on the family.

1. Thou shalt not wait for something to turn up. Pull off thy coat and go to work that thou mightest prosper in thy affairs.

2. Thou shalt not be content to go about thy business looking untidy, for thou should stop and know that thy personal appearance is better than a letter of recommendation.

3. Thou shalt not wait to be told what thou shalt do, for thus may thy days be long in the job which fortune has given thee.

4. Thou shalt not try to make excuses nor shalt thou say to those who chide the, I didn't think.

5. Thou shalt not fail to maintain thy integrity, nor shalt thou be guilty of anything that will lessen thy respect for thyself.

---

[277] Order of Owls. 1915, Apr 1. Mitchell Commercial
[278] Etzler Opera House. 1908, Sept 4. Salem Republican Leader.

6. Thou shalt not covet the other fellow's job, nor his salary, nor the position which he has gained by his own hard labor.

7. Thou shalt not fail to live within thy income nor shalt thou contract any debts when canst not thy own way clear to pay them.

8. Thou shalt fail not to blow thy horn, for he who is afraid to blow his own horn at the proper occasion finds nobody standing to blow it for him.

9. Thou shalt not hesitate to say "No" when thou meanest "No" nor shalt thou fail to remember that there are times when it's unsafe to bind thyself to hasty judgment.

10. Thou shalt give every man great commandment and there is no other like unto it, upon this commandment depends all the law and Profits of the business world.[279]

Sante operated the "Snow Drip", a restaurant with sandwiches and cold drinks.[280] He was a shrewd businessman, wheeling-and-dealing to make his establishments become the exclusive local attraction, and he cornered more markets than just vaudeville and motion picture. Within just a few years, he grew the Opera House large enough to attract big shows. Some of the shows, such as "Fine Feathers", were so entertaining that they ran 156 nights in New York and six months in Chicago.[281]

In 1930, shortly before the time Roy E. Davis was the music minister for Ralph Rader and before Davis took a large part of Rader's congregation, the Odd Fellows attended Ralph Rader's tent revival.[282] Sante Davidson led the singing. The Pentecostal Baptist Tabernacle — and Roy Davis — were there. The "prophet" said that he was Davis' assistant pastor in 1930; so it is quite possible that this could have been the first time Sante Davidson met the "prophet", and it could have been the moment in time that connected the two. It was the first published account of a cooperative effort between Sante Davidson, Rev Roy E Davis and (according to the timeline established by research linking the two men) the "prophet".

---

[279] The Ten Commandments. 1909, Dec 22. Salem Democrat.
[280] The Snow Drip. 1910, Apr 20. Salem Democrat.
[281] Special Attraction – Fine Feathers. 1917, Jan 10. Salem Democrat.
[282] Odd Fellows Attend Rader Tent Meeting. 1930, Sept 26. Jeffersonville Evening News.

The union of fraternal organizations and Christianity were not well received in the community. Rev. Ralph Rader was forced to hold his meetings at the Knights of Pythias Armory,[283] and it's safe to assume Sante Davidson was involved, simply due to his rank. Local ministers saw the non-denominational strategy as a threat, because Rader, Davis, and others were using that platform to grow their new churches. In the case of Roy E. Davis and Ralph Rader, they were growing their churches by persuading members from other congregations to leave their home church. Two days after Roy E. Davis was arrested for violation of the Mann Act, arrested at the ongoing church revival in Jeffersonville, a resolution to prevent this practice was passed. [284]

I began to think about the unusual circumstances during the revival meetings that connected these men. Sante Davidson would have met Rev. Roy Davis for the first time, met the "prophet", who was Davis' assistant pastor at the time, and witnessed federal agents taking Davis away for underaged sex with a minor from another state. After Roy Davis' Pentecostal church was burned and the Davis brothers left town in 1934, leaders of Roy Davis' Pentecostal church (George DeArk and others) became elders in Branham's Pentecostal Tabernacle. Yet, with all of this going on, Sante Davidson joined them as Branham's "choir master"!

His first publicized appearance in the Billie Branham Pentecostal Tabernacle was October 2, 1935.[285] It was not advertised on 8th and Penn streets, however. Sante's participation in Branham's church in 1935 was at the "8th and Graham Street Tabernacle", two and a half blocks away from the "Branham Tabernacle" that exists today.

---

[283] Rader Meetings Are Now On. 1930, Oct 14. Jeffersonville Evening News. "The Jeffersonville Ministerial Association went on record at a regular meeting Monday as 'being entirely out of sympathy with any evangelistic meetings now being held.' The resolution did not specifically name any such meetings. The only series of meetings now being conducted in Jeffersonville is that which has been conducted for the last few weeks by the Rev. Ralph Rader in Warder Park under a tent."
[284] Pastors Refuse to Back Revival. 1930, Oct 14. The Evening News.
[285] Revival at Tabernacle. 1935, Oct 2. Jeffersonville Evening News

SANTE DAVIDSON:

Revival at Tabernacle. 1935, Oct 2. Jeffersonville Evening News
Misc. News. (Sante's car shop). 1923, Mar 14. Salem Democrat
Appointed Deputy Grand Chancellor. 1934, Oct 5. Jeffersonville Evening News
Armory Healing Services Held Tonight. 1925, Oct 12. Jeffersonville Evening News
Sante Davidson is Ill at Residence. 1937, Jul 28. Jeffersonville Evening News
Sante Davidson Shows Improvement in Illness. 1935, Oct 31. Jeffersonville Evening News
Misc. News. (Christmas travel). 1907, Dec 24. Jeffersonville Evening News
Misc. News. (Visits relatives) 1907, Sept 27. Jeffersonville Evening News
Fraternal Ceremonies. 1931, Apr 11. Jeffersonville Evening News
Misc. News. (Choirmaster at Wall Street). 1901, Apr 12. Jeffersonville Evening News
Sellersburg Candidates to be Initiated Here. 1934, Aug 17. Jeffersonville Evening News
Sante Davidson Still Ill. 1942, Dec 10. Jeffersonville Evening News
Former Resident Broadcasts from KTHS Tonight. 1938, Dec 12. Jeffersonville Evening News
Spurgeon Decides to Continue Revival. 1930, Dec 15. Jeffersonville Evening News
Doctor, Theater and Shoemaker Aid Unemployed. 1931, Feb 3. Jeffersonville Evening News
New Union Organized. 1903, Feb 13. Jeffersonville Evening News
Odd Fellows. 1910, Feb 14. Jeffersonville Evening News
Funeral of Miss Howard. 1902, Feb 19. Jeffersonville Evening News
Another Union. 1903, Oct 22. Jeffersonville Evening News
Misc. News (visit George Meadows). 1908, Jan 4. Jeffersonville Evening News
Society. (return to Salem, IN) 1908, Jan 13. Jeffersonville Evening News
Mayor Jacobs Will Make Race for 2d Term. 1934, Jan 17. Jeffersonville Evening News
Hope Lodge K. of P. Installs New Officers. 1934, Jan 19. Jeffersonville Evening News
Tabor Lodge. 1903, Jan 20. Jeffersonville Evening News
Hope Lodge K. of P. Installs New Officers. 1932, Jan 26. Jeffersonville Evening News
A Big Family. 1902, Jan 28. Jeffersonville Evening News
Tabor Lodge. 1903, Jan 29. Jeffersonville Evening News
Don't Lose Your Pluck. 1930, Jan 29. Jeffersonville Evening News
Orphans Enjoy Themselves. 1903, Jan 30. Jeffersonville Evening News
Sante Makes City Property Blossom. 1933, Jul 13. Jeffersonville Evening News
Sante Davidson Landscape Man. 1932, Jul 27. Jeffersonville Evening News
Memorial is set Sunday June 7. 1931, Jun 1. Jeffersonville Evening News
The Shower. 1902, Jun 5. Jeffersonville Evening News
Odd Fellows. 1902, Jun 9. Jeffersonville Evening News
Sante Davidson. 1927, Jun 9. Jeffersonville Evening News
Misc. News. (visit relatives). 1905, Jun 30. Jeffersonville Evening News
Sunday Sessions of Disciples. 1902, Mar 1. Jeffersonville Evening News
Revive Us Again. 1901, Mar 25. Jeffersonville Evening News
Thief Makes a Florist of Mr. Davidson. 1934, May 23. Jeffersonville Evening News
K. of P. Band Plans to Give Free Concert. 1932, May 24. Jeffersonville Evening News
Daughters of Rebekah and Three Lodges Go to Wall Street Church. 1921, May 27. Jeffersonville Evening News
Suddenly Life Extinguished. 1908, Nov 5. Jeffersonville Evening News
Misc. News. (Sante visits Grand Lodge in Indianapolis). 1927, Nov 21. Jeffersonville Evening News
Candidates to be Initiated. 1932, Oct 3. Jeffersonville Evening News
Pastors Refuse to Back Revival. 1930, Oct 14. Jeffersonville Evening News
Misc. News. (eye poisoned). 1905, Jul 21. Jeffersonville National Democrat

Odd Fellows. 1902, Jun 13. Jeffersonville National Democrat

Attention Knights. 1916, Aug 9. Salem Democrat.

Order of Owls. 1915, Apr 1. Mitchell Commercial

Pentecostal Group to Sponsor Program. 1938, Aug 9. Jeffersonville Evening News.

Pentecostal Tabernacle. 1937, Jun 12. Jeffersonville Evening News.

Pentecostal Tabernacle. 1936, Oct 24. Jeffersonville Evening News.

Odd Fellows Attend Rader Tent Meeting. 1930, Sept 26. Jeffersonville Evening News.

Bethany Circle Easter Party. 1917, Apr 18. Salem Democrat.

Misc. News. (Sante sued). 1916, Apr 19. Salem Democrat.

The Snow Drip. 1910, Apr 20. Salem Democrat.

Misc. News. (Sante presented Masonic pin). 1909, Apr 21. Salem Democrat.

The Show. 1909, Aug 4. Salem Democrat.

Program of Band Concerts. 1911, Aug 30. Salem Democrat.

Salem Celebrates Indiana's One Hundredth Birthday. 1916, Aug 30. Salem Democrat.

Misc. News. (Etzler Attraction). 1909, Dec 15. Salem Democrat.

The Ten Commandments. 1909, Dec 22. Salem Democrat.

Misc. News. (Etzler Attraction). 1912, Dec 25. Salem Democrat.

Announcement. 1910, Dec 28. Salem Democrat.

K. of P. Installation. 1914, Dec 30. Salem Democrat.

Misc. News. (Business trip to Jeffersonville). 1909, Feb 3. Salem Democrat.

Misc. News. (shaved moustache) 1911, Feb 8. Salem Democrat.

Masquerade Tonight. 1915, Feb 17. Salem Democrat.

Special Attraction -- Fine Feathers. 1917, Jan 10. Salem Democrat.

Unique Adornment. 1917, Jan 10. Salem Democrat.

Only Real Fourth. 1915, Jul 7. Salem Democrat.

Letter to the Editor. 1917, Jun 6. Salem Democrat.

Misc. News. (Cuts off finger) 1913, Jun 11. Salem Democrat.

Misc. News. (Business trip to Campbellsburg). 1909, Jun 16. Salem Democrat.

Open Air Meetings. 1911, Jun 28. Salem Democrat.

Misc. News. (Men's meeting). 1920, Mar 3. Salem Democrat.

Salem M. E. Sunday School. 1923, Mar 14. Salem Democrat.

Misc. News. (Out of show business). 1911, Mar 22. Salem Democrat.

We Were Notified to Get Our Wagon off the Street. 1910, May 4. Salem Democrat.

Misc. News. (Business prospects) 1908, May 6. Salem Democrat.

Misc. News. (I.O.O.F. Lodge) 1919, May 28. Salem Democrat.

Fourth of July Celebration. 1912, May 29. Salem Democrat.

My Honolulu Girl Highly Praised. 1916, Nov 29. Salem Democrat.

Knights Go to Indianapolis. 1916, Oct 4. Salem Democrat.

K. of P. Celebration. 1916, Oct 11. Salem Democrat.

House of Sign Painting. 1910, Oct 19. Salem Democrat.

Show Season Here. 1912, Oct 30. Salem Democrat.

Misc. News. (paint business bid). 1910, Sept 7. Salem Democrat.

Misc. News. (Sister named). 1909, Sept 8. Salem Democrat.

Misc. News. (Etzler house). 1910, Sept 28. Salem Democrat.

Elect Officers. 1908, May 8. Salem Republican Leader.

Sante Davidson Organizes Choir of Sixty at Wall Street Church. 1921, Apr 8. Salem Republican Leader.

Misc. News. (Sante receives K.of P. pin). 1909, Apr 23. Salem Republican Leader.

Misc. News. (Sante's sister-in-law named). 1908, Aug 7. Salem Republican Leader.

Misc. News. (choir). 1910, Aug 12. Salem Republican Leader.

"My Friend from Arkansas". 1908, Dec 4. Salem Republican Leader.

Etzler Opera House. 1914, Dec 11. Salem Republican Leader.

Sacred Concert. 1915, Dec 31. Salem Republican Leader.

I. O. O. F. Banquet. 1910, Feb 4. Salem Republican Leader.

Misc. News. (Opera House). 1909, Feb 5. Salem Republican Leader.

Misc. News. (Opera House). 1911, Feb 24. Salem Republican Leader.

Annual Celebration. 1910, Feb 25. Salem Republican Leader.

Misc. News. (Visit Mr. and Mrs. Howell). 1909, Jan 1. Salem Republican Leader.

Westminster Chapel. 1912, Jul 12. Salem Republican Leader.

Misc. News. (Visit William H. Gray). 1908, Jul 31. Salem Republican Leader.

Misc. News. (Memorial Service). 1910, Jun 3. Salem Republican Leader.

It Was a Good Show. 1911, Mar 10. Salem Republican Leader.

Misc. News. (Princess Chrysanthemum). 1913, May 2. Salem Republican Leader.

Try the Snow Drip. 1910, May 6. Salem Republican Leader.

Memorial Day. 1910, May 27. Salem Republican Leader.

It Is Excellent. 1913, Nov 21. Salem Republican Leader.

Misc. News. (hauling corn). 1913, Oct 10. Salem Republican Leader.

Misc. News. (opera house). 1909, Oct 15. Salem Republican Leader.

Salem Centennial Hoosiers. 1914, Oct 16. Salem Republican Leader.

Big Minstrels Coming. 1915, Oct 29. Salem Republican Leader.

Etzler Opera House. 1908, Sept 4. Salem Republican Leader.

Mt. Zion. 1913, Sept 19. Salem Republican Leader.

Thos. J. Guernsey. 1924, Aug 23. Courier Journal.

Misc. News. (lotto club). 1925, Apr 19. Courier Journal.

Davidson's Brother Ill. 1923, Aug 26. Courier Journal.

Officers and Members of Tabor Lodge I.O.O.F. 1925, Sept 13. Courier Journal.

Misc. News. (Tabor Lodge). 1902, Jun 26. Courier Journal

CHAPTER 15

WILLIAM BRANHAM AND THE 1940 OLYMPICS

"I used to be a boxer. I had the undefeated title of Bantamweight Championship of the three states[286]"

As the years pass, and I get older, I enjoy traveling. For me, seeing new places and meeting new people are some of life's greatest pleasures. When my wife and I first got married, traveling was a luxury we simply could not afford. She worked hourly at a fast-food restaurant while I worked hourly at a retail store, and there was barely enough extra to visit family. Somehow there was always just enough, though, and food was always on our table. We did manage to get away one or two times a year to visit our loved ones.

At the time, I sympathized with the "prophet" as he told his own stories of early marriage, not being able to scrape two pennies together when he and his wife Hope started out in Jeffersonville. I had seen the pictures of their humble little shack, and sometimes smiled at the thought of how our tiny apartment seemed like a mansion compared to the house we heard that he started with. With the vacuum cleaner plugged into one outlet, we could vacuum the entire apartment using just the distance allowed by the length of the cord. The little shack used in the photographs of the "prophet's" early home, however, didn't even

---

[286] Branham, William. 1954, Feb 20. Expectation.7

need the cord; you could almost clean his entire house with the length of the vacuum cleaner hose!

Now, after learning about the parties they threw, vacation resorts they visited, and their traveling around the country, I became curious as to why he said that. I also wondered about the house in the pictures and tried to imagine all those people crammed inside. One newspaper article in particular[287] described an anniversary party thrown for the "prophet" at their home on Graham Street, which included music, contests, and plenty of guests. The newspaper listed almost fifty familiar names, not including their children or the additional guests that they brought with them or that showed up uninvited. This was far more people than I could fit in my tiny apartment, even if people stood in rows, side to side and front-to-back! The more I researched, the more I realized that things were quite different than we were told.

The "prophet" used to talk about his first wife's death during the 1937 flood. He'd say, *"there is where my sorrows started"*. Learning that Hope Branham died several months after the flood raised many more questions. The "prophet" told an adventurous story about how he fought the raging flood waters by boat to get to her hospital, but the waters would have receded long before her death. His gut-wrenching tale describing scenes from his journey to visit his wife as she lay dying were simply untrue.

> *I pulled and it wouldn't start. And I pulled again and it wouldn't start. And I tried, and I got down in the boat, I said, "God, it isn't but a few more jumps down here till I would sink beneath those falls there, where they were roaring and bubbling, miles of water stretching through there." I said, "I got a sick wife and two babies laying out there in the hospital." I said, "Please, dear God, start this motor." All I could think: "'I will never let my girl go out with a bunch of that trash.'" And I say this with*

---

[287] Rev. Branham Given Anniversary Party. 1936, Apr 15. Jeffersonville Evening News.

all due respects to every church: I find out what she called
"trash" is the cream of the crop.[288]

I was coming to terms with the fact that I could no longer rely on his "Life Story" accounts as being historically accurate. Many parts of his descriptions of those accounts no longer made sense to me, and some events simply could never have happened as he described them. Yet, it was hard to deny that the death of his wife and daughters would have had an impact on his life. It would have had an impact on any person who endured such a tragedy. That part of his tale I still believed, but I could find no evidence that it had any effect at all on the young "prophet", at least based upon examining the historical timeline for 1936-1938.

Looking at the newspaper advertisements, not much changed before and after Hope Branham's death. The "Billie Branham Pentecostal Tabernacle" was still growing. The music program was still thriving. What changed? I knew that the death of his first wife would have been traumatic. I also acknowledged the impact of the traumatic effects of the 1937 flood; it was an experience that would have affected all people that were impacted, especially the poor. But was there a time, after becoming a minister, when the "prophet" was truly poor? It was time to start examining the prophet's personal life. The best place to start was where he told us that *"sorrows started"*.

The 1937 flood was truly devastating. Across eleven states, 125,000 people were rendered homeless during the coldest months of winter. In the city of Jeffersonville alone, over 400 families were homeless. The city itself was nearly obliterated from the map.[289] Except for the bridge to Louisville, Jeffersonville was completely cut off from the outside world. Tent cities were setup to keep the homeless alive in the bitter cold. People were being rescued by boat.

If the "prophet" had a boat, there's no doubt he was assisting — anyone who could help did so to stay alive. There is strength in numbers, and strength meant survival. It was a desperate time, and

---

[288] Branham, William. 1952, Jul 20. Life Story.
[289] The Great 1937 Flood of Louisville and Southern Indiana. Accessed Nov 16, 2018 from *https://filsonhistorical.org/galleries/the-great-1937-flood-of-louisville-southern-indiana/*

everyone in the community came together. Some families lost everything. No doubt many families in the "prophet's" own congregation were homeless and destitute. Even if the "prophet" was wealthy in his first years as an evangelist, many if not all of his congregation members were now extremely poor. Without their weekly tithes coming in, the "prophet's" income would have also dwindled.

While looking through the government records I'd found, I noticed something interesting. As late as 1940, the "prophet" and his son, Billy Paul, were living with his recently widowed mother on 304 E. Maple Street in Jeffersonville, Indiana. Also living with them were six of his siblings.[290] I suddenly realized that part of his "life story" was somewhat true, even if embellished and taken out of historical context. There *were* several Branhams living together under one single roof, just as he described in his "Life Story" accounts. Instead of small children, however, his siblings would have been grown men. I also found it interesting to learn that he was working for the Public Service Company at the time. The "prophet" was a bill collector, collecting money from the poor people in Jeffersonville, while his brother Jesse worked at the dog track among the gamblers. I thought to myself, "This isn't what the 'prophet' described!"

I noticed that Henry Branham was among the siblings listed in the home of Ella Branham at the same time as the "prophet" and his son. Henry was a name that I had recently been curious about and had been collecting any information that I could stumble upon that bore with his name. When the "prophet" was first described by the Associated Press in 1948, it was "Henry Branham" that the news media named as the "healer".[291] I had always wondered, "why did the press name his brother as the 'healer?'"

There is no doubt that the "prophet" went through some hard times. He married Hope Brumbach during the Great Depression. Based on his descriptions of the new automobiles he purchased and the places that he visited, he didn't seem to struggle too much, but those around him would surely have struggled. Still, he had his own set of hardships, and they were such difficult times that no person would have ever wanted to

---

[290] Sixteenth Census of the United States: 1940, Jeffersonville
[291] Brother Branham, the Faith Healer. 1947, Jul 6. St Louis Post Dispatch

trade places. Not only had the "prophet" lost his wife, been forced to become a bill collector, lost his house, and been forced to move in with his mother, he did so during some of the worst of times. Like many Americans, he was faced with the fears of war. The United States hadn't yet joined WWII, but many people feared that U.S. involvement in the war was inevitable.

Suddenly, I stumbled onto something that was very surprising in the local newspapers. Because of the war with Germany,[292] Henry Branham's name made the news! The 1940 Olympics were scheduled to be held in Tokyo, Japan. In March of 1938, however, Japanese military demanded Olympic venues be built of wood instead of steel; they needed the material to produce arms for the war that was already raging with China. The Olympic event was moved to Helsinki, but that was also canceled. With global war spreading, the Olympic games would have been far too dangerous to attend at any location. Local Louisville and Southern Indiana athletes banded together in protest of the cancellation and joined a nation-wide Amateur Athletic Union movement against canceling the 1940 Olympics. The Louisville A.A.U committee received notice the games had not yet been canceled which added fuel to the fire. Soon after, the Louisville athletes joined New Albany and Jeffersonville. Among them was Henry Branham, the "prophet's" brother![293] He was one of two bantamweight boxers from Jeffersonville, Indiana. While the "prophet" was living with his mother, Henry made local headlines and quickly became the center of attention.

Walter Cory, pro boxer, claimed that Louisville's best would struggle against Henry. According to the newspapers, Kenny Barrett was "king of the South", and Henry was his able contester. Barrett had made the quarterfinals in Chicago and lost to Jimmy Joyce from Gary, Indiana. Henry fought his way into the inter-city boxing matches at the Louisville Sports Arena. Henry, along with several others, represented Southern Indiana. In July, he was carded to participate in 30 rounds at the Louisville Amateur Boxing Club.[294] While Jeffersonville was

[292] War vs. Olympics. 1940, Mar 17. The Courier Journal.
[293] Amateurs to Fight to Aid Olympics Fund. 1940, Mar 24. The Courier Journal.
[294] N. A. To Send Tough Team for Bouts Here. 1940, Jul 26. The Courier Journal.

slowly rebuilding from the damage left by the flood, Henry would have been seen as a local hero.

This made me curious about the "prophet's" own claim to be a professional boxer. The "prophet" claimed to have won the bantamweight championship for three states. In fact, he claimed to have had an opportunity for world champion and forfeited. Yet when I looked at old photos of the "prophet", I did not see a boxer. The photographs capture a scrawny man, not a fighter. Nor was I able to find any mention of the "prophet" in the news while his brother was making headlines, and a two-brother-championship-boxing-duo would have made not just local, but also national news. Was the prophet jealous of his brother's success in the championship?

> *I used to be a boxer. I had the undefeated title of Bantamweight Championship of the three states, so—and know what grip is*[295]

> *I was a young fellow and straight in the shoulders; and I'd won the Bantamweight Championship in the Golden Gloves, and went out in professional fighting, and I—I thought I was a big fellow*[296]

Learning that the prophet was a *bill collector* for the Public Service Company was surprising at first, but desperate times call for desperate measures. I felt sorry for all of Jeffersonville, not just the "prophet". The real story of what happened — not only to the "prophet", but to all of Jeffersonville — was far worse than the "Life Story" could ever have captured. I began to wonder why he needed to change the details! The factual history was far more heartbreaking than the story that he described. I was also curious about his temporary change in lifestyle. There was no doubt that the "prophet" had plenty of money before the flood, and he may have been poor for a brief time while living with his mother, but his financial struggles did not appear to last very long. The research painted the picture of a quickly restored, wealthy lifestyle, at least compared to the average American during the Depression.

---

[295] Branham, William. 1954, Feb 20. Expectation.
[296] Branham, William. 1955, Oct 8. The Results of Decision.

I began searching to see how long the "prophet" lived with his mother. I found an article in 1942 Jeffersonville Evening News describing the "prophet". He had caught a wolf northwest of Henryville, and the newspaper told his story and described the "prophet". By 1942, he was living at 922 E. 8th Street. He had worked for the Public Service Company for years, but for at least two months he was no longer a bill collector. He was working as a line patrolman. The interesting part for me, however, was not the wolf caught in a trap. The "prophet" was recognized for owning many hunting trophies![297] By 1942, he was already making big-game hunting excursions, and was planning on another in October of that same year. How was he paying for these excursions on Public Service wages?

When I thought about the "prophet" taking hunting excursions during the Great Depression, a time when most Americans struggled to keep food on the table, in a city where a large percentage of people lost everything to a flood, I became more curious about his role as "pastor". A pastor is a shepherd to his flock, a servant to his congregation. I had a difficult time imagining a pastor who was flaunting trophies from excursions in front of the people of Jeffersonville. Jeffersonville was a town where many were still rebuilding from the tragic loss of all their possessions. But I was beginning to realize that this was no ordinary "pastor", and that he was not ordained as just a "minister". How much of his "mission" aligned with his mentor, Roy E. Davis? It was time to dig even deeper into the early stages of his *public* ministry.

---

[297] Wolf Captured Alive in Den Near Henryville. 1942, Aug 22. Jeffersonville Evening News. "Rev. Branham is the owner of many hunting trophies, including the skins from grizzly and black bears, shot in Alaska, Maine, and the Rocky Mountains, and pelts of several other wild animals taken on his hunting trips. He has another live wolf at his residence, captured last year near Butte, Montana. He contemplates leaving October 15 on another hunting excursion in the Rocky Mountains."

1937 FLOOD:

Flood Waters Still Rising. 1937, Jan 12. Logansport Pharos Tribune.
Hoosier Troops Restore Order in River Ravaged Ares. 1937, Jan 27. Logansport Pharos Tribune.
Residents Flee Jeffersonville as City Is Inundated. 1937, Jan 25. Rushville Republican.
Indiana Flood Refugees Returning to Ruined Homes. 1937, Feb 8. Logansport Pharos Tribune.
Picture Story of Record Flood Waters. 1937, Jan 25. The Kokomo Tribune.
Two Indiana Towns Wiped Out by Floods. 1937, Jan 26. The Times
No Letup of Flood in Sight. 1937, Jan 26. The Times.
11 States Ravaged by Floods. 1937, Jan 22. Logansport Pharos Tribune.
The Great 1937 Flood of Louisville and Southern Indiana. Accessed Nov 16, 2018 from
https://filsonhistorical.org/galleries/the-great-1937-flood-of-louisville-southern-indiana/

1940 OLYMPICS:

War vs. Olympics. 1940, Mar 17. The Courier Journal.
Finland Definitely Cancels 1940 Olympics Because of Europe's War. 1940, Apr 24. The Baltimore
    Sun.
Amateurs to Fight to Aid Olympics Fund. 1940, Mar 24. The Courier Journal.
Peace in Finland Causes New Hope for 1940 Olympics. 1940, Mar 15. The Dayton Herald
1940 Olympics Off. 1940, Apr 24. The Montgomery Advertiser
Sandra Collins. The 1940 Tokyo Games: The Missing Olympics: Japan, the Asian Olympics and
    the Olympic Movement.

HENRY BRANHAM:

N.A. To Send Tough Team for Bouts Here. 1940, Jul 26. The Courier Journal
For Finnish Relief. 1940, Apr 8. The Courier Journal
Amateurs to Fight to Aid Olympics Fund. 1940, Mar 24. The Courier Journal
Lively Evening Seen for Kenny Barrett. 1940, Apr 4. The Courier Journal
Ed Cornwell Welterweight Champion. 1940, Apr 10. The Courier Journal
Brother Branham, the Faith Healer. 1947, Jul 6. St Louis Post Dispatch
Branham, William. 1962, Jul 1. To Take on The Whole Armor of God.
Branham, William. 1955, Jun 26. My Life Story.

WILLIAM BRANHAM AT PUBLIC SERVICE COMPANY:

Sixteenth Census of the United States: 1940, Jeffersonville
Wolf Captured Alive in Den Near Henryville. 1942, Aug 22. Jeffersonville Evening News.
Branham, William. 1950, Feb. Here We Have No Continuing City
Branham, William. 1950, Aug 20. My Life Story.
Branham, William. 1951, July 22. Life Story.
Branham, William. 1951, July 29. The Second Miracle.
Branham, William. 1953, Mar 25. Israel and the Church.
Branham, William. 1953, Apr 5. Go Tell My Disciples.
Branham, William. 1954, Apr 4. Earnestly Contending for the Faith.

CHAPTER 16

WILLIAM BRANHAM AND E. HOWARD CADLE

"No Creed But Christ"

I was thirty-five years old before I realized that one of the best vacation spots in the country was only about a four-hour drive north of Jeffersonville. Lake Michigan, surrounded by beautiful, sandy beaches — yet hundreds of miles from the ocean — is a great weekend getaway. Not far from the northern Indiana border is the big city of Chicago, with a beautiful harbor on Lake Michigan. Chicago has one of the most amazing skylines with towering skyscrapers, mirrored-glass buildings, incredible architecture and more. Best of all, visitors can take in the breathtaking view while lying in the sand and sipping ice-cold drinks on the beach nearby. Afterward, visitors can stroll down the busy streets of Chicago, sampling some Chicago-style pizza, loaded hot dogs and sizzling hot fries. Standing in downtown Chicago, the buildings are so massive that you begin to wonder how they stand on their own. They look as though they'd simply collapse, crushed by their own weight!

When I first visited Chicago, I was still in the "Message". At the time, I had no idea how significant Chicago was to the history of the religion of my family. As I began to research, however, I quickly began to learn that many trails of research led directly to Chicago. The "prophet's" father produced liquor that was likely distributed in

Chicago. Before the Wathen Liquor Ring was taken down, Wathen's drivers were frequently arrested making Chicago deliveries. It was also likely that this unusual business arrangement is the reason Wathen decided to post Charles Branham's bail money.

Chicago is where the "prophet" visited his first World's Fair, and where he got the inspiration for some of his "prophecies". Chicago is home to the "Philadelphia Church" and Joseph Mattsson-Boze, who would help promote the "prophet". Chicago is where the "prophet" would hold huge "healing campaigns", some of which were hosted by the infamous Reverend Jim Jones and People's Temple. The "prophet's" "Latter Rain" theology was heavily marketed from Chicago, from that same church. Chicago itself was the target for what the "prophet" claimed to be "Biblical" prophecy when he alleged that Chicago was the city Nahum saw by vision, in a sermon that was plagiarized from Rev. C. L. Franklin.[298]

> *That great eagle called Nahum, four thousand years ago, went up so high in the Spirit of God until he seen Outer Drive in Chicago, four thousand years later. Said, "The chariots shall rage in the broad ways: they shall run like lightning, they shall seem like torches, they'll justle one against another."* [299]

In all the sermons that I listened to in my life, from all of the pastors in "Message" churches that I attended, I never heard any sermon where the "Outer Drive prophecy" was mentioned. Most "Message" pastors did not include that in their sermons, some never mentioning the "prophecy" at all. Those who did mention the book of Nahum realized that the "prophet" hadn't studied Nahum's vision very well and described the prophecy of Nahum in its correct geographical location. It is widely known that the book of Nahum focuses specifically upon the end of the Assyrian Empire, and its capital city of Nineveh.

When a researcher thinks of Chicago during the prohibition era, they typically think of Al Capone and organized crime. Researchers from the

---

[298] Franklin, C. L. 1953. As the Eagle Stirreth Her Nest.
[299] Branham, William. 1957, Jul 14. As the Eagle Stirreth Her Nest.

Louisville and Southern Indiana area especially, because Capone often frequented the Southern Indiana casinos and had business associates in Louisville. Considering the many times that the "prophet" mentioned his father and the whiskey stills in his "Life Story" accounts, one might even conclude that organized crime in Chicago helped to shape the "prophet's" early life and to influence his ministry to promote teetotalism.

Organized crime was not the only early influence in the "prophet's" life from Chicago, however, at least not directly. The most famous early religious associate for the "prophet" was converted from a life in Chicago organized crime, a man by the name of E. Howard Cadle. Cadle was an evangelist from the 1920's who would influence many in the Louisville and Southern Indiana area, and would eventually influence multiple aspects of the "prophet's" ministry.

Chicago's "Levee" district was infamous for its brothels, gambling, crime, and seedy locations. It was in this district where Al and Frank Capone started their brothel and gambling house, "The Four Deuces". It was the same district where E. Howard Cadle owned his saloon and gambling house.[300]

E. Howard Cadle was a businessman with strong Jeffersonville ties. His mother lived in Utica, not far from the "prophet" and his family. Cadle owned casinos and slot machines in Illinois, Indiana, and Kentucky. He was born just north of Jeffersonville in the town of Salem, Indiana.

About the time Al Capone moved to Chicago from New York, however, E. Howard Cadle suddenly "got religion" and left gambling altogether. He moved his base of operations to Indianapolis, Indiana, and then set out to begin building a religious empire instead of nightlife.

Cadle wanted to create a network of churches and began focusing his attention towards Louisville and Southern Indiana. When Kentucky became a dry state in 1919, Cadle began an evangelistic campaign in Louisville's business district, shortly after Prohibition laws were passed. In January of 1920, Cadle announced that Louisville was chosen for his main Tabernacle, and that others were soon coming.[301] Cadle wanted to erect a chain of tabernacles throughout Southern Indiana and Kentucky.

---

[300] This Mother's Prayers Won. 1921, Oct 29. The Dearborn Independent

By June of that same year,[302] Cadle's new tabernacle was built. He became known to the locals as the "Tabernacle Man". Cadle's combination of business strategy and religion was highly successful, as was his "life story", which he frequently retold. It attracted the attention of big-name evangelists, such as Gipsy Smith.[303] Cadle's crime-to-Christianity story would have been very appealing.

I became curious about this "conversion", however, and wondered if this was a "normal" Christian conversion story. Something about the timeline of E. Howard Cadle's "conversion" made me curious. I thought about his ties to Jeffersonville and Chicago, which coincided with the time Charles Branham was producing liquor for Otto Wathen. I thought about his sudden flight from Chicago during mob control.[304] I considered the fortune he accumulated almost overnight and his ambition to establish a chain of Indiana churches. Knowing that Jeffersonville became a battleground between the Ku Klux Klan and distilleries, I began to wonder about E. Howard Cadle leaving the saloon business. Was it a clean break, as he claimed, after he "got religion?" Or did he switch sides during the heat of the battle?

Examining the timeline, I found that E. Howard Cadle's sudden rise to fame coincided with another historical event. While E. Howard Cadle was boasting about his overnight growth in Indiana, the Ku Klux Klan was boasting about their plans of expansion. They began parading through the streets of cities and states across the nation. In an unprecedented event, the Klan marched on Washington, D.C. in 1920,[305] the same time Cadle was planning his network of churches throughout Indiana. With the knowledge that the "prophet" started his career as an assistant to a high-ranking member of the Klan I began to wonder: how does E. Howard Cadle fit into the picture? How did the rise of the Indiana Klan fit into the picture? Was E. Howard Cadle a member of the Ku Klux Klan?

---

[301] Tabernacle Built Here by Indianapolis Man. 1920, May 28. The Courier Journal

[302] Cadle Tabernacle. 1920, Jun 5. The Courier Journal

[303] To Join Gipsy Smith Party. 1921, Apr 9. The Indianapolis News

[304] Cadle continued his Chicago presence after moving to Indianapolis. Example advertisement American Shoe Repair Company, E. Howard Cadle President. 1920, Jan 18. Chicago Tribune part 2 page 6.

[305] McArdle, Terence. The day 30,000 white supremacists in KKK robes marched in the nation's capital. Accessed 2018, Dec 1 from *https://www.washingtonpost.com/news/retropolis/wp/2017/08/17/the-day-30000-white-supremacists-in-kkk-robes-marched-in-the-nations-capital*

Things began to move quickly after the Indiana Klan was formed. E. Howard Cadle acquired a permit to build a *massive* tabernacle in the State Capital of Indianapolis.[306] It was almost 40,000 square feet and cost $75,000 to build the structure. All said and done, the entire cost of the Cadle Tabernacle was $305,000. In today's money, that is the equivalent to almost four million dollars. It opened in October 1921, and the newspapers announced its grand opening. Gipsy Smith was chosen to preach at the dedication service of the new Tabernacle,[307] and 20,000 people filled the building until it was bursting at its seams. There were so many people that 10,000 were turned away from entering.

Meanwhile, Cadle's evangelistic business continued to grow. He had a six-figure income and a beautiful home that was attended to by servants.[308] Cadle toured from coast to coast, telling his bars-to-tabernacles story, and in November of 1921, his evangelistic business was formally organized. His motto was, *"No Creed but Christ, No Law but Love, No Book but the Bible"*, which gave the public appearance of a devout religious leader. Behind the scenes, however, religion quickly started to mix with politics. Secretary of State Ed Jackson was elected president of the Cadle organization.[309]

Ed Jackson was a name I remembered from my research into the Indiana Ku Klux Klan. Ed Jackson was the 32nd Governor of the State of Indiana. History records his association with the Ku Klux Klan,[310] political scandals and questionable activities. As the Ku Klux Klan took control of the Indiana government, Jackson was accused of favoring Klan-appointed officials.[311] During Jackson's time in office, Klan meetings were publicized in the Indianapolis news — which was strange to me and out-of-character for the secretive group.

As I dug through the archives, I suddenly stumbled across an article that helped connect the dots. The Ku Klux Klan meetings in

---

[306] Permit for Tabernacle. 1921, Jun 23. The Indianapolis News

[307] 20,000 Hear Gipsy Smith Dedicate Cadle Tabernacle. 1921, Oct 10. The Indianapolis Star

[308] Once a Porter, Now Millionaire. 1921, Jun 22. Dunkirk Evening Observer

[309] Jackson Tabernacle Head. 1921, Nov 10. The Indianapolis Star

[310] Gitlin, Marty. 2009. The Ku Klux Klan: A Guide to an American Subculture. "Before the 1924 election, the Indiana Klan sent out 250,000 sample ballots to its members, indicating which candidates to vote for. The result was that Klansman Ed Jackson, an unknown before the primary, won the gubernatorial election"

[311] Charges that D. C. Stephenson, Ex-Klan Dragon, Aided Gov. Ed Jackson to Buy Car Are Reiterated by Ex-Officials of Company That Handled Deal. 1927, Jun 16. The Huntington Press

Indianapolis were held at the Cadle Tabernacle![312] According to the newspaper accounts, the Cadle Tabernacle became the meeting place for strategic Klan operations. Even the religious meetings in the Cadle Tabernacle were centered on Klan agenda, and they played Ku Klux Klan motion pictures during church services.[313] The Ku Klux Klan was praised openly from behind the pulpit. The Imperial Wizard, Hiram Evans, held his first open meeting at the Cadle Tabernacle.[314]

In an eerie glimpse into the future Civil Rights battles that were to come, Evans focused on the "public school problem" in America. It was racism. Different factions in the Klan chose the Cadle Tabernacle to hold public debate. Cadle's Tabernacle became widely recognized as the Klan's official meeting place, so much so that official Klan meetings came to be called "Tabernacle Meetings".[315]

Klan-appointed candidates began taking seats in Indianapolis government. They were bipartisan candidates, both Democrat and Republican, with the same agenda. As Klan-appointed officials took over Indianapolis, E. Howard Cadle announced his own candidacy.[316] Like Jackson, he started under the Republican ticket but then switched to an Independent candidate. The public noticed that Indianapolis government was being replaced by Klan appointees, and linked Klan candidates to the Klan meetings at Cadle Tabernacle. In the end, Cadle was pushed out of his own Tabernacle, and the "prophet" branded his own ministry with a design created by E. Howard Cadle — right down to copying Cadle's evangelistic motto:

We're glad to have you here. We're no denomination. We have no law but love, no creed but Christ, no book but the Bible.[317]

---

[312] Indiana Klan Re-Elects Bossert Grand Dragon. 1924, Sep 18. The Hancock Democrat
[313] For Immigrants to Vote. 1924, Mar 29. Indianapolis News. "He praised the Ku Klux Klan for what he said it had done for the uplift of negros and for its insistence on more restrictions on immigration. More than 1,000 persons attended the meeting. The principal part of the program consisted of a moving picture, "The Traitor Within", which depicts activities of the Ku Klux Klan".
[314] (Hiram W. Evans) To Speak at Cadle Tabernacle. 1924, Feb 12. The Indianapolis News
[315] Large Tabernacle Meeting. 1925, May 4. The Indianapolis News
[316] Wilmeth Will Seek Mayor Nomination. 1924, Nov 6. The Indianapolis News
[317] Branham, William. 1962, Nov 11. Why I'm Against Organized Religion.

There was much to be found about E. Howard Cadle, Ed Jackson, and the sudden rise and fall of the Indiana sect of the Ku Klux Klan, but they were scattered, disconnected pieces of a much, much larger puzzle. I wondered, "How did this information fit into the 'prophet's' real life story?"

I found a 1940 article in the Jeffersonville Evening News newspaper that I found to be very curious. The "prophet" vacated his pulpit for an entire summer. An unknown Rev. N. C. Guthrie took over the "prophet's" pastoral duties.[318] The article mentioned evangelism in Milltown, Indiana, the name of a town that I remembered from recordings of the "prophet". I quickly searched through the transcripts to find all of the "prophet's" statements about Milltown, and to my surprise, E. Howard Cadle was there when the "prophet" was preaching at Milltown![319] Even stranger, when the "prophet" was speaking to an audience in Chicago, IL, he claimed that he pastored a Baptist church in Milltown. I'd already established that he was a Pentecostal minister, not Baptist, and that Milltown was just one of many stops in an evangelistic tour. Why did he want his listeners to think he was a Baptist from Milltown instead of a Pentecostal from Jeffersonville, near Cadle's first Tabernacle chain?

I found something else interesting in a sermon the "prophet" preached *in* the Cadle Tabernacle. Sharing the pulpit with Rev. Jim Jones of Peoples Temple, where he "prophesied" God's "blessing" on Jones' ministry,[320] the "prophet" claimed that E. Howard Cadle was "looking for this day".[321] Was the "prophet" alleging that Jones' involvement in the Cadle Tabernacle meetings were the result of a "spiritual vision" from E. Howard Cadle himself?

---

[318] Rev. Branham Leaves for Sumer. 1940, Apr 29. Jeffersonville Evening News

[319] Branham, William. 1953, Dec 13. What Think Ye of Christ. "A bosom friend of mine down from Milltown, Indiana, where I pastored a little old Baptist church down there. I'd say, "Brother Cadle, I want you this morning, in the face of the Philadelphian Church, tell me Who you think the Son of God is?"

[320] Branham, William (with Jim Jones). 1956, Jun 15. An Exodus. "I believe that God's going pour out here in a few moments, something. I don't whether it's going to be a spontaneous healings, whether it's going to be a filling with the Holy Ghost, whether it's going to be a sending forth of a ministry. I don't know, but something's fixing to happen. Remember, I told you. I never felt this right in the prayer line. Ask anybody. Here's men that's been with me since I was early in the ministry. You never seen that; it picked up and I feel strong enough, look like, till run a mile (See?), run through a troop and leap over a wall. I never felt that way, never come back like that. Something started; something's happening."

[321] Branham, William. 1957, Jun 10. Faith Once Delivered to the Saints. "Your servant E. Howard Cadle, Gipsy Smith, B. E. Rediger, many other great men who stood here looking for this day"

The "prophet" returned to his own Pentecostal Tabernacle after the summer evangelistic tour. The next year, he married his second wife, Meda Broy,[322] in the home of Rev. Carnie Carpenter. Like Cadle, Rev. Carpenter was a United Brethren Church minister. Cadle's Tabernacle chain were all under the United Brethren umbrella and the denomination did not exist in the Louisville and Southern Indiana area until Louisville's first Cadle Tabernacle. Without Howard Cadle, there would not have been a Brethren minister in Jeffersonville to officiate their wedding.

I stumbled across an article in the Nashville newspaper that I found to be interesting. In Nashville, several ministers revolted against Roy E. Davis for giving the false impression of being a United Brethren Minister, and I wondered if the "prophet" was doing the same. According to a letter to the editor in the Tennessean, Davis was attempting to recruit Brethren Church members to his own revival.

Mr. Davis in this communication accused me of several things of which I wish the public to have the right conception of. A committee composed of myself and two of my men paid Mr. Davis a friendly visit on last Saturday night and ask him to please stop using the name of the United Brethren church when he was advertising his meetings as he had been doing for some time. Several times he had spoke of his meetings at the Old United Brethren church, to which was confusing to the public in general. And on one occasion an announcement came out in the paper that read as follows: Republicans of the North Nashville will meet tonight at the United Brethren church, Tenth street and Cheatham avenue, to organize a Hoover club. The Rev. Roy E. Davis, pastor of the church, is heading the organization. This announcement came out in the Wednesday morning's Tennessean. I felt and still feel it was not fair to me, to the United Brethren church, or even to Mr. Davis' church to use the name of another denomination.[323]

The background to E. Howard Cadle was very revealing, but it raised more questions than it answered. Why did the "prophet" choose

[322] Broy-Branham. 1941, Oct 24. Jeffersonville Evening News.
[323] A Further Explanation. 1928, Sep 7. The Tennesseean.

a Brethren minister for his second wedding? Was he joining forces with Cadle? Why did he claim to be a Baptist minister from Milltown? It was time to dig deeper into the "prophet's" early religious connections. The best place to start was by researching an evangelist that toured with the "prophet" starting in the 1940s. He was a man by the name of Fred Francis Bosworth.

E. HOWARD CADLE:

Kostlevy, William. 2001, Feb 28. The A to Z of the Holiness Movement
Yael Ksander. 2008, Apr 21. Howard Cadle. Accessed 2018, Dec 1
    from https://indianapublicmedia.org/momentofindianahistory/howard-cadle/
Retro Indy: Cadle Tabernacle. Accessed 2018, Dec 1 from
    https://www.indystar.com/story/news/history/retroindy/2014/10/10/retro-indy-cadle-
    tabernacle/17026731/
Zeigler, Connie. 2018, May 10. History 301: Cadle Tabernacle: Indy's home of fire and brimstone.
    Accessed 2018, Dec 1 from http://urbantimesonline.com/2018/05/10/history-301-cadle-
    tabernacle-indys-home-of-fire-and-brimstone/
Charges that D. C. Stephenson, Ex-Klan Dragon, Aided Gov. Ed Jackson to Buy Car Are
    Reiterated by Ex-Officials of Company That Handled Deal. 1927, Jun 16. The Huntington
    Press
Hold Shop Meetings. 1919, Jan 27. The Courier Journal
Beiderwolf To Take Charge of Church. 1926, Jan 13. Logansport Pharos Tribune
Klan Meeting Planned. 1926, Apr 15. The Indianapolis News
Tabernacle Built Here by Indianapolis Man. 1920, May 28. The Courier Journal
Real Religion Cannot Be Lost. 1920, Nov 5. The Courier Journal
Cadle Tabernacle. 1920, Jun 5. The Courier Journal
Story of Life Will Be Told. 1920, Jan 4. The Indianapolis Star
Cadle Memorial United Brethren Church. 1920, Jun 12. The Courier Journal
This Mother's Prayers Won. 1921, Oct 29. The Dearborn Independent
Cadle Tabernacle Ready for Dedication. 1921, Oct 8. The Indianapolis News
Teaching Kukluxism. 1921, Aug 27. The Appeal
20,000 Hear Gipsy Smith Dedicate Cadle Tabernacle. 1921, Oct 10. The Indianapolis Star
To Join Gipsy Smith Party. 1921, Apr 9. The Indianapolis News
Choir Upholds Cadle in Split. 1921, Nov 23. The Indianapolis Star
Starts New Life Is Now Wealthy. 1921, Jan 24. The Star Press
Permit for Tabernacle. 1921, Jun 23. The Indianapolis News
Jackson Tabernacle Head. 1921, Nov 10. The Indianapolis Star
Once a Porter, Now Millionaire. 1921, Jun 22. Dunkirk Evening Observer
Letter to the Editor. 1922, Aug 17. News and Observer
Tabernacle Sold by Howard Cadle. 1923, Jun 20. The Indianapolis News
Misc. News. 1923, May 12. The Indianapolis News
Stephenson Criticized. 1924, May 9. The Indianapolis News
Cadle Company Receiver. 1924, Oct 1. The Indianapolis News
Bosworth Party to Return. 1924, Dec 30. The Indianapolis News
Cadle Faces Libel Suit. 1924, Jun 7. The Indianapolis News
Klan the Issue in Indiana Now. 1924, May 16. The Fairmount News
Indiana Klan Re-Elects Bossert Grand Dragon. 1924, Sep 18. The Hancock Democrat
For Immigrants to Vote. 1924, Mar 29. The Indianapolis News
Bossert is Re-Elected. 1924, Sep 6. The Indianapolis News
Wilmeth Will Seek Mayor Nomination. 1924, Nov 6. The Indianapolis News
No Connection with King. 1924, Oct 22. The Indianapolis News
New Klan Chiefs to Quit. 1924, May 16. The Indianapolis News
Ask Receiver for Big Cadle Tabernacle. 1924, Oct 11. The Alexandria Times Tribune
Plot Against Watson Seen by the Old Man. 1924, May 10. The Indianapolis News
Hiram W. 1924, Feb 12. Evans To Speak at Cadle Tabernacle. The Indianapolis News
Klansmen Respond to Call by Stephenson. 1924, May 12. The Indianapolis News

Duvalus Administration. 1925, Nov 10. The Indianapolis News
Klan Debate Challenge. 1925, Jul 27. The Indianapolis News
At Baltimore Convention. 1925, Jul 27. The Indianapolis News.
Large Tabernacle Meeting. 1925, May 4. The Indianapolis News
Renounces All Party Ties. 1925, Mar 26. The Daily Republican
Evangelist to Hold Services at College. 1934, Aug 24. Wilmington News Journal
Cadle's Talk to Close Revival. 1936, Sep 28. The Journal News
Cadle Staff Coming. 1938, Jan 21. The Kokomo Tribune
Cadle Booked. 1939, Aug 1. The Circleville Herald
E. 1939, Nov 22. Howard Cadle. The Decatur Daily Review
Cadle to Hold Church Service at Auditorium. 1941, Jun 6. Kingsport Times

AL CAPONE:
FBI History: Al Capone. Accessed 2018, Dec 1 fromhttps://www.fbi.gov/history/famous-cases/al-capone
America's Most Wanted: The Hunt for Al Capone. 2010, May 1. Accessed 2018, Dec 1 from
    https://www.npr.org/templates/story/story.php?storyId=126419364
Shanahan, Edward. 2013, Aug 19. Al Capone's Haunted Chicago Cullerton Hotel and Paranormal
    Experiences There. Accessed 2018, Dec 1 from
https://www.chicagotribune.com/suburbs/chi-ugc-article-al-capones-haunted-chicago-cullerton-
    hotel-a-2013-08-19-story.html
Chicago Wouldn't be Chicago without Prohibition. 2012, Dec 4. Accessed 2018, Dec 1 from
    http://www.chicagonow.com/chicago-quirk/2012/12/chicago-prohibition/
"Al Capone moves his gang's headquarters to Cicero, Illinois". Timelines.com. Retrieved 2010-03-
    12.

INDIANA KU KLUX KLAN
Fischer, Jordan. 2016, Dec 8. The History of Hate in Indiana: How the Ku Klux Klan took over
    Indiana's halls of power. Accessed 2018, Dec 1 from
https://www.theindychannel.com/longform/the-ku-klux-klan-ran-indiana-once-could-it-happen-
    again
The Golden Era of Indiana. Accessed 2018, Dec 1 from http://historymuseumsb.org/the-golden-era-
    of-indiana
Dunn, Lindsay. The Stephenson Trial: Internal Klan Conflicts Linked to Downfall of Second Klan
    in Indiana. Accessed 2018, Dec 1 from
https://web.archive.org/web/20080130134128/http://www.columbia.edu/~rr91/1402-
    2007/The%20Stephenson%20Trial%20prospectus.htm
Ku Klux Klan: A Secret History, written and produced by Bill Brummel, History Channel, 31 May
    2003.
Leonard J. Moore, Citizen Klansmen: The Ku Klux Klan in Indiana, 1921-1928, Chapel Hill:
    University of North Carolina Press, 1997
Gugin, Linda C.; St. Clair, James E, eds. (2006). The Governors of Indiana. Indianapolis, Indiana:
    Indiana Historical Society Press. ISBN 0-87195-196-7.
Rory McVeigh, "Structural incentives for conservative mobilization: Power devaluation and the
    rise of the Ku Klux Klan, 1915–1925" Social Forces (1999) 77#4 pp: 1461-1496.
Lutholtz, M. William (1993). Grand Dragon: D. C. Stephenson and the Ku Klux Klan in Indiana.
    West Lafayette, Indiana: Purdue University
McArdle, Terence. The day 30,000 white supremacists in KKK robes marched in the nation's
    capital. Accessed 2018, Dec 1 from

https://www.washingtonpost.com/news/retropolis/wp/2017/08/17/the-day-30000-white-supremacists-in-kkk-robes-marched-in-the-nations-capital/?noredirect=on&utm_term=.a11ad65c485b

WILLIAM BRANHAM - ABOUT HOWARD CADLE:

Branham, William. 1952, July 10, I Am the Resurrection and The Life
Branham, William. 1953, Dec 13, What Think Ye Of Christ?
Branham, William. 1954, Mar 21, What Think Ye Of Christ?
Branham, William. 1956, Mar 4, Making A Way
Branham, William. 1956, Apr 3, Shepherd of The Sheepfold
Branham, William. 1956, Apr 5, The Resurrection of Jesus
Branham, William. 1956, Apr 26, Jesus Christ The Same Yesterday, Today, And Forever
Branham, William. 1956, May 13, Teaching on Moses
Branham, William. 1956, Jun 3, The Lamb's Book of Life
Branham, William. 1956, Jun 10, Perfection
Branham, William. 1956, Jun 11, Hear Ye Him
Branham, William. 1956, Jun 12, Life Is the Healer
Branham, William. 1956, Jun 13, Jehovah-Jireh
Branham, William. 1956, Jun 14, God Provided A Lamb
Branham, William. 1956, Jun 15, An Exodus
Branham, William. 1956, Jun 17, Revelation, Book of Symbols
Branham, William. 1956, Jun 21, The Law Having A Shadow
Branham, William. 1956, Jul 26, Love
Branham, William. 1956, Aug 26, Divine Love
Branham, William. 1956, Oct 2, Elisha The Prophet
Branham, William. 1957, May 18, Stand Still
Branham, William. 1957, Jun 10, Faith Once Delivered to The Saints
Branham, William. 1957, Jun 13, Thirsting for Life
Branham, William. 1957, Jun 14, The Queen of The South
Branham, William. 1957, Aug 18, Time-Tested Memorials of God
Branham, William. 1958, Mar 23, Jesus Christ The Same Yesterday, Today, And Forever
Branham, William. 1959, Apr 16, El-Shaddai
Branham, William. 1959, Nov 20, A Prophet Like unto Moses
Branham, William. 1959, Dec 20, Identified with Christ
Branham, William. 1959, Dec 27, A Super Sense
Branham, William. 1960, Jun 11, Faith Is the Sixth Sense
Branham, William. 1961, Jan 1, Revelation, Chapter Four #2
Branham, William. 1961, Jan 12, Questions and Answers
Branham, William. 1962, Oct 14, A Guide
Branham, William. 1962, Nov 4, Blasphemous Names

CHAPTER 17

WILLIAM BRANHAM AND
FRED FRANCIS BOSWORTH

"Brother Bosworth was raised up here in Zion, under Doctor Dowie[324]"

In San Jose, California, there is a museum on Park Ave that is worth visiting if you ever happen to be in the area. The Rosicrucian Egyptian Museum holds the largest collection of ancient Egyptian artifacts in western North America. Inside, you'll find some of the most amazing sights, all significant parts of world history. From statues and hieroglyphs to mummies, household goods to clothing, papyrus documents and more, the museum holds many sights many people in the world will never see or even know existed!

I had the opportunity to visit this museum shortly after I left the "Message". At the time, I didn't fully appreciate priceless value these artifacts represent. Each artifact, each individual piece of history, tells a thousand stories! They tell how the ancient world lived, what the ancient world thought, and how the ancient civilizations progressed. The lessons they learned are passed down through time, all preserved for us to see! The museum displayed a full-scale replica of the Rosetta Stone, a large stele used to translate the ancient Egyptian hieroglyphics and Demotic scripts to ancient Greek which enabled modern translators to interpret the Egyptian hieroglyphs, a language that would have otherwise been lost to time. Large granite and stone tablets were

---

[324] Branham, William. 1952, Jul 25. Experiences.

meticulously carved with images of pharaohs, sphinx, and hundreds of other hieroglyphs depicted as Egyptians under the warm rays flowing from the sun god, Ra.

It was very easy to compare the belief system of the ancient Egyptians to the "Message" religion that I had left. The "prophet" believed that the first "Bible" was the "Zodiac"[325], and that the second "Bible" was the "pyramid"[326] (The Pyramid of Khufu at Giza).[327] This unusual theology would have been strange to other Christians, but for the ancient Egyptians, it would have been readily accepted. As I studied each exhibit, I found it hard to believe that "Message" believers were so uninterested in Egyptian history. If the Great Pyramid was a "bible", shouldn't we have tried to know more about it and its relation to the Zodiac, astronomy, and astrology? The "Message" focused heavily on "faith healing". The "prophet" was known as a "faith healer" and was one of the leaders of the Post WWII Healing Revival. Shouldn't the "first and second Bible" tell us more about faith healing? Wouldn't understanding the ancient culture tell us more about those two Bibles?

In Egyptian mythology, Isis was the goddess of healing. Historians believe that worshippers of Isis rarely prayed to her for healing, however. Instead, they believed in her kindness and willingness *to answer* those who needed healing. The average age of death in ancient Egypt was 19 years old,[328] yet the ancients never questioned the effectiveness of Isis or their faith healing. Even with high rates of infant mortality and premature death, they believed that Isis improved their chances of healing.

This is an idea I had never really thought about! The gravesites in Jeffersonville are *filled* with people who placed their faith in the "prophet" for healing. Those diagnosed with a terminal illness who recovered all believe that their chances were better because of the "prophet". Those who died went to their graves thinking their faith was

---

[325] Branham, William. 1953, Apr 3. The Cruelty of Sin and the Penalty That It Cost To Rid Sin From Our Lives. "He is writing His first Bible. The first Bible was ever written, was written in the skies, the Zodiac."
[326] Branham, William. 1953, Apr 3. The Cruelty of Sin and the Penalty That It Cost To Rid Sin From Our Lives. "The second Bible was written, was written by Enoch, and put in the pyramid."
[327] Branham, William. 1961, Dec 31. "That great pyramid in Egypt is so perfect in the center of the earth, no matter where the sun is, there's never a shadow around it."
[328] Lijas, Ann E M. Old age in ancient Egypt. Accessed 2020, May 17 from https://blogs.ucl.ac.uk/researchers-in-museums/2015/03/02/old-age-in-ancient-egypt/

not as strong as it should have been, never questioning the "prophet" or his power to "heal". Instead, they questioned their own faith. The "prophet" taught that if you weren't healed after he pronounced "Thus Saith The Lord", it was *your* faith at fault.[329] I always wondered where that doctrine came from. As much as I searched, I never could find anything even remotely similar to it in the Bible. The sick had faith in *God* for their healing, not any prophet. And when God declared healing, he never tied His healing results to the faith of the person who was healed.

Once I learned that the "prophet" started the Voice of Healing publication to promote his ministry, I searched to find several early issues. Fortunately, they were available in an online archive. Searching through them, I found a similar article in several of the issues describing *"Why All Are Not Healed"*. Even the very first issue had this disclaimer for those who were not healed in the "prophet's" recent campaigns. That article was written by Rev. Fred Francis Bosworth.

This was a name I as very familiar with in the "Message". The "prophet" mentioned Rev. Bosworth 568 times on the recorded sermons that we had access to hear, the earliest in 1947. I found something strange in the very first recording that is available. The very first words are, *"we're getting some new gadgets for recording".*[330] I had never noticed this sentence when I was a believer in the "Message", yet it was the very first sentence of the very first transcript of the very earliest sermon that we could access. It was evident from the quality of later sermons that they did purchase new recording equipment, but why would the "prophet" announce *new equipment* on the first recording? Certainly, he did not start his ministry with "gadgets" he intended to immediately replace! How many years in the past was the announcement of the old "gadgets" for recording? I wanted to know more about the "prophet's" ministry that we no longer had access to see or hear, and I was curious about F. F. Bosworth, who played such a significant part in the "prophet's" ministry. What made him decide to

---

[329] Branham, William. 1948, Mar 4. The Angel of God. "You come in that attitude, and that's the reason you get healed. That's the reason you're healed, because you come humble. Anyone who comes stiff-necked will never receive nothing from God."

[330] Branham, William. 1947, Apr 12. Faith is the Substance. "We're getting some new gadgets for recording"

tour the world with the "prophet"? How was he so deeply involved, yet never joined the "Message"?

I came across something interesting while researching the Ku Klux Klan activities at the Cadle Tabernacle as I researched E. Howard Cadle and Ed Jackson. Shortly after the Klan started launching their campaign to take control of Indiana government, Fred Francis Bosworth announced his plan for a religious campaign in Indianapolis![331] I knew that this was not enough to tie him directly to the white supremacy group, but I also knew that they would not have invited him if his views did not align with theirs. It was also highly unlikely that he would have accepted their invitation if *his* views did not align with theirs — the Ku Klux Klan activities in Indianapolis had made national news for their recent invasion of Indianapolis government. I found it interesting that Bosworth was recognized in the article for pastoring the Gospel Tabernacle in Dallas, Texas, and that it was about the same time Rev. Roy E. Davis was a pastor in the Dallas / Fort Worth area.

Like the "prophet", F. F. Bosworth was a nationally recognized "faith healer". From the newspaper articles I found it was clear that the Bosworth Brothers Campaigns attracted big crowds from coast to coast. During the time Roy Davis began his evangelistic career in Texas, the Bosworth Brothers began their "healing revivals".[332] F. F. Bosworth was one of the early founders of the Assemblies of God sect of Pentecostalism,[333] a Pentecostal sect that promoted the exclusion of African Americans from the highest levels.[334]

After the Church of God sect of Pentecostalism split to form the Assemblies of God, some Church of God churches became predominately black while the Assemblies became predominately white. This segregation would have been popular with both Roy Davis and the leaders of the Cadle Tabernacle, and I was surprised to see that Bosworth himself was a big name in the denomination during its

---

[331] Evangelist Plans Big Campaign in Cadle Tabernacle. 1924, Nov 3. The Indianapolis Star
[332] Revival Campaign. 1917, February 16. Manitoba Free Press.
[333] Menzies, Robert. 2004. The Spirit and Spirituality: Volume 4. Essays in Honor. "another of those dissenting voices was surely F.F. Bosworth, also an Executive Presbyter of the Assemblies of God."
[334] Newman, Joe. 2007. Race and the Assemblies of God Church: The Journey from Azusa Street to the "Miracle of Memphis". "In addition, a concerted effort to refer African Americans interested in the Assemblies of God to African American groups, such as the Church of God in Christ, was approved at the highest levels of Assemblies of God leadership."

formation and until 1916.[335] I was also surprised to learn that David du Plessis, another one of William Branham's associates, was also part of the organization.

Still, this was not the most startling information to be found about Rev. F. F. Bosworth. Faith healing was not new to F. F. Bosworth when he and his brother began their "healing campaigns". Before starting the Assemblies of God, Bosworth was a member of a strange healing cult that was located just north of Chicago — yet another tie to the Chicago area. Bosworth was a ranking member of "faith healer" John Alexander Dowie's religious commune,[336] which started in the Chicago area and moved to Zion, Illinois. Dowie was a name I was also familiar with; the "prophet" preached to the Zion cult following and claimed that Dowie himself had prophesied about the "prophet's" ministry.

> *How Doctor Dowie, in his death, prophesied that I would come to that city forty years from the time that he died. Not knowing nothing about it, he died on one day, and I was borned on the next. And forty years to the day I entered the city, not knowing nothing about it. Oh, how God's great move is coming together. I hear the sound of abundance of rain.[337]*

It is difficult to say whether the "prophet" first came in contact with Dowie's religious doctrine through his connection to F. F. Bosworth or Roy E. Davis, but it was clear from the "prophet's" statements that he respected John Alexander Dowie as a "prophet" and had respect for the religious cult that Dowie had established. I suddenly realized that through F. F. Bosworth, there were multiple connections being established between the "prophet" and Chicago.

While E. Howard Cadle was building his gambling empire in Chicago, John Alexander Dowie was building a political and religious

---

[335] Poloma, Margaret. 1989. The Assemblies of God at the Crossroads Charisma and Institutional Dilemmas. "The tension between an emerging organization and would-be prophets is not new. One of the early cases may be seen in 1916 with F. F. Bosworth's dismissal. Bosworth challenged the tenet of the new sect which asserted that tongues was the only initial evidence of Spirit baptism. Although this challenged cost him his Assemblies of God credentials, like du Plessis and Cunningham, Bosworth reportedly remained on good terms with the emerging denomination.

[336] "Christ the Healer." Accessed 2017, April 22 from *http://healingandrevival.com/BioBosworth.htm.*

[337] Branham, William. 1951, Sept 29. Our Hope is in God

empire. His following grew to such a population that they outgrew Chicago. Dowie purchased land north of the city that would eventually become known as Zion City. Zion City, a religious cult commune, was fully controlled by John Alexander Dowie. It had its own government, utilities, distribution, retail, and more, with Dowie holding supreme authority.[338]

During this time, F. F. Bosworth was the band director for the city, its religious activities, and its evangelistic outreach program.[339] Dowie's followers believed him to be the *"return of Elijah the prophet from the Old Testament"*. The nation recognized him as a mentally unstable "faith healer" titled the "Richest Man in the West",[340] but Chicago recognized him as a political threat.

As F. F. Bosworth toured the country with Dowie, whose nickname was quickly becoming *"Elijah III"*, Dowie pushed his agenda like a Chicago mob boss. In a meeting at Madison Square Garden in New York City, Dowie threatened New York officials.[341] He boasted that he had gained political control of Chicago, that he was able to sway 50,000 political votes, and that soon he would have control of New York City. At the height of his wealth and power, John Alexander Dowie had accumulated $15,000,000, which was over $425,000,000 in today's money. According to the newspapers, Dowie had built his half-billion-dollar (in today's money) empire in just ten years simply by promoting himself as a biblical "Elijah" faith healer. At first, I wondered why F. F. Bosworth would switch from believing Dowie's "Elijah" to Branham's "Elijah", but then, a much more disturbing thought struck me. Had Roy E. Davis and other Klan leaders realized that religion could be weaponized[342] to sway politics?

---

[338] Zion City, The Remarkable Community Established by the Most Thoroughly Denounced Man In America, John Alexander Dowie. 1903, Oct 17. The Indianapolis News.

[339] Bosworth is named in articles describing Dowie's evangelism, such as New York City.

[340] A Record $15,000,000 Profit Makes John Alexander Dowie, Alias Elijah III, The Merchant Prince of Faith Healers. 1902, November 30. Brooklyn Daily Eagle.

[341] Eleventh Commandment as Given Out By Dowie. 1903, Oct 29. Austin American Statesman.

[342] St. Petersburg court declares books by U.S. missionary Branham extremist. Accessed 2020, May 24 from *rapsinews.com/judicial_news/20200521/305831637.html*. "Brochures authored by XX century U.S. missionary William Branham have been defined as extremist literature … In April of 2017, an examination by experts of St. Petersburg State University revealed that the texts contained "technics of neuro-linguistic programming" aimed to set up the spectre of an enemy and insult the feelings of certain religious believers and priests. The results of the expert examination served as the basis of the claim, according to the statement."

Shortly before Roy E. Davis moved his base of operations to Louisville from Tennessee, F. F. Bosworth faced a very devastating, highly publicized failure in his "faith healing" campaigns. A man that Bosworth claimed to be "cured" had died of the same disease that brought him to the "healing campaigns".[343] According to his widow, the victim did not die for lack of faith; the victim was very faithful. Bosworth's only response to news media was, in my opinion, a poor defense. He insinuated that the man could have been cured of one disease and die of another. Bosworth went on to tell the news media of a previous failure, wherein a deaf man was "healed" but failed to hear. According to Bosworth, the "spirit" told him to avoid tobacco, and when the man did not listen to the "spirit", his deafness returned.

Reminded of the Egyptians and Isis, I began to wonder: Was Bosworth's "god" also so powerless that he didn't realize the man had two illnesses? Did this "god" not have the power to both "heal" and "take away the sin"? Suddenly I began to understand why Bosworth published "unhealed" disclaimers in the "prophet's" newsletter. He was familiar with the angry mobs that grew from a failed "healing".

Seeing the political and financial power of men involved with the "prophet's" ministry changed the way that I viewed his meetings. Up until this point, I only thought of the "Message" as a religion. I had never considered its political power, or the amount of money that flowed through those meetings. Even early in my research, I had discovered a handful of people that the "prophet" had "healed" who still died.[344] Thinking about the crowds of people that filled auditoriums to see the "healers", and how they must have been viewed by Cadle, Bosworth, Dowie, Davis, and other big names in the healing revival, my stomach began to churn. These were not the "faithful". They were assets to persuade, influence, control, and financially deplete. Did the "prophet" view them in the same way?

---

[343] Man Dies Believing Himself "Cured". 1927, May 28. Altoona Tribune
[344] Why I Left the Tongues Movement. Accessed 2020, May 17 from
http://www.bereanresearchinstitute.com/03_Doctrines/D.0030_14_Why_I_Left_the_Tongues_Movement_-_Alfred_H._Pohl.html. "Time went on, the campaign ended, and Mr. Branham and his party were gone. Then we began to see the results being tested by time. It was a difficult time for us, and particularly for me. For one by one these that I had personally seen "healed" and declared so by the "healer," died. Our faith was severely tested. Relatives of the deceased ones would ask, "Why?" What could we tell them?"

It was time to focus my attention once again to the "prophet's" early ministry, and more closely examine his personal lifestyle. I'd already learned that the "prophet" was not nearly so poor as he had often described, but I also did not see any signs of an abundance of wealth during his early years. I decided that there were only three possibilities: 1) either the "prophet" was so fully devoted to his spiritual beliefs that he decided to mass-persuade others to also devote themselves, or 2) the "prophet" was seeking wealth or power, or worse 3) *other* men were using the "prophet" for their own wealth, power, and strategic purpose.

I knew that the first option should be very easy to prove or disprove. If the "prophet" were fully devoted, that devotion would be manifested in his life off-stage. The stage *persona* would match the person. I had already exhausted most of my resources for learning about the "prophet's" personal life directly, and they seemed as one might expect. They were his own descriptions of himself, using his own advertisements, titles and subject matter that he himself created and gave to newspapers. For a minister, his early life was simply "ministry". If I was going to gain any insight into his life off-stage, I knew that I would need to begin examining people in his inner circle who were not in the public eye or part of the stage act. I knew that the best place to start was with the "prophet's" immediate family, those who did not travel with him in his evangelistic career.

FRED FRANCIS BOSWORTH

Perkins, Eunice M. 1927. Fred Francis (Joybringer) Bosworth - His Life Story (2 ed.). Bosworth.

Against Dowie Individually. 1906, April 27. Bismarck Tribune.

Goff, James R. 1988. Fields White unto Harvest. University of Arkansas Press. ISBN 1-55728-025-8.

Barnes III, Roscoe. 2009. F. F. Bosworth: The Man behind "Christ the Healer." Cambridge Scholars Publishing.

"Christ the Healer." Accessed 2017, April 22 from http://healingandrevival.com/BioBosworth.htm.

Southwick, George W. Controversy in Zion. Truth in History Ministries.

King, Paul L. 2006. Genuine Gold. Word & Spirit Press.

Blumhofer, Edith. 1985. The Assemblies of God: A Popular History. Gospel Publishing House. Accessed 2017, May 25 from: http://edmundc.weebly.com/uploads/2/5/3/9/25397277/__assemblies_of_god-a_popular_history_aog.pdf.

Newman, Joe. 2007. Race and the Assemblies of God Church: The Journey from Azusa Street to the "Miracle of Memphis."

Oliver, Jeff. 2017. Pentecost to the Present: The Holy Spirit's Enduring Work in the Church. Bridge-Logos.

Our Story. Accessed 2017, May 30 from http://www.thelakesassembly.com/our-story.html.

Revival Campaign. 1917, February 16. Manitoba Free Press.

F. 1917, February 24. F. Bosworth. Winnipeg Tribune.

Special Services at Boulevard Tabernacle. 1918, January 15.

To Hold Big Revival at Cadle Tabernacle. 1924, November 3. Huntington Herald.

Misc. News. 1920, January 24. Courier Journal Louisville

Misc. News. 1910, November 15. Pittsburgh Press.

Misc. News. 1920, November 19. Pittsburgh Press.

Texas Evangelist Opens Midway Gospel Meetings. 1921, February 21.

Big Tent. 1921, August 20. Chicago Daily Tribune.

Prayer Meeting Officially Opens Valley Tabernacle. 1921, October 13. Pittsburgh Daily Post.

Sick Seek Aid of Evangelist Bosworth At Valley Meet. 1921, October 17. Pittsburgh Daily Post.

What Others Say. 1924, September 24. Press and Sun Bulletin Binghamton, NY.

'Healer' Will Anoint Lame, Sick Tonight. 1927, May 11. Altoona Tribune.

Ottawa Accords A Sendoff to the Bosworth Brothers Such as Is Rarely Seen Here. 1924, May 27. Ottawa Journal.

Widow Tells of Invalid's Strong Faith. 1927, May 28. Altoona Tribune.

Bosworth Has Nothing to Say. 1927, May 28. Altoona Tribune.

Aged Lawyer Anointed by Evangelists. 1927, May 13. Altoona Tribune

Bosworth "Faith Cures" Continue as Ministers Attack His Methods. 1927, May 16. Altoona Tribune

'Faith Healer' Meet Marked by Surprises. 1927, May 16. Altoona Tribune

Widow Tells. 1927, May 14. Altoona Tribune

Man Dies Believing Himself "Cured". 1927, May 28. Altoona Tribune

Rev. F. F. Bosworth and his Wife Are Guests. 1931, Mar 17. Altoona Tribune

Took $3400. 1927, May 10. Altoona Tribune

Healer Will Anoint Lame, Sick Tonight. 1927, May 11. Altoona Tribune

Misc. News. 1932, Nov 16. Angola Herald

Bosworth Bros. 1924, Nov 1. Great Evangelists at Indianapolis. Brazil Daily Times

JOHN ALEXANDER DOWIE - EARLY MINISTRY

J. Franklin, Catholics versus Masons, Journal of the Australian Catholic Historical Society 20 1999, 1-15.

A Lecture. 1876, October 18. Sydney Morning Herald.

Free Christian Addresses. 1880, August 28. Sydney Morning Herald.

A Curious Action for Libel. 1882, June 20. The Age Melbourne

Healing by Faith – The Ministry of John A. 1888, June 14. Dowie. San Francisco Chronicle.

A Healer. 1888, July 14. Oakland Tribute.

No Miracles Yet. 1888, July 19. Oakland Tribune.

Methodist Clergy. 1888, July 31. Oakland Tribune.

Miracles Galore. 1888, July 31. Oakland Tribune.

Not "Invited. 1889, January 11. Oakland Tribune.

Preached in A Big Tent. 1890, July 28. Chicago Tribune.

Did Not Forget the Collection. 1891, May 25. Chicago Daily Tribune.

Claims He Raised the Dead. 1891, September 17. Central Times Dunn, NC.

Dowie Winds Up. 1891, November 10. Pittsburgh Daily Post.

A Medial View. 1891, November 10. Pittsburg Daily Post.

Mr. Dowie Again. 1892, February 1. Pittsburgh Post-Gazette.

Had A Very Small Audience. 1892, October 17. Pittsburgh Dispatch.

Latter Day Miracles. 1894, April 8. Inter Ocean Chicago.

A Divine Healing Home. 1894, December 4. San Francisco Chronicle.

John Alexander Dowie, the "Faith Healer," Is Arrested. 1895, January 6. The Inter Ocean.

Dowie Heard in His Own Defense. 1895, January 23. The Inter Ocean Chicago.

Parliamentary Elections. 1880, September 1. Sydney Morning Herald.

News of the Day. 1880, June 23. Sydney Morning Herald.

The Case of Mr. J. A. Dowie. 1882, June 20. The Age Melbourne

JOHN ALEXANDER DOWIE - LOS ANGELES/SAN FRANCISCO HISTORY

A Suit for Slander. 1890, June 11. San Francisco Chronicle.

Crazed by Dowie's Meetings. 1890, June 18. Oakland Tribune.

Just Lays on Hands. 1891, May 23. Chicago Tribune.

"Healing Hand" Dowie Turned Out. 1894, June 25. Chicago Daily Tribune.

JOHN ALEXANDER DOWIE - ZION CITY COMMUNE AND ENTERPRISE

He Will Call It Zion. 1895, June 7. The Inter Ocean.

The Cop Took the Healer. 1895, July 23. Los Angeles Herald.

"Dr. Dowie Rejoices." 1895, August 15. The Inter Ocean.

Divine Healers in Jail. 1899, August 9. Montgomery Adviser.

Faith Healing in Chicago. 1899, August 20. New York Times.

Dr. Dowie Fears Assassination. 1899, August 22. New York Times.

Wants Only A Million. 1899, November 25. Lawrence Daily World Lawrence, KS.

Dowie Attacks Editors. 1899, December 11. The Inter Ocean.

Dowie to be Guarded. 1899, December 28. Montgomery Adviser.

A Good Thing in Zion. 1900, January 3. Inter Ocean.

Misc. News. 1900, May 1. Indianapolis Journal

Misc. News. 1901, May 22. The Decatur Herald.

A Record $15,000,000 Profit Makes John Alexander Dowie, Alias Elijah III, The Merchant Prince of Faith Healers. 1902, November 30. Brooklyn Daily Eagle.

Zion City in Receivers' Hands. 1903, December 17. Cheyenne County Rustler. St. Francis, KS.

A Prophet for Profit. 1902, January 6. Honolulu Adviser

A Dowie Dupe on Trial. 1902, Feb 21. Perry Daily Chief.

Labor Outbreak. 1902, March 19. Star Gazette.

Smallpox Routs Healers. 1902, April 8. Leavenworth Times.

Prayers Could Not Save Dowie's Daughter. 1902, May 15. Coffeeville Daily Journal.

Dowie Would Buy Jerusalem. 1902, June 8. The Times Pennsylvania.

Does Dowie Need Money. 1902, September 23. Abilene Daily Chronicle.

Dowie Plans More "Zion" Cities. 1903, October 8. Lebo Enterprise.

Lame, Halt, and Blind Rushed. 1903, October 21. Xenia Daily.

Dowie At White House. 1903, November 10. Los Angeles Times.

His Ready Money About Exhausted. 1903, December 2. The Tennessean.

Dowie Is Stricken. 1905, September 30. Spokane Press.

Dowie Surrenders Leadership of his Church. 1905, December 18. San Francisco Call.

CHAPTER 18

WILLIAM BRANHAM'S
MARRIAGE AND DIVORCE

"Your vow is until death you separate, and there's nothing else in the world will permit you to marry (in the Bible) until your companion is dead. That's right. Their only grounds! There's no remarrying nowhere at all, except a dead companion[345]"

T he Department of Records in the Jeffersonville, Indiana, Courthouse is unlike the record archives found in other courthouses in the area. Jeffersonville still allows public access to all of their historical record books. Just ten miles away in New Albany, for instance, the courthouse keeps their archives in a storage facility without immediate public availability. Access is only granted if the requestor has a specific case number. For researchers like me who are attempting to piece together unknown history, it makes finding *anything* impossible. If the history is *unknown,* then the case numbers are also unknown. In my personal experience, the departments of records in courthouses in Southern Indiana and Louisville, Kentucky were very unhelpful in providing any means to *find* a case number for historical research purposes. It's difficult, because the records are mostly hand-written, and cannot be searched by software programs. At the Jeffersonville Courthouse, however, a person can freely walk into

---

[345] Branham, William. 1962, May 27. Questions and Answers.

the building and browse the stacks of books, open any record book and read, take pictures or write down notes. Records are stored in neatly organized rows, about 15 books high. They are organized chronologically, from the early 1800's until recent years when Indiana legal records transitioned from paper to digital storage.

At first, I was overwhelmed by the amount of information available to me and had no idea where to begin! There were marriage licenses, divorce dockets, civil lawsuits, criminal trials, and more. It would take a lifetime to read through everything in these books that interested me! These books were written in real time, as each case came in, without knowing which cases or names would come later — so indexing them was impossible. Names were written as they came into the courts. Names were not alphabetized, and indexes are scattered throughout the list of people in random order. Worse, they are written in cursive, sometimes by people with very poor handwriting. Cases are added in order by date of hearing, not by case number and date of hearing and were not in the name index in the front. To find a case, you literally must hunt through pages, one by one, until you find the case number in the front of the book.

Many times, this painful exercise offered very little value towards the research, though some of the records I found offered small pieces of the puzzle. For instance, searching through the archives might yield a tiny historical fact, such as finding the "prophet's" brother Melvin divorcing Hope Brumbach's sister Charlotte[346] — which could have just as easily be found on one of the genealogy websites. But finding the record in the courthouse along with the notes taken and the log of events for each case did offer some value. Learning more about Melvin and Charlotte's divorce did give insight into the "prophet's" personal life.

In the "Message", divorce and remarriage was a very touchy subject. Each pastor had a different opinion on what they felt the "prophet" permitted and what he rejected. Most "Message" pastors were very strict towards the women in the religion while being somewhat lenient with the men. If you were female, and divorced your husband, you were forced to be single until the day of your death. Some pastors claimed that a divorced female could only join in the "Rapture" if their husband

---

[346] 22685. Charlotte Hazel Branham vs. Melvin F. Branham. 1945, Mar 3. Clark County Court.

took them back. Some took this further to say that a divorced woman would only be a servant, once in heaven.[347] Other pastors in the "Message" taught the general fundamentalist Christian views on divorce and remarriage: Men and women, equally, were not permitted to remarry after divorce unless their spouse died. Still others taught that men *could* remarry, but *women could not*, regardless of whether their spouse was alive. Each pastor who differed and held a slight variation of opinion claimed that their version was exactly what the "prophet" taught.

Even while in the "Message", I noticed that these opinions varied among those who learned from the "prophet's" actions, and that they were vastly different from those who learned from the prophet's sermons. My grandfather, for instance, taught his church that "Marriage and Divorce" was a "mystery",[348] and that if the "prophet" had not preached the sermon with that title, the church would never have known what God wanted. I always wondered, why was that necessary when we had the Bible? If the "prophet's" actions in later years did not align with his sermons, what of his early years?

I knew that this was one subject that could offer some insight into the "prophet's" personal life, and that it might give a glimpse into the difference between the views of the "prophet's" stage personas. If the "Message" pastors were not wrong in their opinion of what the "prophet" taught, even if they were polar-opposite in their own opinions, then the "prophet" must have had conflicting doctrines in his sermons. I had seen the differences in the transcripts and had listened to them on multiple occasions using the recordings that we could access. In some instances, the "prophet" did not permit remarriage after divorce until the death of a spouse.

Your vow is until death you separate, and there's nothing else in
the world will permit you to marry (in the Bible) until your

---

[347] According to former members, this doctrine was used by my grandfather in private consultation, and he claimed that it came directly from William Branham.
[348] Branham, William. 1965, Apr 10. The Easter Seal. "Go home and open these Seven Seals that are given." And here they are, the true mystery of marriage and divorce, and the serpent's seed, and all of these things that's been fussed about. It's THUS SAITH THE LORD"

companion is dead. That's right. Their only grounds! There's no remarrying nowhere at all, except a dead companion [349]

In other instances, there were circumstances in which remarriage after divorce was permitted. Usually, those circumstances were only valid if the person seeking remarriage was male. In some cases, the conflicting doctrines were only a few months apart.

> *See, she has got a living husband, so no man can marry her. Care what she does and who she is, she's got a living husband, there is no grounds for her at all. But, it's not, for him. "Causes her," not him. Get it? You have to make the Word run in continuity. See, nothing saying he couldn't, but she can't. See, "causes her," not him. That's exactly what the Bible says, "causes her." It is not stated against him to remarry, but "her." Why? Christ in the type. Notice, it is stated that he cannot remarry, only a virgin.* **He can remarry** [350]

Learning that the marriage between "prophet" and his second wife was performed by a United Brethren minister during the time of the "prophet's" public affiliation with E. Howard Cadle (the man who introduced that denomination of faith to Southern Indiana), I knew that the "prophet" would have been adopting the fundamentalist view on remarriage. Considering the criminal sex scandal of Roy E. Davis during his mentoring the "prophet", I wasn't certain that those same views would have been present in his early ministry. Davis was living with an underaged teenager, and if his criminal past were fully exposed, the "prophet" would have known that Davis had abandoned his first and second wives to live with the girl in his parsonage. The question was whether his affiliation with Cadle would have convinced the "prophet's" *person* and not simply contributed content for the stage persona.

I found it interesting that the "prophet" never mentioned being affiliated with the United Brethren in the sermons that we had access to hear. It was but one of many surprises found while researching his 1941

---

[349] Branham, William. 1962, May 27. Questions and Answers.
[350] Branham, William. 1965, Feb 21. Marriage and Divorce

marriage to Meda Broy. The marriage certificate between the "prophet" and Meda was the first official document in which the "prophet" claimed to have been born in 1909. On earlier documents, he claimed to have been born in 1908, while his parents believed that he was born in 1907. The 1909 birth year is significant to the version of the "Message" movement that I grew up in. I wondered why he decided to change his birth year after working with E. Howard Cadle. Also, I wondered why he would choose Brethren minister Carnie Carpenter to perform his wedding instead of his own Pentecostal assistant pastor?

Reading through the United States Census documents, I discovered that the "prophet" and his son lived with his siblings after the 1937 flood, and that his brother Jesse worked at the casino. I knew that tracing Jesse's life would also lead to good insight into the "prophet's" off-stage views; there were many sermons speaking about the sins of casinos and gambling.[351] I found a marriage license for Jesse in the 1938 marriage license book at the courthouse.[352] Jesse had divorced three months before the wedding that same year, and the "prophet" performed the wedding of Jesse and Agnes Gullett. That marriage lasted only a few months, even though Jesse had a child with Agnes. A little over a year later, Jesse married Mary Merryman.[353] Jesse falsely claimed on his marriage certificate to Mary that he had only been married once before, and the "prophet" signed it! The "prophet" had performed Jesse's third wedding, knowing that he had been divorced twice before!

The Clark County Memorial Hospital sued Jesse for services provided for professional care to Mary.[354] I wondered: "Was Jesse physically abusive?" I was not able to find the divorce lawsuit transcripts. I was, however, able to find a record of Jesse Branham being arrested in 1945.[355] As brawls broke out in resorts on Highway 62, nine were arrested at the Woodview Inn. Henry Branham, the boxer and soon-to-be mistaken for "faith healer" was also among those involved.

---

[351] Branham, William. 1963, Jan 19. The Way of a True Prophet. "The casinos, and so forth, was so great in the city," or because that they might set on the street corners and watch the passing of the other sex, lust."
[352] Marriage License: Jesse E. Branham and Agnus Gullett. 1938, Aug 1. Clark County Courthouse
[353] Marriage License: Jesse E. Branham and Mary Merryman. 1941, Feb 1. Clark County Courthouse
[354] Hospital Seeks $356.95 in Suits. 1942, Aug 15. Jeffersonville Evening News.
[355] Two Disturbances Cause Arrests at Resorts on No. 62. 1945, Dec 10. Jeffersonville Evening News.

Even more surprising, as I searched through the newspaper archives for the "prophet's" siblings and local acquaintances; I found that the "prophet's" brother, Howard, was *still* involved with the liquor industry long after the healing campaigns began. During the early part of William Branham's ministry, Howard traveled with the "prophet" both in the United States and abroad as a "Faith Healing" evangelist, and he is featured in many of the early photographs used for marketing and for Branham's newsletter, The Voice of Healing. Howard posed for many of the photographs, familiar faces such as Gordon Lindsay, Ern Baxter, Jack Moore, and others. During this time, as early as March of 1948, Howard Branham remained actively brewing, promoting, and selling liquor. In 1948, he found himself at the center of legal issues as Robert Hutsell and Earl Neal filed an injunction against Paul Jacob's and Howard Branham's Beech Grove night club and dance hall.[356] This continued until as late as 1952. In March of 1952, Howard proudly advertised his tasty "Irish Shillelagh", an Irish mixed drink, at his nightclub, the Galway Bay.[357] Howard had partnered with Harold Stockhoff and Kenneth Miller and invited everyone to "Greetin's on St. Patrick's Day March 17th Bock Beer"

...

The 1965 sermon, "Marriage and Divorce", is one of the most controversial sermons preached by the "prophet". Many children in the "Message" are required to listen to the "prophet's" instructions on the subject, including his misogynistic statements concerning women. Many parents forced their adolescent girls to listen as the "prophet" taught them to believe that they are capable of becoming morally lower in virtue than any hog, dog, or any other animal.[358] In the "Creation Theology" presented in this sermon, the "prophet" claimed that they, as females, were designed by Satan himself.[359] This sermon is used in

[356] Beech Grove Target in Injunction Suit. 1948, Apr 7. Jeffersonville Evening News.
[357] Irish Shillelagh. 1952, Mar 14. Jeffersonville Evening News.
[358] Branham, William. 1965, Feb 21. Marriage and Divorce. "There is no hog, no dog, or no other animal, designed like her or can stoop as low as she can stoop. Now, that is true."
[359] Branham, William. 1965, Feb 21. Marriage and Divorce. You may question me about Satan being her designer, but that's the Truth. Satan designed her. He still does it.

some countries to defend their belief in polygamy; the "prophet" claimed that the "Bible" described a "covenant of polygamy".[360]

According to my grandfather, the "prophet" explained his reason for preaching the sermon "Marriage and Divorce" to him privately. He claimed that before this sermon, "Message" believers did not know remarriage after divorce was forbidden. Therefore, God *forgave* specific (men) who remarried, as long as they didn't divorce and remarry yet again. A year before, it had been made public that the "prophet's" son was remarried after divorce, and the "prophet" claimed that it was after an annulment, not a divorce.[361] It seemed all too coincidental to me, especially since the "prophet" said that *"he could but she can't"* towards the end of his "Marriage and Divorce" sermon.

I found the civil court docket for the separation in the records section of the Courthouse. It was filed with action "Divorce", not annulment. Billy Paul Branham divorced Ollie May (Christopher) Branham on September 23, 1953.[362] They were only married for about a month when May Branham filed for divorce.[363] According to the court record, she filed the divorce suit through Jesse Branham. By this time, I realized that the "prophet's" life off-stage did not match his *words* on stage. In many public sermons, the public figure would have been preaching against his own brother who stood on the platform with him! But I was curious: what did locals think about a Pentecostal minister performing weddings for the divorced and re-divorced?

I found an article in the Louisville, Kentucky, newspaper describing the ministers in Jeffersonville that were creating a moral dilemma for

---

[360] Branham, William. 1965, Feb 21. Marriage and Divorce. Then when the double covenant was made by man and woman, through sex, another covenant altogether (not the original covenant, but another covenant), now what's introduced? Polygamy, in all. Then, after the beginning, polygamy was introduced both in man and in beasts; after the beginning, the fall. God now, secondarily, sets a new nature again, by sex. God created the first without sex. Do you believe that? [Congregation says, "Amen. "—Ed.] Now it's another covenant with nature, He sets it in another order, by sex. Second covenant: one male, many females; one buck deer, a whole harem of does. Is that right? One bull, a whole herd of cattle, cows; one rooster, a yardful of hens. Is that right? One David, after His Own heart, with five hundred wives; with a hundred children born to him, in one year, of different Women, a man after God's Own heart. One Solomon, with a thousand wives. But notice now, it wasn't so at the beginning, but now it's "after" the beginning. The woman has done this, then she just becomes what she is now. See?.

[361] Branham, William. 1964, Aug 30. Questions and Answers #3. "We annulled the wedding, the father of this girl and myself. We annulled the wedding, but he was married just the same. He's my boy setting here listening at me now.

[362] 28713. May Branham vs William Branham. 1953, Sept 23. Clark County Courthouse

[363] Marriage License: William Paul Branham and Ollie May Christopher. 1953, Aug 2. Clark County Courthouse

187

Louisville churches. Jeffersonville, which was at that time a gambling town, was known throughout Kentucky and Indiana for "easy marriages". According to Louisville's Judge Kirby, at least 90% of the divorcees in Louisville had been married in Jeffersonville.[364] He urged legislators to consider laws to abolish "easy marriages", or as some called them, "quick marriages".

Shortly after Jesse divorced his second wife, this law became a reality for citizens of Indiana.[365] State legislators agreed that the problem in Jeffersonville was a threat to society. So, in 1940, they passed a law that required waiting for a blood test. If the couple had a sexually transmitted disease, they were told "No", and could not be married. This made me even more curious about the "prophet" performing Jesse's third marriage in 1941. Was the "prophet" helping Jesse bypass the health and legal system?

...

If the "prophet" joined forces with E. Howard Cadle, it was only temporary. As far as I could tell, the "Pentecostal Tabernacle" never became a "Cadle Tabernacle" or "Brethren Tabernacle". Instead, in 1945, it was renamed "Branham Tabernacle". The very first mention of "Branham Tabernacle" in the newspapers was October 13, 1945. I wondered: "Why did the name change?"

It was time to expand my research to a much larger scope of research. If the "prophet" was already connected to E. Howard Cadle and Fred Francis Bosworth, he was already deeply involved with his "faith healing" evangelistic campaigns. Yet in the "Message", we were told that his "gift of healing" was not given to him until 1947. That's what the "prophet" said in his "Life Story" accounts.

> *Immediately, after coming out of the, here, going right into Israel where there's never been any fanaticism, or carrying on, or anything, right into virgin territory. And I believe that there'll be a wakening of those Jews for about a million or two*

---

[364] Divorcees Stir up Family Rows. 1919, Jan 25. Courier Journal
[365] It's Not So Easy Now to Marry in Haste. 1 940, Feb 25. Courier Journal."

188

to receive the baptism of the Holy Ghost. Jesus Christ will come on the scene as certain as anything. Even in the prophecy He said, "Over Jerusalem there'd be an ensign lifted up in the last days," another sign. And for the first time for twenty-five hundred years, the oldest flag that's in existence today, is the six-point star of David, is flying over Jerusalem today. And a strange thing of that, that you might not know, the very day the Angel of the Lord called me out, May the 6th, 1947, and issued the gift to pray for the sick, was the very same day that Israel become a nation for the first time for twenty-five hundred years. Oh, I believe there's something in it. I just can't keep from believing that we're near the end of time. [366]

I knew that it was time to start digging into the history of the "prophet's" ministry from 1945 to 1947. What happened during this timeline? Did he leave Pentecostalism? Did he become a United Brethren minister? "Maybe", I thought, "He became a Baptist minister, and his 'Life Story' accounts were partially accurate. Maybe he just failed to mention that he was a *Pentecostal-turned-Baptist-turned-Pentecostal!*"

The many, many links to the Ku Klux Klan, white supremacy, and African American exclusion, through multiple people involved with the "prophet's" early ministry, were too many to ignore. I thought: *"If the 'prophet' was rebranding his Tabernacle name to his own name, he was preparing for the second phase of a much bigger plan"*. What was that plan? How did it fit with E. Howard Cadle and the Indiana Klan? How did it fit with Roy E. Davis, and the Georgia Klan? and what was Roy Davis doing after being extradited to Arkansas *before* reconnecting with William Branham?

I needed to search for the missing timeline, and I knew that it would not be easy. The "prophet" said that his "gift of healing" came in *May* of 1947, yet the earliest transcripts of "healing campaigns" were dated *April* 1947 — before this "gift" was supposed to have been "given". The first of the transcripts mentioned "new gadgets for recording",

---

[366] Branham, William. 1950, Jul 11. Ministry Explained.

implying there were "old gadgets" — and we had no access to a single sermon by the "old gadgets". Where did they go?

JESSE BRANHAM:
Marriage License: Jesse E. Branham and Agnes Gullett. #233, 1938, Aug 1. Clark County
    Courthouse
Agnes Wilma Branham and Infant vs. Jesse Edward Branham. #19, 964. 1939, Mar. 25. Clark
    County Courthouse
Marriage License: Jesse Branham and Mary M. Merryman. 1941, Feb 1. Clark County Courthouse
Hospital Seeks $365.95 in Suits. 1942, Aug 15. Jeffersonville Evening News
Two Disturbances Cause Arrests at Resorts on No. 62. 1945, Dec 10. Jeffersonville Evening News.
Woman Seeks $5,000 Alimony. 1953, Sept 24. Jeffersonville Evening News.

BILLY PAUL BRANHAM:
May Branham vs. William Branham. #28713, 1953, Sept 23. Clark County Courthouse
Woman Seeks $5,000 Alimony. 1953, Sept 24. Jeffersonville Evening News.

JEFFERSONVILLE "EASY JEFFERSONVILLE "EASY MARRIAGES"
Divorcees Stir up Family Rows. 1919, Jan 25. Courier Journal
It's Not So Easy Now to Marry in Haste. 1940, Feb 25. Courier Journal."

WILLIAM BRANHAM PERFORMING WEDDINGS FOR DIVORCED
Marriage License: Jesse E. Branham and Agnes Gullett. #233, 1938, Aug 1. Clark County
    Courthouse
Agnes Wilma Branham and Infant vs. Jesse Edward Branham. #19, 964. 1939, Mar. 25. Clark
    County Courthouse
Marriage License: Jesse Branham and Mary M. Merryman. 1941, Feb 1. Clark County Courthouse
Charlotte Hazel Branham vs. Melvin F. Branham. #22, 685, 1945, Mar 3. Clark County Courthouse
Marriage License: Henry Branham and Leslie Davis. 1946, Nov 2. Clark County Courthouse
Marriage License: Rudolph Broy and Inez Asher. 1946, Nov 22. Clark County Courthouse

CHAPTER 19

WILLIAM BRANHAM'S
MISSING TIMELINE

"The very day the Angel of the Lord called me out, May the 6th, 1947[367]"

Breaking free from the religion of my family was an extremely difficult journey. The "Message" was my life. It was more than just my "faith", it was my community. I was raised to believe the "prophet". My father was raised to believe the "prophet". My grandfather, a former Methodist minister, believed the "prophet" and pastored the "prophet's" church in Jeffersonville for over 50 years. My grandfather was converted to the "Message" at a revival held in Macon, Georgia. He often told the story about the "prophet's" "supernatural" abilities in that meeting; about how the "prophet" had the power to "discern" names, addresses, and diseases. On stage, the "prophet" accurately told a woman her name, address, and disease. When she returned to her seat, right in front of my grandfather, she was astonished! Not only had he known her name, address and disease, he knew the impossible! According to my grandfather, the lady said that she had changed addresses *just the week before* and that the "prophet" not only knew her address, he knew her *new* address!

I vividly remember the crowd at the Branham Tabernacle when my grandfather told his "conversion" story. Like myself, everyone in the

---

[367] Branham, William. 1950, Jul 11. Ministry Explained.

building praised and worshipped God for this event, even though we were never there. We were *"happy to believe and eager to receive"*.

I never will forget the sinking feeling I had the first time I saw a "prayer card". For over thirty years, I'd heard recordings of the "prophet" when he would accurately "discern" a person's name and address and tell them whether or not they were a Christian. But it felt entirely different seeing the handwritten note the "discerned person" gave the ushers before the "healing" meeting. We were told that the card was only necessary for identifying a position in line to see the "prophet", and that the "angel of God" was the "One" giving the "prophet" a name, address, and disease. According to my grandfather, however, the woman had written her *old* address on the "prayer card", not her *new* address. Seeing the "prayer card", combined with everything else I had discovered, made me become very uncomfortable. If the cards were used only to keep the line in order, then why did the "prophet" need the people to write down *everything* the "angel" was going to help "discern"? Why not just give them a piece of paper with a number?

"Faith Healers" practicing "discernment" using "prayer cards" were common during that era, and the practice was not unique to William Branham. A. A. Allen, Jack Coe, Oral Roberts, and many others used "prayer cards" in their meetings.[368] All of the "healers" claimed that these cards were used to keep people in order, by number. But many "healers" who practiced "discernment" collected the information they "discerned" *before* the meeting started.

In the "Message", we thought those other "healers" were "fakes", because they used these deceitful practices. I never knew that our "prophet" was using the same technique as other "prophets"! Listening to the recordings of the prayer lines was a much different experience without this information. I shuddered to think that even Rev. Jim Jones had what many claimed to be a very accurate "gift of discernment" — especially after I learned that William Branham helped launch Jim Jones' "faith healing" ministry at the Cadle Tabernacle in Indianapolis in 1956.[369] How did the "prophet" convince my grandfather to join the

---

[368] Example: Reverberations Accessed 2020, May 17 from *https://forums.ssrc.org/ndsp/2013/11/12/prayer-card/*
[369] Reiterman, Tim and John Jacobs, Raven: The Untold Story of Jim Jones and His People,

"Message"? In the "Message", we were taught that the "prophet" was given his gift of "discernment" on May 6, 1947, and that this exact day held "spiritual significance". According to the "prophet", it was the same day that Israel became a nation.

> *And a strange thing of that, that you might not know, the very day the Angel of the Lord called me out, May the 6th, 1947, and issued the gift to pray for the sick, was the very same day that Israel become a nation for the first time for twenty-five hundred years.*[370]

I never really thought about the fact that the "prophet" claimed to have this gift on sermons recorded in *April* 1947 before this "gift" would was "given", or that in that same sermon he claimed to be able to "heal" cross-eyed children without God's assistance![371] I also never knew that "The Voice of Healing" was created in April of 1948 to promote his own campaigns. It came as a surprise to me that the very first issue of The Voice of Healing would contain disclaimers as to why some people that the "prophet" "healed" never improved. This was only supposed to be one year into the "prophet's" "healing" ministry! I wondered: How long had the "prophet" claimed to have the "gift of healing" and "discernment"?

We were never told that the "prophet" was the original publisher of The Voice of Healing or that subscribers were sending letters, including their names and addresses. We were never told that subscribers were asked to notify the "prophet" when their address changed, or that subscribers were offered a deal for a gift subscription — giving the "prophet" the names and addresses of other people. The newsletter advertised many other "healers" with the "gift of discernment". Was the "prophet" selling names and addresses to other healers? Was the Voice of Healing business established to help create "faith healing" ministries? Was all this nothing more than a pyramid scheme?

---

[370] Branham, William. 1947, Apr 12. Faith is the Substance
[371] Branham, William. 1947, Apr 12. Faith is the Substance. "I'll take any cross-eyed child you've got in this meeting, you bring it up here without even praying for it, and just let me look at it straight in the eyes like that, I'll make its eyes come straight."

194

Something about the timeline was bothering me. I'd already established that the Billie Branham Pentecostal Tabernacle was actually planted by Roy E. Davis and filled with congregants from his church from before he was extradited on criminal charges. I'd also established that Davis was a high-ranking member of the Ku Klux Klan, and was working with multiple white supremacy groups. I'd learned that the "prophet" was working with E. Howard Cadle, and discovered the history of the Ku Klux Klan's invasion of Indiana government in the mid 1920's. I'd learned that F. F. Bosworth had a background in healing cults, healing revivals, and worked with a leader who used religion for political influence, power, and money. I'd also learned that Bosworth was doing "damage control" for those "healed" who never improved — some of which who died. I'd discovered that shortly after working with Cadle, the "prophet" and his second wife Meda were married by a United Brethren minister, which was a direct result of E. Howard Cadle planting Brethren Churches in the area. But if the "prophet" wanted people to think his "healing" ministry started in 1947, and that his Pentecostal experience started long after leading Roy Davis' Pentecostal church congregation, I wondered: "What wasn't he wanting us to see?" Why did the name of the Pentecostal Tabernacle change to Branham Tabernacle in 1945? Was he still working with Roy E. Davis and the Ku Klux Klan?

I began to study the early photographs of the "prophet's" early church and noticed something that I had never seen before. As many times as I had looked at the early congregation posing inside the church, for as many years as I had seen that photograph, I had never noticed that one person in the photograph was *completely blacked out!* I couldn't believe my eyes! Someone had meticulously covered the person in dark, black ink, so carefully that they did not leave a trace of the body. A casual glance made it look as though the figure was a shadow from another person, yet it sat erect. It was not cast from another person blocking light.

Who was the mysterious figure, inked out of the early Billie Branham Pentecostal Tabernacle photos? It was clear that part of the "prophet's" timeline had been erased. Was this figure involved with whatever was erased from the timeline?

When the name of the "prophet's" church was changed, and the first advertisement of the "Branham Tabernacle" was published in the newspapers, I noticed a familiar name. The name Rev. Robert Doherty was listed in the advertisement.[372] It was a name I knew well, though it did not seem to fit with the timeline of this 1945 newspaper article. The "prophet" claimed to have "healed" Doherty's daughter, Betty.[373] Yet he also claimed that his "gift of healing" came in 1947 — two years after 1945. The story of her "healing" was published in a pamphlet no longer available to "Message" believers that was entitled "*I Was Not Disobedient to the Heavenly Vision*". I had never read the pamphlet. A former "Message" minister had a copy of the tract and was able to let me read it for the first time.

The author of the publication — the "prophet" — sounded much different than the illiterate, backwoods "prophet" that I grew up hearing. The words written were eloquent and refined, very formal. It was not the "Kentucky Hillbilly" English that the "prophet" used in the ministry I grew up hearing. To my surprise, the "prophet" was sending a message to readers about a vision of *"white robed people"*!

> *This book of testimonies is for the glory of our Lord Jesus Christ. It is for that purpose only that I write it. It was in the month of March, 1945, one morning about 3:00 A.M. that our Lord Jesus Christ gave me a vision. ... I was then brought to a plain where a platform was erected. Seemingly, it was under a large tent or auditorium. There were curtains drawn in back of the platform. The Lord then told me to pull back the curtains and when I did I saw a great mountain of the bread of life. He then said, "Feed these," and turning around I saw white-robed people coming from everywhere, making up a large audience.[374]*

I couldn't believe my eyes! I was looking for clues into what happened with Roy E. Davis and his involvement with the Ku Klux Klan, searching for the "missing years" after 1939 when Davis was

---

[372] Misc. Church Advertisements. 1945, Oct 13. Jeffersonville Evening News. "Rev. Robert Doherty, St. Louis, guest speaker."

[373] Branham, William. 1952, Aug 17. Expectancy. "I went to St. Louis first, where little Betty Daugherty was healed"

[374] Branham, William. 1945. I Was Not Disobedient to the Heavenly Vision.

extradited to Hot Springs, Arkansas. As I looked at the 1945 date of the publication and read about this "white robed vision" and healing campaign, I thought about the version of the "Message" that we were told and how different it was from recorded history. Being raised to believe his "healing ministry" started in 1947, it was very difficult for me to see the 1945 date. Before reading this, I'd have assumed that his attempts at healing during the early 40's had failed, and that the "prophet" was trying to claim he didn't yet have the "gift". This tract confirmed that he *did* have a "healing" ministry before 1947, and that he was fully aware of his "gift".

I knew by now that leaders of the "Message" were hiding something, but I'd never considered hiding an entire healing campaign that was for "white robed people!" The Ku Klux Klan were known as the "white knights", and every single member was given a white robe!

...

The research trail for Roy E. Davis had grown cold. I'd traced him through Texas, Oklahoma and Arkansas, from 1914-1917. Largely thanks to his highly publicized and unusual immoral and criminal activities, I'd traced him through Georgia, South Carolina, and Tennessee. Due to his rank of official spokesperson for the Ku Klux Klan and his living a dual life, with multiple wives in multiple states, I'd tracked him through Tennessee, Kentucky, and Southern Indiana where he planted the "prophet's" church. But after Roy E. Davis was extradited from Jeffersonville to Hot Springs, Arkansas in connection with murder and grand theft auto, Davis himself appeared to have gone into hiding. There was no trace of him to be found! "Roy Davis" is a common name, and there were numerous "Rev Roy Davis" listings. There were over 36,000 records to examine in just *one* of the many archive tools.

I began searching multiple keywords, multiple names familiar to the "Message". By sheer accident, I stumbled onto a Rev. Roy E Davis in the Los Angeles Times. Former Congressman William D. Upshaw had helped this Roy E. Davis pose as an FBI agent to secure donations for an orphanage. William Upshaw was a name I was intimately familiar with. Former Congressman Upshaw was one the more famous people that the "prophet" claimed to have "healed".

Suddenly, all the pieces to this puzzle were starting to make sense. The Ku Klux Klan, the liquor and criminal activity, the healing campaigns, the Knights of the Flaming Sword. The "crippled" Congressman, seen posing with his crutches in many photographs. It made sense why leaders of the "Message" would erase years of the "prophet's" early ministry, and why the "prophet" himself would change or erase so many stories of past experiences.

I turned back to the photograph of the early church congregation and examined it more closely. I could see the "prophet" standing in the middle of the photograph holding his bible in his left hand as he often posed for the camera. Several people were standing on either side of him, filling the platform from the back wall of the church to the first pew. There were several people sitting in the pews, twisted awkwardly to show their faces to the camera. I looked closely at the figure that had been inked out, sitting next to one of the structural columns of the building.

Suddenly, I noticed it. Next to the figure that had been blacked out, erased from the photograph, was a single crutch leaning against the pew beside him. Was the figure that had been erased the former Congressman Upshaw? Was this the single crutch that he posed with in all the photographs I'd seen of the former Congressman?

PRAYER CARDS

Blanton, Anderson. 2013. Reverberations: New Directions in the Study of Prayer. Accessed 2018, Dec 20 from *http://forums.ssrc.org/ndsp/category/materiality/*

Randi, James. 1989. The Faith Healers.

Schiffman, Nathaniel. 2005. Abracadabra! Secret Methods Magicians and Others Use to Deceive Their Audience

Harrell, David Edwin. 1985. Oral Roberts: An American Life

1962, Aug 3. Keys to a "Healer's" Kingdom. Life.

Harrell, David Edwin. 1979. All Things Are Possible: The Healing and Charismatic Revivals in Modern American

THE VOICE OF HEALING

Branham, William. 1948, April. How the Gift Came to Me. The Voice of Healing

Bosworth, Fred Francis. 1948, April. Why All Are Not Healed. The Voice of Healing.

Branham, William. 1948, May. How the Gift Came to Me. The Voice of Healing

Bosworth, Fred Francis. 1948, May. Why All Are Not Healed. The Voice of Healing.

Branham, William. 1948, July. An Appraisal of the Freeman Healing Campaign in Salinas, California

Branham, William. 1948, July. The Policy of the Voice of Healing

Branham, William. 1948, July. News of the Roberts Meeting

Branham, William. 1948, July. Testimonies from the Healing Campaigns

1945 vs 1947 "GIFT OF HEALING" AND CAMPAIGNS

Branham, William. 1954, July 18. The Great Coming Revival and the Outpouring of the Holy Spirit

Branham, William. 1955, Jan 9. Beginning and Ending of the Gentile Dispensation

Branham, William. 1959, Oct 4. Who Is This?

Branham, William. 1945. I Was Not Disobedient to the Heavenly Vision

Branham, William. 1950, Jan 15. Believest Thou This

Branham, William. 1950, July 16. Believest Thou This

Branham, William. 1950, Aug 13. The Resurrection of Lazarus

Branham, William. 1952, Aug 17. Expectancy

199

CHAPTER 20

WILLIAM BRANHAM AND CONGRESSMAN UPSHAW

"And I never heard in my life of this gallant man, Mr. Upshaw[375]"

The city of Atlanta, Georgia at night is absolutely breathtaking. Towering skyscrapers touch the clouds as a million tiny windows of light glow like embers of a dying campfire. Some of the taller skyscrapers are dimly light and sit behind the shorter ones like faintly glowing shadows with shiny pointed hats. No matter how many times I see it, I still feel like a child in an amusement park every time, wanting to take in every attraction all at once. Growing up in the "Message", I thought of Georgia as an anchor in a life of uncertainty. No matter where we moved to live with other "believers", from Arizona to South Carolina, I'd always come back to Georgia to spend summers with family members. If I was lucky, I'd get to see the lights of the city at night as we passed through Atlanta.

I had no idea at the time, how fundamental the history of Atlanta was to the "Message". It was just as important as Chicago, possibly more so, considering the historical figures that impacted the city of Jeffersonville, Indiana and the prophet. If not for Atlanta, Roy Davis would never have come to Louisville, Kentucky or fled authorities to setup his base of operations in Indiana. If not for the men in Atlanta

---

[375] Branham, William. 1951, Jul 19. Who Hath Believed Our Report?

organizing campaigns against the liquor industry, the "prophet's" father might never have produced whiskey for the Wathen Liquor Ring. In a way, one might even say that politics in Atlanta impacted the nation enough to create prohibition-era Chicago, cause a saloon-to-salvation E. Howard Cadle, and cause white supremacists to invade Indiana government. Atlanta is where the Ku Klux Klan was reborn in 1915, and in more ways that I could even imagine at this stage of my research, created the perfect storm that birthed an Indiana "prophet".

It's difficult to imagine, but the city of Atlanta was a modern marvel long before Roy E. Davis arrived in the city from Texas to create his double-life. By 1900, the city's horizon was already filled with skyscrapers. Horses and buggies strolled the streets below as trolleys carried a massive workforce to and fro as they traveled from their homes to their jobs and back again. By 1915, there were about 600,000 people in the quickly spreading metropolis.

Just one year into the First World War, a fuse was ignited in Atlanta that would burn for decades. The war between races exploded into the forefront with the release of D. W. Griffith's film, *Birth of a Nation*. The film told the story of a villainous, psychopathic "mulatto", the offspring of a sexual union between black and white. "Heroes" in white robes rushed in to save the day as the interracial villain terrorized the town.

Shortly after the film was released, 15 men gathered on Stone Mountain just north of Atlanta to organize the 1915 Ku Klux Klan. Very little is known about the 15 men who gathered that day. They were led by William Joseph Simmons, but the secretive nature of the Klan's formation remains a mystery. Like the hooded "heroes" in *Birth of a Nation*, the men who joined the Ku Klux Klan masked their true identities to instill fear in their opposition. To oppose the Klan and be outspoken was very dangerous during that time. Anyone could be watching or listening. It could be your neighbor. Your coworker could be a Klansman. You'd better be looking over your shoulder, because the politician in office, the laborer in a factory, the police force, *anyone* could be watching. Those who crossed the lines in the sand that were drawn by the Ku Klux Klan were terrorized at night by men in white robes. Many were killed, especially those without white skin.

At the other end of the chronological fuse that was lit in Atlanta was an explosion into the battle for Civil Rights in the late 1940s. I'd spent hours studying that side of the timeline and was surprised how closely the timeline aligned with "spiritual topics" in key sermons by the "prophet". From the "prophet's" statements against Martin Luther King[376] to the students seeking equality in the school systems and more,[377] it was easy to see that current politics of the era created subject matter for the "prophet". All one need do is line up the sermons by date in one column and line up milestones in the battle for Civil Rights in another column.

According to his own account to the Shreveport Times newspaper, Roy E. Davis was one of the fifteen men who created the Ku Klux Klan that day on Stone Mountain.[378] I knew that Roy E. Davis was the official spokesman for the Ku Klux Klan as late as 1923, and that he worked closely with William Joseph Simmons. I also knew that Roy Davis worked with Simmons to create other white supremacy groups, such as the Knights of the Flaming Sword. I was curious about the other men among the fifteen. Who were they?

Finding William D. Upshaw helping Roy E. Davis secure donations for an orphanage in Los Angeles was the key to unlocking a goldmine of information. Former Congressman Upshaw was a key figure in the "Message". He entered one of the "prophet's" healing revivals confined to a wheelchair,[379] and the "prophet" healed him before the watchful eyes of the visitors in the auditorium. According to the "prophet", Upshaw had been confined to beds and wheelchairs for sixty-six years.[380]

---

[376] Branham, William. 1963, Jul 21. He Cares Do You Care. "And I think that Martin Luther King is Communistic inspired, which is going to lead about a million people to a absolutely a death trap."

[377] Branham, William. 1963, Jun 28. O Lord Just Once More. "It's just because they want to go to school. They got schools. Let them go to school. That's right. … a colored man is satisfied in the state he is in, so they don't need those things"

[378] Ku Klux Klan Active in Shreveport Area. 1961, Feb 10. The Times. "Davis said that he is the only Klansman who can boast having all the degrees of the Klan conferred on him. He said that he helped write the constitution, by-laws, and ritual of the original Klan when it was revived in 1915.

[379] Branham, William. 1951, May 1. Exhortation of Divine Healing. "That's how our brother Senator here was healed. When I was standing here looking at him out there over the audience, I seen a—a bench come down and right over, kinda this way from that clock, I suppose, be north. Right in here I seen a bench and I seen a man there, and I seen the people applauding him. I seen him with a big kind of a collar on. I seen a young man fall on a hayrack or something there and hurt his back, begin to talk to my... And there It went. And I looked down, and I found the man. He was setting back in the audience there in a wheelchair … When I went out then I seen Mr. Upshaw healed and happy"

[380] Branham, William. 1954, Jun 20. Divine Healing. "Congressman Upshaw, after being in a—a congressman for seventeen years, in the White House, and had been a cripple in the wheelchair, and an invalid, beds and

202

As Upshaw raised out of his wheelchair, the faith in Branham as a healer raised with him. Each and every person in that meeting — many of which traveled from miles around and other states — went home to tell about the famous figure healed in one of the "prophet's" meetings. Each person they told went to work and told others. Like a highly contagious virus quickly spreading through a thickly populated city, the "prophet's" name spread from person to person. Each person who heard the name, especially those in need of healing, wanted to know more.

Learning that Upshaw was working with Davis in the mid 1940s opened the door to several paths of research, but it also raised many questions. Had they worked together since their days in the rebirth of the Ku Klux Klan, or had they just re-united? Was the former Congressman's "healing" genuine, or was it part of a much bigger plan?

...

William D. Upshaw was raised in rural Cobb County, Georgia, just outside of Atlanta. An accident had left him bedridden for seven years, from 1888 to 1895. A gifted public speaker in the early 1900s, he often spoke from a wheelchair, but his physical disability was not a life sentence. As early as 1915, Upshaw was once again mobile. In an interview with the Shreveport Times, Congressman Upshaw admitted that his days of disability were behind him, and that he was no longer confined to a "rolling chair".[381]

As a fundamentalist Christian with powerful connections, Upshaw used his political influence attempting to wage war against alcohol. He was one of the key leaders of the anti-saloon league,[382] and Upshaw helped Georgia become a dry state in 1907. He had earned quite a reputation as the editor of the Golden Age publication, a weekly paper well-known for its noble and moral tones. He was also a nationally recognized revivalist, one who could attract large crowds. His combination of politics and religion was very popular in the South. By

wheelchairs for sixty-six years"
[381] Mr. Upshaw Objects to Being Called "Dr.". 1915, May 8. The Times. "I was on bed for seven years dictating letters for the papers, and it stayed with me for a while nearly twenty years ago when I used to lecture from a rolling chair."
[382] William D. Upshaw Says That the Hardman Prohibition Bill Is Sure to Pass. 1910, Mar 9. The Atlanta Constitution.

the time he became a Georgia Congressman in 1919, he already had the ability to sway political votes in cities across the nation. That fact was evident by simply examining the trail of dry states in the wake of his revivals.

From the time he regained his mobility in 1895 through the early 1900s, he used the wheelchair as part of his own stage persona. In speeches and sermons around the nation, Upshaw balanced his time between his wheelchair and crutches. He had a huge setback in March of 1910, when a fall from a buggy broke one leg. Though it hurt him physically, it may have helped him strategically — it further enhanced his ability to gain the sympathy of the crowd.

Upshaw's national popularity increased until he became a common household name. He became known as the "Georgia Cyclone"[383] for his ability to storm through a city like a whirlwind. Posing with his crutches, Upshaw's photo was published in newspapers across the nation. I became curious as to why the "prophet" said that he never heard of Congressman Upshaw. In the Jeffersonville, Indiana town of distilleries, Upshaw would have been public enemy number one! During the same year that the Ku Klux Klan was formed on Stone Mountain in 1915, Upshaw announced his run for public office. The battle against the liquor industry was soon to have a powerful ally in Washington, D.C.

Finding Roy E. Davis and William D. Upshaw together in 1943 was too big of a coincidence to ignore. Davis was also well-connected in Atlanta, and his Ku Klux Klan activities were publicized in newspapers across the state. Upshaw, a prominent member of Atlanta government, would have known all about Davis' sketchy past even without being involved with the Ku Klux Klan. His knowledge would have not only come from the newspaper descriptions of Davis' dual life and criminal past. Both men were nationally recognized revivalists,[384] and they would have also known each other in religious circles just as much as they would have in political circles.

Looking through the newspapers of the early 1920s, it was very easy to find articles about Roy Davis and William Upshaw. In fact, it was

---

[383] Orator-On-Crutches. 1915, May 13. The Mansfield Enterprise.
[384] Georgia Congressman A Law Maker by Day and Revivalist At Night. 1919, Jun 11. The Charlotte Observer.

overwhelming; there were simply too many articles in too many newspapers, from too many cities in too many states. As an official spokesman for the Ku Klux Klan, Roy Davis held lectures throughout Georgia and the surrounding states. In 1921, however, I noticed a significant change in acceptance of Davis and the Klan. Though the Ku Klux Klan was very popular shortly after its birth, that popularity would quickly fade as the organization became more violent and terroristic. By the early 1920s, its appeal was quickly fading.

In September 1921, New York World ran a series of articles exposing the Ku Klux Klan[385] for their violence and hatred. According to the publication, the Ku Klux Klan had silently infiltrated America. Membership had quickly grown to over 500,000 members. The Ku Klux Klan had suddenly become a political and terroristic invisible empire — a force to be reckoned with. Governing bodies were now being controlled by Klan forces, and that control was secretive, outside of public view. The Klan was suddenly exposed as an anti-Catholic, anti-Jewish, anti-Black terrorist organization inciting violence in American cities. William Joseph Simmons had silently gained control of the United States.

New York World's exposure of the Ku Klux Klan gained national attention. As a result, a federal investigation was suddenly requested by multiple states in the country.[386] The House opened an investigation, and William Joseph Simmons was called to testify before Congress.[387] In a stroke of legal genius, Upshaw put an instant halt to the investigation, saving the Ku Klux Klan from an immediate government shutdown. Upshaw urged Congress to investigate *all* secret orders that were growing in the United States — knowing full well that many members of Congress were also members of secret orders.

In a public display of support for the Ku Klux Klan, Upshaw himself testified. Congressman Upshaw told members of Congress that William Joseph Simmons was one of the "knightliest, most patriotic" men that he knew.[388] His speech brought a swift, dramatic end to the Congressional

---

[385] The Ku Klux Klan. 1921, Sept 5. New York World.

[386] Searchlight to be Thrown on Ku Klux Activities by Secret Service Officials. 1921, Sep 9. Oxford Public Ledger.

[387] Sweeping Denial Made by Simmons of Charges Brought Against Klan in House Investigations. 1921, Oct 13. The Atlanta Constitution.

[388] Wants Every Sect Order Investigated. 1921, Oct 13. The Chronicle.

investigation of the Ku Klux Klan,[389] and secured their right to continue their clandestine operation. If not for Congressman Upshaw, the Ku Klux Klan would never have existed past that Congressional inquiry. During the course of the investigation, government officials seized all of the Ku Klux Klan records. Documentation obtained from newsletters sent from Klan Headquarters confirmed that William D. Upshaw was secretly a member of the Ku Klux Klan.[390]

The pieces of the puzzle were coming together clearly. William Upshaw and Roy Davis were using their evangelism to promote Ku Klux Klan agenda, and the Klan-published newsletters painted them as heroes. Upshaw claimed that 39,000,000 persons in the United States had alien (un-American) thought.[391] William D. Upshaw and Roy E. Davis moved their base of their operations to Los Angeles. It should come as no surprise that when the "prophet" held meetings in the Los Angeles area, Roy E. Davis — the "prophet's" mentor — sent William D. Upshaw to the "healing revival" for a famous name to become an attraction in the healing revivals. William Upshaw — who had not needed a wheelchair for several decades — came to the meeting for the "prophet" to claim the "healing" of a man confined to a wheelchair. More specifically, confined to *beds* and *wheelchairs* for *sixty-six years*.

While searching through the newspaper archives for articles about William Upshaw, I found something interesting. An article in the Louisville, Kentucky newspaper also described the "healing". [392] Shortly after posing as an invalid healed in the "prophet's" healing revival, William Upshaw came to Jeffersonville, Indiana to help restore the "prophet's" image. This was a story that I had never heard while in the "Message" and was very surprised that the story had been lost to time. The "prophet" had falsely claimed to have raised a man from the dead during revival meetings in Canada,[393] and the Evening News had set the record straight.

I decided to take a step back from the research of the 1940s to trace the links between Roy Davis and William Upshaw after the two left the

---

[389] Ku Klux Klan Inquiry Has Sudden, Dramatic Closing. 1921, Oct 18. Altoona Tribune.

[390] Norfolk Chief of Police Said to Be Member Ku Klux. 1921, Oct 12. Durham Morning Herald. "Upshaw a member. Information Gained From News Letters Sent From Klan Headquarters"

[391] 39,000,000 Persons with Alien Thought in U.S. Says Upshaw. 1923, Dec 14. The Fiery Cross.

[392] Pastor, No Longer Using Crutches Still A Militant Dry at Nearly 85. 1951, Sep 23. Courier Journal.

[393] Rev. Branham in the News. 1947, Jul 23. Jeffersonville Evening News.

Atlanta Ku Klux Klan. In archives of the Louisville newspaper, I found that Upshaw was in Louisville in 1927[394] — the same time that Roy E. Davis was setting up his base of operations in Louisville.

This took place during the time that Indiana Governor Ed Jackson was under investigation for accepting bribes to favor Klan-appointed officials.[395] By that time, Indiana Klan leader D. C. Stephenson had begun confessing the clandestine operations of the Indiana Ku Klux Klan, and had shared records proving that Jackson had bribed government officials. Jackson left office disgraced before a presidential run was possible. William D. Upshaw and Roy E. Davis had come into the Jeffersonville, Indiana area in what appeared to be an opportunistic moment in time. The Indiana Klan was in disarray and primed for hostile takeover. Had Davis not been extradited for crimes committed in Arkansas, the Indiana Klan might have looked entirely different.

Riding the wave of popularity caused by his backing of the Prohibition Party, William Upshaw announced his own run for President of the United States.[396] It was easy to see that even more pieces of the puzzle were coming together, and the faces in the puzzle were beginning to show. William Upshaw was running for President on a platform of Prohibition. The Davis brothers were setting up camp in the midst of Indiana Klan disarray, next to the liquor distilleries. Roy E. Davis escaped magically from every criminal charge and almost overnight had created a nationally recognized "faith healer". I could see the picture forming, but I did not like the image that it presented.

...

In the "Message", we were so focused on "healing" that we often lost focus on the bigger picture. Sermons brought so much excitement of the "Rapture" that we were expecting any day for God to take us to heaven where we would receive brand-new bodies free from aches and pains. Then after the sermon, we'd beg and plead with God to fix these

[394] Pastor, No Longer Using Crutches Still A Militant Dry at Nearly 85. 1951, Sep 23. Courier Journal. "Mr. Upshaw, ordained a Baptist Minister at 72, first came to Louisville nearly 50 years ago to attend a meeting of the Southern Baptist Convention. He came back here in 1927."
[395] Jackson Cries "Blackmail" at Stephenson. 1927, Jul 14. Muncie Evening Press.
[396] Upshaw Wins Prohibition Party Nomination for President Following Neck-and-Neck Race. 1932, Jul 8. Indianapolis News.

broken bodies that we'd be leaving behind. It reminded me of packing brand new suitcases to leave for vacation and making the whole family wait while we took the old ones to a repair shop!

At first, I thought I was the only one to notice that in the photographs taken, William Upshaw barely used his crutches. He placed his full weight on his injured leg. But as I researched, I found that others had also questioned the Congressman for years. Members of Congress noticed that he barely touched his crutches to the ground, as early as 1936. They also observed that with the use of modern bracing made from whale bone, Upshaw really didn't need the crutches at all. One member of Congress claimed that he saw William Upshaw running across the floor, without his crutches even touching the ground!

> *Old Will was telling about those crutches of his and why he has to wear them. It seems that because he is such an expert crutch-walker, touching them lightly and nimbly to the ground, some of them have thought the crutches were part of a costume. He had a row in Washington once when he was in Congress because a man said he ran lightly up the aisle ignoring the crutches. It burned him to be accused of ignoring the crutches merely because he had mastered the trick of getting the most out of them with the least effort.* [397]

I could have been angry that William Upshaw plotted with Roy Davis to enter Branham's meeting in a wheelchair, or that these men were using religion as a means to a political end. Instead, I thought about a man forcing himself to hold crutches in public for several decades, only to die a few months after claiming to be "healed". I thought of their victims, the faithful followers who thought God would ignore years of earnest prayer and only listen if a "healer" was involved. I also thought about how crushed the faithful would have been to watch Upshaw "healed", right before the time of his death, unable to make use of his seemingly useless "healing" from his grave after having received a "new body" on the other side.

---

[397] Fair Enough. 1936, Jul 18. The Morning News.

WILLIAM D. UPSHAW - DEFENDING KU KLUX KLAN

Defends Klan in Congressional Inquiry into the Ku Klux Klan:

Associated Press. 1921, October 11. Congress Has Started Klan Investigation. The New Bern Sun Journal.

House Rules Committee Ready for Klan Investigation Today. 1921, October 8. The Washington Post.

Upshaw Explains Kuklux Attitude. 1921, October 11. The Washington Post.

Associated Press 1921, October 8. Congressman Backs Klan. The Courier Journal.

Wants Every Secret Order Investigated. 1921, October 13. The Chronicle.

Ku Klux Klan Inquiry Has Sudden, Dramatic Closing 1921, October 8. Altoona Tribune

Urge Congress to Investigate Secret Orders. 1921, October 15. Asheville Citizen.

With Mask Off, Klan Is Week, Congress Hears 1921, October 12. Chicago Daily Tribune.

Upshaw Describes Aftermath of Probe of the Ku Klux Klan. 1921, October 28. The Atlanta Constitution.

Klan Hearing Begins by Rules of Committee of Congress Today. 1921, October 11. The Atlanta Constitution.

Congressional Probe of K. K. Klan Blows Up. 1921, October 18. The Charlotte Observer.

Congress Drops Inquiry into Ku Klux Klan. 1921, October 18. The Decatur Herald.

Ku Klux Klan Inquiry Ends. 1921, October 22. The Washington Post.

The Secret Orders. 1921, October 8. The New Bern Sun Journal. 321

Searchlight to Be Thrown on Ku Klux Klan Activities by Secret Service Officials. 1921, September 9. Oxford Public Ledger

WILLIAM D. UPSHAW - KU KLUX KLAN MEMBER

Associated Press 1921, October 12. Norfolk Chief of Police Said to Be Member Ku Klux. Durham Morning Herald.

WILLIAM D. UPSHAW - SPEAKING ENGAGEMENTS, ACCIDENT, WALKING

"Earnest Willie." 1942, November 15. The Anniston Star.

"Hon. William D. Upshaw." 1921, July 28. Wilmington News- Journal.

WILLIAM D. UPSHAW - EVANGELIST

Upshaw Closes Church Campaign. 1936, April 13. Alton Evening Telegraph.

Congressman Upshaw Speaks Twice Today. 1918, December 29. Asheville Citizen Times.

WILLIAM D. UPSHAW - ANTI-SALOON LEAGUE

Thomas R. Pegram, "Hoodwinked: The Anti-Saloon League and the Ku Klux Klan in 1920s Prohibition Enforcement," in Journal of Gilded Age and Progressive era Vol. 7, Issue 1.

Delanceyplace. 2016, March 30. Political Alliances – The KKK and the Anti-Saloon League. Retrieved from *http://bigthink.com*

Hanson, David. 2016, March 30. KKK and WCTU: Partners in Prohibition. 322

WILLIAM D. UPSHAW - REPORTER FOR THE GRAPHIC

Upshaw is Cub Reporter. 1929, July 27. Macon Chronicle-Herald

"Louis Sobol, 90, Dies; Broadway Columnist by THE ASSOCIATED PRESS; Published: February 10, 1986". The New York Times. 1986-02-10. Retrieved 2010-05-20.

WILLIAM D. UPSHAW - SECOND CONGRESSIONAL RUN

Upshaw Is Ruled Ineligible to Run. 1928, June 24. The Anniston Star.

Georgia Democrats May Bounce Upshaw. 1928, August 12. The Independent Record.
Upshaw Sees Prohibition Successful by Year 1940. 1927, March 5. New Castle News.
Upshaw Broomed. 1927, March 9. Kingsport Times. Suspends Prohibition Campaigns to Fight
    Communism
Forum Writer Urged to Support Townsend. 1936, January 18. The Salt Lake Tribune.
Committee Gets Laugh. 1936, June 24. The Emporia Gazette. Another Congressional Run
Russell Wins. 1942, September 10. The Hutchinson News. First Wife Dies
Last Rites for Mrs. Upshaw. 1942, May 22. The Index-Journal 323

WILLIAM D. UPSHAW - SECOND WIFE
KKK and WCTU: Partners in Prohibition. 2016, March 31.
Retrieved from http://www.alcoholproblemsandsolutions.org/Controversies/KKK- and-WCTU-
    Partners-in-Prohibition.html
Upshaw to Wed Official of WCTU. 1946, October 5. The Post- Standard.
Dry Leaders to Wed. 1946, October 6. Medford Mail Tribune. Ex-Congressman Upshaw to Wed
    WCTU Leader. 1946, October
8. Harrisburg Telegraph. Biography
William D. Upshaw "The Georgia Cyclone" our candidate for President in 1932." 1942, November
    15. The Anniston Star. Retrieved from http://www.prohibitionists.org.

WILLIAM D. UPSHAW - MISC
Hon. W. D. Upshaw Endorses Sargon. 1930, Jan 28. Lincoln Evening Journal.
Upshaw to Tour State for Drys. 1933, September 23. The Courier Journal.
WCTU Leaders, 60 and 80, To Wed. 1946, October 8. Wilkes- Barre Evening News.

WILLIAM D. UPSHAW "SICK" DURING ORHPANAGE SCANDAL
W. D. Upshaw Reported Critically Ill. 1943, December 31. The Index-Journal.

ROY E. DAVIS - USSHER-DAVIS ORPHANAGE
Child Problem to Mount, Says Superior Judge. 1943, September 17. The San Bernardino County
    Sun
Orphanage School at Upland Slated to Open Sept. 15. 1943, August 8. The San Bernardino County
    Sun

USSHER-DAVIS ORPHANAGE - LILY GALLOWAY CONNECTION
Burnett Union WCTU to Hold Lunch. 1944, May 8. Long Beach Independent
Upshaw to Wed Official of WCTU. 1946, October 5. The Post Standard.
W.C.T.U. Meet Will Attract Record Crowd. 1928, October 7. The San Bernardino County Sun.

USSHER-DAVIS ORPHANAGE CRIMINAL TRIAL
Orphanage Head Named in Grand Theft Charge. 1944, February 28. The San Bernardino County
    Sun
Davis Faces Charge of Mail Tampering. 1944, February 26. The San Bernardino County Sun
Orphanage Said to Be Result of Pastor's Vision – Assuredly Came to Rev. Roy Davis After He Had
    Eaten Peach. 1944, April 20. The San Bernardino County Sun
Upland Evangelist Before U. S. Judge. 1944, April 19. The San Bernardino County Sun
Complaints Filed Against Orphanage Head of West End. 1944, February 22. The San Bernardino
    County Sun
Summons Issued for Rev. Roy E. Davis. 1944, February 1. The San Bernardino County Sun
Accused Pastor Demands Writ. 1944, April 27. The San Bernardino County Sun

Orphanage Benefactor Questioned, Pictured as 'Disillusioned'; Funds Raising Investigation. 1944, February 20. The San Bernardino County Sun

Two Counts Are Dropped After Court Hearing. 1944, May 6. The San Bernardino County Sun

Orphanage Head Asks Reduction in $16,000 Bail. 1944, March 4. The San Bernardino County Sun

Habeas Corpus Petition Denied. 1944, April 29. The San Bernardino County Sun

Minister Charged. 1944, March 15. Nevada State Journal. Minister, Wife Seek Damages – Rev., Mrs. Davis Ask for Sum of

$25,000. 1945, February 18. The San Bernardino County Sun

CHAPTER 21

WILLIAM BRANHAM AND THE AMERICANIZATION PROJECT

"These last days, true Church-Bride comes to the Headstone, will be the super Church, a super Race[398]"

Sunday services in the "Message" were not like the services in other churches. Visitors to a "Message" church, expecting to hear a sermon about the words of Jesus Christ were in for quite a surprise! The focal point of each sermon was usually not what Jesus did for us; instead, most sermons were focused upon what the "prophet" said we must do if we wanted to be included in the "Rapture". If we failed on any of his main points, we were reminded that we'd suffer the same fate as other Christians who did not believe the "Message". Believing in Christ for salvation was not sufficient — we also had to believe the "prophet", and we had to adhere to the rules that he established using his sermons from 1947 to 1965.

One of the rules frequently mentioned by the "prophet" was concerning the drinking of alcohol. Like some other fundamentalist Christian churches, the "Message" strictly forbade the drinking of alcohol but took it a step further in forbidding the use of alcohol in any form. The drinking of liquor, wine, or beer was harshly condemned by the "prophet", but most pastors in the "Message" also condemned cooking with alcohol. Some condemned even the *appearance* of

---

[398] Branham, William. 1962, March 18. The Spoken Word Is the Original Seed

drinking, though the "prophet" casually raised his glass for cheers. I had among my collection of the "prophet's" photographs a funny picture of the "prophet" and his family around the dinner table, each smiling ear-to-ear and raising their stemmed glasses for the camera. We laughed at those types of photographs, because we just knew that the "prophet" would never be drinking alcohol.

I often wondered why the "prophet" forbade wine, while most men and women in the Bible drank wine, and even recommended it. One of the greatest miracles of the New Testament was a story about the Christ turning water into wine — *to drink*! The "prophet" often reminded us of Bible verses describing sin associated with drunkenness, but I always wondered why he did not remind us of the many passages that were supportive of drinking alcohol or wine. Even more confusing was the fact that we all drank wine for communion in church, even the children, in commemoration of the "Last Supper". Yet we were forbidden to drink wine at our own supper at home. If communing with wine at home was sinful, wouldn't communing in church with wine also be sinful?

I was surprised when I began researching the many things that we drank or used that were either made from or with alcohol. Some of the things we used had large concentrations of alcohol. Vinegar was used for cooking or cleaning by most "Message" families, as was vanilla extract and soy sauce. All included some alcohol content. Energy drinks, which many men in the "Message" drank, had as much as 6% alcohol. Alcohol for medicinal purposes was strictly forbidden, yet many of us used mouthwash which contained as much as 70% alcohol to fight bacteria. Many families swore by NyQuil and other cough syrups, which contained 10% or more alcohol. Some canker sore medicines were 90% alcohol. I compiled a list, a long list, of common household products that many of us ingested, not knowing that they were made with alcohol. It was very surprising. While "Message" pastors condemned other families for taking a shot of whiskey for a cold or flu, they themselves took medicines with alcohol! All the while, they were preaching that the "prophet" could heal, and that we could receive healing from listening to the "prophet's" voice and should not have needed the liquor for our ailments in the first place! Unsurprisingly, the stance against alcohol taught in Message churches has roots in the early history of William Branham's ministry and that of his early associates.

...

When I learned that former Congressman Upshaw was helping Roy Davis pose as an FBI agent[399] to secure donations for an orphanage, and that Roy Davis claimed to have had a "vision"[400] for the orphanage scheme, I wanted to know more about this "vision" and what those donations were used for. Davis had a long trail of accusations and convictions for swindling people out of their money, and I had no doubt that he was up to no good. But I was curious as to why a respected former Congressman of the United States would join him in doing so. There had to be much more to this "vision" that met the eye, and Upshaw's involvement had to be for purposes other than religion.

According to the San Bernardino, California newspapers, William D. Upshaw and Roy E. Davis had convinced a wealthy Elizabeth Ussher to donate $8,500 to build an orphanage. In today's money, that is almost $125,000. It was no small amount of money that she had entrusted with the two men. She donated most of the money after Roy Davis posed as a Federal Agent in July of 1943, and later thousands more during a "prayer meeting" on the grounds of the orphanage site. Somehow, their scam was exposed, and it was made public that the men were not as respectable as they had claimed, and the money was not being used for the purposes in which it was intended. Before long, all donors were attempting to get their money back, which resulted in a criminal investigation and a court trial.

During the trial, attorneys for Elizabeth Ussher informed the court that Ussher was not the only victim defrauded, and that Davis was armed with a firearm — which was a felony in California. I wondered: what did Davis need with a firearm in an evangelistic meeting or a children's orphanage? Multiple people witnessed Davis posing as a Federal Agent. One of them, a Baptist minister, witnessed Davis making the claim as many as ten times. Rev. John Williams testified to

---

[399] Witnesses Say Davis Claimed to be F.B.I. Man. 1944, Apr 22. The San Bernardino County Sun
[400] Orphanage Said to be Result of Pastor's Vision. 1944, Apr 20. The San Bernardino County Sun

the court that the records seized by government officials were not correct, and that the money was being used for an unknown purpose. He told the jury that Davis kept two sets of accounting books; one book was for the public to see, and the other was to be kept private.

The name of the other witness called to testify was a name that I was already familiar with. Mrs. Lily Galloway of Santa Monica was present with William Upshaw and Roy Davis at the time that Davis claimed to be a Federal agent. Lily Galloway was a name I stumbled onto while researching Congressman William Upshaw as he led the battle against liquor in the Prohibitionist Party. Mrs. Galloway was also very vocal in the fight against alcohol. But this was not where I had first heard her name. Mrs. Galloway was also a witness claiming that former Congressman William D. Upshaw was healed in a revival by the "prophet"!

Lily Galloway married William Upshaw shortly after the criminal trial of Roy E. Davis. She was the state spokesperson for the Women's Christian Temperance Union (W.C.T.U.), well-known in the Los Angeles and San Bernardino area.[401] In terms of the fight against alcohol, Galloway would have been the female equivalent of William Upshaw in his work with the Anti-Saloon League. Elizabeth Ussher was also a member of the W.C.T.U. and was very vocal in her support.[402] The W.C.T.U. was very active in the Los Angeles and San Bernardino Area and participated with other women's activist groups in surrounding cities. One of those groups was the Women's Relief Corps, a fraternal organization of women invited for ceremonial purposes to the W.C.T.U. conferences.

After being extradited to Hot Springs, Arkansas on charges of grand theft, Rev. Roy E. Davis took a leadership role in the Upland Baptist Church.[403] Posing as a "Federal Agent" pastor, Davis convinced several wealthy people to purchase the Monte Vista Resort to use as an orphanage. William D. Upshaw was the treasurer, a financial administrator of the orphanage. According to witness testimony, this would have made Upshaw an accomplice to the crime since Upshaw

[401] Burneit Union WCTU to Hold Lunch. 1944, May 8. Long Beach Independent.
[402] Grauman Plans Women's Week. 1927, Oct 9. Los Angeles Times.
[403] 1943, Sept 17. Child Problem to Mount, Say Superior Judge. The San Bernardino County Sun

would have been the person keeping the dual (public and private) accounting.

Roy Davis was invited to speak at a W.R.C. meeting in Ontario, California.[404] His subject was "Things We Are Fighting For", and he acted as the principal speaker for the San Bernardino members. This would have likely been where he met Ussher, and also where he would have used his claim to have been a Government agent. At any rate, Roy Davis convinced Elizabeth Ussher to invest her wealth, and the Ussher-Davis Children's Orphanage opened Sept 15, 1943.[405] According to the newspapers, William D. Upshaw took an active role in charge of the "Department of Americanism". This made me curious. Why would an orphanage need a "Department of Americanism?" This made me even more curious as to the motive behind the orphanage and made me suspect that the orphanage was likely a front for the Klan. The Fiery Cross (Ku Klux Klan) newspaper quoted Upshaw as claiming many United States Citizens had "alien thought". Was this the beginning of an attempt at thought reform?

"Americanism" was a term I frequently encountered when researching the Ku Klux Klan. White supremacy groups claimed that allowing African Americans in white schools, jobs, and marriages was "un-American", and therefore promoted their agendas as "Americanism". I also came across several articles describing the many orphanages, non-profit organizations, and other entities created as disguises for white supremacy groups after white supremacy in America went underground. The practice was so widespread that it required a special committee in Washington, D.C. to unravel the spiderweb of connections.

I thought back to an article I had found in the Shreveport Times, where Roy E. Davis testified that he was present when the Constitution and Laws of the Ku Klux Klan were written. The Klan promoted themselves as a "Christian" organization, but it was evident that their structure was much more complicated than a simple group of Christians seeking to uphold their belief system. In meetings, lectures,

---

[404] 1943, Dec 11. W.R.C. Federation Meeting Attended by San Bernardino Group. The San Bernardino County Sun
[405] Orphanage School at Upland Slated to Open Sept 15. 1943, Aug 8. The San Bernardino County Sun

publications, and public response, the Ku Klux Klan claimed to promote "True Americanism" or "Pure Americanism" — implying that any who did not support these believes were "un-American".[406]

To most people, "Americanism" simply means being supportive of American values. But like a cult with overloaded keywords, the Ku Klux Klan used "True Americanism" or "Pure Americanism" to tout white supremacy. I found that the codeword was also used by historians in books, articles, websites, and other publications. Others were familiar with the Klan's usage of "Americanism".

Knowing that both William Upshaw and Roy Davis were high-ranking members of the 1915 Ku Klux Klan, I also knew that both men were fully aware of the loaded meaning of the word "Americanism" and the meaning it would convey to readers of the San Bernardino newspaper when they described the "Department of Americanism" for the Ussher-Davis orphanage. Roy Davis himself claimed to have written the Klan's constitution. I also knew that Los Angeles elite donors would have known that Upshaw's "Americanism" position was unusual for an orphanage, and that the white supremacy groups in the area would have immediately recognized the keyword when it was advertised. Then, it suddenly struck me. The research into the Ku Klux Klan wasn't the only time I'd heard that term!

I'd heard the term "Americanism" in the "Message" when the "prophet" spoke harshly against specific public figures. The "prophet's" sermons often singled out specific public figures, and his voice resounded strongly against them. Even children in the "Message" held the same disregard for those condemned by the "prophet" today as his disregard in the 1940s, 1950s, and 1960s. They were names I knew more by his condemnation than their actual fame. Elvis, Arthur Godfrey, Pat Boone, Lucille Ball, and the Beatles were a few of the people on Branham's list of infamy. I never thought about why he disliked them so, or why he considered them to be "un-American". Suddenly, I found myself taking a crash course on pop culture in American history.

Arthur Godfrey was a strong supporter of Civil Rights. Elvis Presley was also a strong supporter of Civil Rights. The "I Love Lucy"

---

[406] Constitution and Laws of the Knights of the Ku Klux Klan. 1921. "a fervent devotion to pure Americanism"

television program was controversial for their attempt at breaking racial barriers with an interracial marriage. The "prophet" used each of them as examples of the opposite of "Americanism". Pat Boone strongly supported Martin Luther King, Jr. The "prophet" claimed that Martin Luther King, Jr. and the Civil Rights movement were "inspired of Satan" and "communistic". I had no idea until I did that research how much the white supremacy groups protested against public figures such as these, or that "communistic" was also used as a term for propaganda against those opposing white supremacy. During the Communist Scare, these claims carried quite a bit of weight; it was more difficult to prove that you were *not* communist than it was to prove that you *were.*

Knowledge of Davy Crockett, arguably a significant figure in American history, was considered "so-called Americanism" by the "prophet", meaning that those who studied the history of the Crocket were only *pretending to be* American. I was surprised to learn that the Davy Crockett television show was played by Fess Parker. Parker's television shows broke down racial barriers, and it was among the few television programs that had African Americans in key roles. Ernie Ford received hate mail from white supremacists for hosting African Americans on his show, and his was yet another name that the "prophet" condemned. There were many others, similarly popular in the entertainment industry, that the "prophet" could have picked to condemn — some of which might have deserved more than a little scorn. Thousands of names across the same genres, some equally famous, could have been chosen to ridicule in his sermons, and some of the others were not even Christians! Why did the "prophet" choose those who were Civil Rights activists and supporters to condemn?

The patterns I began noticing were far too frequent to be coincidental. I noticed key figures in the "Message" who came from cities where Roy Davis was most active. By comparing the timeline of Davis' fight against Civil Rights, I began to find answers to some very strange statements made by the "prophet". Even more unusual was the fact that the "prophet's" sudden rise to fame happened about the same time that Davis completed his mission in California and moved back to Texas to begin an operation that was much, much larger and more effective.

I had to pause, though, to consider this initiative for creating "Americanism" in the youth, and what it implied. Children were being trained to be what the Ku Klux Klan considered to be "true American", to support beliefs which those who opposed the Klan would consider "white supremacy". How much of this training was used on me? How much of this training did I expose my children to as we listened to the recorded sermons of the "prophet" every Wednesday, two times on Sunday, and many days between?

It was time to examine the "prophet's" sudden rise to fame in 1947 and try to understand how and why he became a recognized leader in the Post WWII Healing Revival. From what I'd discovered so far, there were many attempts at a ministry, and more than one previous "version" of a "prophet". Why was the 1947 version the only one that succeeded and would be remembered? What was it about 1947 that changed? And if this ministry remained connected to Roy E. Davis and William D. Upshaw — which it did — what was their motive and agenda?

ROY E. DAVIS, WILLIAM D. UPSHAW IN CALIFORNIA:

Child Problem to Mount, Say Superior Judge. 1943, Sept 17. The San Bernardino County Sun

W. R. C. Federation Meeting Attended by Sand Bernardino Group. 1943, Dec 11The San Bernardino County Sun

Orphanage, School at Upland Slated to Open Sept 15. 1943, Aug 8. The San Bernardino County Sun

Trial of Minister Opens on Impersonation Charge. 1944, Apr 19. Los Angeles Times

Pastor Denies Charge of Posing as F. 1944, Apr 21. B. I. Man. Los Angeles Times.

Minister Charged. 1944, Mar 15. Nevada State Journal

Upland Pastor, Acquitted of Theft Charges, Sues Police Chief, 21 Others for Half Million. 1944, Sept 12. The San Bernardino County Sun

Orphanage Head Named in Grand Theft Charge. 1944, Feb 28. The San Bernardino County Sun

Witnesses Say Davis Claimed to be F. 1944, Apr 22. B. I. Man. The San Bernardino County Sun

Habeas Corpus Petition Denied. 1944, Apr 29. The San Bernardino County Sun

Davis Faces Charge of Mail Tampering. 1944, Feb 26. The San Bernardino County Sun

Orphanage Head Asks Reduction in $16,000 Bail. 1944, Mar 4. The San Bernardino County Sun

Two Counts are Dropped After Court Hearing. 1944, May 6. The San Bernardino County Sun

Orphanage Benefactor Questioned, Pictured as 'Disillusioned'; Funds Raising Investigated. 1944, Feb 20. The San Bernardino County Sun

Orphanage Said to be Result of Pastor's Vision. 1944, Apr 20. The San Bernardino County Sun

Accused Pastor Demands Writ. 1944, Apr 27. The San Bernardino County Sun

Summons Issued for Rev. 1944, Feb 1. Roy E. Davis. The San Bernardino County Sun

Complaints Filed Against Orphanage Head of West End. 1944, Feb 22. The San Bernardino County Sun

Upland Evangelist Before U. 1944, Apr 19. S. Judge. The San Bernardino County Sun

Minister, Wife Seek Damages. 1945, Feb 18. The San Bernardino County Sun

Summons Issued for Rev. 1945, Feb 1. Roy E. Davis. The San Bernardino County Sun

Attorneys for Radio Station Seek Davis. 1945, Jan 31. The San Bernardino County Sun

LILY GALLOWAY, WOMEN'S GROUP CONNECTION:

Burneit Union WCTU to Hold Lunch. 1944, May 8. Long Beach Independent.

Grauman Plans Women's Week. 1927, Oct 9. Los Angeles Times.

Upshaw to Wed Official of WCTU. 1946, Oct 5. Post Standard.

Program for W. 1940, Sept 28. C. T. U. Convention Announced.

W. 1928, Oct 7. C. T. U. Meet Will Attract Record Crowd.

Pastor, No Longer Using Crutches, Still a Militant Dry at Nearly 85. 1951, Sept 23.

PUBLIC FIGURES CONDEMNED BY BRANHAM INVOLVED IN CIVIL RIGHTS:

1964, Civil Rights -- and the Beatles? Accessed 2019, Jan 3 from
   http://greenlining.org/blog/2013/1964-civil-rights-and-the-beatles/

The Beatles banned segregated audiences, contract shows. Accessed 2019, Jan 3 from
   https://www.bbc.com/news/entertainment-arts-14963752

Remembering how the Beatles helped break down racial segregation. Accessed 2019, Jan 3 from
https://faroutmagazine.co.uk/
remembering-how-the-beatles-helped-break-down-racial-segregation-by-refusing-to-play-1964/

The Beatles: Fab Four AND Civil Rights Activists: NPR. Accessed 2019, Jan 3 from
   https://www.npr.org/2011/09/18/140573236/the-beatles-fab-four-and-civil-rights-activists

Paul McCartney Meets Women Who Inspired Beatles' 'Blackbird'. Accessed 2019, Jan 3 from
   https://www.rollingstone.com/music/music-news/paul-mccartney-meets-Women-who-inspired-beatles-blackbird-57076/

Mirken, Bruce (11 September 2013). "1964, Civil Rights – and the Beatles?". Greenling Institute.

Berger, Maurice. 2010. For All the World to See: Visual Culture and the Struggle for Civil Rights

Kennedy, Stetson. 1990. Jim Crow Guide to the U.S.A.: The Laws, Customs, and Etiquette Governing the Conduct of Nonwhites and Other Minorities as Second-Class Citizens

TogetherWeServed - Arthur Godfrey, CDR. Accessed 2019, Jan 3 from
   https://navy.togetherweserved.com/usn/servlet/tws.webapp.WebApp?cmd=ShadowBoxProfile&type=EventExt&ID=231775

Deane, Pamela. 2014. James Ewards: African American Hollywood Icon. 2013. Arthur Godfrey. Accessed 2019, Jan 3 from *http://purehistory.org/15-arthur-godfrey/*

Landay, Lori. 2010. I Love Lucy. Wayne State University Press.

Davies, Jude. Smith, Carol R. 1998. Race, Gender, and the American Mother: Political Speech and the Maternity Episodes of I Love Lucy and Murphy Brown.

Breaking Barriers - PBS. Accessed 2019, Jan 3 from https://www.pbs.org/wnet/pioneers-of-television/pioneering-programs/breaking-barriers/

Love in Technicolor: Interracial Families on Television: NPR. Accessed 2019, Jan 3 from
   https://www.npr.org/sections/codeswitch/2014/02/15/276526212/love-in-technicolor-interracial-families-on-television

10 Scandalous TV moments that aren't so scandalous anymore. Accessed 2019, Jan 3 from
   https://www.nydailynews.com/entertainment/tv/10-scandalous-tv-moments-aren-scandalous-anymore-article-1.2442196

Bertrand, M. T. (2009). Race, Rock, and Elvis. University of Illinois Press.

Graham, Allison. 2003. Framing the South: Hollywood, Television, and Race During the Civil Rights

Wallace, Marcie. Elvis Presley: A Revolutionist. Accessed 2019, Jan 3 from
   https://www.lagrange.edu/resources/pdf/citations/2012/11_Wallace_History.pdf

Elvis Presley and Racism. Accessed 2019, Jan 3 from *https://www.elvis.com.au/presley/elvis-not-racist.shtml*

Elvis and Race in 1950s America. Accessed Jan 3 from *http://teachrock.org/lesson/elvis-and-race-in-1950s-america/*

If I can Dream: The Elvis tribute to Martin Luther King, Jr. Accessed 2019, Jan 3 from
   https://nationalpost.com/pmn/news-pmn/if-i-can-dream-the-elvis-tribute-to-martin-luther-king-jr

Nantais, David. 2011. Rock-A My Soul: An Invitation to Rock Your Religion.

Fensch, Thomas. 2001. The FBI Files on Elvis Presley. Cookville: New Century Books.

Schnider, Scott. Icons of Rock: An Encyclopedia of the Legends Who Changed Music Forever. Westport,

Connecticut: Greenwood Press, 2008.

Breaking Racial Barriers on "Daniel Boone" - PBS. Accessed 2019, Jan 3 from
   https://www.pbs.org/wnet/pioneers-of-television/video/breaking-racial-barriers-on-daniel-boone/

Hoffer, Richard. FORREST GRIER GUMPTIOUS ROSEY GRIER, THE FORMER NFL STAR, JUST KEEPS STUMBLING INTO FAME - Sports Illustrated. Accessed 2019, Jan 3 from
   https://www.si.com/vault/1995/03/20/8092877/forrest-grier-gumptious-rosey-grier-the-former-nfl-star-just-keeps-stumbling-into-fame

Elliott, Joe. FESS PARKER'S "DANIEL BOONE" TAUGHT US WHAT IT MEANT TO BE AN AMERICAN. Accessed 2019, Jan 3 from

221

http://www.cinemaretro.com/index.php/archives/9552-FESS-PARKERS-DANIEL-BOONE-TAUGHT-US-WHAT-IT-MEANT-TO-BE-AN-AMERICAN.html

Gallager, Charles A. 2017. Race and Racism in the United States

2015, Jun 18. Pat Boone, Civil Rights musician, seeks conservative revolution.
https://www.washingtontimes.com/news/2015/jun/18/pat-boone-civil-rights-musician-seeks-conservative/

I Had a Dream by Pat Boone - Songfacts. Accessed 2019, Jan 3 from
https://www.songfacts.com/facts/pat-boone/i-had-a-dream

2009. True to the Core. (Interview by Pat Boone). Accessed 2019, Jan 3 from
https://www.wnd.com/2009/01/87550/

Rabaka, Reiland. 2016. Civil Rights Music: The Soundtracks of the Civil Rights Movement.

2016. Journey to the past with Pat Boone. (quote from Jesse Jackson) Accessed 2019, Jan 3 from
https://entertainment.mb.com.ph/2016/12/04/journey-to-the-past-with-pat-boone

CHAPTER 22

WILLIAM BRANHAM'S
OVERNIGHT FAME

"We're getting some new gadgets for recording[407]"

One of the best benefits of consulting for clients that have a global scale of operations is the travel that comes with the work. Seeing new places, meeting new people, and learning new cultures can be very exciting, even if the travel is mainly for work. Conventions are often held in big cities that are filled with entertainment, and convention hosts specifically chose these locations to create excitement that might raise attendance. I've had the opportunity to visit Las Vegas for multiple clients over the years and can truly say that though I've tried very hard, the architectural wonders of the Strip in Las Vegas cannot be captured by a camera.

Each massive hotel is like a city in and of itself, filled with shopping malls, restaurants, bars, Broadway shows, concerts, and other attractions. From the moment I entered the lobby of any one of the hotels in Las Vegas, I was overwhelmed by the artistic design. I could spend hours looking at just the lobby! From magnificent paintings to finely detailed woodwork, from thousands of carefully placed light bulbs to carpet woven into a masterpiece of design; the resort hotels are simply breathtaking. That same careful attention to detail carries on through every aspect of design in every feature of every hotel.

---

[407] Branham, William. 1947, Apr 12. Faith is the Substance.

The city is filled with entertainment. Visitors to any attraction in the city expect to pay a lot for their entertainment, while the entertainers are expected to draw crowds large enough to fund the unbelievable operating expenses. To thrill-seeking visitors, the city is nothing more than entertainment. But to the entertainers, it is nothing more than a business. If visitors stopped paying, there are very few entertainers who would continue their show.

I suddenly thought about the similarities to the "divine healers" entertaining crowds with their preaching. They also had to be entertaining in their speeches and had to run their operations like a business to offset the huge expenses. Why didn't they hold the prayer lines in hospitals, clearing out the sick wards? If their success rate was as high as they advertised, insurance companies would pay *them* for the money they saved from doctors and expensive operations. The healthcare problem in this country would not even exist! I thought about the cost of holding one of these meetings. From travel, to rent, to hotels, and food; the revival meetings would have been very expensive. Yet the "prophet" said that he never took an offering! How could he afford to stay in hotels like London's Piccadilly,[408] one of the most expensive in the world?

One day, a former "Message" believer shared with me their findings of the tax records for "Voice of God Recordings", which was the headquarters for the "Message" faith. I was very surprised to see that they had accumulated over $100,000,000 in assets.[409] I was even more surprised the former "Message" believer shared the tax records of a brand-new organization that none of us were aware even existed. The year after $100,000,000 came into Voice of God Recordings, *"Jehovah Jireh Foundation"* was established, and the large sum of money was transferred to the new organization. I wondered: how many times had that type of financial transaction happened in the past, yet none of us had any idea? The leaders of the organization were brazen — openly stating that the new organization was created for the sole purpose of moving funds.

---

[408] Branham, William. 1960, Mar 4. Thirsting for Life. "I said, 'We're going to stay, I believe, they said at the Piccadilly Hotel.'
[409] Form 990. 2012. Voice of God Recordings.

To provide funding and support to expand, add to, and enrich the services, programs, activities, facilities, and mission of Voice of God Recordings.[410]

Searching the transcripts of the sermons, I found a time when the "prophet" was frustrated with the Internal Revenue Service. In a rare glimpse into the finances for his healing campaigns, the "prophet" described the business side of his ministry. In 1962, he owed over $300,000 in taxes.[411] In today's money, that is almost 2.5 million dollars owed to the United States government! In the 1960's, this would have placed the "prophet" in the tax brackets of the wealthiest Americans, not the poor and humble as he claimed. Anyone earning over $200,000 was taxed at a very high rate. Assuming he was taxed at 70%, which was common for the wealthy, this would mean that he earned $428,571.42 that year. And the people of that era were willing to pack out auditoriums to see this genre of entertainment!

Like my business associates traveling to Las Vegas, people of the 40's, 50's, and 60's would travel miles to see a revivalist. They had no idea as to the business operating behind the stage persona in any one of the revival campaigns. Unlike Vegas, this was a business without huge operating overhead. Nor were very many people aware of $428,000 that was brought in from the offering plates. In today's money, the "prophet" would have earned over 3.5 million dollars!

I quickly got a calculator and started doing the math on his income versus expenses. Even while staying at luxurious hotels like the Piccadilly, paying his hosts for the auditoriums and tent rentals, advertising expenses, and covering the salaries of multiple men, this amount of income was far more than he could spend. I began to wonder: Where was all the "prophet's" money going? If the "prophet" had this much income, after expenses, I knew I needed to dig deeper.

...

---

[410] Form 990. 2012. Jehovah Jireh Foundation.
[411] Branham, William. 1962, Nov 24. All Things. "And they said they was going to make me, that I owed them with delinquency, and with all of my meetings, three hundred and something thousand dollars."

The more articles describing Roy Davis' involvement with white supremacy groups I stumbled across, the more I realized that Roy Davis and William Upshaw were securing funds for their "Americanization" of the United States through the Ku Klux Klan. I found it strange how similar these two men were to the "prophet" — their public faces were that of humble, sincere ministers, yet what was seen on the outside did not resemble what was inside. In 1944, both civil and criminal accusations against Roy Davis were stacking up quickly. Some of his charges were felonies. They included impersonation of a Federal officer, iillegal weapons, fraud, and mail tampering.

Government agents were turning over every stone in their investigation, while news reporters were having a field day with the unusual circumstances behind their investigation. Others working in the Ussher-Davis Children's Orphanage were charged with grand theft. Finally, Roy Davis, his wife, and others were arrested. Bail was set at $16,000 -- unusually high for a simple orphanage scam. According to the details that would come out during the trial, the Feds knew all about Davis' criminal past. They also knew all about Roy Davis and William Upshaw being involved with the Ku Klux Klan. Then, as abruptly as it all started, and, matching the same pattern since the early 1900's, charges were suddenly dropped![412]

Roy Davis was somehow able to convince a jury that he knew nothing of the misuse of funds. William D. Upshaw simply disappeared, and never seemed to be accused at all — Upshaw was mysteriously absent from most of the reports of the trial. In a turn of events that would shock newspaper reporters, Roy Davis was eventually acquitted, and sued local officials for a half a million dollars.[413] In February 1945, the couple sued for an additional $25,000 for Mrs. Davis. Then, the constant stream of articles in newspapers suddenly stopped. Shortly after the lawsuits, Davis disappeared from California. The next year, William D. Upshaw married trial witness Lily Galloway.[414]

---

[412] 1Two Counts are Dropped After Court Hearing. 944, May 6. The San Bernardino County Sun
[413] Upland Pastor, Acquitted of Theft Charges, Sues Police Chief, 21 Others for Half Million. 1944, Sept 12. The San Bernardino County Sun
[414] Upshaw to Wed Official of WCTU. 1946, Oct 5. Post Standard.

In the United States, a wife can refuse to testify against her husband by simply invoking "spousal privilege".

That same year, the "prophet's" "Heavenly Vision" tour began, and 1945 tracts were published. Shortly after Roy Davis sued Los Angeles officials, in March of 1945, the "prophet" had a vision of "white robed people", published it in a tract, and started out in the revival trails.

> *This book of testimonies is for the glory of our Lord Jesus Christ. It is for that purpose only that I write it. It was in the month of March, 1945, one morning about 3:00 A.M. that our Lord Jesus Christ gave me a vision. This He has done many times and I most humbly praise Him for it. {...} The Lord then told me to pull back the curtains and when I did I saw a great mountain of the bread of life. He then said, "Feed these," and turning around I saw white-robed people coming from everywhere, making up a large audience. The following night, after the vision was over, I explained it to my church just as the Lord had given it to me.[415]*

According to the tract, he had already had a healing ministry until 1940. This seemed to confirm what I had already found with in research. Then, for five years, the "prophet's" ministry was put on hold, which explained the gap in my research. But in 1945, the "prophet" claimed to have been given a "double portion" of the "power to heal" in 1944.

> *Then one year ago, while I was standing in my yard the Spirit came to me again; I was told that God had forgiven me and that a double portion of the Power to heal would be given me. In this book are some of the things He did on my first trip for Him.[416]*

This version of the stage persona describing how the "prophet's" "gift" came was vastly different than the version used in later years. I

---

[415] Branham, William. 1945. I Was Not Disobedient to the Heavenly Vision.
[416] Branham, William. 1945. I Was Not Disobedient to the Heavenly Vision.

had listened to countless sermons describing an "angel" meeting the "prophet" in a cave in 1947. In fact, the "cave" where that happened was a sacred place for those of us in the "Message".[417] We never knew that he had a "healing" ministry before 1947. We never heard the story of how the "gift of healing" came in his yard, as it said in the 1945 tract. Is this why the 1945 tract was so difficult to find?

I found an article in the July 1947 issue of the Everyday Magazine in the St. Louis-Dispatch. Rev. Kidson of Houston, Texas was managing the "prophet's" revival meetings at that time. Kidson also claimed the "gift" was given two years prior, which would have been in 1945. Only $60 rent was required to collect two large suitcases full of cash. Kidson described the hefty men who carried the money from the meetings.

> *But first a collection had to be taken to defray the $60 rent for the tent, even though it wasn't being used, and the rent for the gym. So far the people in Houston, Tex., had been kindest in showing their appreciation but Brother Kidson had no doubt that the people of Vandalia could outdo them. (A man at the hotel later told us it had taken two husky men to carry in the boxes of offerings from the kind people of Vandalia the night before). As the collection was taken, the audience stood and sang Brother Branham's favorite hymn, "All Things Are Possible, Only Believe" and Brother Branham entered.[418]*

The newspaper reporters were very thorough in their investigation, and it was evident that they had not only attended the large meeting, but also had done some research on the "prophet" before he arrived. Like other "faith healers" of the era, the "prophet" claimed to feel "vibrations" coming from the hand of the sick and afflicted. He even said that it had stopped his watch, as he explained getting an expensive Longines watch.[419] Today, these watches sell for *thousands* of dollars![420] After feeling the "vibrations", he would ask a "demon" to depart from

---

[417] A Prophet's Cave. Accessed 2020, May 17 from http://www.williambranhamhomepage.org/thecave.htm
[418] Brother Branham, the Faith Healer. 1947, Jul 6. St. Louis Post Dispatch Sun.
[419] Branham, William. 1947, Nov 2. The Angel of the Lord. "The vibrations stopped my watch. I can't pray for people with a watch on. I can show it to you this afternoon. It'll stop it every time, vibrations over that brand new Longines watch. It'll—it'll stop; the vibration would stop it. 47-1102"
[420] Men's Watches. Accessed 2020, May 17 from https://shop.us.longines.com/watch-selector/men.html

the person. None in the audience were permitted to watch what went on during the "healing". The "prophet" told the people that if they opened their eyes, the "devils" would enter their bodies. Newspaper reporters found humor in this statement, having kept their eyes open to report the findings and experienced no "demon activity".

> *Then he prays for the demon to depart. It is essential that everyone keep his head bowed during the prayer: should you raise it, the liberated devils may enter your body. During the evening's prayers, heads were kept dutifully bowed, except for those of photographers and reporters, who apparently considered themselves filled with devils beyond redemption and continued with their work.*[421]

It wasn't difficult to see how the pieces of the puzzle were coming together. By comparing the "prophet's" timeline with the timeline for Roy Davis, I could see that the two timelines aligned perfectly, like zipping a zipper. Still, there was much more work to do, and more pieces of the puzzle to find. Where did Roy E. Davis go after he left California? How did he and Upshaw use the money which they had secured in California? How did the "prophet" use the hundreds of thousands of dollars he was collecting? Even his expensive jewelry could not account for all this money!

It was becoming more and more difficult for me to call him "the prophet". He was William *Marrion* Branham, but even that was questionable — his draft card, signed by himself, was submitted as *"William Marvin Branham"*. Who was this man I once respected as a "prophet"? Could I believe anything that he said? Could I believe anything that anybody said about him? When I approached my grandfather to discuss my initial findings, he was very upset. I will never forget his words to me: *"People have known these things for years, John, what does it hurt for you to believe it anyway?"* He then proceeded to shun my family from the religion, instantly severing all relationships. If my grandfather knew there were issues, then who else knew?

---

[421] Brother Branham, the Faith Healer. 1947, Jul 6. St. Louis Post Dispatch Sun.

It was time to dig deeper into his early ministry and the men who helped lift him into fame and fortune. The men who enabled William Branham were no doubt controlling, and possibly creating, details for Branham's stage persona. The best place to start researching was with his (alleged) first campaign manager, Rev. W. E. Kidson.

WILLIAM BRANHAM AND MONEY, CLAIMING NEVER TAKING OFFERING
Voice of God Recordings IRS Form 990's
Jehovah Jireh Foundation IRS Form 990's
Branham, William. 1953, Nov 8. Life Story
Branham, William. 1954, Jun 20. Divine Healing
Branham, William. 1956, Jul 26. Love
Branham, William. 1956, Aug 16. Working of the Holy Spirit
Branham, William. 1959, Apr 24. Faith of Abraham
Branham, William. 1960, Feb 21. Hearing, Recognizing, Acting on the Word
Branham, William. 1962, Jul 1. Take on the Whole Armor of God
Branham, William. 1962, Jul 8. A Super Sign.
Branham, William. 1965, Anointed Ones at the End Time.
Branham, William. 1949, Jul 8. I Was Not Disobedient to the Heavenly Vision
Branham, William. 1950, March. Gifts and Callings are Without Repentance
Branham, William. 1950, Jul 13. Obey the Voice of the Angel
Branham, William. 1950, Aug 20. My Life Story
Branham, William. 1951, May 7. Expectations
Branham, William. 1951, Jul 17. The Manifestation of the Spirit
Branham, William. 1951, Jul 22. The Second Miracle
Branham, William. 19151, Jul 29. The Second Miracle
Branham, William. 1951, Sept 30. Expectation
Branham, William. 1952, Jul 13. Early Spiritual Experiences
Branham, William. 1952, Aug 10. I Am the Resurrection and the Life
Branham, William. 1953, Jun 8. At Thy Word
Branham, William. 1953, Aug 30. Why I Am A Holy-Roller
Branham, William. 1951, Jul 22. The Second Miracle
Branham, William. 19151, Jul 29. The Second Miracle
Branham, William. 1951, Sept 30. Expectation
Branham, William. 1952, Jul 13. Early Spiritual Experiences
Branham, William. 1952, Aug 10. I Am the Resurrection and the Life
Branham, William. 1953, Jun 8. At Thy Word
Branham, William. 1953, Aug 30. Why I Am A Holy-Roller
Branham, William. 1955, May 1. Fellowship
Branham, William. 1957, Jan 6. Jehovah Jireh
Branham, William. 1958, Jun 20. Queen of the South
Branham, William. 1959, Apr 24. Faith of Abraham
Branham, William. 1960, Jul 23. Speak to the Rock
Branham, William. 1961, May 15. A Greater than Solomon is Here
Branham, William. 1962, Jul 19. Life
Branham, William. 1963, Nov 15. World Falling Apart
Branham, William. 1963, Nov 17. Once More
Branham, William. 1964, Apr 18. Paradox
Branham, William. 1965, Aug 1. Events Made Clear with Prophecy

CHAPTER 23

WILLIAM BRANHAM AND W. E. KIDSON

"It had taken two husky men to carry in the boxes of offerings from the kind people of Vandalia the night before[422]"

As a sub-sect of Pentecostalism, the "Message" shared many beliefs with other Pentecostal churches. Pentecostal founders like William Seymour and Charles Fox Parham were mentioned but we never really talked about their history, or the impact Pentecostalism had on the "Message". We read books about William Branham that were written by those supporting him, not realizing that their version of history was taken directly from his speeches or from private discussions they had with him. After learning that many of these "historians" never investigated Branham's version of "history" for accuracy, it became difficult for me to trust anything written about William Branham whether it was supportive or critical of his ministry. It was very disturbing. But the deeper I dug into Pentecostalism itself, the more disturbing this trend became.

The founder of modern Pentecostalism, Charles Parham, was involved with scamming investors during his creation of the religion. Parham was caught on the business-end of "Chemical Gold",[423] a product that allegedly turned ordinary materials into "gold from God".[424]

---

[422] Brother Branham, the Faith Healer. 1947, Jul 6. St. Louis Post Dispatch Sun.
[423] 1902, November 6. Alchemist in Prison. The Wilkes-Barre Record.
[424] 1902, November 7. Could Make Gold. Sedalia Democrat.

He modeled his new religious movement after movements founded by two notorious cult leaders who were exposed as having become rich from the contributions of their own faithful followers: cult leaders named Frank Sandford and John Alexander Dowie.[425] Sandford was arrested after nearly killing the members of his commune due to starvation after taking ownership of all their possessions.[426] He had taken so much from them that they literally could not put food on their own tables, while he himself was living like a king. John Alexander Dowie, who also took ownership of his commune's possessions, was nicknamed the "Richest Man in the West".[427]

When Pentecostal founder Charles Parham was accused of sodomizing young boys in his commune, William Seymour seized his opportunity to make money. Newspaper reporters described the scene that they witnessed during the Pentecostal Revival and described Seymour's pockets as being so filled with money that it fell out as he walked along Azusa Street.[428] Five and ten dollar bills ($137 - $272 in today's money) were being stuffed into his pockets by the faithful as he walked through the revival crowd.

There was so much information in the libraries and internet archives about William Branham, the religion, his peers, and the history. Why did we only read those who wrote positively about that history? Why did authors critical of these men and their ministries base their "history" on the claims made by the dishonest rather than investigate for themselves? A few trips to a local library would have given any of the "Message" historians facts that were much more accurate. In today's world, a few internet subscriptions for any one of the many historical archives will produce the same result as a visit to the local library. But we were so caught up in the emotion created by Pentecostal-style preaching that none of us even thought to check if the "history" being given to us was true!

---

[425] Goff, James R. Jr. (1988). Fields White unto Harvest: Charles F. Parham and the Missionary Origins of Pentecostalism. University of Arkansas Press. ISBN 1-55728-025-8.

[426] "Holy Ghost" Leader Guilty of Starving Members of His Sect. 1911, December 9. Oregon Daily Journal.

[427] A Record $15,000,000 Profit Makes John Alexander Dowie, Alias Elijah III, The Merchant Prince of Faith Healers. 1902, November 30. Brooklyn Daily Eagle.

[428] Borlase, Craig. 2006. William Seymour: A Biography. "Those that were there remembered seeing how Seymour would wonder among the crowds in the mission with five and ten dollar bills wafting out of his pockets, the man frequently failed to notice as people placed them there."

...

Searching the national archives for the trail of Roy E. Davis was difficult. As I'd already learned, Roy Davis was a very common name. I had to search with other keywords to filter the results into hundreds of hits rather than thousands, and even then, I was forced to read almost every article. Fortunately, by adding "Ku Klux Klan" to the filters, I learned that the Roy Davis I was looking for became much easier to find.

After Roy Davis sued Los Angeles officials, he moved operations back to his home state of Texas where it all began. Claiming to be a "Baptist" preacher filled with the Pentecostal gifts, he formed new alliances with Pentecostal churches. After what I'd learned about William Branham, this disgusted me. Both men were using the same dishonest tactics to lure unsuspecting people into their snare.

Somehow managing to escape his trail of criminal history, Roy Davis embedded himself into Fort Worth elite.[429] He was on the executive committee of the Ft. Worth Chamber of Commerce. In a letter to the editor of Branham's "The Voice of Healing" newsletter, Roy Davis referred to William Branham as his "Timothy", referring to the Biblical protege of the Apostle Paul. By now, the revival business had grown so large that Branham promoted others as editor of the publication and was now listed as "Associate Editor". After everything that had happened with Davis, I was very surprised that Branham would allow Roy Davis' letter to be published. I was also surprised by an unusual statement in his letter, *"Until recently, I was working with the Assembly of God, though not a member with them"*. This seemed like such an odd thing to say, and out of context. Little did I know that this statement would turn out to be vitally important in understanding how the "healing ministry" was related with the "Americanization" agenda.

A researcher digging for information concerning the assassination of President John F. Kennedy stumbled upon my website and became

---

[429] Davis, Roy. Wm. Branham's First Pastor. 1950, Oct. The Voice of Healing. "I am a member of the Ft. Worth, Texas Chamber of Commerce, and on the Executive Committee of same. I was born and reared near this Texas city, converted near there, and ordained to preach the Gospel in a well-known Baptist church of Texas. Until recently, I was working with the Assembly of God, though not a member with them."

interested in my research on "Americanism", Davis, Upshaw, Branham and the Ku Klux Klan. Suddenly, I found myself collaborating with others who had mounds of research to share with me, including F.B.I. Files[430] that had been made available through the Freedom of Information Act. They had many pieces of the puzzle that I did not have, and apparently, I had many pieces that they were looking for. The information I had stumbled onto by finding William Upshaw's "Americanization" project was the key to tying our research together!

FBI informants testified that Roy Davis had separated from the Atlanta Ku Klux Klan and had started a new Ku Klux Klan organization in Arkansas, Texas, and Louisiana. One of the FBI files mentioned a publication by Roy Davis entitled *"50 Reasons Why You Should Be A Member of the OKKK"*.[431] I searched the archives for a copy of the publication and found it in a historical research site online. It was a combination of religion, propaganda, white supremacy, and bigotry like none I had ever seen. I was surprised how many of the religious points in Davis' publication that I could identify from the "prophet's" sermons. To be certain, I couldn't picture the "prophet" saying some of these things in a public speech, but if he was Reverend Roy E. Davis' "Timothy", how many of these things did he say in private?

By the time of Roy Davis' criminal trial in Los Angeles, William Branham had moved into the parsonage on 8th Street in Jeffersonville, Indiana. Branham followed Roy Davis' pattern of using letters to the editors of newspapers to recruit others and to support his own doctrinal positions. I was surprised at how polished William Branham's English was in the letters to the editor. They were not the broken "Kentucky English" used in later sermons. He continued to speak clearly and articulately as though he were educated. I pulled out my copy of the "*I Was Not Disobedient*" tract and began to examine it more closely. I found that it was also very well written. If a person were to listen to a 1965 sermon of William Branham and then read his 1945 tract, they would assume that two different people were speaking and writing. Even more interesting was the description of the vision. He claimed

[430] Citizens Committee for Americanism in the Arts. 1962, Mar 5. F.B.I.
[431] United States Government Memorandum to SAC, NEW ORLEANS from SA, ROBERT EDWARD LEE Subject THE WHITE KNIGHTS OF THE KU KLUX KLAN of MISSISSIPPI. 1964, Feb 20. F.B.I.

that at his "Tabernacle", the "*fowls*" would no longer eat his "*bread*". Therefore, he was to go west, and feed the "*white-robed people*". Was this a coded message to meet Roy Davis and William Upshaw out west? One of those people he was to meet was Rev. Robert Daugherty. He continued to describe his revival campaigns, and I found it odd that his "healing" fame had reached St. Louis by 1945.

After his "vision" about his church not eating his "bread", the "prophet" renamed his church from "Pentecostal Tabernacle" to "Branham Tabernacle". The first advertisement for "Branham Tabernacle" was in 1945, and Robert Daugherty was guest speaker listed in that advertisement. It was as though the renaming of the Billie Branham Pentecostal Tabernacle was ceremonial, and Rev. Daugherty came into town to dedicate the new church. I wanted to know more about this Rev. Daugherty.

...

Rev. Robert Daugherty was a United Pentecostal preacher.[432] When he visited the new "Branham Tabernacle", he no doubt believed William Branham's claims to have been a converted Baptist minister who was new to Pentecostalism. It was the same strategy Roy Davis was using to build a new sect of the Ku Klux Klan in the Southern United States.[433] For both Roy Davis and William Branham, that strategy was highly successful. Pentecostal ministers eagerly accepted the men's claims to be new converts, simply based upon the number of times they frequented the same venues. They presented themselves as "Baptist open to the Pentecostal theology". William Branham's brother Howard[434] and son Billy[435] traveled to assist with "prayer cards". Branham claimed to speak with the "gift of tongues",[436] which many Pentecostals believed to be evidence of the Holy Spirit. The "vision"

---

[432] Mrs. W. H. Peters. 1948, May 13. The Current Local.
[433] Old Fashioned Revival. 1950, Mar 16. Hood County News. "Evangelist R. E. Davis, of Fort Worth. Dr. Davis is an outstanding evangelist. He is a Baptist preacher filled with the Holy Ghost and fire."
[434] Branham, William. 1953, Nov 30. Has the Lord Spoken Only To Moses? "I told Howard, I said, "What prayer cards did you give out?"
[435] Branham, William. 1951, Apr 14. The Angel of the Lord. "Where's Billy? How many did you give out today? A hundred?"
[436] Branham, William. 1955, Sep 11. The Unwelcomed Christ. "I said, "Yeah. Yeah, I spoke in tongues."

commissioning his "gift of healing", that he claimed to have received in his yard gradually transitioned to a story of an "angel" in his room. As the campaign tour entered Arkansas, where Roy Davis was building his sect of the Ku Klux Klan, William Branham suddenly connected with Rev. W. E. Kidson.

Reporters were interested in interviewing those the "prophet" had healed in the revivals. It was obvious that they were skeptical, and even more obvious that they were having difficulty finding any evidence to support Branham's miraculous claims. According to reporters, not a single person who was present to testify had actually been healed. Rev. Kidson defended the "prophet", alleging that those healed were uninterested in the sermons, came for their "healing", and then disappeared.[437] According to Kidson, they had simply left the meeting and did not return.

Using the same sort of disclaimers that F. F. Bosworth had used to explain why people were not being healed, Kidson reminded people that they might "lose their healing" if they were not careful. I wondered how many people interviewed by reporters were afraid they might have "lost their healing" due to "lack of faith" or were too embarrassed to tell the reporters that their faith did not "work".

I could tell by the writer's tone that William Branham and his campaign team did not like having the reporters present. Anyone watching the collection plates could see the money flowing in, but the reporters were curious enough to dig deeper and find out about large suitcases full of cash. This was not the kind of publicity that fills auditoriums. Yet somehow, Kidson was able to tactfully dodge every single critical question asked, and reporters were unable to publish their much-anticipated exposure of swindling.

When I learned that W. E. Kidson left his church to manage the "prophet", I wanted to know more. Why would a leader of the U.P.C.I. quit his church for a "faith healer" in 1945, especially if people were "losing their healing"? Kidson was very well connected. He was a Pentecostal leader in Dallas Texas,[438] where Davis would soon base his Ku Klux Klan operations. He was on the same board with Rev. B. H.

---

[437] Brother Branham, the Faith Healer. 1947, Jul 6. St. Louis Post Dispatch Sun.
[438] Head Pentecostal Church Board. 1937, Oct 1. The Jackson Son.

Hite of St. Louis, a close associate of Rev. Robert Daugherty. Also on that board was Rev. Harry Morse of Oakland, CA., very near the area Davis and Upshaw had just left, and Rev. J. H. Reeter of Vandalia, IL, who opened the door to the "prophet's" Vandalia "healing" campaigns. I found it very strange that William Branham was already famous for his "gift of healing" — so much so that Robert Daugherty sent a telegraph in 1945,[439] and Branham's overnight fame came *before* his pamphlet was published. How long had the "prophet" been a "faith healer", and just how far had his ministry spread? How did W. E. Kidson, the "prophet's" first campaign manager, create "fame" *before* the "gift"? This "gift" wasn't supposed to come until 1947!

...

As early as 1929, W. E. Kidson was a recognized name among the Pentecostal faith. Before taking his position in Dallas, TX, he pastored a church in Louisiana, MO.[440] By 1930, he was named General Secretary of the Pentecostal Ministerial Alliance. Kidson toured Pentecostal churches in West Texas, and likely would have been familiar with Roy E. Davis of West Texas during the early years of Pentecostalism. During that era, when Pentecostalism was spreading, Pentecostal evangelists worked together closely with one another. Kidson was deeply involved in Pentecostal operations, not only in Texas,[441] but also in other states.

Kidson was very mobile, with offices in multiple cities. By 1940, he had moved his main office to Dallas, Texas,[442] but he also had a home in Shreveport, Louisiana, which would later become a stronghold for both Roy Davis' sect of the Ku Klux Klan and William Branham's "Message". Though he sold his home in 1942,[443] Kidson would frequently return to Shreveport.

---

[439] Branham, William. 1945. I Was Not Disobedient to the Heavenly Vision. "About three weeks from the time of the vision, I received a telegram from a minister in St. Louis, Mo., by the name of Rev. Robert Daugherty. He asked me to come at once because his little daughter, Betty, was dying."

[440] Pentecostal Body to Meet Here in Annual Session. 1929, Oct 13. The Times Sun.

[441] Pentecostal Church Ministers Training College May Be Established Here. 1934, Apr 12. The Jacksonville Daily.

[442] Pentecostal Officers to be Announced. 1937, Oct 26. The Jacksonville Sun.

[443] Misc. 1942, Feb 15. The Times. "Phone W. E. Kidson"

By the time Kidson agreed to manage William Branham's "healing" campaigns, Kidson was very familiar with "divine healing" and "healers".[444] In his role as General Secretary, he was involved in the ordination of many other pastors, evangelists, and healers. Some of the evangelists were women,[445] which would have been forbidden in later versions of the "Message". I was surprised that William Branham claimed that his stance against female ministers was why he left Davis' church in Jeffersonville[446], yet he partnered with Kidson who was also working with female ministers.

In 1941, W. E. Kidson moved his base from Dallas to Houston. He was the pastor of the Houston Gospel Tabernacle when he launched the "prophet" into overnight fame.[447] But William Branham was not the only "healer" whose career W. E. Kidson would help create. And Branham was not the only "healer" whose "commission story" would be changed to include an "angel". Kidson managed other "healing" evangelists such as A. D. Van Hoose of Evansville, Indiana, who claimed to have had an angelic visitation.[448] Kidson advertised "City Wide Revival(s) of Power" with phrases such as "Don't Miss His Experience, 'I Met An Angel!'", and called the services of other evangelists, "Miracle Services".

W. E. Kidson knew the business, and he knew it well. I wondered, "Why did W. E. Kidson help create new 'healers' if William Branham was the 'Messenger' for our 'age'?" Finding Roy Davis' plan to create a new Ku Klux Klan was very disturbing, but seeing both Roy Davis and William Branham at the very same time start to pose as *Baptists just learning about the Pentecostal faith*" was even more disturbing. At first, I wondered how men like W. E. Kidson could not see through their stage persona and realize what was happening. Visiting Jeffersonville, Kidson and others would surely have known about Branham's "Pentecostal Tabernacle". Were they really as unaware as they seemed?

---

[444] Divine Healing Service Tonight at Convention. 1937, Oct 27. The Jackson Sun.
[445] Women Speak. 1937, Oct 25. The Jackson Sun.
[446] Branham, William. 1961, Jan 12. Questions and Answers. "said, 'Doctor Davis, in all due respects to the Baptist faith, and everything that I have been ordained to, I did not know that it was in the doctrine of the Baptist church to ordain women. That was one thing that was left out of it.'"
[447] Rev. William Branham. 1947, Apr 14. Camden News.
[448] City Wide Revival of Power! With A. D. Van Hoose. 1961, Feb 25. Arizona Republic. "Don't Miss His Experience, 'I Met an Angel'"

Or were these men, who intimately knew the "prophet", part of the plan?

It was time to search for those missing sermons, the ones recorded with the "old gadgets for recording". If the very first sentence of the very first sermon that William Branham preached that we had access to hear started with the words, *"We're getting some new gadgets for recording"*, then surely there were sermons prior to this that used old gadgets. I knew that it was unlikely I'd find the actual recordings, but with access to newspaper archives, it should be very easy to find the revival trail of William Branham and his campaign team. There must be a reason why those sermons were no longer available. What was that reason? What was William Branham and his later campaign team hiding?

REV. FRANK SANDFORD

New Religious Sect Started – Holy Ghost and Us Society Established Down East. 1899, Jul 12. The Times Richmond Virginia.

"Elijah" Sued for Loan. 1910, Oct 22. Washington Herald.

Holy Ghost and Us Follower Crazed. 1906, August 13. Fairbanks Daily Times.

Famine and Insanity In 'Elijah's' Colony. 1906, October 14. Minneapolis Journal.

Hypnotized A Pretty Girl. 1910, June 15. Great Falls Tribune.

"Holy Ghost and Us," A Society at Shiloh. 1900, November 17. Brooklyn Daily Eagle.

Starvation Cleaning Out "Holy Ghost and Us" Band. 1906, October 15. Spokane Press.

"Elijah" Is Returning. 1909, May 24. Burlington Free Press.

Holy Ghost Colony. 1910, May 10. Chillicothe Constitution Tribune.

Frank Sandford is "Elijah". 1910, November 6. Evening Statesman.

"Holy Ghost" Leader Guilty of Starving Members of His Sect. 1911, December 9. Oregon Daily Journal.

Hoodwinked Him. 1911, December 13. Seattle Star.

REV. FRANK SANDFORD - AS ELIJAH

Sandford Is A Sure Prophet. 1906, November 16. Reno Gazette.

Earth's Last Throne. 1909, July 14. Point Pleasant Register.

Holy Ghosters All at Sea; No Place on Earth to Land. 1910, July 28. Evansville Press.

The Religious Grafter. 1911, December 20. Allentown Democrat..

REV. FRANK SANDFORD - DOOMSDAY

Believe They Know That the Judgement Day Will Come Next September. 1909, July 9. Daily Republican.

Earth to Be Destroyed At 10:20 A. 1909, July 9. M. Sept. 15. Vicksburg Evening Post.

"Holy Ghost and Us" Society Prepares for the Ascension. 1909, July 12. Arkansas City Daily Traveler

Earth Ends on September 15. 1909, July 13. Evening Star.

Misc. news. 1909, September 14. The Eugene Guard.

End Due Tomorrow. 1909, September 14. Webb City Register.

Maine Man Said World Would Come to End Today. 1909, September 15. Iola Register.

REV. FRANK SANDFORD - FLOATING COMMUNE

Gospel Ship is Back in Port. 1910, May 23. Leavenworth Post.

Holy Ghosters All at Sea; No Place on Earth to Land. 1910, July 28. Evansville Press.

Misc. news. 1910, July 16. Manitoba Morning Free Press.

"Holy Ghosters" All at Sea; No Place on Earth to Land!" Wichita Beacon. 1910, August 2.

"Holy Ghosters" Are All Out at Sea. 1910, August 10. Ohio County News.

Holy Ghosters on Ship Get Nothing, Says Deserter. 1910, September 16. Washington Herald.

Endure Privations on Religious Craft. 1911, October 22. Anaconda Standard.

REV. FRANK SANDFORD - INDICTMENT, PRISON

Arrest Holy Ghost Leader. 1910, Oct 26. Indianapolis Star.

"Elijah" Sandford Was Indicted. 1911, December 11. Evening Star.

Evangelist Indicted. 1911, December 8. Salina Daily Union.

Says "Lord Will Protect Me". 1911, December 9. Seattle Star.

"Holy Ghoster" Found Guilty. 1911, December 9. Iowa City Press Citizen.

Sandford Has Refused to Have Legal Help. 1911, December 9. Scranton Truth.

Holy Ghost and Us Leader Sentenced to Pen. 1911, December 18. East Oregonian.

Elijah Gets 10 Years in Cell. 1911, December 18. La Grande Observer.

"Elijah II" Out of Penitentiary. 1918, September 8. Daily Arkansas Gazette.

Leader of Peculiar Sect Released from Government Prison. 1918, November 25. Oregon Daily Journal.

REV. FRANK SANDFORD - FAITH HEALING

Jan 7. Raised from Dead – Remarkable Case in a Religious Community in Maine. 1900, Wichita Daily Eagle.

Doubts Resurrection Story. 1900, Feb 6. Inter Ocean.

"Holy Ghost and Us," A Society at Shiloh. 1900, November 17. Brooklyn Daily Eagle.

CHARLES FOX PARHAM

Goff, James R. Jr. (1988). Fields White unto Harvest: Charles F. Parham and the Missionary Origins of Pentecostalism. University of Arkansas Press. ISBN 1-55728-025-8.

Healing and Pentecost. Accessed 2017, April 17 http://healingandrevival.com/BioCFParham.htm.

A. P. Pentecostal Movement Is About to Turn 100. 2000, December 31. St. Louis Dispatch.

In Tower of Babel. 1901, January 27. The Inter Ocean.

They Pray Ceaselessly. 1901, March 16. Lawrence Daily Journal.

"Stone's Folly" for a Pest House. 1901, May 17. Topeka Daily Capital

Misc. News. 1901, August 17. Evening Star Independence, KS

Misc. News. 1901, December 13. Hoisington Dispatch.

Missionary Work. 1901, January 22. Topeka Daily Capital

The Gift of Tongues. 1901, June 9. Anaconda Standard.

CHARLES FOX PARHAM - MODELING AFTER SANFDFORD

Goff, James R. Jr. (1988). Fields White unto Harvest: Charles F. Parham and the Missionary Origins of Pentecostalism. University of Arkansas Press. ISBN 1-55728-025-8.

1900, November 3. How Parham Rode. The Topeka Daily Capital.

Nelson, Shirley. The Story of Shiloh. Accessed 2017, April 17 from
http://www.christianity.com/church/church-history/timeline/1901-2000/the-story-of-shiloh-11630697.html.

CHARLES FOX PARHAM - MODELING AFTER DOWIE

Healing and Pentecost. Accessed 2017, April 17 from
http://healingandrevival.com/BioCFParham.htm.

CHARLES FOX PARHAM - ARK OF THE COVENANT

1902, February 3. Wants the Ark of the Covenant. Pittsburg Daily Headlight. (Pittsburg, KS).

CHARLES FOX PARHAM - CHEMICAL GOLD

1902, November 6. Alchemist in Prison. The Wilkes-Barre Record.

1902, November 7. Could Make Gold. Sedalia Democrat.

CHARLES FOX PARHAM - MODELING AFTER ZION CITY

1907, July 27. Dowie's Right-Hand Gets Pinched for Misuse of Mails. Oregon Daily Journal.

1906, November 3. Kansas Faith Cure Worker Loses Out. Topeka Daily Capital.

1906, September 29. Want "Elijah's Robes." The Tennessean.

1907, September 24. Devil Dance at Zion City. Vancouver Daily.

242

CHARLES FOX PARHAM - AS "ELIJAH"
1906, November 3. Kansas Faith Cure Worker Loses Out. Topeka Daily Capital.

CHARLES FOX PARHAM - SODOMY
MacArthur, John. Tongue Tied Part 2. Accessed 2017, April 19 from
https://www.gty.org/library/Print/Blog/B131010.
Bunker, Michael. 2002. Swarm of Locusts – The Jesuit Attack on the Faith. Writers Club Press.

CHARLES FOX PARHAM - 1925 DOOMSDAY
Charles Fox Parham Facts. Accessed 2017, April 17. from
http://biography.yourdictionary.com/charles-fox-parham.

CHARLES FOX PARHAM - HOUSTON
Synan, Vinson. 1971. The Holiness-Pentecostal Tradition: Charismatic Movements in the
Twentieth Century. Wm. B. Erdmans Publishing Co.

CHARLES FOX PARHAM - KU KLUX KLAN
Goff, J.R., Fields White unto Harvest, Fayetteville, University of Arkansas Press, 1988.

JOHN ALEXANDER DOWIE - END OF LIFE
Dowie Is Stricken. 1905, September 30. Spokane Press.
Dowie Surrenders Leadership of his Church. 1905, December 18. San Francisco Call.

W. E. KIDSON:
Garett Healing Campaign on At Johnston Station. 1949, May 27. Enterprise Journal
Thousands Attend Vandalia "Faith Healing" Services. 1947, Jun 28. The Decatur Herald
Elect Church Officers. 1940, Nov 3. The Jackson Sun
New Officers Named by Pentecostal Ministers. 1930, Oct 25. St. Louis Star and Times.
Ministerial Body to Meet in Overland. 1965, Oct 9. St. Louis Post Dispatch
Pentecostal Conference. 1941, Mar 2. The Jackson Sun
Divine Healing Service Tonight at Convention. 1937, Oct 27. The Jackson Sun
Mrs. Cutkomp Rites Monday. 1963, Oct 20. The Times
Association to Convene. 1963, Oct 5. Arizona Republic
Graveside Services for Willis Infant. 1950, Mar 1. The Baytown Sun
Churchmen of the Pentecostal Faith in Annual Session Here. 1937, Oct 22. The Jackson Sun
Pentecostal Church Holds Conference in Vandalia. 1939, Nov 24. The Decatur Daily Review
Misc. Properties for Sale. 1942, Feb 15. The Times
Pentecostal Conference in Mission Study. 1937, Oct 24. The Jackson Sun
Bay Area Conference. 1960, Jun 25. Oakland Tribune
Churchmen to Meet. 1933, Aug 17. El Paso Times
Mrs. Cutkomp Funeral Today. 1963, Oct 21. The Times
Officers Named at Session of Pentecostal. 1940, Oct 30. The Jackson Sun
Revival of Power! 1961, Feb 25. Arizona Republic.
Brother Branham, the Faith Healer. 1947, Jul 6. St. Louis Post Dispatch Sun.
Crowd of 1500 at Pentecostal Services Here. 1937, Oct 25. The Jackson Sun
Opens Meeting. 1947, Apr 14. The Camden News
Pentecostal Body to Meet Here in Annual Session. 1929, Oct 13. The Times
Prayer Service in Roadhouse Church Oct 31. 1969, Oct 26. Jacksonville Journal Courier
International Ministerial Association 3 Great Days. 1960, Jun 25. The San Francisco Examiner
Harvest Festival at Full Gospel Church. 1963, Dec 5. Oakdale Leader

Pentecostal Church Holds Conference in Vandalia. 1934, Apr 12. The Jacksonville Daily Journal

Misc. News. 1952, Jun 3. Lubbock Evening Journal

Misc. Property Sales. 1942, Feb 25. The Times

Heirport. 1977, Nov 17. The Baytown Sun

Pentecostal Meeting Opens Here Tomorrow. 1940, Oct 23. The Jackson Sun

Church to Hold Annual Parley Here in October. 1940, Aug 1. The Jackson Sun

Pentecostal Officers to be Announced. 1937, Oct 26. The Jackson Sun

White. 1962, Feb 26. The Akron Beacon Journal

Revival at Pentecostal Church Begun by Houston Evangelist. 1952, Jun 8. Lubbock Avalanche Journal

Head Pentecostal Church Board. 1937, Oct 31. The Jackson Sun

New Officers Pentecostal Church Named. 1937, Oct 28. The Jackson Sun

CHAPTER 24

WILLIAM BRANHAM'S LOST 1947 SERMONS

"Most healings are of the gradual type[449]"

When William Branham connected with W. E. Kidson, a whirlwind of events created the perfect storm. The success of Branham's revivals of the 1930's and early 1940's was limited by the small crowds in mostly rural churches. By 1946, he was holding "healing revivals" all across the United States. In the fall of 1946, W. E. Kidson launched a "healing" campaign that would quickly change William Branham from a small-town preacher to an internationally recognized "faith healer".

When I thought about the "prophet's" early years as a "faith healer", in the "Message", I thought about late 1947 and 1948. We were told that an "angel" gave him his "gift of healing" in May of 1947, and that the 1947 availability of the tape recorder was "God's gift" to the "bride". There were only six recordings in 1947, five of them after November.[450] When the "prophet" described getting "new gadgets" for recording in April, I just assumed they weren't needed until November. I never considered that they might be replacing the old "gadgets".

The 1947 "healing" campaign trail began Jan 15 in Camden, Arkansas, at the Apostolic Tabernacle.[451] Nine back-to-back services

---

[449] Minister Holds Healing Services; Hundreds of Cures Are Reported. 1947, Sep 29. St. Louis Post Dispatch Mon. St
[450] The Table. Accessed 2020, May 17 from branham.org

were held. Six days later, the campaign made its way to Shreveport, Louisiana.[452] In a city where Roy Davis, William Upshaw, and W. E. Kidson were already familiar faces, the "prophet" packed 2000 people into Byrd High School. Reporters were eager to interview those "healed", but they were unable to find any who were actually cured. The "prophet" pronounced "healing" for those arriving in ambulances, but according to newspaper reporters, they left the meeting in those same ambulances. A blind woman was "healed" yet remained blind. According to the reporters,[453] promises of healing were accepted just as eagerly as an actual healing. They were only able to find one single person who even sounded remotely better, having a stomach trouble and later eating a hearty breakfast after being "healed".

The reporters had many opportunities to see a "miracle" performed. They were present as the "prophet" placed his hands on the sick and afflicted. But after watching the "healed" leave in the same condition they arrived, their reports were written with a very skeptical tone. One crippled woman tried to walk after being "healed", but nearly fell to the ground when she tried to walk. A cancer patient in a cot was pronounced "healed" but was back in the cot when he left for home. There were many who "claimed" their "healing", but none miraculously healed with a change in condition that was visible to the eye. Not a single person was actually healed in the meeting. Instead, they were sent home to "claim" healing.

Branham's next publicized meeting was in March, in Santa Rosa, California.[454] A week-long series of meetings was held at the Saturday Afternoon Clubhouse. By June, news spread through Pentecostal assemblies, throughout the United States and Canada. Pentecostals were expecting a "move from God" after the 1907 Azusa Street Revival and believed Branham's revivals held their answer to prayer. They placed "spiritual significance" on the 40 years from 1907 to 1947,[455] and decided that William Branham's sudden fame forty years later was destined by God. The number "40" is spiritually significant to some

[451] Great Healing Revival. 1946, Apr 25. St. Louis Dispatch
[452] Ailing Crowd Jams Byrd Auditorium Again. 1947, Jan 30. The Times
[453] 2,000 Crowd Byrd High to Hear 'Healer'. 1947, Jan 29. The Times
[454] Evangelist Here Tuesday. 1947 Mar 30. The Press Democrat
[455] Apostolic Church of Pentecost. 1947, Jun 14. The Vancouver Sun

Christians.[456]   Pentecostal ministers started spreading the news that Pentecost was "coming of age" and announced that the "prophet" was coming to Canada.

Shortly after the California meetings, the "prophet" held a healing revival in Vandalia, Illinois.[457] Reporters, still eager to find a "healing" to report, followed him to the meetings. From January to the end of June, they had seen many people listen to William Branham claim that they were "healed", yet none of the severe cases showed any signs of "miracle". Only a handful of "slightly healed" cases were reported that could be verified. They were questionable, at best.

One case of interest in the Vandalia meetings was Walker Beck, a boy nearly everyone that was present in the meetings recognized. The "prophet" would have never known that young Beck was familiar to the crowd when he pronounced him "healed" in the meeting. Walker Beck was severely injured in a horrific accident on Dec 6, 1938.[458] The car of an oilfield worker traveling at almost 80 mph struck Beck, throwing him 125 feet through the air. Beck was rendered both deaf and mute, and nearly died.

Nine years later in that Vandalia meeting, the "prophet" said that Beck was healed because he could utter the sound "dada".[459] This caught the attention of former magician James Randi, who recognized some of the strategies the "prophet" had used in his meetings. Randi noticed that they were similar to things he did during his stage act as a magician. Randi had built a reputation exposing frauds during the spiritualist movement and was collecting similarities between "faith healers" and stage magicians that he would later publish in a book. When the well-recognized Beck wasn't healed, it presented quite a problem for William Branham, W. E. Kidson, and the Branham campaigns. Apparently, William Branham claimed that Beck wasn't healed because he smoked a cigarette after the meeting[460] — a tactic I had earlier found that was also used by F. F. Bosworth. Both the

---

[456] The Number 40 in the Bible. Accessed 2020, May 17 from
https://www.guideposts.org/inspiration/miracles/gods-grace/the-number-40-in-the-bible
[457] Brother Branham, the Faith Healer. 1947, Jul 6. St. Louis Post Dispatch Sun.
[458] Auto Kills Fayette Boy. 1938, Dec 6. The Decatur Herald
[459] Randi, James. 1987. The Faith Healers
[460] Randi, James. 1987. The Faith Healers

reporters and Randi knew this wasn't much of an excuse for a man claiming to have been empowered with a "gift" from God to "heal".

Though the reporters present were unable to find any "healed", they were able to find people who "witnessed" healings in the meeting.[461] Some said that an eight-year-old mute was "healed" and that she was able to speak a few words after her "healing". Others said crossed eyes were straightened, and deaf were made to hear. One Rev. Borror reported several cases of healing, from abandoning crutches to cancers "falling out",[462] but the reporters following the campaign trail were still unable to find any verifiable healing. Not a single first-hand account from a person who was actually "healed" could be located.

Reporters continued attending the revivals, patiently waiting to report a "miracle". In fact, they watched 1100 of the 2500 people in the meeting go through one of the "healing" lines. The revival, watched very closely by reporters, ended without any visible miracle. I wondered, "If someone was healed in the meeting, why didn't the person healed tell the reporters and offer proof to validate their claim?"

Even with the lack of verifiable "healings", the excitement continued to grow and spread. Those who attended the "healing" revivals and witnessed people being pronounced "healed" were eager to tell others. From minister to minister, elder to elder, and church members to townspeople, news of this "prophet" from Jeffersonville, Indiana spread from coast to coast. Some people who attended the meetings did return claiming to be healed. One person claiming to be healed was Minister L. R. Mitchell's wife, who claimed to be cured of epilepsy, and her name was used in the newspapers for advertisement.[463] The paid newspaper advertisements, however, failed to mention those who left *without* healing. The advertisements were worded in such a way that it sounded like *anyone* could be healed, not just a handful of unverifiable cases.

In August, the "healing" revival moved through Saskatoon, Canada.[464] William Branham continued pronouncing "healing" on thousands of

---

461 Healer Ends Revival with More Sensational Cures. 1947, Jul 1. Journal Gazette
462 Branham claimed that cancer was a "demon" that could "fall out". Example: 1947, Dec 7. Experiences.
"That cancer turned white, fell off of his neck, and rolled over my feet."
463 By Way of Testimony. 1947, Jul 5. The Journal Times
464 At Apostolic Church. 1947, Aug 2. The Third Page.

people. Saskatoon reporters were able to find people to testify of their healing and suddenly it began to sound as if something miraculous *was* taking place. Mary Bruce claimed that she could speak better after the meeting. Another woman ate a regular meal after being healed of stomach trouble, and yet another claimed that she gained hearing in one deaf ear. In one of the meetings, William Branham claimed to have raised people from the dead in his hometown in Jeffersonville, Indiana — from the undertaker's parlor — causing a flurry of questions to the news media back home.

There were so many questions that the Jeffersonville Evening News published an advertisement to set the record straight. In no uncertain terms, the Jeffersonville News rejected Branham's claim as false, and denied ever having reported any such account. The Branham Campaign organizers were very clever in their advertising. They used the number of people pronounced "healed" by William Branham, not the actual number of *confirmed* "healings". Advertisements made statements like, "35,000 cases of healing have been wrought".[465] Jack Moore, from Shreveport, Louisiana, helped promote the Branham Campaigns.

At the end of August, the "prophet" left Saskatoon and toured through Calgary.[466] The Branham revivals had attracted so much attention and gained such a large following that the campaign team rented the Victoria Pavilion Exhibition Grounds to hold all the people. The revival had Calgary bursting at its seams! There were so many people that it was difficult to find hotels with vacancy.[467]

As the revival continued, the failed healings started to catch up with William Branham and his team. Mrs. Clyde Kidd, "healed" of tuberculosis, died in a Calgary hotel.[468] Newspaper reporters decided to investigate, and published their findings. When questioned, William Branham denied praying for the woman[469] who said he had "healed" her shortly before her death. But taxi records confirmed her visit to the meetings, placing his denial in question.

---

[465] Apostolic Church. 1947, Aug 2. Star Phoenix.
[466] Full Gospel Church. 1947, Aug 9. Calgary Herald.
[467] Tourists Flee Mountain Cold. 1947, Aug 27. Calgary Herald
[468] Vancouver Woman Dies After Claiming Faith Healing Cure. 1947, Aug 27. Vancouver Sun.
[469] Faith Healer Denies Praying for Woman. 1947, Aug 28. Vancouver Sun.

I found it odd when reading William Branham's response to the press. He said, *"I prayed for the sick individually at the pavilion and did not try to help to cure the audience en masse"*. I remembered several recordings where William Branham *did* pray for the audience after a "healing line",[470] and it was one of his common techniques. It was also surprising to read him using the words *"en masse"*, which was not a phrase that later versions of his "Kentucky" stage persona would have even known. All of the words used by William Branham during his early ministry were much different from the words which made up his later "Kentucky English".

After leaving Calgary, William Branham held meetings in St. Louis, Missouri. He teamed up with "Little" David Walker, a 13-year-old evangelist.[471] They advertised "signs", "miracles", and "wonders". In my opinion, the public following he attracted were more focused upon their ailments than they were upon the Bible. Matthew 16:4 described *"An evil and adulterous generation seeks for a sign"*, yet William Branham's campaign advertisements used big, bold words claiming, *"SIGNS"*, *"WONDERS"*, or *"MIRACLES"*. According to the advertisements, young David Walker preached the sermons, and the "prophet" held prayer lines after the meetings.

Reporters witnessed several people who showed visible signs of improvement, but not all were "miracles". The vast majority of "cures" were people being told to leave and find healing later. In an interview, William Branham told reporters that most "cures" were of the "gradual type" — meaning that the reason reporters were unable to find any people cured was because their healing was not instant.

> *Most of the cures reported at the meetings were of the gradual type. The Rev. Mr. Branham spent considerable time over the serious cases and announced in almost every case that "the demon" or "the spirit" which had been causing the illness and fled the afflicted body. He could tell this, he said, by vibrations he felt in his hand and through a change in color of the hand.*[472]

---

[470] Branham, William. 1951, Oct 3. Believest Thou This. "Pour over these people. Heal every one of them, Lord God, with Your great Divine power. May it sweep over this audience; in the Name of Jesus."
[471] Wm. Branham & The Atom. 1947, Sep 20, St. Louis Post Dispatch Sat.
[472] Minister Holds Healing Services; Hundreds of Cures Are Reported. 1947, Sep 29. St. Louis Post Dispatch

This was a side of the "prophet's" ministry that I'd never seen or heard of before. We were told that people were *instantly* healed,[473] and that thousands of crutches were carried away from the meetings by the truckloads![474]

When I thought about his "healing campaigns", I thought about "getting the 'Message' out to the people". We were told that the "healing" was only to attract the people to the "Message". Yet the boy preacher who traveled with William Branham was not old enough to know sound theology, and *he* was attracting people to the "healing"; he was giving the "message" during the sermon. It wasn't about the sermon; it was about the crowd!

In early November, the revival continued to Phoenix, Arizona,[475] where meetings were scheduled for eight Sundays straight. In the days between, William Branham held revivals as far away as Vancouver, British Columbia, in Canada. He would preach on Sunday[476] at Phoenix, Arizona, and then spend Wednesday through Saturday back in Vancouver. He also held meetings in the surrounding areas of each major event. While in Vancouver, he'd travel over 100 km to Chilliwack, British Columbia[477] for yet another series of revivals. Testimonies of healing continued to pour in, many of which were printed in local newspapers. But suddenly, newspaper reporters noticed something very unusual. Some of the people testifying that William Branham had healed them were repeats of previous "healings"![478]

A crippled Helen Gledhill, for instance, entered the "healing line", and was told that the "evil spirit" was cast out from her. She was "healed", but then returned to another meeting in a stretcher. Once again, she was "healed", walking from the room. Her mother, Ethel Gledhill, claimed that "the spirit" came back and crippled her. She entered the November revival, and was "healed" a second time. Her

Mon. St

[473] Branham, William. 1947, Dec 7. Experiences. "And God healed her instantly, right then"

[474] Branham, William. 1955, Nov 15. Blind Bartimaeus. "Seven truckloads of crutches and—and wheelchairs, and things that they had packed their loved ones on, was picked up off the grounds, after one prayer. Seven truckloads; to clean the grounds for the next meeting."

[475] Notice! Branham healing Services Returning to Phoenix Tomorrow. 1947, Nov 1. Arizona Republic

[476] Noted Evangelist. 1947, Nov 1. The Vancouver Sun

[477] Pentecostal Tabernacle. 1947, Nov 5. The Chilliwack Progress

[478] Girl 'Cured' Second Time by Healer, Only 'Miracle' Here. 1947, Nov 6. The Vancouver Sun

mother suffered from anemia and pneumonia and was confined to her home, unable to work. I wondered: was William Branham's campaign team paying the poor and needy to claim "healing"?

I started to compile a list of newspaper advertisements for meetings held by the Branham Campaigns, and compared it to the handful of sermons that we had access to hear. Just as I suspected, there were many, many sermons that we did not have access to hear. Also, as I suspected, many of them were before the "new gadgets for recording".

> 1946, Fall. Houston, TX. Gospel Tabernacle
> 1947, Jan 15. Camden, AR. Apostolic Tabernacle (19 sermons)
> 1947, February. Texas. (Locations Unknown)
> 1947, March 31. Santa Rosa, CA. Saturday Afternoon Clubhouse
> 1947, April 1. Santa Rosa, CA. Saturday Afternoon Clubhouse
> 1947, June 26. Vandalia, IL. Tent (8 sermons)
> 1947, July 3. Vandalia, IL. Vandalia High School
> 1947, July. Missouri. (Locations Unknown)
> 1947, July. Manitoba, Canada. (Locations unknown)
> 1947, July 25. Saskatoon, Saskatchewan. Apostolic Church (8 sermons)
> 1947, August. Edmonton, Alberta. (Locations unknown)
> 1947, August. Edmonton, Alberta. (Locations unknown)
> 1947, Aug 20. Calgary, Alberta. Victoria Pavilion (7 sermons)
> 1947, Sept 21. St. Louis, MO. Kiel Auditorium (8 sermons)
> 1947, Nov 4. Vancouver, BC. St. Giles United Church (4 sermons)
> 1947, Nov 9. Phoenix, AZ. Shrine Auditorium (7 sermons)

I knew that I would never find them all, yet I had identified over seventy sermons preached in 1947, not even counting all the church invitations mentioned in the newspaper reports. That number also didn't count any of the meetings from the previous year of the same revival tour, which started in the fall of 1946. The wire tape recording was widely popular in the United States in 1946 but was also available for his 1945 meetings. Where were those recordings? As part of the "prophet's" income, I couldn't imagine them being "lost" or "misplaced" — they would have been recorded, mass-produced, and sold. The master copies of those sermons would have been kept under lock-and-key by the campaign team; it was yet another source of income. Were these sermons being removed to conceal failed healings discovered by news reporters?

It was time to start investigating The Voice of Healing, the newsletter publishing company that William Branham created to advertise his own healing revival meetings. The publication seemed to have been a critical part of the creation of his stage persona, yet in the "Message", we barely even discussed them. Many people had never seen a single issue. I thought to myself, "Maybe those issues held some clue as to why the early sermons were erased from existence!"

1946-1947 HEALING CAMPAIGNS:

Great Healing Revival. 1946, Apr 25. St. Louis Dispatch
Ailing Crowd Jams Byrd Auditorium Again. 1947, Jan 30. The Times
Vandalia Healer Near Collapse. 1947, Jul 1. The Decatur Herald
Branham to Hold Meet Elsewhere. 1947, Jan 30. The Times
Opens Meeting. 1947, Apr 14. The Camden News
Apostolic Tabernacle. 1947, Jan 25. The Camden News
Healing Services in Liberty Hall. 1947, Dec 18. El Paso Times
Branham Healing Campaign Stirs the City. 1947, Aug 23. Calgary Herald
Noted Evangelist. 1947, Nov 1. The Vancouver Sun
Tourists Flee Mountain Cold. 1947, Aug 27. Calgary Herald
Branham Campaign Prayer Meetings. 1947, Oct 11. The Vancouver Sun
Notice! Branham healing Services Returning to Phoenix Tomorrow. 1947, Nov 1. Arizona
    Republic
1Boy Evangelist Flails at Sin and Wins 100 to Repentance. 947. Sep 28, St. Louis Post Dispatch
    Sun.
Prayer Meetings for Noted Minister's Visit. 1947, Oct 11. The Vancouver Sun
By Way of Testimony. 1947, Jul 5. The Journal Times
Rev. William Branham. 1947, Jul 26. Star Phoenix
Healer Ends Revival with More Sensational Cures. 1947, Jul 1. Journal Gazette
2,000 Crowd Byrd High to Hear 'Healer'. 1947, Jan 29. The Times
Faith Healer Meeting Goes to Liberty Hall. 1947, Dec 18. El Paso Herald Post
Girl 'Cured' Second Time by Healer, Only 'Miracle' Here. 1947, Nov 6. The Vancouver Sun
Faith Healer Denies Praying for Woman. 1947, Aug 28. The Vancouver Sun
Opens Meeting. 1947, Apr 14. The Camden News
Full Gospel Church. 1947, Aug 9. Calgary Herald
Minister Holds Healing Services; Hundreds of Cures Are Reported. 1947, Sep 29, St. Louis Post
    Dispatch
Apostolic Church of Pentecost. 1947, Jun 14. The Vancouver Sun
Evangelist Here Monday, Tuesday. 1947 Mar 30. The Press Democrat
Pentecostal Tabernacle. 1947, Nov 5. The Chilliwack Progress
Rev. Wm. Branham in Salem Nov. 18 thru 21. 1947, Nov 15. Statesman Journal
Healer to Hold Services Here. 1947, Dec 14. El Paso Times
Miracle Claimed Here. 1947, July 15. Winnipeg Free Press
Zion Church. 1947, Sep 27. Winnipeg Free Press

VANDALIA INVESTIGATION:

Randi, James. 1987. The Faith Healers
Auto Kills Fayette Boy. 1938, Dec 6. The Decatur Herald
Church Debate in Vandalia. 1923, Dec 20. The Decatur Herald
Continue Revival Meetings. 1937, Apr 18. The Decatur Daily Review
Presbyterians Plan Session in Vandalia. 1935, Jan 19. The Decatur Daily Review
Thousands Attend Vandalia 'Faith Healing' Services. 1947, Jun 28. The Decatur Herald
Revival Service. 1937, Apr 14. The Decatur Daily Review
Pentecostal Church Holds Conference in Vandalia. 1939, Nov 24. The Decatur Daily Review
Presbyters to Open Session in Vandalia. 1935, Jan 19. The Decatur Herald
Revival Meet. 1937, Jun 4. The Decatur Herald
Brother Branham, the Faith Healer. 1947, Jul 6. St. Louis Post Dispatch Sun.
Pentecostal Church Holds Conference in Vandalia. 1939, Nov 24. The Decatur Herald

'LITTLE' DAVID WALKER:

Little David Miracle Boy Preacher. Accessed 2019, Jan 23 from:
http://www.dealpentecostal.co.uk/Little%20David%20Miracle%20Boy%20Preacher.pdf
Boy from Heaven? 1948, May 1. Long Beach Independent
"Little David" Manager Removed by Court. 1949, May 26. The Alexandria Times Tribune
Boy Preacher Overworked by Minister, Parents Charge. 1948, Apr 29. The Courier Journal
Judge Ousts Manager of Boy Evangelist. 1949, May 26. The Akron Beacon Journal
Wm. Branham & The Atom. 1947, Sep 20, St. Louis Post Dispatch Sat.
Boy Evangelist in Custody Fight. 1948, Apr 29. The Edwardsville Intelligencer
Boy Evangelist Flails at Sin and Wins 100 to Repentance. 1947, Sep 28. St. Louis Post Dispatch Sun.
Parents File Suit to Regain Custody of Boy Evangelist. 1948, May 17. The Fresno Bee The Republican
7,500 Persons Hear 13-Year-Old-Preacher Deliver Sermon Here. 1948, Sep 29. St. Louis Star and Times Mon.
Minister Holds Healing Services; Hundreds of Cures Are Reported. 1947, Sep 29. St. Louis Post Dispatch Mon. St
Mother Asks Custody of Boy Evangelist Son. 1948, Jun 17. The News Herald
"Little David" Parents Endorse Management of Raymond G. Hoekstra. 1949, Apr 9. The Indianapolis Star
Boy Evangelist. 1948, Apr 29. The Edwardsville Intelligencer

CHAPTER 25

WILLIAM BRANHAM'S
VOICE OF HEALING

"Not to the exclusion of other evangelical truths[479]"

One of my favorite places for a family vacation is just off the coast of Florida. You can almost taste the air as it blows across the salty ocean waters. I could spend hours upon hours sitting in the sand in the shade listening to the rhythmic sound of the waves crashing in. For me, there is healing in every single part of the experience, from the cleansing saltwater air to the soothing sounds of the seagulls and the refreshing rays of the sun. Something about the water brings a feeling of peace, no matter how tightly wound I become from the stress of life. I used to laugh at these televangelists and "healers" who held big meetings along Florida's coast. I knew what they were up to! I often thought, "Our 'prophet' would never do that!" But I was surprised as I started examining William Branham's early rise to fame, and even more surprised as I started examining names of those who joined Branham's revival trail and the locations that they chose in sermons we no longer had access to hear.

There were many men who joined William Branham in his early campaigns. They sat on the stage with him as the group toured. They were religious entertainers on stage, like a carnival moving from town to

---

[479] Inter-Evangelical Policy of the Branham Campaigns. 1948, Apr. The Voice of Healing.

town. Each one of them had a history just as interesting and "supernatural" as William Branham's own "Life Story", and they made big money by selling their own special version of religious entertainment. Many of them cross-promoted, and William Branham bragged of their "supernatural" powers in his publications. Yet most of them never joined the "Message". I wondered, "Why?"

On July 6, 1947, the St. Louis Post-Dispatch published their investigative report on William Branham's "healing" revival. Reporters who were increasingly skeptical over the lack of "miracles" in Branham's meetings focused their attention to the failed healings. Suddenly, just days after their investigative report, the St. Louis Post-Dispatch changed their attention to a new "Prophet of Healing".[480] Avak Hagopian, whose world-wide "healing" fame drew crowds of thousands, had just landed in Palm Springs, California. He came to the United States after holding massive "healing" meetings in Iran, Cairo, New York, and Los Angeles, California.

Avak Hagopian was brought to America by a millionaire named Krikor Arakelian to heal his son, but as thousands of people poured into Palm Springs seeking their own healing, the scene turned into complete chaos. For months on end, Avak prayed for Arakelian's paralyzed son while a multitude of other people gathered in Palm Springs for their chance with the "healer". Avak stayed in the luxurious home of the Arakelian family, "treating" only 30 people per day. The situation grew so dire that the police force had to call in reserves to bring order back to the city. Bars started selling food, peddlers opened food stands, and still there was not enough food for the multitude of people. Yet as Avak "healed" the multitude, and many claimed "healing", Arakelian's son remained crippled. Avak doubled his appointments, "healing" 60 people per day.[481] Then, after a few weeks, he took a vacation in the mountains.[482]

Hundreds of people camped outside the Arakelian home during Avak's mountain retreat. Demand for Avak was so great in the United States that the U.S. government got involved. Representative George

---

[480] Avak - The New Prophet of Healing. 1947, Jun 29. St. Louis Post Dispatch Sun.
[481] Appointments for Avak Number 700. 1947, May 23. Tucson Daily Citizen.
[482] Weary Healer Plans Vacation. 1947, Jun 6. The San Bernardino County Sun

Smathers introduced new laws[483] intended to extend Avak's visa. Yet still, even with all the "healing frenzy", Arakelian's son remained crippled.

Tom Kardashian, Kim Kardashian's great grandfather, sponsored Avak's tour through the U.S. and Canada.[484] Tom pledged to build a temple in Los Angeles for Avak. I was a little surprised when I found that William Branham admitted that the same people sponsoring Avak Hagopian had "sent up in Indiana" to sponsor his own "healing" tour.[485] I was even more surprised when I found photographs of the "prophet" touring with Avak Hagopian. The "prophet" was wearing an expensive suit and had slicked-back hair, a far cry from the "Kentucky Hillbilly" persona he later would incorporate into his ministry. Sadly, Arakelian's son was never cured by either Avak or William Branham. The family eventually moved to a secluded area, where Avak could "rest", and the boy's condition was never again reported.

William Branham continued to tour the United States and Canada, starting the year in Miami, Florida with "Little David". The Branham / Walker meetings were timed perfectly with Avak's healing tour and together, they took photographs for an article no longer available to people in the "Message".[486] After Miami, the Walker / Branham tour made its way to Tampa, Florida. Just as they did during their meetings in Indianapolis at the Cadle Tabernacle, in St. Louis, and in Miami; the dynamic "healing" duo packed the auditorium. But as young David Walker was entering his "Divine Healing" career, William Branham was at the height of his own career and was already in very high demand. The tour continued through Pensacola, Florida; and William Branham's campaign team advertised William Branham as America's "Voice of Healing".[487] Just days later, that title became the name of the "prophet's" newsletter.

---

[483] Introduce Law to Aid Avak. 1948, Aug 10. The Desert Sun

[484] Oppenheimer, Jerry. 2017. The Kardashians: An American Drama.

[485] Branham, William. 1947, Nov 2. The Angel of God. "They flew a boy, who prays for the sick, by the name of Avak. They brought him from Cairo over to pray for a man by the name of Arakelian. The same time they sent for him, they sent up in Indiana and had me to come to a woman with cancer."

[486] Branham, William. 1948, Mar 4. The Angel of God. "Many of you has heard of Avak. You know, they come over here that time. Well, we've been trying to meet each other for some time. We met a few days ago in Florida, and put our pictures together and said, "...?... American...?... consults Divine healing."

[487] The Truth of Divine Healing. 1948, Mar 30. Pensacola News. Journal. "Rev. Branham has preached to capacity audiences all over this continent. He has the voice of healing".

The Voice of Healing publication was originally created to promote the William Branham Campaigns. William Branham was the publisher, and it was printed from Shreveport, Louisiana. But the first issues of the publication did not mention Avak or "Little" David anywhere in the articles contained within. Apparently, the first issue was created as an attempt to reorganize and rebrand the Branham campaigns and its newsletter; the first issue contained legal verbiage intended to cease all previous committees and publications. I wondered: "Where are the copies of the previous publications?" And why were David Walker and Avak Hagopian not included in this new publication?

> *After much prayer, Brother Branham has decided to form a committee which should direct the policy of the Branham healing campaigns and the publication of The Voice of Healing. This will supersede all previous arrangements. This committee, besides Rev. Branham, includes Rev. Jack Moore and Rev. Gordon Lindsay. All correspondence concerning campaigns should be directed to Branham Healing Campaigns, Box 4097, Shreveport, Louisiana.[488]*

After the Pensacola meetings, Rev. F. F. Bosworth joined Branham's revival tours.[489] Bosworth, already well-known for his own "faith healing" career, brought yet another attraction to the meetings. From Florida, the group headed to Kansas City, Kansas, where they filled the Memorial Hall. Then they moved on to the small town of Sedalia, Missouri, where they packed the Convention Hall at Liberty Park. The newspapers made it sound as if a convoy of ambulances followed the group as they went from town to town.[490] Ern Baxter, who attended the revivals in Canada, joined the campaign.[491] From there, the tour went through Oregon, landing at Eugene from May 18-23. Then, after Eugene, William Branham took a break from the revival tours.[492]

---

[488] Inter-Evangelical Policy of the Branham Campaigns. 1948, Apr. The Voice of Healing.
[489] Rev. And Mrs. F. F. Bosworth Work with Branham Party. 1948, May. The Voice of Healing.
[490] Meeting Draws Large Crowds. 1948, Apr 18. The Sedalia Democrat. "while others have been brought by ambulance from out of town"
[491] Evangelistic Tabernacle. 1948, May 8. The Vancouver Sun
[492] Brother Branham Takes Extended Rest. 1948, July. The Voice of Healing.

The fourth issue of Voice of Healing contained an article that described William Branham's "early part of his healing ministry". I was still surprised that he even had a "healing" ministry before April 1947.

> *Rev. William Branham has returned to his home to rest for a period of time. So great has been his burden for the sick and the suffering that it is difficult for him to withdraw from the multitudes when there are so many needing his ministry. In the early part of his healing ministry, our brother would pray for the sick till one or two in the morning, or until he would drop from sheer exhaustion.*[493]

The version of the "Message" I was raised to believe included an "angel" coming the "very day" that Israel became a nation. Reading this issue of The Voice of Healing and learning that the modern State of Israel was born May 14, 1948,[494] it was difficult to trust anything that I had been told. Articles in the early issues of The Voice of Healing had even more confirmations that Branham's ministry started long before the stage persona we knew described, and more confirmation that history had purposefully been erased.

During his rest "at home" in July, the Jeffersonville Evening News tried to contact William Branham to verify some claims that he had made during the revival meetings in Canada. William Branham had claimed to raise a man from the dead — from the undertaker's parlor — in Jeffersonville, Indiana. The local newspapers in the small town, intimately familiar with local events, knew this was not true. According to the Jeffersonville Evening News, William Branham was "absent" and a "substitute minister" was conducting services.

> *The Evening News yesterday afternoon received an unusual telegram from Ted Shrader, reporter for the Winnipeg Tribune, Winnipeg Manchester, Canada, which it reproduces herewith:*

---

[493] Brother Branham Takes Extended Rest. 1948, July. The Voice of Healing.
[494] The State of Israel Is Born. 1948, May 14. The Palestine Post.

REVEREND WILLIAM BRANHAM OF JEFFERSONVILLE CLAIMS THAT HE RAISED A MAN FROM THE DEAD IN A JEFFERSONVILLE UNDERTAKING PARLOR. CAN. YOU PLEASE WIRE DETAILS WHETHER OR NOT THIS IS TRUE? WHAT WAS MAN'S NAME? CAUSE OF DEATH? NAME OF MORGUE? WHEN IT HAPPENED? (SIGNED) TED SHRADER WINNIPEG TRIBUNE

This newspaper keeps abreast of local news in Jeffersonville and Clark County, and has been doing so for nearly 75 years, but nowhere in its annals appears such a startling occurrence, and the WINNIPEG newspaper was sent a wire saying that we could not substantiate this reported phenomenon.

Stories of the healing powers of Rev. Branham, practiced in different parts of the country, have come to this newspaper. Crowds flock to be healed by him in every city he has visited, according to accounts. It is understood that he still retains his position as head of Branham's Tabernacle located at 804 Penn Street, where a substitute minister is conducting services in his absence.[495]

The media frenzy continued, especially when William Branham stopped touring. A rumor quickly spread that Branham had died, and reporters from all over the country were contacting Jeffersonville news media for information concerning his death. The local news media was well informed about the "prophet's" schedule, not only by the campaign advertisements but also from the numerous people contacting reporters as Branham went from city to city claiming to heal the sick and raise the dead. When rumors spread that he himself had died, the Jeffersonville Evening News issued a correction.

REV. WILLIAM BRANHAM IS VERY MUCH ALIVE
The Associated Press was today checking a rumor that Rev. William Branham, Jeffersonville faith healer, had died unexpectedly while on

---

[495] Rev. Branham in the News. 1947, Jul 23. Jeffersonville Evening News.

tour. Inquiry disclosed the Rev. Mr. Branham to be very much alive.
He was preparing to leave for Chicago, Illinois, to fill a week's
engagement of faith healing lectures.[496]

There was very little that reporters could do to stop the momentum
of the Branham campaigns. The revival was quickly growing. I was
surprised as I noticed the ministers joining in the revival tours. Some of
them were familiar faces whose ministries were launched by the
Branham Campaigns, yet previously I had no idea how closely
connected they were in the "prophet's" early ministry. It was news to
me how much they promoted each other to establish their careers. Some
of them were on the editorial staff of his newsletter, The Voice of
Healing. There were so many pieces to the puzzle coming together that
it was almost unbelievable!

The most surprising part of my research was learning that the
Kardashian family were connected to William Branham's early ministry
and learning that close relatives of the Kardashian patriarchs continued
to work with and promote William Branham's revival campaigns and
ministry for decades. I wanted to know more about this family, the
family history, and why they would suddenly decide to take interest in a
Jeffersonville, Indiana preacher who claimed to be an uneducated
Kentucky hillbilly!

---

[496] Rev. Branham Is Very Much Alive. 1948, Apr 26. Jeffersonville Evening News.

AVAK HAGOPIAN:

Rawiszer: church is really a cult. 1985, Feb 14. Rhinebeck NY Gazette

Church or cult? Poughkeepsie Journal. 1985, Feb 17

Large Crowd Waits to See Avak. 1947, Jun 4. Santa Cruz Sentinel

Crowd Awaits A Miracle as Faith Healer Prays Over Paralytic Sufferer. 1947, May 12. La Grande Observer

Healer. 1947, May 24. The San Bernardino County Sun

Awaits Outcome. 1948, Apr 20. The Gaffney Ledger

Shocked by Hagopian. 1985, Mar 6. Poughkeepsie Journal

Church Leader Says He Talks with God. 1985, Feb 17. Poughkeepsie Journal

In Palm Springs. 1947, Jun 7. The Logan Daily News

Lure of valley water once prompted international influx of ill. 2006, Mar 8. The Desert Sun

Avak to Tour, Heal by Faith. 1947, Oct 13. The Eugene Guard

Death Takes Well Known Village Man. 1951, Mar 2. The Desert Sun

Persian Faith Healer Must Leave or Face Deportation. 1954, Aug 27. The News Tribune

Appointments for Avak Number 700. 1947, May 23. Tucson Daily Citizen

In Brief. 1947, Nov 3. The Morning Call

Permit Sought. 1948, Aug 4. Medford Mail Tribune

Introduce Law to Aid Avak. 1948, Aug 10. The Desert Sun

E. 1947, Oct 14. P. Sick Around Avak 'Faith Healer', at Union Depot. El Paso Herald Post

Healer Who Sees Visions of Christ Visits Syracuse. 1949, Nov 30. The Post Standard

Crowd Swarms Around Faith Healer. 1947, Jun 2. Cumberland Evening Times

Death Takes Arakelian, Wine Maker. 1951, Feb 27. The Los Angeles Times

Avak Accepts City on Faith. 1947, Oct 31. The Minneapolis Star

No Housing for People Who Seek Faith Healer. 1947, May 21. The Plain Speaker

St. 1947, Jun 29, Avak - The New Prophet of Healing. Louis Post Dispatch Sun.

Agents Arrest Avak. 1948, Apr 7. Charge Visa Violated. The Tennessean

To Leave Country. 1948, Apr 5. The Petaluma Argus Courier

Healer 'Lays On' Restoring Hands. 1947, May 9. The Daily Herald

People: John B Murphy, Back Home. 1947, Jul 14. Oakland Tribune

Faith Healer Enroute To Florida for Visit. 1948, Jan 18. The Decatur Herald

Avak, the Miracle Healer. 1947, May 13. The Decatur Herald

Avak Prays Over Invalid. 1947, May 8. The Minneapolis Star

Weary Healer Plans Vacation. 1947, Jun 6. The San Bernardino County Sun

Faith Healer Afraid to Return to Native Iran. 1948, Apr 30. El Paso Herald Post

Immigration Service Has No Faith In 'Faith Healer's' Trip. 1947, Nov 29. The Indianapolis Star

Faith Healer Holds Public Service. 1947, Sep 10. The Palm Beach Post

Avak to 'Sightsee' in Twin Cities. 1947, Oct 30. The Minneapolis Star

News Cameras Record Events in Various Places of the World. 1947, Sep 12. The Chronicle Telegram

Faith Healer Tells Methods. 1947, May 7. The Decatur Daily Review

Sick Flock to Faith Healer. 1947, May 22. The Minneapolis Star

Faith Healer. 1947, May 31. The Courier Journal

'Healer', Patient Remain in Retreat. 1947, Jul 6. Argus Leader

E. 1947, Oct 14. P. Sick Seek Avak, the Healer. El Paso Herald Post

Avak Prays. 1947, May 10. Argus Leader

Iranian Healer Says U. 1947, Nov 7. S. Refuses Visa Extension. The Indianapolis Star

Faith Healer Delays Rest, Starts Cures. 1947, May 11. The Press Democrat

Avak Worried Can't Practice in Mexico If He Gets There. 1947, Nov 29. The Decatur Herald

Victory for Faith Healer. 1947, May 27. Traverse City Record Eagle
Faith Healer Grows Weary. 1947, May 30. Reno Gazette Journal
Visa Extended for Faith Healer. 1948, Jan 15. Reno Gazette Journal
Armenian Faith Healer Ordered Out of U. 1947, Nov 6. The Edwardsville Intelligencer
Faith Healer Avak Contemplates Own Destiny as Mexico Withholds Visa. 1947, Nov 30. Oakland
    Tribune
Avak, Faith Healer, Tries Mass Cures of Sick, Maimed. 1947, Sep 22. The Pittsburgh Press
Village May Again Become Avak's Home. 1948, Nov 12. The Desert Sun
Faith Healer's Prayers Aid Crippled. 1947, Sep 3. The Rhinelander Daily News
Avak To Await Divine Call. 1947, Nov 8. The Bakersfield Californian
Avak, Two Servants Are Arrested on Deportation Charges. 1948, Apr 6. The Fresno Bee The
    Republican
Avak Presents $2952 As Offering to Chest. 1947, Oct 5. The Los Angeles Times
Mystic to Hold Faith Healings. 1947, Sep 17. The Daily Herald
Avak Arrives in California. 1947, Jul 15. The Evening Sun
Deportation Hearing to Begin for Avak. 1948, Apr 9. Tallahassee Democrat
Throngs of Sick Seek Armenian Faith Healer. 1947, May 19. The Morning News
Persian Mystic Must Leave U. 1954, Aug 28. S. The San Bernardino County Sun
Avak and Patient in Secret Retreat. 1947, Jun 10. The Des Moines Register
Avak Will Go to Mexico. 1947, Nov 9. The Honolulu Advertiser
Healer's Success Averred. 1947, Nov 19. Medford Mail Tribune

1948 BRANHAM CAMPAIGNS:
The Full Gospel Mission. 1948, Apr 17. The Lethbridge Herald
Little David: Phenomenal Boy Preacher. 1948, Jan 20. The Miami News
Branham Healing Campaign. 1948, May 16. The Eugene Guard
Evangelistic Tabernacle. 1948, May 8. The Province
Little David. 1948, Feb 15. The Tampa Tribune
The Greatest Evangelical Meetings. 1948, Mar 30. Pensacola News Journal
Meeting Draws Large Crowds. 1948, Apr 18. The Sedalia Democrat
Branham Healing Campaign. 1948, May 16. The Eugene Guard
Little David. 1948, Feb 14. The Tampa Times
Evangelistic Tabernacle. 1948, May 8. The Vancouver Sun
The Greatest Evangelical Meetings. 1948, Mar 31. Pensacola News Journal
Remember These Dates. 1948, Mar 26. The Sedalia Democrat
Meeting Draws Large Crowds. 1948, Apr 23. Sedalia Weekly Democrat

1948 ISRAEL:
The State of Israel Is Born. 1948, May 14. The Palestine Post.

WILLIAM BRANHAM'S 1947 "GIFT OF HEALING" CLAIM
Branham, William. 1954, July 18. The Great Coming Revival and the Outpouring of the Holy
    Spirit.
Branham, William. 1955, Jan 9. Beginning and Ending of the Gentile Dispensation.
Branham, William. 1959, Oct 4. Who Is This?
Branham Claims "Gift of Healing" came in 1946:
Branham, William. 1954, Aug 9. The Manifestation of thy Resurrection to the People of this Day
Branham, William. 1961, July 30. Gabriel's Instructions to Daniel.

THE VOICE OF HEALING:

264

Branham, William. 1948, April. Inter-Evangelical Policy of the Branham Campaigns. The Voice of Healing.

Branham, William. 1948, April. How the Gift Came to Me. The Voice of Healing.

Branham, William. 1948, April. Eighteen Days of Branham Meetings in the Northwest Yield Great Results. The Voice of Healing.

Branham, William. 1948, April. List of Staff. The Voice of Healing.

Moore, Jack. 1948, April. Miami Meetings. The Voice of Healing.

Branham, William. 1948, April. Schedule of the Branham Healing Campaigns. The Voice of Healing.

Branham, William. 1948, May. Branham Campaigns Stir Pensacola and Kansas City. The Voice of Healing.

Branham, William. 1948, May. Rev. and Mrs. F. F. Bosworth Work with Branham Party. The Voice of Healing.

Branham, William. 1948, May. Kansas City Times Gives Fine Report of Branham Meeting. The Voice of Healing.

Branham, William, Gordon, Lindsay. 1948, May. The Ministry of Angels and the Appearance of the Angel to William Branham. The Voice of Healing.

Branham, William. 1948, May. Three Wonderful Days at Sedalia, MO. The Voice of Healing.

Branham, William. 1948, May. Branham Party News. The Voice of Healing.

Branham, William. 1948, May. The Rumor of Brother Branham's Death. The Voice of Healing.

Branham, William. 1948, May. Rev. Oral Roberts Present at Kansas City Meeting. The Voice of Healing.

Branham, William. 1948, May. Rev. J. Ern Baxter to Become Canadian Editor of the Voice of Healing. The Voice of Healing.

1948, July. Five Great Days in Eugene, Ore. The Voice of Healing.

1948, July. Brother Branham Takes Extended Rest. The Voice of Healing.

CHAPTER 26

WILLIAM BRANHAM AND THE KARDASHIAN FAMILY

"They flew a boy, who prays for the sick, by the name of Avak. They brought him from Cairo over to pray for a man by the name of Arakelian. The same time they sent for him, they sent up in Indiana and had me to come[497]"

From 1915 to 1917, the Ottoman Empire systematically exterminated 1.5 million citizens living within their empire. It became known as the Armenian Genocide,[498] because most people killed were of Armenian descent. Like the Jewish people during the Holocaust; men, women, and children were starved, beaten, and killed at the hand of Ottoman leaders. The Ottoman oppressors treated the people like animals, forcing them to plead and beg for survival. The Turkish government claimed to be "deporting" the Armenians, but it was later learned they were removing food, shelter, and means for survival. They were not deporting them; they were effectively wiping the Armenians from existence.

In Constantinople, three hundred Armenian leaders, writers, skilled thinkers, and working professionals were murdered in the streets; while five thousand of the lower-class Armenians were slaughtered in their own neighborhoods. Afterward, Turkish soldiers began to systematically find, torture, and destroy all remaining Armenians. The

[497] Branham, William. 1947, Nov 2. The Angel of God.
[498] Kifner, John (7 December 2007). "Armenian Genocide of 1915: An Overview". The New York Times.

Ottoman Empire feared the Armenians would collaborate with the Russians, and used military force to prevent Russian assistance. In the aftermath, the Armenian population was almost completely obliterated. Only those who fled the country stood any chance at survival.

A group of Armenian Christians were already familiar with exile and managed to survive. According to historians, they were religious rebels, rejecting the orthodox faith of their homeland. Their sect believed in modern-day prophets and migrated to California after a person claiming to operate a prophetic gift convinced them to leave. Shortly before the First World War broke out, they boarded the SS Brandenburg for America.

Among these Armenian exiles were the Kardaschoffs, who would later become known as the Kardashians.[499] In September of 1913, Tatos Kardashian, his wife Hanna, and their family came to the United States for refuge. After arriving, Tatos officially filed a declaration of intent to become a U.S. citizen.[500] Shortly thereafter, in 1923, he filed his petition for naturalization.[501] He had migrated from Kars, Russia, and was a Los Angeles citizen. Once naturalized, he legally changed his name from "Tatos" to "Tom" and embraced his new American life.

Tatos was married to Hanna Shakarian, the aunt of Demos Shakarian. [502] Demos Shakarian was a long-time, close friend and business associate of William Branham. [503] The Kardashians and Shakarians had sponsored Avak Hagopian[504] to come from Iran to "heal" Krikor Arakelian's son, and they were connected to the Arakelian family through the marriage of Arthur Kardashian. Krikor was the "godfather" of the vineyards, with connections to Chicago – yet another of many trails leading back to Chicago. More than one thousand

---

[499] Oppenheimer, Jerry. 2017. The Kardashians: An American Drama.

[500] Declaration of Intention: Tatos Kardashian. 1913, Sept 30. U.S. Dept. of Labor.

[501] Petition for Naturalization: Tatos Kardashian. 1913, Oct 6. U. S. Dept. of Labor.

[502] Oppenheimer, Jerry. 2017. The Kardashians: An American Drama. "His son, Demos Shakarian, took over the business but would earn his greatest fame as a Pentecostal evangelist who believed in miracles and healings, and in the early sixties would found a global organization for Pentecostal Christian businessmen called the Full Gospel Businessmen's Fellowship International.

[503] Branham, William. 1957, Jun 14. The Queen of the South. "My good friend, Brother Demos Shakarian"

[504] Oppenheimer, Jerry. 2017. The Kardashians: An American Drama. "Earlier, in the late forties, Robert and Tom's grandfather, Tatos Kardashian, then the family patriarch who dominated the Kardashian household, had helped sponsor and pledged to build a temple in Los Angeles for an Armenian faith healer and mystic, twenty-year-old robed and bearded Avak Hagopian.

Armenians in the San Joaquin Valley considered Arakelian to be their leader. [505] Sadly, even all his wealth and power could not heal his son.

Learning from historian authors that the Kardashian family had ties to white supremacy, [506] I began to examine this unusual connection to William Branham's ministry in light of the impact that Roy E. Davis would have had in the state for both white supremacists and fundamentalist religion. The Kardashians placed unusual emphasis on modern-day prophecy, [507] which was a key point in Roy E. Davis' criminal trial in the mid-1940s. Davis' defense of impersonating a Federal Agent, mail fraud, concealed weapon, and swindling was ... "prophecy". He had publicized his "vision" story, claiming he went into a trance while eating a peach and claimed that the "vision" he received gave him a "great desire" to rescue parentless children and give them a home.

> *After I finished the peach, there was a vision. I saw a diffused view of the orphanage. A great desire arose in me. I wanted to see the parentless children have a home — a real home*[508]

Roy Davis and former Congressman William D. Upshaw had convinced several people to fund an "orphanage", which became known as the Ussher-Davis Children's Orphanage. Based upon the F.B.I. Documents I had reviewed, it became apparent that Roy Davis was raising funding to launch the Third Wave of the Ku Klux Klan.

This "vision" would have been very popular in Los Angeles, especially within the Armenian community. From the descriptions of the religious sect that the Kardashian family was involved with, it appears that the Kardashians' and Shakarians' religious views would have aligned with Davis' Pentecostal extremism. But Davis' published propaganda did not just include religious views, it also mixed religion

---

[505] Grape Leader Battles Suit. 1931, Feb 2. San Francisco Examiner.

[506] Oppenheimer, Jerry. 2017. The Kardashians: An American Drama. "For a time Kardashian had actually teamed up with another financial backer of the mystic, one Clem Davies, an avowed anti-Semite, whose books included such titles as *The Racial Streams of Mankind.*"

[507] Oppenheimer, Jerry. 2017. The Kardashians: An American Drama. "about the kind of prophetic word that convinced the family to get out of Armenia"

[508] Orphanage Said to be Result of Pastor's Vision. 1944, Apr 20. The San Bernardino County Sun

with white supremacy. I wondered, "Would the Kardashian family have supported a proponent of white supremacy?

I found a book describing the Kardashian family and their history. According to Jerry Oppenheimer's *The Kardashians: An American Drama*, this would have been aligned with the views of the Kardashians at that time. The Kardashian family were strong supporters of Rev. Clem Davies, an outspoken white supremacist. Interestingly, Clem Davies and members of the Kardashian family also worked with Avak Hagopian.

The sprawling Kardashian family had arrived in America from their village in Armenia in the early 1900s. It was in California where Tatos Kardashian met his future wife, Hamas Shakarian, the matriarch and the great-grandmother of the famous Kardashian siblings. Hamas's brother, Isaak Shakarian, had made a fortune in the dairy business in Downey, California. His son, Demos Shakarian, took over the business but would earn his greatest fame as a Pentecostal evangelist who believed in miracles and healings, and in the early sixties would found a global organization for Pentecostal Christian businessmen called the Full Gospel Businessmen's Fellowship International. {...}
Earlier, in the late forties, Robert and Tom's grandfather, Tatos Kardashian, then the family patriarch who dominated the Kardashian household, had helped sponsor and pledged to build a temple in Los Angeles for an Armenian faith healer and mystic, twenty-year-old robed and bearded Avak Hagopian. For a time, Kardashian had actually teamed up with another financial backer of the mystic, one Clem Davies, an avowed anti-Semite whose books included such titles as "The Racial Streams of Mankind, What is Anglo-Israel?" And "Pre-Adamic Races". He was a known member of the Christian Identity Movement, using strange interpretations of biblical scripture to "prove" white superiority and to demonize Jews. The anti-Semitic hate that Davies spewed

269

seemingly didn't conflict with Tatos Kardashian's old-world views of Jews.[509]

If Oppenheimer was correct, the sudden surge of the masses to see faith healers Hagopian and Branham in Palm Springs would have not only been aligned with the Kardashian and Shakarian ideology, it would have been a fantastic business opportunity. It should come as no surprise that Demos Shakarian, Tatos' nephew, founded the Pentecostal Full Gospel Businessmen's Fellowship International after witnessing the sheer number of people this type of religious entertainment could attract.

On the recordings still available to the public, William Branham never mentioned the Kardashians or Shakarians by name when discussing Avak Hagopian. Instead, he would mention Avak's sponsors sending for him, sponsoring his own "healings".

> *And I have many thousand miles of flying ahead of me. I have ... going up on the ... plumb down from Vancouver, work down the coast as far as California, coming back to Fresno where I'm to go tomorrow, to the Armenian people. They flew a boy, who prays for the sick, by the name of Avak. They brought him from Cairo over to pray for a man by the name of Arakelian. The same time they sent for him, they sent up in Indiana and had me to come to a woman with cancer.[510]*

Transcripts now include several *"[Blank spot(s) on tape-Ed.]"*, and when talking about the publicity events, significant words were "unintelligible", replaced with "..." and "?". It was clear that all mention of the Kardashian and Shakarian families had been removed from the early recordings of William Branham's sermons, and from the number of sermons I had found missing from the list of transcripts, some entire sermons had been removed.

Branham often mentioned how "they" (Kardashians and Shakarians) had offered him a Cadillac or custom Packard, and claimed that he

[509] Oppenheimer, Jerry. 2017. The Kardashians: An American Drama.
[510] Branham, William. 1947, Nov 2. The Angel of God.

"refused" it.[511]   Yet Branham did accept a Cadillac from Minor Arganbright, Vice President of the Full Gospel Businessmen's Association[512] — which meant that he accepted the Cadillac from the Shakarians and/or the Kardashians. But at the time I first saw the article of William Branham receiving the Cadillac, I was unaware that it was from the same people that he claimed to have refused the car.

Oppenheimer described how Pentecostalism was woven through the Shakarian / Kardashian family and even described the family attendance in the Pentecostal "healing" meetings.[513] But I was surprised to learn that the family had roots in white supremacy — especially as having ties to "mystic" white supremacy evangelists like Clem Davies.   I remembered back to Roy E. Davis holding meetings in Jeffersonville describing himself as a "converted mystic", and John Alexander Dowie who promoted himself as a "Christian mystic". I should have known by William Branham's statements about "fortune tellers", pyramids and the Zodiac, that mysticism flowed throughout the "Message" that we were taught, but still it came as a surprise.

Learning the ties to the Kardashian, Arakelian, and Shakarian families filled in even more pieces of the puzzle. From the moment my research began, I'd always wondered where the "prophet" got the money to fund such huge advertising campaigns and pay for the accommodations for the big healing events. He always claimed that he couldn't scrape two pennies together, yet it took significant funding to generate these massive crowds. Examination of the ministries of the hundreds of other ministers and evangelists who joined the "prophet" on the platform revealed that if substantial amounts of money were not behind William Branham, these individuals would not have been behind him either.

---

[511] Branham, William. 1952, Aug 17. Expectancy. "And here, some time ago somebody wanted to give me a Cadillac car. And I said, 'Do you mean to tell me that I have…' I said, 'Brother, I'm glad you got one.' One said, 'We just gave Avak one; why not give you one?' I said, 'Look, brother, you mean to tell me that I'd go down through Arkansas, and some of them poor little women out there pulling that cotton sack, and their back broke, and eating fat bacon, perhaps, and—and corn meal for breakfast, and say, 'There goes Brother Branham,' going down the street out there in a Cadillac car?' I said, 'Not me, brother. That don't run in my blood to do that.' No, sir."

[512] William Branham and Money. Accessed 2020, May 17 from
http://en.believethesign.com/index.php/William_Branham_and_Money

[513] Oppenheimer, Jerry. 2017. The Kardashians: An American Drama. "Demos Shakarian preached about miracle healing — Kardashian was hoping there was some authenticity to the stories he had heard over the years about cancer victims being miraculously made well through the power of prayer and a healer's touch."

Suddenly, I noticed the bigger picture that was being formed. This picture included much, much more than simply a business strategy to fund the Branham campaigns. While William Branham published self-promoting articles for his ministry, he also promoted other "healers" and "prophets". He helped establish their stage personas and launch their careers, using stories and titles like his own. At the same time, he collected names, addresses, and testimonies for the newsletter he published, and that information was worth more than gold to a "healer" practicing "discernment"!

William Branham promoted many other "healers" who claimed to have the "gift of discernment", such as Oral Roberts. Some of them were only filling tents of three thousand people in comparison to Branham's crowds of thirty thousand, and they were struggling to survive. With the names and addresses collected as they sold and promoted The Voice of Healing, however, a large database of personal information quickly grew. It wouldn't have surprised me if access to this information were sold to participating evangelists in the revival — especially considering the unethical tactics I had already discovered. With this information, any evangelist could collect "prayer cards" like Branham, and claim to "discern" the names, addresses, and diseases of their visitors while having inside information! Using the same newsletter to collect the names, William Branham published the testimonials for the ministers who used his advertising, making it beneficial to both parties!

Subscribers who read the testimonials were asked to send gift subscriptions to others, enabling the collection of even more names and addresses. Hundreds of evangelists joined the quickly growing movement, filled with excitement as the crowds began to overflow tents into auditoriums. It was such a powerful strategy that the "healing revival" became known as the "Voice of Healing Revival",[514] and William Branham was recognized as the leader of the revival.[515]

Clem Davies organized healing campaigns in downtown Los Angeles shortly after publishing his book, "Racial Streams of

---

[514] Crowder, John. 2006. Miracle Workers, Reformers, and the New Mystics. "Known simply as the healing revival, Voice of Healing Revival, or Latter Rain Revival"
[515] Liardon, Roberts. 2000. God's Generals. "Branham became the leader in the Voice of Healing revival, which originated in the late forties."

Mankind". It was then announced that Tom Kardashian and William Perumean were going to sponsor the youth,[516] and big names among the youth began to spring up as revivalists. It was at this time that three-year-old Marjoe Gortner began his career. He made millions of dollars before exposing the tactics used in the healing meetings.[517] I began to understand why William Branham started his career with "Little" David Walker and Avak Hagopian. The "Voice of Healing Revival" was packing auditoriums and generating massive amounts of revenue. It clearly was an opportunity for "Gospel Businessmen".

But the "Voice of Healing Revival" would soon be known by another name. As hordes of people swept across the United States and Canada joining in the frenzy, another children's orphanage became interested in William Branham. This particular orphanage would leave a long-lasting mark on religion in America. I knew that my research would eventually shift towards the Sharon Orphanage in North Battleford, Saskatchewan. First, however, I needed to know more about Clem Davies. If I was reading Oppenheimer correctly, Davies played an integral role in helping kick-start William Branham's ministry, and there was no question that Branham's sudden rise to fame came shortly after working with the Kardashians. Yet there was not a single mention of Clem Davies on any transcript or any publication related to William Branham. There was a reason why the names Kardashian, Shakarian, and Davies were scrubbed from every recording and every transcript. I wanted to know why.

---

[516] Mystic to Hold Faith Healings. 1947, Sep 17. The Daily Herald. "Arakelian recently announced that Tom Kardashian and William Perumean, Los Angeles businessmen, had taken over sponsorship of the youth."
[517] Marjoe. 1972. Documentary.

ARMENIAN GENOCIDE

Alikhani, Keshvar. 25 Rare, Chilling Photos of the Armenian Genocide. Accessed 2019, Apr 7 from *https://www.ranker.com/list/armenian-genocide-pictures/keshvaralikhani*

Derderian, K. (1 March 2005). "Common Fate, Different Experience: Gender-Specific Aspects of the Armenian Genocide, 1915–1917". Holocaust and Genocide Studies. ISSN 8756-6583.

Kifner, John (7 December 2007). "Armenian Genocide of 1915: An Overview". The New York Times.

Rummel, RJ (1 April 1998). "The Holocaust in Comparative and Historical Perspective". IDEA – a journal of social issues. ISSN 1523-1712.

Herzig, Edmund; Kurkchiyan, Marina (2004). The Armenians: Past and Present in the Making of National Identity. Routledge. p. 47. ISBN 978-1-135-79837-6.

Akçam, Taner (2006). A Shameful Act: The Armenian Genocide and the Question of Turkish Responsibility. New York: Metropolitan Books. ISBN 0-8050-7932-7.

Balakian, Peter (2003). The Burning Tigris: The Armenian Genocide and America's Response. New York: HarperCollins. ISBN 0-06-019840-0.

Gust, Wolfgang (2013). The Armenian Genocide: Evidence from the German Foreign Office Archives, 1915–191. Berghahn Books. pp. 653–54. ISBN 978-1-78238-143-3.

Bozorgmehr, Der-Martirosian, Sabagh, "Middle Easterners: A New Kind of Immigrant," p. 352.

THE KARDASHIAN / ARAKELIAN / SHAKARIAN CONNECTIONS

Oppenheimer, Jerry. 2017. The Kardashians: An American Drama.

Declaration of Intention. 1921, Nov 8.

Petition for Naturalization: Tatos Kardashian. 1923, Nov 15

Petition for Name Change: Tatos Kardashian to Tom Kardashian. 1927, Mar 4

EXCLUSIVE: Keeping Up with The Kardashians circa 1900! How Kim's ancestors heeded Prophet's warning of looming slaughter to escape rural Armenia for a new live in the U.S. Accessed 2019, Apr 7 from *https://mamul.am/en/news/65577*

Smith, Dean. Was Kim Kardashian's family saved by a 165-year-old prophecy? Accessed 2019, Apr 7 from https://opentheword.org/2015/02/08/was-kim-kardashians-family-saved-by-a-near-two-hundred-year-old-prophecy/

Family Relationship of Hamas Shakarian (1896-1987) Great Grandmother to Kim Kardashian. Accessed 2019, Apr 7 from https://famouskin.com/famous-kin-chart.php?name=44542+hamas+shakarian&kin=43765+kim+kardashian

Shakarian, Cynthia. 2017, Nov 10. The Shakarian Legacy: How A Humble Dairyman Inspired the World! Demos Shakarian

The Happiest People on Earth, the story of Demos Shakarian as told to John and Elizabeth Sherrill, Steward Press, Chuppaqua, New York, 10514, 1975

Anderson, Allan. 2013. An Introduction to Pentecostalism: Global Charismatic Christianity

Val Fotherby: The awakening giant. London (UK) (Marshall Pickering), 2000. ISBN 0-551-03234-0

Zeigler, J. R. "Full Gospel Business Men's Fellowship International". The New International Dictionary of Pentecostal and Charismatic Movements

Branham, William. 1955, Mar 11. The Seal of the Antichrist.

Branham, William. 1957, July 27. He Was to Pass That Way.

Branham, William. 1964, Mar 21. He Was to Pass This Way.

MARJOE GORTNER / 'LITTLE' DAVID WALKER

Marjoe. 1972. Documentary.

Harrell, David (1975). All Things are Possible. Ontario: Indiana University Press. p. 234. ISBN 0253100909.

Cooper, Travis (2013). "Marjoe Gortner, Imposter Revivalist: Toward a Cognitive Theory of Religious Misbehavior". Penteco Studies.

Schafer, Jason. 2015, Feb 27. "'A lot of people do bad things': The bizarre tale of child evangelist turned conman, Marjoe Gortner". Dangerous Minds.

Little David Miracle Boy Preacher. Accessed 2019, Jan 23 *from: http://www.dealpentecostal.co.uk/Little%20David%20Miracle%20Boy%20Preacher.pdf*

Boy from Heaven? Long Beach Independent. 1948, May 1

"Little David" Manager Removed by Court. 1949, May 26. The Alexandria Times Tribune

Boy Preacher Overworked by Minister, Parents Charge. 1948, Apr 29. The Courier Journal

Judge Ousts Manager of Boy Evangelist. 1949, May 26. The Akron Beacon Journal

Branham & The Atom. 1947, Sep 20, Wm. St. Louis Post Dispatch Sat.

Boy Evangelist in Custody Fight. 1948, Apr 29. The Edwardsville Intelligencer

Boy Evangelist Flails at Sin and Wins 100 to Repentance. 1947, Sep 28. St. Louis Post Dispatch Sun. St

Parents File Suit to Regain Custody of Boy Evangelist. 1948, May 17. The Fresno Bee The Republican

7,500 Persons Hear 13-Year-Old-Preacher Deliver Sermon Here. 1948, Sep 29. St. Louis Star and Times Mon.

Minister Holds Healing Services; Hundreds of Cures Are Reported. 1947, Sep 29. St. Louis Post Dispatch Mon. St

Mother Asks Custody of Boy Evangelist Son. 1948, Jun 17. The News Herald

"Little David" Parents Endorse Management of Raymond G. 1949, Apr 9. Hoekstra. The Indianapolis Star

Boy Evangelist. 1948, Apr 29. The Edwardsville Intelligencer

CHAPTER 27

WILLIAM BRANHAM AND CLEM DAVIES

"Now, counting the time, we find that we have exactly (Listen.) seventeen years left[518] "

There are many days that I wish I could go back in time and relive moments of my childhood. There are so many questions I have about conversations I remember. As a child, I only got the "children's version" of each story, and I wish that I could hear the adult version. I vividly remember the times that I heard my grandfather speak behind the pulpit, and many of those statements were recorded for all to hear. But my grandfather also had a very private life, which looked much different from the public version. There were stories about the "prophet" he told in public, but there were also memories he shared with our family about the "prophet" and his family, in private.

I can remember riding with my grandfather and my father on a road trip deep into Kentucky when Grandpa told one of his favorite jokes about a football player. I can remember like it was yesterday, Grandpa saying, *"Calhoon say he don't want that ball!"* and then laughing until his sides hurt. This was from a recording of what my grandfather said was the "prophet's" favorite comedian. It was called "Laughing With 'Em" (my Grandpa called it, "The White Negro"). It was a recording of

---

[518] Branham, William. 1961, Aug 6. The Seventieth Week of Daniel.

a Baptist minister telling jokes involving situations with African Americans in the Mississippi Delta. Grandpa had a cassette tape which was copied from the record, and several friends also had copies. I learned later that the recording was made in 1971, six years after William Branham's death, and that it would not have been this *exact* recording that Branham had heard.

Still, as my research turned towards white supremacy, this was very troubling. I never thought about that recording as being "racist", and never thought about how even the title itself would have been considered racial profiling. These were jokes poking fun at the African American culture, "laughing with _them_", and though it seemed harmless enough, I know now just how wrong this was. We never gave it a second thought while in the "Message". If this kind of humor was loved by the "prophet", then it must not be sinful!

When I learned that the Kardashian Family was involved with the early stages of the Healing Revival, and that they were sponsoring "faith healers" Avak Hagopian and William Branham, I wanted to know why. How did the Los Angeles elite hear about an Indiana preacher? Why did they choose to sponsor him, above all the other "faith healers" of the era? In the photograph of William Branham standing in an expensive white suit with Avak Hagopian, there was a third man standing. Who was this man in the photo with William Branham and Avak Hagopian? Learning that Tatos Kardashian also sponsored white supremacist Clem Davies was the key to many doors of research. Davies published books on British Israelism and taught Christian Identity doctrine. These ideologies were strongly anti-Semitic and promoted by the Ku Klux Klan. This type of theology is used to promote a racial interpretation of Christianity, usually by white supremacists, and by comparison William Branham's "Serpent Seed" doctrine was no different.

I found it interesting that Davies was in Los Angeles at the same time as Roy E. Davis, and that Davies had organized Avak's tour through 34 states and 3 Canadian provinces starting Oct 13, 1947. This was about the time that William Branham's "faith healing" career was launched into full steam. I began to wonder: was Clem Davies a member of the Ku Klux Klan? Would Davies have been aligned with "Americanization" and the white supremacy agendas of Roy E. Davis?

...

Clem Davies earned his fame in Victoria, British Columbia, in the early 1920's.[519] He was a pastor of the Centennial Church, and in the early 1920's, he was quite popular. His sermons were unlike those of other preachers of the time; Davies made his sermons appealing for those who were tired of the traditional sermon. Similar to William Branham's "Message" doctrine,[520] Clem Davies' version of Christianity was militant[521] and opposed to organized religion.[522] It was also very popular. In fact, it was so popular that his congregation grew until his small church overflowed and filled the Victoria City Temple.

In the Victoria City Temple, his sermons continued to stray even further from the ordinary. They began to include discussions on sex, race, and bloodline.[523] They also included the fundamental elements of his Christian Identity doctrine, which was similar to William Branham's "Serpent Seed" theology.

Clem Davies' sermons had to be censored, and at times, children under 16 were forbidden. Davies was deeply involved with White Supremacy and the Ku Klux Klan, and Klan agenda made its way into his sermons. In 1924, he threatened that the Ku Klux Klan would become militant if the "Oriental problem" was not stopped.[524] In 1925, he began preaching about joining the Ku Klux Klan, apparently holding membership drives.[525] There was no question that Davies was a member of the Ku Klux Klan — he openly declared his allegiance.

---

[519] Marks First Year of Pastorate at Centennial Church. 1923, Oct 13. Victoria Daily Times.

[520] Branham, William. 1955, Oct 8. The Results of Decision. "This morning when we was stand at the Christian Business Men, Brother Hicks had us all singing, "Onward Christian Soldiers"

[521] Centennial: Life a Recounting. 1923, Sep 8. Victoria Daily Times. "A sermon for militant Christians"

[522] Branham, William. Church Age Book. "He was militant against any form of organization. Also, his life history, wherein he served the Lord"

[523] Commencing A Series of Health Lectures. 1926, Jan 9. Times Colonist. "Commencing a series of lectures on birth control and eugenics, raise betterment and heredity. Dr. Clem Davies speaks on "Applying Science to Marriage." Should we marry just for love? How can we know whether we have chosen the right partner for our own health and happiness and the happiness and health of our children? NO CHILDREN UNDER 16 SHOULD HEAR THESE DISCUSSIONS"

[524] Roy, Patricia. The Oriental Question: Consolidating a White Man's Province. "Late in 1924 Davies gave a sermon on 'British or Oriental Columbia — which?' Two thousand people, including many MLAs, attended while others heard him over the radio warn that the Ku Klux Klan was growing in the province and would "take the law into its own hands unless legislators realized the gravity of the economic and oriental problems.'"

[525] Will Preach on Ku Klux Klan at Sunday Service. 1925, Nov 14. Times Colonist. "Shall we join the Ku Klux Klan?' Will be the theme of an address by Rev. Dr. Davies."

Clem Davies was a prominent lecturer as well as a preacher and a Klansman[526]. He gave public speeches concerning British-Israelism, which gained an even more diverse crowd. British Israelism is the pseudo-archaeological notion that the people of the British Isles are "genetically, racially, and linguistically the direct descendants" of the Ten Lost Tribes of ancient Israel from the Christian Bible.

Rev. Gordon Lindsay, Branham's campaign manager, was also active in Davies' British-Israelism,[527] and spoke during public conventions. In the late 1940s, Davies began working with the Kardashians to support Avak Hagopian and William Branham. Coincidentally, this was during the time Roy E. Davis and William D. Upshaw were in Los Angeles, preparing for what would later become the Third Wave of the Ku Klux Klan.

As I began to study the ministry of Clem Davies, it brought back several painful memories. We were taught to believe the "prophet" had a "revelation" about Russian invasion.[528] We believed that "women voting" would cause the destruction of the United States at the hand of Russia.[529] I was shocked to see that this was a popular notion among white supremacists of the 40's and 50's.[530] They were weaponizing religion to use fear for political agenda, and their sermons were not simply religious -- they were politically motivated. Even the "prophet's" use of the Giza Pyramid was popular among the white supremacy groups; this was a subject Clem Davies also discussed during lectures. One advertisement suggested that Davies and his peers used "Pyramid Dates" to predict world disaster.

---

[526] Barkun, Michael. 2014. Religion and the Racist Right: The Origins of the Christian Identity Movement. "Clem Davies, a prominent British-Israel preacher from Victoria, British Columbia. By the time he arrived in Los Angeles, Davies had a long right-wing and anti-Semitic past, including involvement with the Ku Klux Klan"

[527] Annual Conference of Anglo-Saxon Christian World Movement. 1940, Aug 17. The Vancouver Sun. "The convention will open with the British Israel church service in the auditorium on Sunday at 11 a.m. Rev. Gordon Lindsay of Portland, Ore., will deliver the address."

[528] Branham, William. 1960, Dec 7. The Pergamean Church Age. "And how many in here remembers me just keep...have you stand, and say it over, I'd tell you, "Watch Russia! Watch Russia, the king of the North! Watch Russia, king of the North! Watch Russia, king of the North!"? How many has heard me just say, just wave that over, over?"

[529] Branham, William. 1960, Nov 13. Condemnation by Representation. "Women, given the right to vote, elected President-elect Kennedy, was the woman's vote, the wrong man; which will finally lead to full control, of the Catholic church, in United States. Then the bomb comes that explodes her."

[530] Dr. Clem Davies Ministry. 1948, Nov 13. Los Angeles Times. "Are ONE BILLION asiatics no being dragooned by Moscow for the Armageddon March?"

279

"SPIRITUAL AWAKENING FOR THE NEW WORLD ORDER": THE ELECTION MIRACLE!
Its meaning in the Great Pyramid and Bible Prophecy — How will it affect finance — business and economics? Will next Wednesday (Pyramid Date Nov 10th) Date the start of Final World Economic Collapse?[531]

Davies also organized and sold tickets for speaking engagements on cruises, touring countries such as Cuba and the South Pacific.[532] I began to think about William Branham's trips with the Christian Businessmen group. I always pictured a very humble, very spiritual trip to save the lost. I never thought about William Branham and his associates taking "glorious holidays" and "cruises", and I always assumed his audience were native converts. I never even considered the possibility of the group selling tickets for vacations with the evangelists. We were never told this part of the "prophet's" "life story". We were never told about the key individuals who were behind the revivals, and we were certainly never told that they were involved with white supremacy.

By 1948, countless ministers and evangelists had joined in the revival, many of them with the "gift of healing". As new "faith healers" joined in the revival, William Branham began to advertise their ministries in his "Voice of Healing" publication. Issues of Voice of Healing were now representing several "men of God" with special "sign-gift ministries.[533] The "Message" I'd heard was always scornful towards other "healers". We called them *"carnal impersonators"*. But in 1948, William Branham ran the newsletter,[534] and subscribers sent him letters that he would read, answer, and sometimes publish.

I began to understand why the "prophet" said that he had *"boxes of testimonies"*,[535] though we weren't allowed to see any of them. I was surprised when I noticed that the "prophet" also authored articles in the

---

[531] Dr. Clem Davies. 1948, Nov 6. Los Angeles Times.

[532] Last Call for Cuba! 1948, Oct 13. Los Angeles Times.

[533] Voice of Healing changed its description to state, "An Inter-Evangelical Publication of the Latter-Day Sign-Gift Ministries. Example: The Voice of Healing. July 1948.

[534] William Branham was listed as the publisher of The Voice of Healing in 1948

[535] Branham, William. 1953, Nov 6. Do You Now Believe? "Who has performed right in our own meetings, testimonies that would make boxes of testimonies. And anyone you read in any book or any literature that's been published by us, they are bona fide testimonies backed up by doctors and law"

Voice of Healing,[536] and I was surprised by how articulate he was. I continued to wonder what year he began claiming to have only a 6th-grade education. His writing skills in 1948 were very good. He also published articles written by Gordon Lindsay that were allegedly prophetic. Following Davies' strategy, Lindsay continued to tout themes of fear about impending invasion or world disaster and presented his own doomsday predictions. Using random number associations between the Bible and modern events, Lindsay warned readers to prepare for Armageddon.[537]

I never realized how often we were subjected to the same type of fear. As I searched through the transcripts, I realized that William Branham often used this same strategy for his own doomsday predictions. In May of 1954, William Branham used number association for the alleged doomsday year of 1954.

> *But look, let's take historically speaking. The first two thousand years, the world order come to a climax, and God destroyed the world with water. You know that? Then it come forth as a new world. And the second two thousand years, it came to its end again and God sent Jesus. Is that right? This is the end of the next two thousand years, 1954. And the Gospel, Jesus said, "The work would be cut short." For what? "The elect's sake, or no flesh would be saved," it would so wicked. So we're at the end time. And then the seventh, in type, is the Millennium, a thousand years.[538]*

In May of 1962, the "prophet" used fear to claim there was only a "month or so" remaining

> *Wished I could come here for about two or three weeks just on Bible teaching of prophecy and things. See where we're living, friends. What's the matter with people? Can't you see we're at the end time? It's all over. The next thing will be a sweep*

[536] Example: Believest Thou This: Message by Rev. William Branham Continued from Last Month. 1948, Sept. The Voice of Healing.
[537] The World in Prophecy. 1948, August. The Voice of Healing.
[538] Branham, William. 1954, May 13. The Mark of the Beast.

that'll grab that little group together. In a month or so she'll be gone, as soon as she's gathered together. Well, we're at the end. There's no hopes left nowhere. Run to Christ, people.[539]

Even his 1977 doomsday prediction, for which he would be remembered,[540] was based on random number association.

Now, counting the time, we find that we have exactly (Listen.) seventeen years left, and we will have the same span of time given to us as God dealing with us in the power of the Holy Spirit since A.D. 33 until 1977, the same span of time of 1954 years. God deals with us the same as He did with the Jews. See? How about that? Now, mark down in your book a little Scripture here I want to give you. Leviticus 25, begin with the 8th verse. God calls a jubilee every forty-ninth year; the fiftieth year was the jubilee. We know that. We understand that. From the first jubilee of Leviticus 25:8, in 1977 will be the seventieth jubilee, making exactly 3,430 years. Jubilee means the going up, the release.[541]

I was very surprised to see that William Branham had been using themes of fear and world destruction since 1948. Clem Davies and those who held similar views on British-Israelites were claiming that the fuse to Armageddon had already been lit. It was evident that Branham held no exception to this common theme, and that he was using the same fear tactics to captivate his own audience.

The Red Scare was an effective way to draw crowds. People feared the unknown, and these religious entertainers were presenting an escape from that fear — all while channeling it to create even more fear. Sermons were focused upon Armageddon, and Biblical prophecy was rewritten to apply to modern events. Davies took this approach to extremes, using screen illustrations to display his doomsday predictions.

---

[539] Branham, William. 1959, Jun 13. Thirsting for Life.
[540] LFP LONGFORM: Inside the doomsday cult-inspired world of London's abusive street preachers. Accessed 2020, May 17 from https://lfpress.com/news/local-news/lfp-longform-inside-the-doomsday-cult-inspired-world-of-londons-abusive-street-preachers/
[541] Branham, William. 1961, Aug 6. The Seventieth Week of Daniel.

As strange as it might sound, crowds were eager to learn more about their impending doom, and he continued to gain attention.

This sudden surge of "faith healers", "prophecy", and doomsday predictions caught the attention of a group of men in Battleford, Saskatchewan. They had visited the revivals in Vancouver, BC, and created the formula for a new breed of Pentecostalism. A "revival" broke out at the Sharon Orphanage, and it spread throughout the ranks of "divine healers" in the United States and Canada. It would become known as "Latter Rain" and would remain controversial for years to come.

CLEM DAVIES
Will Preach in Chicago Temple. 1933, Aug 12. The Victoria Daily Times
Will Preach on Ku Klux Klan At Sunday Service. 1925, Nov 14. Times Colonist
Palestine Partition - the Fuse to Armageddon. 1948, May 1. The Los Angeles Times
Davies Condemns Mussolini, Hitler. 1937, Mar 31. The Vancouver Sun
Life a Recounting. 1923, Sep 8. The Victoria Daily Times
Last Call for Cuba. 1948, Oct 13. The Los Angeles Times
Red-Yellow Peril! The Los Angeles Times. 1948, Nov 13
Rev. 1925, Jan 26. Clem Davies Starts Political Organization. The Province
Wonders of the World. 1933, Jul 22. The Victoria Daily Times
Will Stalin Crash to His Doom in Palestine? The Los Angeles Times. 1949, Jun 4
Roy, Petricia. The Oriental Question: Consolidating a White Man's Province, 1914-41
Barkun, Michael. Religion and the Racist Right: The Origins of the Christian Identity Movement
Milestones to Armageddon. 1940, Nov 16. The Vancouver Sun
Present-Day Events and Bible Prophecy the Los Angeles Times. 1941, Oct 25
Dr. 1925, Dec 12. Davies to Revive Klan. Times Colonist
Annual Conference of Anglo-Saxon Christian World Movement. 1940, Aug 17. The Vancouver
    Sun
Commencing a Series of Health Lectures. 1926, Jan 9. Times Colonist
Clem Davies Foresees Climax on Oct 22. 1937, Sep 27. The Vancouver Sun
Dr. 1937, Apr 24. Clem Davies to Continue Lectures. The Vancouver Sun
Second Talk on Big Fair. 1933, Jul 29. The Victoria Daily Times
Russian Enigma to be Discussed. 1941, Jun 14. The Los Angeles Times
The Election Miracle! The Los Angeles Times. 1948, Nov 6
Clem Davies. 1923, Oct 13. The Victoria Daily Times
The Future of Mankind. 1940, Aug 17. Gordon Lindsay Clem Davies The Vancouver Sun
The Nine-Month Orbit of Financial Disaster! The Los Angeles Times. 1948, Dec 4
Avak to Conduct Healings in L. 1947, Sep 16. A. The Californian
ROY E. DAVIS, William D. Upshaw IN CALIFORNIA:
Child Problem to Mount, Say Superior Judge. 1943, Sept 17. The San Bernardino County Sun
W. 1943, Dec 11. R. C. Federation Meeting Attended by Sand Bernardino Group. The San
    Bernardino County Sun
Orphanage School at Upland Slated to Open Sept 15. 1943, Aug 8. The San Bernardino County
    Sun
Trial of Minister Opens on Impersonation Charge. 1944, Apr 19. Los Angeles Times
Pastor Denies Charge of Posing as F. 1944, Apr 21. B. I. Man. Los Angeles Times.
Minister Charged. 1944, Mar 15. Nevada State Journal
Upland Pastor, Acquitted of Theft Charges, Sues Police Chief, 21 Others for Half Million. 1944,
    Sept 12. The San Bernardino County Sun
Orphanage Head Named in Grand Theft Charge. 1944, Feb 28. The San Bernardino County Sun
Witnesses Say Davis Claimed to be F. 1944, Apr 22. B. I. Man. The San Bernardino County Sun
Habeas Corpus Petition Denied. 1944, Apr 29. The San Bernardino County Sun
Davis Faces Charge of Mail Tampering. 1944, Feb 26. The San Bernardino County Sun
Orphanage Head Asks Reduction in $16,000 Bail. 1944, Mar 4. The San Bernardino County Sun
Two Counts are Dropped After Court Hearing. 1944, May 6. The San Bernardino County Sun
Orphanage Benefactor Questioned, Pictured as 'Disillusioned'; Funds Raising Investigated. 1944,
    Feb 20. The San Bernardino County Sun
Orphanage Said to be Result of Pastor's Vision. 1944, Apr 20. The San Bernardino County Sun
Accused Pastor Demands Writ. 1944, Apr 27. The San Bernardino County Sun

Summons Issued for Rev. 1944, Feb 1. Roy E. Davis. The San Bernardino County Sun
Complaints Filed Against Orphanage Head of West End. 1944, Feb 22. The San Bernardino County Sun
Upland Evangelist Before U. 1944, Apr 19. S. Judge. The San Bernardino County Sun
Minister, Wife Seek Damages. 1945, Feb 18. The San Bernardino County Sun
Summons Issued for Rev. 1945, Feb 1. Roy E. Davis. The San Bernardino County Sun
Attorneys for Radio Station Seek Davis. 1945, Jan 31. The San Bernardino County Sun

CHAPTER 28

WILLIAM BRANHAM AND THE MANIFEST SONS OF GOD

"Not a man, God! But it'll come through a Prophet[542]"

I was starting to recognize a much different picture of the "Message religion" than that which I was raised to believe. Things were not as they had seemed. The original Branham Tabernacle was Pentecostal, not Baptist. The deed was titled "Billie Branham Pentecostal Tabernacle" and did not change its name until 1945. Elders, teachers, and congregation had been a part of Roy E. Davis' Pentecostal church and had transitioned to attending the Billie Branham Pentecostal Tabernacle after a series of criminal investigations forced Roy Davis and his brother Dan Davis from town. During the time that William Branham was an elder and evangelist in Roy Davis' Pentecostal church (and likely in Dan Davis' church and Mission in Louisville, Kentucky) Roy Davis was extradited multiple times on charges ranging from sex with a minor to swindling and grand theft. I'd learned that Davis had an extensive criminal history — before, during, and after William Branham worked directly with him. Yet William Branham continued to work indirectly with him and speak very highly of him in public.

I'd learned that since the early 1920's, Roy Davis was an official spokesperson for the Ku Klux Klan. I'd learned that he was working

[542] Branham, William. 1965, Nov 27. Trying to Do God a Service Without It Being God's Will.

closely with Congressman William D. Upshaw, and that Upshaw was also a ranking member of the Klan. I'd learned that Upshaw was very (physically) mobile before entering Branham "healing" campaigns posing in a wheelchair, and that William Upshaw and Roy Davis had once again joined forces in the mid 1940s, provided they ever even separated. They joined together in an attempt to "Americanize" (indoctrinate) youth with Ku Klux Klan ideology. I'd learned that part of that plan included establishing a children's orphanage just east of Los Angeles, shortly before William Branham connected with the Los Angeles elite. I'd learned that the minister from L.A. working with Branham was Clem Davies who openly promoted the Ku Klux Klan in Canada and in the United States. I'd learned that Clem Davies was working with Gordon Lindsay, the "prophet's" campaign manager. But when I learned yet *another* orphanage was a fundamental part of William Branham's historical timeline, I wanted to know more about this "orphanage" and its history.

...

In late summer of 1943, another orphanage scheme was announced in the Saskatoon news by men who *appeared to be* unconnected to William Upshaw, Roy Davis, or Clem Davies. A "Four Square" minister by the name of Herrick Holt was asking for a quarter of a million dollars to erect an orphanage.[543] The Foursquare Church belonged to another Pentecostal Sect whose central figure was Aimee Semple McPherson. Branham spoke highly of her in his sermons.[544] McPherson's headquarters was located in Los Angeles — which was geographically a tie to both Roy Davis and Clem Davies. Hedrick Holt would have been in communication with McPherson and/or her group. McPherson herself was nearing the end of her life, suffering from numerous health problems, which created the perfect opportunity for another central figure to enter the scene.

---

[543] Orphanage Scheme Under Way at North Battleford. 1943, Oct 30. Star Phoenix
[544] Example Branham, William. 1959, Dec 16. What is the Holy Ghost? "Notice. And then, the same time that the nominal church was having their revival, what taken place? The Full Gospel was having a revival. There come forth the Bosworth brothers, Smith Wigglesworth, and Dr. Price, Aimee McPherson, all those."

Like Davis and Upshaw's orphanage, Herrick Holts' orphanage plans included a school. Holt had not yet secured the money, but stressed it was a "faith" project, and he claimed that he would get the funding regardless of whether it seemed impossible. Architectural plans required a large tract of land; large enough to supply housing, training, and work for one hundred boys and girls. The extensive plans occupied thirty-four acres.

I found it very interesting that the plans were announced shortly after Davis and Upshaw announced *their* orphanage. The Sharon Orphanage was announced in October of 1943, and the Davis/Upshaw orphanage in August of 1943. Both orphanages were "faith funded", and both had plans to include a school that was isolated from the public-school system.[545] By May of 1944, the project had doubled in expense to a half-million dollars. In today's money, that is 7.2 million dollars. In September of the same year, Herrick Holt announced his plans to purchase the Mounted Police barracks, along with 2,000 acres for the orphanage and connected facilities.[546]

By May of 1946, the Sharon Orphanage and Schools were quickly growing and exercising custody of twenty-eight children. Herrick Holt assured town leaders the school was "undenominational", but Protestant.[547] In the same way I wondered about Roy Davis and William Upshaw creating a "Department of Americanism" for their orphanage, I was curious as to why an orphanage would need to advertise that it was connected (or disconnected) from denominations at all. What did the orphanage have to do with religion? I also wondered why and how this "undenominational" orphanage and school became connected to William Branham.

In the summer of 1947, William Branham's campaign toured Canada with his new "angelic" "commission" story was introduced when W. E. Kidson managed the campaign team.[548] The Branham Campaigns held meetings in Saskatoon, Saskatchewan, which was the home of the Elim Tabernacle.

[545] North Battleford to Get Orphanage and School. 1944, May 13. Star Phoenix
[546] Prem. T. C. Douglas Inspects Northern Mental Hospital. 1944, Sep 5. Star Phoenix
[547] Sharon Orphanage Homes Care for 28 Children. 1946, May 9. Star Phoenix
[548] Full Gospel Church. 1947, Aug 9. Calgary Herald

Saskatoon was a strategic location for multiple reasons. Geographically speaking, it sat along the Trans-Canada Highway. From a religious standpoint, it was a religious center for Pentecostal meetings.[549] The Pentecostal Assemblies of Canada often held meetings at the Elim Tabernacle, and it was home of the Bethel Bible College, founded by George Hawtin. At the time of the Branham meetings, Hawtin had just resigned under pressure from the school he founded, adding to the perfect storm.

George Hawtin was sympathetic to the ideologies of white supremacy, which would eventually lead to his disgrace. Over the years, Hawtin would make a name for himself due to his unusual religious doctrine as well as for his work in promoting the "supreme white race". According to Hawtin, "blacks" were created to serve the "superior race" of "whites".

> *George Hawtin of Battleford, Sask., issued a written apology for distributing the 40-page booklet after a complaint about it to the Saskatchewan Human Rights Commission. Entitled "The Living Creature: Origin of the Negro", the booklet says God created a superior race of whites who are meant to rule. Blacks were created "in God's wisdom" to serve whites, it says.[550]*

Religious historians describe the events that took place after Branham's meetings in Saskatoon, Saskatchewan. George Hawtin joined forces with Herrick Holt and began working with the Sharon Orphanage. Percy G. Hunt resigned from Bethel Bible School to join Hawtin at the orphanage. Branham's campaign tour continued from Saskatchewan to Calgary, and finally to Vancouver. George Hawtin, Herrick Hunt, and several students from the "orphanage" followed William Branham to Vancouver for the meetings. As reporters — fully aware of the questionable tactics being reported in the meetings throughout the United States — covered the unusual events in the meetings with skepticism, the men from the Sharon Orphanage claimed

---

[549] Pentecostal Group to Convene Here. 1940, Jan 30. Star Phoenix
[550] A Lesson for Racist. 1989, May 11. The Province

to "witness" several "healings" and supernatural events. Suddenly, the Branham campaign had "witnesses!" I wondered: Why were Hawtin, Hunt, and seventy students from an orphanage following William Branham? Did they really "witness" genuine healings?

I found an article written by Alfred H. Pohl, one of the men from the Bethel Bible School who attended Branham's meetings. Pohl described what he witnessed in Branham's meetings in the Bible School and described his own private visits to the dorm rooms. After Branham left town, many of the "healed" started dying. Pohl, who was both a strong supporter and promoter of the meetings, was left to answer the very difficult questions — both from reporters and from family members who had lost loved ones that were supposed to have been "healed".[551]

Meanwhile, reporters were growing extremely curious as to the finance and intentions of the orphanage and "school". The Sharon group continued to purchase land, aircraft, busses, and other resources. Mysteriously, these purchases were funded by donors from the United States.[552]

"How was it done?" reporters asked of Holt. "What did he use for money?" They now had cottage homes, a trade school, hospital, and even a vacant airport building. The same month of Branham's Vancouver meeting, the leaders of the Sharon Orphanage formed an "interdenominational" Bible college. The "orphanage" began publishing a newsletter, promoting a combination of the doctrines of William Branham and Franklin Hall. Franklin. Hall had published a book on "spiritual fasting",[553] and toured the continent holding revivals. Shortly before William Branham teamed up with "Little" David, Hall had teamed up with Jack Walker, "Little" David's father, to establish a daily "fasting center" in San Diego. Like Branham, Hall held

---

[551] Why I Left the Tongues Movement. Accessed 2020, May 17 from http://www.bereanresearchinstitute.com/03_Doctrines/D.0030_14_Why_I_Left_the_Tongues_Movement_-_Alfred_H._Pohl.html. "Time went on, the campaign ended, and Mr. Branham and his party were gone. Then we began to see the results being tested by time. It was a difficult time for us, and particularly for me. For one by one these that I had personally seen "healed" and declared so by the "healer," died. Our faith was severely tested. Relatives of the deceased ones would ask, "Why?" What could we tell them?"

[552] Scenes at Orphanage and Aviation School. 1947, Dec 17. Saskatoon Star Phoenix. "Revenues for the venture were made available by offerings of interested people said to represent many areas in Canada and the United States."

[553] Hall, Franklin. 1946. Atomic Power with God, Thru Fasting and Prayer.

conventions with the 12-year-old preacher, addressing crowded auditoriums.

The more connections I found, the more questions I had. This was no ordinary "orphanage". Why was a Canadian "orphanage" promoting American ministers in their newsletter? Was this an attempt to counter the media's attempt to expose the unethical tactics and backgrounds of the men involved with the Branham campaigns?

The meetings Branham held in Vancouver were organized by Ern Baxter, who toured with Branham from 1947-1953. Shortly after the meeting, in 1948, Baxter's secretary, George H. Warnock, started attending revivals at the Sharon Orphanage. The revivals gave birth to a movement known as the "New Order of the Latter Rain". The movement based its theology, loosely, on a passage from the Old Testament in the Christian Bible. The quickly growing sect repurposed a prophecy from the book of Joel in the Old Testament that stated, *"He will cause to come down for you the rain, the former rain, and the latter rain in the first month"*.

It was a passage we heard often in the early years of the "Message". William Branham frequently taught about *"The locust, the cankerworm, the caterpillar, the palmerworm"* from that passage. Entire sermons Branham preached were based upon Joel's prophecy. Towards the end of his ministry, William Branham started claiming that Joel's prediction was being fulfilled, and that the Son of God was being made manifest. God was appearing in the form of a "prophet".

> *The Elijah of this day is the Lord Jesus Christ. He is to come according to Matthew the seventeen-...Luke 17:30, is, the Son of man is to reveal Himself among His people. Not a man, God! But it'll come through a Prophet.*[554]

Ern Baxter's personal secretary, George Warnock, began promoting William Branham's more extreme doctrines under the name, "Joel's Army",[555] or the "Manifest Sons of God". This movement was

---

[554] Branham, William. 1965, Nov 27. Trying to Do God a Service Without It Being God's Will.

[555] Southern Poverty Law Center, Klanwatch Project, Militia Task Force. 2008. Intelligence Report: A Project of the Southern Poverty Law. Accessed 2020, May 28 from https://www.splcenter.org/fighting-hate/intelligence-

supposed to demonstrate God revealing Himself in the form of a prophet. I was surprised when I noticed the names of the people who were involved. Key figures in the "Message" cult following helped to spread parts of the "Latter Rain" theology.[556] But I was more surprised to learn what they created, and how many people died because of their creation. Most of all, I was surprised that sermons with the title "Manifested Sons of God" were renamed, [557] apparently to conceal all traces of William Branham's connection to Jim Jones.

report/2008/todd-bentley%E2%80%99s-militant-joel%E2%80%99s-army-gains-followers-florida. "Through Cain came all the smart, educated people down to the antediluvian flood — the intellectuals, bible colleges," Branham wrote in the kind of anti- mainstream religion, anti-intellectual spirit that pervades the Joel's Army movement "

[556] Example: Roy Borders, campaign manager. 1949, Jan 22. The Temple of the Latter Rain. Calgary Herald.

[557] Manifested Sons of God. Accessed 2020, May 28 from *https://www.williambranham.com/manifested-sons-of-god-60-0518* "This Message by Brother William Marrion Branham called Manifested Sons Of God was delivered on Wednesday, 18th May 1960 at the Branham Tabernacle in Jeffersonville, Indiana, U.S.A. The tape, number 60-0518, is 2 hours and 5 minutes, and consists of 2 cassettes. This message is available in book format (Adoption)."

WILLIAM BRANHAM AND METAPHYSICS

Branham, William. 1947, April 12. Faith is the Substance

3-The Sharon Orphanage Connection Accessed 2019, May 1 from
   http://abc-history.blogspot.com/2008/02/before-i-was-born-my-father-ramon-haas.html

Bowman, Robert M. Jr. Word-Faith Movement. Accessed 2019, May 1 from
   https://www.watchman.org/profiles/pdf/wordfaithprofile.pdf

Word-Faith Heresy is Blinding. Accessed 2019, May 1 from
   https://www.delreychurch.com/blog/post/word-faith-heresy-is-blinding

Kovak, Ivan P. 2018. The Falsehoods of Christianity: Volume Two: (A Layman's Perspective),
   Volume 2 (Branham as one of Marilyn Hickey's "Word of Faith" favorites)

Kozar, Steven. 2017, Jan 9. The Word of Faith Cornucopia of False Doctrine. Accessed 2019, May
   1 from *http://www.piratechristian.com/messedupchurch/2016/12/the-word-of-faith-
   cornucopia-of-false-doctrine*

SHARON ORPHANAGE AND SCHOOL

A Lesson for Racist. 1989, May 11. The Province

Evangelistic Tabernacle. 1948, Feb 21. The Province

Sharon Camp Opens July 5. 1949, Jun 24. Star Phoenix

The Temple of the Latter Rain. 1949, Jan 22. Calgary Herald

Institute Will Erect New School. 1939, Apr 4. Star Phoenix

Orphanage Scheme Under Way at North Battleford. 1943, Oct 30. Star Phoenix

Philadelphia Church. 1950, Jan 7. Chicago Tribune

Pentecostal Group to Convene Here. 1940, Jan 30. Star Phoenix

North Battleford Hangar, Planes, Burn. 1948, Jun 11. Star Phoenix

Latter Rain Convention: The Hawtin Party. 1949, Sep 3. St. Louis Star and Times

2,000 Take Part in Daily Rites at Religious Camp. 1949, Jul 23. Star Phoenix

Obituary: Roy H. 1982, Jul 29. Borders. The Courier Journal

Sharon Orphanage Homes Care for 28 Children. 1946, May 9. Star Phoenix

Elim Tabernacle. 1933, Jan 28. Star Phoenix

Full Gospel Church. 1947, Aug 9. Calgary Herald

Giant Spiritual Feast Coming to Dayton. 1966, Oct 29. The Journal Herald

Orphanage Farm Barn Destroyed. 1949, Sep 12. Star Phoenix

Private Orphan Homes Opposed. 1950, Mar 28. The Leader Post

Local Boy Makes Good. 1948, Feb 25. Richmond Review

Youngsters Sent Home. 1948, Jan 15. Star Phoenix

Annual National Convention: Independent Assemblies of God. 1948, Oct 23. Edmonton Journal

Housing Situation Easier as More Suites Available. 1949, Sep 2. Star Phoenix

Prem. 1944, Sep 5. T. C. Douglas Inspects Northern Mental Hospital. Star Phoenix

Scenes at Orphanage and Aviation School. 1947, Dec 17. Star Phoenix

North Battleford Faces Serious Water Situation. 1945, Apr 4. Star Phoenix

North Battleford to Get Orphanage and School. 1944, May 13. Star Phoenix

CHAPTER 29

WILLIAM BRANHAM AND
A. W. RASMUSSEN

"Without even praying for it[558]"

When most believers of the "Message" think of William Branham, they think of the "prophet". Believers of the "Message" are convinced to believe that William Branham is "Elijah" from the Old Testament, returning in modern times. When most believers of the "Message" think about the "prophet", they think about the sermons and the "healing" lines. Since William Branham's death in 1965, he has been immortalized through over a thousand recorded sermons and transcripts that are distributed to all parts of the globe by Branham's two sons and their "non-profit" organization, Voice of God Recordings. Believers of William Branham think of him often, painting pictures in their minds that were created mostly from the details and "history" that was created for Branham's stage persona. But the personality given to the "prophet" using only his words is far from accurate.

My family remembers a much different person. I grew up with stories of a laughing, joking man. According to the stories told by my grandfather, father, aunts, and uncles, William Branham was a much different man than his stage persona. My family described William Branham as a man that was full of fun, often pulling pranks to make

---

558 Branham, William. 1947, Apr 12. Faith is the Substance.

others laugh. I can remember the excitement in their eyes and the emotion that filled the air when they told and re-told the stories more than I can remember the details of the stories themselves. William Branham held a special place in each of their hearts, and most of my family was unaware of the very sinister things going on behind the scenes.

My grandfather was a close friend of William Branham. My aunts and uncles grew up with Branham's sons and daughters. They remember what the family was like in the early years, long before ankle-length skirts were enforced for women[559] and before shorts were forbidden for men. They had photographs of William Branham and his family posing for the camera wearing outfits that would later be forbidden by virtually every preacher in the religious cult called the "Message". William Branham's son wore shorts, as did William Branham. Both posed for photographs in their shorts, even though shorts were condemned by the stage persona. William Branham's daughters wore skirts above the knees, which would have caused them to be labeled as "prostitutes" by every "Message" pastor that I had heard. At least one church I visited had forced a young woman out of the church for wearing a "scandal skirt", a skirt with a slit in the back that exposed part of her upper calves. Men and women who were close to the "prophet" lived by his actions, not by his words. Men and women who knew William Branham only by the stage persona presented on the recordings lived their lives by his words and not his actions.

I always knew the "Message" that I raised my children in was different from the "Message" that my grandfather raised his in. I wasn't aware, however, of how much it had changed before my grandfather joined, or of the tactics used to grow and spread the "Message". When I discovered the testimony of the son of Raymon A. Haas, something unusual caught my eye. When William Branham was teaching the "Latter Rain" theology to those at the Sharon Orphanage, it included metaphysics. Haas claimed Branham could move objects in the air.[560] I

---

[559] FAQ. Accessed 2020, May 17 from https://stillwaterscamp.org/faq "Skirt lengths must be below-mid calf. Ankle-length skirts are required for all activities"

[560] The Sharon Orphanage Connection. Accessed 2019, Apr 20 from http://abc-history.blogspot.com/2008/02/before-i-was-born-my-father-ramon-haas.html "One of Branham's teachings was the ability to use the "Spirit of God" to make things move on their own accord. My dad related to me he had tried this, just once, and said that things in the room moved on their own but the air had become cold, dark and heavy.

remembered a story I heard on the very first sermon we had access to hear. One person stood before William Branham, claiming not to believe. Suddenly, William Branham asked everyone in the room to turn their backs to him. With their backs turned, Branham claimed he could move a bracelet in the air with his mind. Just when it got interesting, the tape was spliced, and I was unable to hear the rest of the story — it was missing from both the recording and the transcript. Then, in an obviously different recording, his voice said, *"I'll take any cross-eyed child you've got in this meeting you bring it up here without even praying for it and just let me look at it straight in the eyes like that I'll make its eyes come straight"*.[561] I wanted to hear what the people said when they turned back around! I also wanted to hear if anyone said, *"Hey! Why did you have us turn our backs! I wanted to see what happened!"* Learning that his brother Howard toured with him — while still running a bar back in Jeffersonville — I knew that this was most certainly a favorite bar trick.

Whether anyone in the room turned to see what happened or not, the strategy worked. Branham's unusual doctrine had made an impact on those at the Sharon Orphanage and the "Latter Rain Revival" quickly started to spread from Battleford. The "Voice of Healing Revival" followed closely on its heels, making it nearly impossible to distinguish the two; men from both camps were cross-pollinating and many of them truly felt that both groups were one and the same.

George Warnock started teaching Branham's "Manifest Sons of God" doctrine, and it began to propagate into both "revivals". As a close associate of Ern Baxter who worked so closely with William Branham that the revivals became known as the *Baxter-Branham Campaigns"*, George Warnock would have been a respected figure. When he taught Branham's "Manifest Sons" theology, listeners would have assumed that other participants in the revival believed the same theology. Before long, both the "Voice of Healing Revival" group and

---

It scared him and he never tried it again. After this he rejected this teaching by Branham but he maintained many other principles taught by Branham and the Latter Rain Movement and incorporated many of the Branham / Latter Rain Movement principles into the fabric of his teachings to the Assembly of the Body of Christ. In this way he carried forward some of these Branham doctrines."

[561] Branham, William. 1947, Apr 12. Faith is the Substance.

the "Latter Rain Revival" group became indistinguishable. Many evangelists were part of both "Latter Rain" and "Voice of Healing".[562]

I found an article in the March 2018 issue of "The Canadian Mantle", a magazine promoting the Independent Assemblies of God (I.A.O.G). The I.A.O.G was organized in 1918 as the "Scandinavian Assemblies of God in the United States of America", established by Rev. A. W. Rasmussen.[563] Rasmussen was a name I was very familiar with in the "Message". William Branham often spoke with or of "Brother Rasmussen" and "Brother Boze" from the platform and referred to both men as not only business associates, but close friends. Page 5 of the magazine had an article that listed the timeline of events in "Latter Rain". According to this list, A. W. Rasmussen invited George Hawtin to speak at the I.A.O.G. convention[564] after the revivals at the Sharon Orphanage, Rasmussen described the men of the Battleford revival as if they were heroes. Both the Hawtin brothers and Hunt were invited to speak concerning their formula for revival. Three meetings were held each day, and the two Hawtins split to cover more ground.[565] Before long, William Branham's name was familiar throughout the I.A.O.G. I suddenly wanted to learn more about "Brother Rasmussen", the Independent Assemblies of God, and the New Order of the Latter Rain.

...

A. W. Rasmussen was, according to William Branham, a close friend and business associate.[566] Rasmussen was also one of the strongest supporters and promoters of William Branham, and his "Message" — at least during the time Branham worked closely with members of the Latter Rain movement. Rasmussen continued to invite

---

[562] Example: T. L. Osborn, Editor for Voice of Healing. Accessed 2020, May 29 from
https://churchwatchcentral.com/2017/04/03/todd-bentley-and-his-generals-kenneth-hagin-tl-osborn-oral-roberts.
Todd Bentley and His Generals: Kenneth Hagan, T. L. Osborn, Oral Roberts. "The men that came out of the NOLR's VHM that helped develop the CGM and CRM
were men like TL Osborn, Oral Roberts and Kenneth Hagin.
[563] History of the Independent Assemblies of God. Accessed 2020, May 17 from *http://www.iaogi.org/styled-5/index.html*
[564] 2018, Mar. The Canadian Mantle. The Latter Rain Movement of '48
[565] Annual National Convention of the Independent Assemblies of God. 1948, Oct 23. Edmonton Journal.
[566] Branham, William. 1956, Apr 3. Shepherd of the Sheepfold. "I was happy tonight to meet Brother Rasmussen, a very dear friend"

William Branham to speak or join events in which William Branham spoke for years to come.

Rasmussen may have been new to William Branham's unusual doctrines, but he was no stranger to Pentecostalism or Christian fundamentalism. About the same time the Azusa Street Revival was exciting the early Pentecostals in 1906, Scandinavian Baptists broke out in a revival in Chicago. As a result, many of the Scandinavian churches joined the Pentecostal faith. Among those who joined was Rev. A. W. Rasmussen. In 1918, Rasmussen founded the Independent Assemblies of God (I.A.O.G) under the title "Scandinavian Assemblies of God", which joined the Independent Pentecostal Churches in 1935. For about five years he ran the organization from Brooklyn, NY, holding two services, one in a Scandinavian language and one in English, and working with revivalists from coast to coast. As a result, Rasmussen became well connected in Pentecostal circles. In November of 1941 Rasmussen took a leadership position in Chicago's Philadelphia Church.[567] It was the same church that organized William Branham's "Chicago Campaign", and the same group that would later host Jim Jones' Latter Rain revivals. From Chicago, Rasmussen would continue to unify the I.A.O.G. while working with Canadian groups. In 1945, Rasmussen relocated to Edmonton, Alberta and started the Edmonton Gospel Temple.[568] Interestingly, the Edmonton Gospel Temple provided a "Masonic Temple Club Room", further connecting Branham and his associates to the Masonic Order — a subject I was very interested in. While Rasmussen worked in Edmonton, Joseph Mattsson-Boze took his place in Chicago at the Philadelphia Church. Church directories in Chicago, however, continued to list Rasmussen as "Pastor".

Branham's tour through Canada in 1947 gave birth to the Latter Rain movement at the Sharon Orphanage in North Battleford, Saskatchewan. William Branham was both a catalyst and supporter. Though he would later distance himself from the main branch of Latter Rain, Branham would continue to work closely with Rasmussen and Boze while teaching specific doctrines from the Manifest Sons of God

---

[567] Pastor and Family Leave for Chicago. 1941, Nov 5. Brooklyn Daily Eagle.
[568] Edmonton Gospel Temple. 1945, Jun 2. Edmonton Journal. "NOTE: All future services will be held in the Masonic Temple Club Room"

sub-sect of the Latter Rain movement. Those who did not know the difference would have mistakenly suspected that William Branham was teaching the same Latter Rain version being taught in the sect originating from the Sharon Orphanage, but those in that particular sect (not its branches) would have disagreed. William Branham himself spoke about the main branch of the Latter Rain sect as if it were old news.

After the birth of the Latter Rain, Rasmussen invited Latter Rain leaders George Hawtin and Percy Hunt to speak at I.A.O.G conventions and advertised the men involved in the revival at North Battleford as heroes of the faith. Both Hawtins and Hunt were invited to share their "formula" for revival to the I.A.O.G, and afterward, Rasmussen began to merge his sect of the Assemblies with the Latter Rain Movement.

The revival at the Sharon Orphanage made an impact on Rasmussen and his multiple congregations. As the revival began to spread, Rasmussen became instrumental in propagating it throughout the United States. On many occasions, Rasmussen would hold Latter Rain revivals in Edmonton one week and then continue them with Joseph Mattsson-Boze in Chicago the next. Then he'd return to Edmonton to tell of the events that happened in Chicago's Latter Rain revivals.[569]

Not everyone agreed with the Latter Rain movement, however, and eventually it would nearly split Pentecostalism in half. Church leaders began to realize the very dangerous way in which Latter Rain leaders were given authority. The Assemblies of God met in Seattle Washington to halt the danger, at which time the extremist views presented by ministers in "The New Order of the Latter Rain" were rejected.[570] After the resolution was passed, Rasmussen separated his Independent Assemblies of God from the main branch of Assemblies, and became fully dedicated to spreading the Latter Rain version of William Branham's "Message".

---

[569] Edmonton Gospel Temple. 1950, Apr 1. Edmonton Journal. "Rev. A. W. Rasmussen Returning from the Philadelphia Church of Chicago will tell of the GREAT REVIVAL DAYS in that city in these services.
[570] 1949, Sept 9-14. Minutes and Constitution with Bylaws: Assemblies of God, the Twenty-third General Council. "That we disapprove of those extreme teachings and practices, which, being unfounded Scripturally, serve only to break fellowship of like precious faith and tend to confusion and division among the members of the Body of Christ, and be it hereby known that this 23rd General Council disapproves of the so-Called "New Order of the Latter Rain"

A. W. RASMUSSEN:

3-The Sharon Orphanage Connection Accessed 2019, May 1 from *http://abc-history.blogspot.com/2008/02/before-i-was-born-my-father-ramon-haas.html*

History. Accessed 2019, May 1 from *www.iaogi.org/styled-5/index.html*

Rasmussen, A. W. 1973. The Last Chapter.

Faupel, William D. Windows from the North - Canadian Contributions to the Pentecostal Movement.

Assemblies of God International Fellowship. Accessed 2017, May 30 from http://Encyclopedia.com

IAOGI. Accessed 2017, May 30 from *http://areyoureadyministries.com/id5.html*

Accessed 2017, May 30 from the wayback machine https://web. 1940-1944. archive. org/web/20160428051535/http://pc-onclark. org/history_1940_1944

The Brooklyn Daily Eagle. 1941, Nov 8. Minister's Bride.

Chicago Tribune. 1951, May 12. Philadelphia Church.

The Minneapolis Star. 1942, Oct 10. Philadelphia Church.

New Castle News. 1972, Jun 3. Rev. Rasmussen will speak in Tabernacle.

The Decatur Daily Review. 1977, May 7. Midwest Bible College Introduced.

York Daily Record. 1974, Jun 22. Guest Speaker.

Chicago Tribune. 1950, Aug 26. Philadelphia Church. 1974, Aug 14. The La Crosse Tribune. Minister to Speak.

Chicago Tribune. 1951, Feb 24. Philadelphia Church.

Democrat and Chronicle. 1944, Apr 29. Missionary Day Highlight of Convention.

The Minneapolis Star. 1938, May 21. Philadelphia Church.

The Berkshire Eagle. 1963, Aug 16. Full Gospel Church Names Speaker for Camp Grounds.

Chicago Tribune. 1950, Sep 9. Philadelphia Church.

Edmonton Journal. 1950, Feb 4. Edmonton Gospel Temple.

The Pantagraph. 1977, Apr 20. Midwest Bible College to Open In Former School.

Chicago Tribune. 1950, Dec 30. Philadelphia Church.

The Minneapolis Star. 1943, Mar 20. Philadelphia Church.

Chicago Tribune. 1950, Nov 25. Philadelphia Church.

Chicago Tribune. 1951, Dec 29. Philadelphia Church.

Democrat and Chronicle. 1959, Jun 27. 15 Great Days of Spiritual Refreshing.

Chicago Tribune. 1950, Dec 2. Philadelphia Church.

Chicago Tribune. 1950, Sep 30. Philadelphia Church.

Chicago Tribune. 1951, Nov 17. Philadelphia Church.

Alton Evening Telegraph. 1970, Sep 26. International Convention.

Chicago Tribune. 1951, Sep 29. Philadelphia Church.

The Daily Chronicle. 1954, Mar 19. Fellowship Chapel Announces Grand Opening.

The Brooklyn Daily Eagle. 1941, Nov 5. Pastor and Family Leave for Chicago.

Chicago Tribune. 1950, Dec 16. Philadelphia Church.

Chicago Tribune. 1949, Oct 1. Assembly of God.

Arizona Republic. 1943, May 29. Reorganized Latter Day Saints.

The Courier News. 1961, Jul 29. Christian Assembly.

Star Tribune. 1966, Jun 23. Full Gospel Meeting Set.

The Dispatch. 1942, Feb 14. Philadelphia Pentecostal Church.

The Minneapolis Star. 1943, Mar 20. Misc. News.

Chicago Tribune. 1951, Nov 10. Philadelphia Church.

Chicago Tribune. 1951, Jan 13. Philadelphia Church.

Chicago Tribune. 1950, Jul 29. Philadelphia Church.

The Brooklyn Daily Eagle. 1940, Jul 18. Famous Evangelist Tent Meeting Speaker.
The Canadian Mantle. 2018, Mar. The Latter Rain Movement of '48
Chicago Tribune. 1950, Feb 11. Philadelphia Church.
York Daily Record. 1972, Oct 6. Dover area class selects officers.
The Brooklyn Daily Eagle. 1951, Mar 3. Marantha Temple Services.
The Minneapolis Star. 1944, Jan 15. Hear Rev. A. W. Rasmussen.
The Minneapolis Star. 1944, Jan 22. Philadelphia Church.
Chicago Tribune. 1950, Dec 23. Philadelphia Church.
The Pantagraph. 1971, Oct 16. Dirksen Library Plans Unveiled.
The Indianapolis Star. 1975, May 31. Rev. Rasmussen Will Speak at Church Services.
Chicago Tribune. 1951, Jun 9. Philadelphia Church.
Chicago Tribune. 1951, Dec 8. Philadelphia Church.
Chicago Tribune. 1951, Feb 17. Philadelphia Church.
The Courier News. 1939, Apr 24. Club News.
The Chillicothe Constitution Tribune. 1956, May 26. Music Festival to Begin Belin U. Week.
Edmonton Journal. 1950, Apr 1. Edmonton Gospel Temple.
The Brooklyn Daily Eagle. 1941, Apr 26. Revival Continues in 5th Week.
New Castle News. 1978, May 27. Preachers sees 'dawn of new age'
The Brooklyn Daily Eagle. 1941, Jun 7. Hear Evangelist Lloyd L. Smith.
Florida Today. 1977, Nov 19. World Outreach for Christ Inc.
Chicago Tribune. 1950, Mar 25. Philadelphia Church.
Chicago Tribune. 1898, Nov 27. Misc. News.
Chicago Tribune. 1951, Mar 17. Philadelphia Church.
Chicago Tribune. 1951, Apr 28. Philadelphia Church.
The Daily Telegram. 1966, Jul 22. Deliverance Convention.
The Winona Daily News. 1974, Aug 16. To Attend Meet.
The Daily Leader. 1977, May 5. Bible College to Open In Bloomington.
Statesman Journal. 1970, Jul 17. Northwest Regional Convention of the Independent Assemblies of
    God, Int.
Chicago Tribune. 1951, Jun 2. Philadelphia Church.
The Minneapolis Star. 1952, Aug 16. 5th Avenue Temple Church.
Chicago Tribune. 1952, Feb 2. Philadelphia Church.
Democrat and Chronicle. 1944, May 6. Pentecostal.
Chicago Tribune. 1951, Nov 24. Philadelphia Church.
Chicago Tribune. 1950, Nov 11. Philadelphia Church.
The Brooklyn Daily Eagle. 1951, Mar 3. "Miracles are Happening"
Chicago Tribune. 1951, Mar 10. Philadelphia Church.
Chicago Tribune. 1886, Apr 17. Michigan-Purchase of an Evening.
Chicago Tribune. 1950, Sep 2. Philadelphia Church.
Chicago Tribune. 1952, Feb 16. Philadelphia Church.
The Brooklyn Daily Eagle. 1941, Jun 6. Sees Nazi Victory Over Norwegians A Hollow Triumph.
Chicago Tribune. 1950, Oct 28. Philadelphia Church.
Chicago Tribune. 1949, Jul 23. Philadelphia Church.
Chicago Tribune. 1951, Nov 3. Philadelphia Church.
The Brooklyn Daily Eagle. 1951, Mar 5. Opening Services Set for Marantha Temple.
Chicago Tribune. 1953, Apr 4. Philadelphia Church.
The Brooklyn Daily Eagle. 1941, Jun 28. Pentecostal Assembly Holds Revival Meetings.
Chicago Tribune. 1951, Sep 15. Philadelphia Church.
The Minneapolis Star. 1943, Mar 6. Philadelphia Church.
Chicago Tribune. 1949, Sep 24. Assembly of God.

Chicago Tribune. 1950, Dec 9. Philadelphia Church.

Chicago Tribune. 1951, Dec 15. Philadelphia Church.

Chicago Tribune. 1951, Dec 22. Philadelphia Church.

Democrat and Chronicle. 1944, Mar 18. Pentecostal Host Plans Convention.

Statesman Journal. 1970, Jul 15. Assemblies of God Will Meet Today.

Chicago Tribune. 1951, Feb 3. Philadelphia Church.

Edmonton Journal. 1945, Jun 2. Edmonton Gospel Temple.

Statesman Journal. 1970, Jul 16. Northwest Regional Convention of the Independent Assemblies of God, Int.

The Brooklyn Daily Eagle. 1941, Jul 26. Don't Fail to Hear.

The Brooklyn Daily Eagle. 1941, Dec 10. Salem Pentecostal Church Gets New Assistant Pastor.

The Courier News. 1936, Sep 28. Poultry and Supplies.

The Pantagraph. 1977, May 10. Midwest Bible College to Open in Former School.

Chicago Tribune. 1951, Apr 7. Philadelphia Church.

Arizona Republic. 1943, Jun 5. Miscellaneous.

The Woodstock Sentinel. 1923, Nov 29. Chapter Masons Entertained by Knights Templar.

Branham, William. 1953, August 30. Why I Am A Holy Roller.

Branham, William. 1955, October 06. The Power of God.

Branham, William. 1956, April 03. Shepherd of the Sheepfold.

Branham, William. 1956, June 17. Revelation Book of Symbols

Branham, William. 1956, October 01. The Ministry Explained.

Branham, William. 1957, August 07. Hear Ye Him.

Branham, William. 1957, August 09. Blind Bartimaeus.

Branham, William. 1957, August 11. Expectations and Leadings of the Spirit.

Branham, William. 1957, August 11. The Greatest Gift of the Bible

Branham, William. 1957, July 25. Hear Ye Him.

Branham, William. 1957, July 28. Thirsting for Life.

Branham, William. 1957, March 23. God in His Word.

Branham, William. 1957, May 16. We Would See Jesus.

Branham, William. 1958, September 27. Why We Are Not A Denomination.

Branham, William. 1959, June 10. As I Thought on My Way.

Branham, William. 1960, August 02. El Shaddai.

Branham, William. 1960, June 06. To Whom Would We Go.

Branham, William. 1961, January 23. Be Not Afraid, It Is I.

Branham, William. 1961, May 20. From That Time.

Branham, William. 1962, July 22. Show Us the Father and It Sufficeth Us.

Branham, William. 1962, July 28. God Has Provided A Way.

Branham, William. 1963, January 18. Spirit of Truth.

CHAPTER 30

WILLIAM BRANHAM AND GEORGE J. LACY

"In Washington DC in the Religious Hall of Arts[571]"

In the "Message", there were two videos we held sacred. The first was the 1953 video, "Twentieth Century Prophet". The second was the 1954 video, "Deep Calleth to the Deep". These were the only two films available to the public with real-life footage of William Branham and the Branham healing campaigns. I found this unusual, considering the fact that they had video recording equipment. The Branham family even had personal video recording equipment, given to them by believers who undoubtedly wanted it to be used in the revivals. But "Twentieth Century Prophet" and "Deep Calleth to the Deep" were the earliest — and latest — sets of video footage of the "prophet" in action that we were allowed to see.

Reverends LeRoy and Paul Kopp traveled to Jeffersonville to speak with William Branham while the film crew captured the scene. In the video, those of us who never knew William Branham in person could see inside the "prophet's" home for a glimpse into his personal life. The Reverends Kopp listened as the "prophet" told his "supernatural" story. I remember watching in awe as William Branham told about how the "pillar of fire" came down over his head. This was a story we heard often, both from the accounts told by William Branham in his sermons

---

[571] Branham, William. 1958, Mar 14. Love

and from our pastors who re-told what William Branham described in his sermons.

We were told that it happened during a debate that William Branham was reluctant to attend. In his sermons, he described how that of the many photographs taken by photographers, God only allowed *one single photo* to be developed: one which had a halo above his head. He described how that George Lacy, "Head of the F.B.I.", came to verify that it was "supernatural" and sent the photo to Washington, D.C. Now that I had found so many factual errors in Branham's testimonies, I began to wonder how many of the details from these stories were true? Now that I was beginning to see the business side of the Branham Campaigns, and being made aware of the types of men who associated with William Branham, I began to wonder, "Was all of this nothing more than a publicity stunt?"

When I learned that the Assemblies of God had publicly rejected the religious movement that William Branham himself (and unknown financial supporters from the United States) had ignited from Canada and that F. F. Bosworth, who was a member of Branham's campaign team, was a founding Father of the Assemblies of God, I began to wonder how this would impact their crowd size. This would have had a very negative impact in the meetings, both for attendance and for income. I began searching for news articles about F. F. Bosworth immediately after "Latter Rain" began to spread into the United States, and I found an article in the January 1950 issue of The Voice of Healing.

The Branham Campaign had scheduled a meeting in Houston from January 10-27. They advertised the upcoming revival meetings using scenes from the 1947 "healing" campaigns at the St. Louis Kiel Auditorium with "Little David" and the Shrine Auditorium in Phoenix, Arizona. The article invited everyone to attend their Houston, Texas meetings in January.

On January 24, the debate was announced in the newspapers.[572] Both sides claimed the other challenged them to the debate. I found it odd that William Branham told newspaper reporters that *"he alone would represent his side"*, because it was the opposite of what he

---

[572] Pastor and 'Faith Healer' Plan Debate 1950, Jan 24. The Baytown Sun.

described when he told the story in his stage persona.[573] In the sermons, Branham said that F. F. Bosworth could go -- but only if he didn't argue.

After holding a conference with the other Baptist pastors in the area Rev. W. E. Best said that he would debate once the challenge was formally issued. I also found it interesting that Rev. Best was concerned for his own safety in a "non-argumentative discussion" with ministers of the "Gospel".[574] If the campaigns were humble, Pentecostal revival meetings, there should be no fear of physical harm! Rev. Best told reporters that he might need police protection in the Sam Houston coliseum — all while William Branham continued to claim that "he alone would represent his side". Did Rev. Best have inside knowledge about William Branham and the men he associated with?

William Branham claimed in his sermons that "God" would not allow any pictures — with the exception of his "halo" photograph — to develop. *"Every one of them was perfect negative".*[575] The Houston Press covered the debate on January 24, 1950, however, and I suddenly learned that this was not the case.[576] Photographs did develop, and I could see Rev. Best and Rev. Bosworth arguing with each other. Rev. Best explained that he was *"not opposed to divine healing"* but was *"opposed to 'divine healers' as such"* and quoted the Apostle Paul's description of deceivers in the last days. I was shocked as I looked at the number of photographs that *did* develop. There were several! But I was even more shocked at the violence that erupted in the meetings. Ministers of the "Gospel" were described swinging their fists as if they were in a boxing ring! Rev. Best was apparently justified in his fear of the men Branham associated with.[577]

---

[573] Branham, William. 1950, Jul 14. At Thy Word. "Doctor Best of the Baptist Tabernacle at Texas, he made the challenge and put it in the paper, and said if I didn't come and debate it with him, that I was afraid to take up for what I believed. And he knew then that I didn't believe it if... Well, that was just Satan trying to work on me. So I—I wasn't going to argue with him. And he kept on. He put it in the paper the next day, said, "Well, that shows that they're... They can't back up what they talk about, these Pentecost people and holy-rollers, and so forth." Said, "They can't back up what they're talking about." And Mister Bosworth, he's about seventy-three, but that was just too much for him. He couldn't stand that. He said, "Brother Branham, let me go over there." Mister Best is a young man, about thirty. And I said, "Brother Bosworth, you may go if you don't argue."

[574] Preachers Will Hold Debate on Faith Healing 1950, Jan 24. Longview News Journal.

[575] Branham, William. 1954, Jul 20. It is I, Be Not Afraid. "Almighty God would not permit one of them to be developed. Every one of them was perfect negative."

[576] Baptist Cleric to Challenge 'Miracle Man' Hofferbert, Louis. 1950, Jan 24. Houston Press.

[577] Baptist Cleric to Challenge 'Miracle Man' Hofferbert, Louis. 1950, Jan 24. Houston Press. "Suddenly a fist

Immediately after the fight broke out, the Baptist ministers fled the building. It wasn't until after the debate that William Branham took the platform. After a brief speech, William Branham also quickly fled the scene.[578] The reporters described his military-style exit from the building into the night. During this short speech, a photographer took a photo of William Branham, men behind him, and a light above his head. This light, we were taught in the "Message", was the "pillar of fire" from the Bible. We were told that it was "evidence" that God was with the "prophet".

The Sam Houston Coliseum hosted many famous acts, some of which were captured in pictures and video. Fortunately, archives of those photographs and videos were now online for me to examine, though it took some time to find them. When I did, it was difficult for me to believe that anyone attending that brief encounter would have for a second believed that this light was in any way supernatural. In fact, not a single person who attended any night-time event in the Houston Coliseum would have believed it. For its time, the lighting in the Houston Coliseum was quite advanced.

From an NBA basketball game, to the legendary John Lennon, Paul McCartney, and the Beatles, the Coliseum's lighting gave the audience a bright view of the stars. Some of the lights could be turned on and off independently, and arrays of lighting could be positioned in various ways. Watching the archived, colorized videos of events held in the Houston Coliseum, a viewer doesn't often notice the lighting. But when the video is paused, and cropped, and made black and white, it is entirely different. Photographs captured at just the right angle in the Houston Coliseum could be made to look unusual, even supernatural. In today's modern world of technology, we'd think nothing of a photograph like this; we are all familiar with light and its effect on the camera. But in the days of yesteryear, a photograph with a "halo" was special!

---

lashed out. It struck Martin Jones, 1315 Shearn, a salesman in a downtown store across the nose and inflicted a slight cut.
[578] Baptist Cleric to Challenge 'Miracle Man' Hofferbert, Louis. 1950, Jan 24. Houston Press. "As the Rev. Branham left the platform a group of followers quickly surrounded him and the group marched in almost military fashion to a rear door and the evangelist disappeared into the night."

This "supernatural" photograph got a lot of mileage, and Branham's campaign team seized the opportunity. Over time, they began to enhance the photograph, darkening it to remove the men in the background — who appear to have seen nothing unusual as they sat staring solemnly into the audience — and later colorized, cropped, and altered the photograph to remove surrounding details. Growing up in the "Message" I saw images of the "halo" photograph, in color, hang in people's homes, and even in churches. There were even those who worshipped the image. Was this "light" really supernatural? I knew that if I had been shown any other photograph of such a light, my initial impression would be that the image captured man-made "lighting", not a supernatural "pillar of fire".

I was also curious about the rest of William Branham's story. Branham claimed that George J Lacy, the "head of the F.B.I.", issued a statement confirming it to be "supernatural".[579] Afterword, according to William Branham, it was hung in the "Religious Hall of Art" in Washington, DC as the only supernatural photograph ever captured on film. I wanted to learn more about this George J. Lacy and his position in the Federal Bureau of Investigation. It only took a few searches through the Texas newspaper archives to find a wealth of information on Mr. Lacy.

...

In 1921, George J. Lacy was Chief of the Identification Bureau of Texas.[580] He became superintendent during a time when black female prisoners were segregated from white.[581] In 1923, Lacy found himself in trouble when he was accused of physical assault. R. V. Hogan claimed he saw George Lacy beating an African American.[582] Hogan heard the black man beg for mercy as Lacy knocked him down and continued to kick him. Other witnesses described being beaten by Lacy

---

[579] Branham, William. 1958, Mar 12. Jesus Christ The Same Yesterday, Today, and Forever. "George Lacy said, "I've been your critic too, Mr. Branham." But said, "I said it was psychology." But said, "The mechanical eye of this camera won't take psychology." That's the head of the FBI in fingerprint and documents. Yes. It was absolutely there."
[580] Goose Creek Merchant Attacked and Robbed. 1921, Jun 5. The Houston Post.
[581] Criminal Investigation Office to be Enlarged. 1921, May 31. The Houston Post.
[582] Witness Declares Lacy Beat Him Up. 1923, Mar 1. The Houston Post.

for making whiskey. One witness claimed that Lacy had struck his only eye, and he was kicked down the stairs while blinded. Lacy was discharged February 15, 1923 after the allegations were confirmed. The board declared, *"No man has a right to take advantage of his authority to show brutality towards helpless prisoners"*.[583]

Somehow, Lacy was magically able to bounce back. Newspapers published an in-depth article describing Lacy's work with the Texas fingerprint system.[584] Lacy opened a private practice, named the "Lacy Fingerprint Bureau of Houston". This was not what I pictured when I thought about the "Head of the F.B.I.". I began to wonder, *"Was Lacy also a member of the Ku Klux Klan?"* During the 1950s, the Ku Klux Klan were installing men into positions of power throughout Texas, and I knew that with his abusive background, it would have made him a prime candidate. I also knew that it was unlikely George Lacy was ever accepted into the FBI after receiving a dishonorable discharge. Still, I wanted to know more about the man that William Branham used to "confirm" the "supernatural" photo.

In May of 1934, W. W. Sterling, George J. Lacy, and H. J. Rafin established a nonprofit organization for crime detection.[585] W. W. Sterling was Governor Ross S. Sterling's appointed Secretary of State of Texas. The Ku Klux Klan's invasion of public office in Texas has been widely studied since the assassination of President John F. Kennedy. It is well known that police brutality against African Americans was a problem throughout the Southern United States. But in Texas, where Roy E. Davis had based his operations, men like Lacy beating African Americans was very common. At the same time, it is extremely difficult to find any information about those who escaped prison time. The Ku Klux Klan is a very secretive group, and any documentation about its members and their Klan-related activities, for all intents and purposes, does not exist. Or so I thought.

To my surprise, in Texas, where Lacy and Sterling were operating, Klan activity has been well documented.[586] In Houston specifically, the

---

[583] Civil Service Examiners Uphold Chief in Lacy Row. 1923, Mar 2. The Houston Post.
[584] Applying Fingerprint Identification System to Court Cases. 1923 2, Jun 3. The Houston Post.
[585] Corporation Formed for Crime Detection. 1934, May 4. The Eagle.
[586] Guardians Against Change: The Ku Klux Klan in Houston and Harris County, 1920-1925 Volume 8. No 1. Houston History.

Ku Klux Klan's primary agenda was allegedly "moralism" and resistance to change. The Klan in Houston was so violent that Klan members were identified and asked to end the violence. Among those named as members in 1923 was Governor Ross S. Sterling, brother of Lacy's business partner, W. W. Sterling. Ross Sterling was among those who joined the Ku Klux Klan in its early days and was asked to end Klan-attributed violence.

Soon after his organization was established, Lacy was asked to test ballistics in criminal trial.[587] He was also asked to administer truth serum.[588] Though he wasn't a Federal Agent, Lacy's ties to the Texas government enabled him to operate at a state level. By 1938, Lacy had advanced to position of president of the Texas division of the International Association for Identification.[589] Still, his assisting in a criminal trial was far from a federal position. Lacy always remained a private investigator, throughout the rest of his career, helping to examine documents for attorneys in criminal trial.

I found it interesting to read some of the things Lacy said in his interviews. Awful statements, and in my opinion, highly inaccurate.

> *"You can study a man and know pretty well how he will act under certain circumstances," said George J. Lacy, head of the Houston scientific crime laboratory. "But there's no telling what a woman will do. And she has no reason herself for what she does. {...} "The reason," said Lacy, "is because she has less sense. There is 'honor among thieves' but not when they are women thieves," both Lacy and Leonard said. "When a man drops to a criminal life, he can get low, but he can't get as low as a woman criminal," Lacy declared.* [590]

This was exactly what I'd heard William Branham state in is sermons. Branham's sermons were filled with derogatory statements

---

[587] Barrow Gunds Tested by Ballistics Expert. 1934, May 30. El Paso Times.
[588] Truth Serum Will Be Given Amnesia Victim. 1934, Jun 2. Austin American Statesman.
[589] Fort Worth Selected as Convention City. 1938, Jun 23. The Corpus Christi Caller Times.
[590] Don't Bet on Lady Desperado; She Might Kiss You or Fire A Slug In Your Heart. 1938, Jun 22. Lubbock Morning Avalanche.

against women, and he claimed that every crime committed was because of women.

When, she's guilty of every sin that was ever committed, she is the cause of it. Right. Now, I'm not, I'm not speaking of rights. She is guilty. She is the one that caused every baby to be born blind. She is the one that caused every grave to be dug. She is the one that caused sin, sickness, sorrow. A ambulance can't ring unless a woman caused it. No crime can be done, no sin, no death, no sorrow, no suffering, but a woman done it.[591]

I was shocked the first time that I read the full report[592] written by George J. Lacy concerning the "halo" above William Branham's head. It did not mention the "pillar of fire". It did not mention the "supernatural". The photographer did not "rush the photo" to the F.B.I. None of the things we believed, not a single aspect of the story that we were trained from birth to accept, was accurate in any way. Gordon Lindsay, of Branham's campaign team, made the request for Lacy to examine the photograph. In his report, Lacy described the scientific method used to confirm that the photo was not retouched and that the negative was not altered. He summarized his findings by simply stating that light in the coliseum had been captured by the film. The same exact way that any professional would describe the photographs of the lighting above the head of the Beatles, basketball players, and any other attraction from the same venue. Should they have access to see the photographs in the archives of the Houston Coliseum records, they might even compare them to Branham's photograph, describing similarities. And they would have laughed at the notion of a "Religious Hall of Art" in Washington, DC, because there was no such "hall".

Learning about the ties to the Ku Klux Klan in Houston, Lacy's brutal beating of African Americans, and the publicity gained from the debate and photograph, I suddenly thought back to the Reverends Kopp, who also appeared to be helping Branham gain publicity. Who were

---

[591] Branham, William. 1963, Nov 10. Souls that Are In Prison Now.
[592] Lacy, George J. 1950, Jan 29. Report and Opinion - RE: Questioned Negative

they? Why did these two men, who weren't in the "Message", decide to make this video? Did they really believe the "halo" story, after having been in the bright lights themselves?

REV. W. E. BEST
Hofferbert, Louis. 1950, Jan 24. Houston Press. Baptist Cleric to Challenge 'Miracle Man'
The Baytown Sun. 1950, Jan 24. Pastor and 'Faith Healer' Plan Debate
Longview News Journal. 1950, Jan 24. Preachers Will Hold Debate on Faith Healing
The Waco News Tribune. 1950, Jan 24. Baptists Rap 'Miracles'.
Lubbock Evening Journal 1-24-1950. Faith Healing Debate is Set.

WILLIAM BRANHAM'S "HALO" PHOTOGRAPH
Lacy, George J. 1950, Jan 29. Report and Opinion - RE: Questioned Negative
Branham, William. 1950, July 14. At Thy Word.
Branham, William. 1950, August 20. Believe Ye That I Am Able to Do This
Branham, William. 1951, May 2. The Angel of the Lord
Branham, William. 1951, May 9. Testimony.
Branham, William. 1951, July 17. The Angel of the Lord.
Branham, William. 1951, Sept 23. The Principles of Divine Healing.
Branham, William. 1952, July 13. Early Spiritual Experiences.
Branham, William. 1952, July 25. Experiences.
Branham, William. 1952, Aug 10. Jesus Christ the Same Yesterday, Today, and Forever.
Branham, William. 1952, Aug 17. Do You Now Believe
Branham, William. 1953, Mar 26. Israel and the Church.
Branham, William. 1953, May 7. Expectations.
Branham, William. 1953, May 8. God Commissioning Moses.
Branham, William. 1953, May 9. The Pillar of Fire.
Branham, William. 1953, Jun 3. God Commissioning Moses.
Branham, William. 1953, Jun 4. The Angel of the Lord.
Branham, William. 1953, Nov 14. Africa Trip Report.
Branham, William. 1953, Nov 29. Testimony.
Branham, William. 1954, Mar 1. The Angel of the Covenant.
Branham, William. 1954, Jul 20. The Maniac of Gadara.
Branham, William. 1954, Sept 2. South Africa Testimony.
Branham, William. 1955, Feb 27. The Healing of Jairus Daughter.
Branham, William. 1955, April. Blind Bartimaeus.
Branham, William. 1955, Jun 8. Abraham.
Branham, William. 1956, Apr 14. Blind Bartimaeus.
Branham, William. 1957, Jun 13. Thirsting for Life.
Branham, William. 1957, Aug 10. Jehovah Jireh.
Branham, William. 1957, Dec 12. The Door of the Door.
Branham, William. 1958, Jan 27. Jehovah Jireh.
Branham, William. 1958, Mar 2. Door to the Heart.
Branham, William. 1958, Mar 12. Jesus Christ the Same Yesterday, Today, and Forever.
Branham, William. 1958, May 8. Expectations
Branham, William. 1958, May 10. Have Faith in God.
Branham, William. 1958, May Jun 12. We Would See Jesus
Branham, William. 1958, Jun 19. Can We See Jesus
Branham, William. 1960, Feb 10. The Revelation That Was Given to Me
Branham, William. 1960, Mar 29. It Is I Be Not Afraid
Branham, William. 1961, Feb 12. It Is I Be Not Afraid
Branham, William. 1961, Mar 12. Jehovah Jireh.
Branham, William. 1962, Jun 28. A Greater Than Solomon Is here
Branham, William. 1963, Jun 5. Greater Than Solomon Is here

Branham, William. 1963, Jun 6. Show Us the Father.

Branham, William. 1964, Apr 12. A Court Trial

Branham, William. 1964, Apr 18. A Paradox.

GEORGE J. LACY:

George J. Lacy: ASQDE President - 1956-1960. Accessed 2019, May 1 from
    http://www.asqde.org/about/presidents/lacy_g.html

The Austin American. 1926, Jun 28. Ponzi Mystery.

The Marshall News Messenger. 1935, Jul 11. Crime Detection Methods Explained.

Volume 8. No 1. Houston History. Guardians Against Change: The Ku Klux Klan in Houston and
    Harris County, 1920-1925

The Houston Post. 1921, May 31. Criminal Investigation Office to be Enlarged.

The Houston Post. 1923 2, Jun 3. Applying Fingerprint Identification System to Court Cases.

El Paso Times. 1934, May 30. Barrow Gunds Tested by Ballistics Expert.

The Marshall News Messenger. 1936, Jun 10. Indict.

The Houston Post. 1923, Mar 1. Witness Declares Lacy Beat Him Up.

The South Bend Tribune. 1962, Nov 9. Obituaries: George J. Lacy.

The Eagle. 1934, May 4. Corporation Formed for Crime Detection.

Lubbock Morning Avalanche. 1938, Jun 22. Don't Bet on Lady Desperado; She Might Kiss You or
    Fire A Slug In Your Heart.

The Houston Post. 1923, Apr 22. Identification is a Modern Science.

The Houston Post. 1921, Jun 5. Goose Creek Merchant Attacked and Robbed.

The Austin American. 1937, Aug 13. Program Arrangements Announced for Identification
    Convention Here.

The Corpus Christi Caller Times. 1938, Jun 23. Fort Worth Selected as Convention City.

Austin American Statesman. 1934, Jun 2. Truth Serum Will Be Given Amnesia Victim.

The Houston Post. 1923, Mar 2. Civil Service Examiners Uphold Chief in Lacy Row.

The Galveston Daily News. 1934, May 30. Ballistics Test is Relied on To Reveal Slayers.

The Corpus Christi Caller Times. 1938, Jun 22. Police Chiefs of State Name Beaumont Man as
    President.

CHAPTER 31

WILLIAM BRANHAM AND THE BIRTH OF THE MESSAGE

"I am God's Voice to you[593]"

W hen the "Latter Rain Revival" began to spread throughout the United States and Canada, William Branham's fame also began to spread. At risk of being caught in the middle of the religious argument, Branham tried to distance himself from the "Latter Rain" movement when speaking to specific crowds. It was quickly causing a major split in Pentecostalism. Many of his invitations and business associates were deeply involved with "The New Order of the Latter Rain", however, and he could not simply abandon them. From a business standpoint, it would have seemed foolish not to ride the wave. "Latter Rain" was growing increasingly popular among some fundamentalists, even while under scrutiny, and "Latter Rain Revivals" were still filling tents and auditoriums.

New leaders quickly emerged, careers were launched through just a "prophecy" and the "laying on of hands".[594] New teachers emerged, fueling the flame ignited by Branham's Canada meetings and the Sharon Orphanage support. Branham's teachings on prophecy,[595]

[593] Branham, William. 1951, May 5. My Commission.
[594] Althouse, Peter. 2003. Spirit of the Last Days: Pentecostal Eschatology. "The difference was that the laying on of hands and the restoration of apostles and prophets were not dominant beliefs in early Pentecostalism. Laying on of hands was given greater theological weight by the Latter Rain Revival."
[595] Branham, William. 1947, Apr 12. Faith is the Substance. "But if I come in the Name of the Lord Jesus, in the

dispensationalism,[596] restoration,[597] and judgment[598] spread quickly throughout the movement. It did not take long to notice that many of the churches that William Branham frequented were also "Latter Rain" churches. Nor did it take long to recognize the fact that many familiar names were spreading the new and unusual theology that William Branham himself was creating or copying from others. New churches were created and named after the movement, with "Latter Rain" in their names.[599] Many "Latter Rain" churches sponsored Branham's campaigns in major cities.[600] As time progressed, "Latter Rain" became known as the "Message of the End Time",[601] and the movement's theology became known as the "Latter Rain Message". Missionaries began to share the "Latter Rain Message"[602] with other countries. Before long, "Latter Rain Message" became a popular topic and with that "Message", rejection of mainstream religion became popular among its participants.

I found a document at Fuller Theological Seminary listing the papers from the office of Rev. Joseph Mattsson-Boze.[603] Joseph Mattsson-Boze, a close friend and business associate of William Branham, was a heavy promoter of the "Latter Rain" when speaking in his Philadelphia Church in Chicago and through his newsletter, "The Herald of Faith". Among the documents was a collection of sermons and manuscripts directly related to the "Latter Rain". Interestingly, a number of Branham's sermons were chosen by Joseph Mattsson-Boze as important to the "Latter Rain". Fifteen manuscripts from the years 1956 through 1962 are included in the list Mattsson-Boze composed.

Teaching on Moses (5/13/56)
Revelation, Book of Symbols (6/17/56)

---

name of prophecy"
[596] Branham, William. 1947, Apr 12. Faith Is the Substance. "Someday God would give the gift back to the church for the Gentiles before the ending of the Gentile dispensation, like He did for the Jews."
[597] Branham, William. 1948, Mar 4. The Angel of God. "I know the next thing to happen is the restoration of the gifts to the Church"
[598] Branham, William. 1950, Jul 11. Ministry Explained. "And when the judgment strikes the earth, and the atomic powers rock the nations, we'll ride above the waves into Glory"
[599] Example: Latter Rain Message at the Latter Rain Chapel. 1952, Feb 23. Tampa Bay Times.
[600] Example: Philadelphia Church in Chicago.
[601] Example: Hear the Message of the End Time. 1951, Feb 3. Arizona Republic.
[602] Example: Fellowship Temple. 1951, Feb 3. Arizona Republic. "Latter Rain Message for Latter Rain Church"
[603] The papers from the office of Joseph Mattsson-Boze from Fuller Theological Seminary

The Handwriting on the Wall (1/8/58)
Palmerworm, Locust, Cankerworm, Caterpillar (8/23/59)
Let Us See God, (11/29/59)
Hearing, Recognizing, Acting on the Word (2/21/60)
He Careth For You (3/1/60)
God's Wrapped Gift (12/25/60)
The True Easter Seal (4/2/61)
The Ever-Present Water from the Rock (7/23/61)
Message of Grace (8/27/61)
Respects (10/15/61)
You Must Be Born Again (12/31/61)
The Key to the Door (12/31/61)
A Guide (10/14/62)
Remembering the Lord (12/9/62)
The Falling Apart of the World (12/16/62)
Standing in the Gap (6/23/63)
We Have Seen His Star and Have Come to Worship (12/16/63)
Shalom (1/12/64)
God is Identified by His Characteristics (3/11/64)
Going Beyond the Camp (7/19/64)
The Seed of Discrepancy (1/18/65)
The Anointed Ones at the End Time (7/2/65)
The Rapture (12/4/65)

A letter to the editor of the Windsor Star from an excited participant in the "Latter Rain" set the stage for a theme that would run throughout a number of William Branham's sermons. In August of 1949, William Branham held a series of meetings in Windsor, Ontario. As his "faith healing" fame quickly spread, critics like James Randi quickly arose, questioning Branham's "healing" power. These questions rang even louder since numerous "faith healers" in the "Latter Rain" and "Voice of Healing" revivals were using "prayer cards" for "discernment". The author of the letter described his own experience in the Branham campaigns.

> *Coming to Windsor this Sunday (August 21) is Rev. William Branham whom God is using in praying for the sick. No building is large enough to hold the crowds that come wanting*

to be prayed for. Many hundreds are turned away daily. Bro. Branham couldn't heal a sick headache, but God can. He prays the prayer of faith and the Lord does the healing. He is only an instrument in the hands of a great and wonderful God.

I have been to his meetings and have seen the Lord make crippled legs straight, heard a small boy, eight or nine years of age, blind, shout for joy, "I see, I see"

Cancers disappear; T.B. People are healed; hopeless bed-ridden people jump from their beds and shout praises to God.

Now can anyone say, I don't believe it? If so, come to the Windsor Arena August 21 to 25 and see for yourselves.

Bring your sick, your blind, and your deaf ones. Come believing, get rid of your sin and God will heal your bodies. He never fails.

"A BELIEVER"
Both well, Ont.[604]

The letter from "a believer" sounded very much like a letter from a promoter of the meetings. I noticed that the author of the letter to the editor qualified their statements concerning the "healing" just as William Branham and F. F. Bosworth were accustomed to doing. *"Get rid of your sin and God will heal your bodies"*. Like the other sermons, if a person was not healed in the meetings, then their own "sin" was the fault — not the healer.

Branham himself must have known that the letter, which was intended to attract the crowds, would also attract the critics who were aware of his current track record in "healing". To halt the critics, Branham introduced a story repeated often about a pastor who questioned his abilities in the Windsor meeting. Branham claimed that the man wrote a disease on his "prayer card" that he did not have, and was *struck to the floor by God.*[605] In 1953, he claimed the man was *given the disease he wrote* (Tuberculosis), [606] which he would suffer with for the rest of his life. In 1956, Branham claimed that the man did

[604] God's Healing Power and Witnesses. 1949, Aug 19. The Windsor Star.
[605] Branham, William. 1950, Jan 10. Moses.
[606] Branham, William. 1953, May 8. God Commissioning Moses.

not fall to the floor. Instead, he *ran screaming.*[607] In 1957, Branham claimed that the man *died a year later.* Parts of the recording were missing or unintelligible.[608] Later in 1957, Branham claimed that the man also *got cancer,* and that he did not die. He was *still alive, in critical condition.*[609] In 1958, Branham claimed the man got cancer, not tuberculosis, and *died six months later.*[610] The next month, Branham claimed that the man did not run screaming or die, he was *struck down paralyzed and was still alive.*[611] In 1961, Branham claimed that the man was not alive, but *died six weeks later.*[612]

I knew that it was highly unlikely that I would ever find out the whole truth about what happened in Windsor, if I was even able to discover any evidence at all. But I also knew that if the story was used to silence critics as early as 1950, the divisions caused by "Latter Rain" were significant. I thought back to LeRoy and Paul Kopp, from the video used to promote the "Message", "20th Century Prophet". This video was frequently used when recruiting converts to the "Message", and it was made about the time that the "Latter Rain" was strongly rebuked by many Christians as "heretical". It seemed all too coincidental that the "Windsor story" and the Kopp's promotion of Branham would emerge during this time period. I wanted to learn more about the Reverends Kopp.

...

LeRoy Kopp was a minister from Brown County, Kansas. In 1914, shortly after marriage, he became mentally ill.[613] He was sent to a sanitarium, but physicians had a difficult time keeping him under control. He'd escape, get thrown in jail, and be returned to medical supervision.[614]

---

[607] Branham, William. 1956, Dec 9. Jehovah Jireh
[608] Branham, William. 1957, Jan 27. Blind Bartimaeus
[609] Branham, William. 1957, Jun 30. Thirsting for Life.
[610] Branham, William. 1958, Feb 8. The Queen of the South
[611] Branham, William. 1958, Mar 30. Christ Knocking at the Door.
[612] Branham, William. 1961, Feb 12. Jehovah Jireh.
[613] Rev. Mr. LeRoy Kopp Ill. 1914, May 1. Brown County World.
[614] Misc. News. (Escaped Sanitarium). 1914, Jul 16. Fairview Enterprise

He was a minister in the United Brethren Church,[615] the denomination Branham appears to have been affiliated with when he married Meda Broy and was working with E. Howard Cadle. LeRoy Kopp was ordained as a pastor while he was still in high school. By 1915, he was released from mental health supervision once again, and started working as an evangelist. Apparently, his ministry paid well. Shortly after starting his ministry, he purchased the Hamlin Reporter newspaper and announced that he would be changing the direction of the news that was published. He stated that he did not approve of the news that was published in the Hamlin Reporter, and he said, *"If we continue printing the Reporter, we will not advertise anything but what we feel is honest and upright, and will not even insert news which we feel is of a degrading sort."*[616] In 1916, he started preaching a "doomsday" version of Christianity.[617]

LeRoy's religious newspaper was not well respected, and competing newspapers let him know about it. They said that he was right — judgment was coming — just not in the way in which he claimed.

Rev. LeRoy Kopp is experiencing some trouble in keeping his religious paper going. He has no job office and not many people care to pay the price for a paper devoted to a particular form of religion. But the reverend gentleman believes the Lord will help him out if his faith is strong enough, so he will move the paper to Fairview and he has sold part of his household furniture to pay the cost. Brother Kopp should listen to the story of the negro brother who had faith and tried to pick up the red hot stove when told that the Lord wouldn't let it burn him. If the Lord sees that there is need of a religious paper at Fairview no doubt He will see that it is supported but it is suspected the Reverend Mr. Kopp has relied upon his own judgment concerning the long felt want. — Leavenworth Times[618]

---

[615] Returned to Sanitarium. 1914, Jul 16. Morrill Weekly News. "was ordained pastor of the United Brethren church at Sabetha while attending high school at that town. Afterward he took up evangelistic work."
[616] U. B. Pastor-Editor Will Change Paper to Religious Publication. 1915, Dec 15. Topeka State Journal
[617] Judgment Day Soon? 1916, May 11. Horton Headlight.
[618] Faith vs. Judgment. 1916, Mar 9. Fairview Express.

Not long after, LeRoy moved to Auburn, Nebraska.[619] He and his family auctioned off part of his belongings, packed up, and left town. This was first of a series of moves and changes in his life. LeRoy moved to Los Angeles, joined the Four-Square Gospel[620] (of which Herrick Holt, creator of the Sharon Orphanage sect was affiliated), became an evangelist, and moved to Wichita. As part of the Foursquare Pentecostal movement of the 1930's, LeRoy's church held speeches defending the "faith healers".[621] Before long, he was touring the country holding revivals himself.[622] By 1936, LeRoy rose through the ranks to become the vice chairman of the Angelus Temple Evangelists, a leader in the Foursquare sect.[623] About the time Roy E. Davis and William D. Upshaw moved to the San Bernardino area, LeRoy started broadcasting on the radio.[624]

In the late 1940's, LeRoy became pastor of the Los Angeles Calvary Temple.[625] He added a grade school to the Temple's ministries, and the United Fundamentalist Bible Institute. The Temple would be the host of multiple Branham campaigns in Los Angeles. As chairman of the revival committee, LeRoy was in the perfect position to promote the "prophet".

But LeRoy was not the only evangelist in the Kopp Family. His brothers Vernon and Paul were also evangelists. Vernon worked as a missionary stationed in Africa.[626] In connection to research about the "Message" movement, however, his brother Paul Kopp was more interesting.

...

---

[619] Misc. News. 1917, Sept 13. The Robinson Index
[620] Foursquare Revival. 1931, May 8. Wichita Citizen.
[621] Foursquare Tabernacle. 1933, Jul 28. Covina Argus. "Some objections to Divine Healing Answered"
[622] Rev. Kopp Opens Revival Campaign. 1935, May 16. Visalia Times.
[623] Misc. News. 1936, Oct 22. Fairveiw Enterprise. "Rev. LeRoy Kopp, formerly of Fairview is now vice chairman of the Angelus Temple Evangelists."
[624] Rev. LeRoy M. Kopp Radio Evangelists of Los Angeles, Calif Opens Meeting at the Foursquare Church. 1946, May 4. Minneapolis Star.
[625] Calvary Temple Anniversary Date. 1949, Feb 26. Los Angeles Times.
[626] Misc. News. 1920, Jan 15. Fairview Express. "Rev Vernon Kopp, a missionary and stationed at the Danville Mission in Africa"

In 1943, Paul Kopp was in San Francisco. By the time Davis and Upshaw set up camp for the Ussher-Davis Children's Orphanage, however, Paul Kopp was in San Bernardino, California. He was there at the same exact time Roy Davis and William Upshaw were in the area posing as "Baptists", and seeking help for their mission. Upshaw was holding public discussions on his "Americanization" project, addressing the city with speeches with titles such as "Americanism that Will Save America"[627] During this time, Paul Kopp pastored the First Baptist church.[628]

In August of 1943, The San Bernardino Sun announced the orphanage scheme that Davis and Upshaw started which appears to have been a front for Ku Klux Klan funding. Upshaw himself was in charge of the "Americanization", and was soliciting involvement from the Baptist community, with which Paul Kopp was affiliated.[629]

It was during the time of this "Americanization" scheme that Paul Kopp was asked to step in as interim pastor of the First Baptist Church of San Bernardino.[630] There is no doubt that Kopp would have been involved with Upshaw's "Americanization" efforts. Not only was Kopp the interim pastor of the Baptist Church, Kopp was also affiliated with the Los Angeles City Baptist Mission Society,[631] and with the Women's Christian Temperance Union,[632] with which William Upshaw and his second wife, Lily Galloway, were deeply involved. Galloway was president of the organization.

It seems very unlikely that Paul Kopp was *not* aware of the highly publicized court trial involving Davis and Upshaw. Newspapers were filled with details, and it would have been the talk of the town. Roy E. Davis, William Upshaw, and Lily Galloway were the center of attention.

---

[627] Downtown Evangelistic. 1944, May 27. The San Bernardino County Sun. "Americanism that Will Save America', William D. Upshaw former Georgia Congressman"

[628] First Baptist. 1944, May 27. The San Bernardino County Sun.

[629] "Arrangements are being made to secure the majority of the faculty members from the Southwestern Baptist Theological seminary at Ft. Worth Texas. Former Representative William D. Upshaw is an active part of the organization."

[630] Baptists Secure Interim Pastor. 1943, Dec 26, San Bernardino County Sun. "The Rev. Paul Kopp, young Baptist minister, has been called by the First Baptist Church of San Bernardino as interim pastor."

[631] Baptists Secure Interim Pastor. 1943, Dec 26, San Bernardino County Sun. "Recently the Rev. M [sic] Kopp resigned as pastor of the Bayshore Baptist church in San Francisco to become affiliated with the Los Angeles City Baptist Mission society"

[632] W. C. T. U. Members Meet Friday; All Invited. 1944, Dec 7. San Bernardino County Sun. "Rev. Paul Kopp will offer the devotionals."

Yet the former Congressman Upshaw would have been actively engaged with Paul Kopp's church while working with Davis to build the next wave of the Ku Klux Klan. Paul Kopp and his brother LeRoy Kopp helped to promote William Branham's ministry with a short film, "Twentieth Century Prophet".

...

I paused to catch my breath, completely shocked at the many connections that tied every aspect of Branham's early ministry, fame, and fortune together. Roy Davis was starting an orphanage as a front for the Klan. William Upshaw was holding conferences for the "Americanization" project. Paul Kopp, director of evangelism for the Northern Baptist convention, was involved in the same community, at the same time. His brother, LeRoy, head of the Calvary Temple, was involved in the promotion of ministers and evangelists featured in Branham's "Voice of Healing" publication.[633]

I considered the publicity of the Houston debate and the photo which was "verified" by George J. Lacy. Lacy had a history of physically abusing African Americans and was partnered with men having connections to the Ku Klux Klan. He likely was a member himself. I shook my head at the publicity stunt created using that photo, shortly after the "Latter Rain" created a potential black eye for the ministry.

I reflected on the contribution of the Kopp brothers, who began helping to promote the "prophet" after the "Latter Rain" controversy began to pose a threat to his success. Roy Davis was promoting William Branham in the Voice of Healing magazine after the "Latter Rain" movement began, as the Assemblies of God sect of Pentecostalism — and Pentecostalism in general — began to split due to disagreement about the "Latter Rain" movement. Former Congressman Upshaw helped to promote William Branham as a "healer" by posing in one of the "healing" meetings in a wheelchair that he didn't need — *at LeRoy Kopp's Calvary Temple in Los Angeles!*

---

[633] Example, Page 2. 1949, Sept. The Voice of Healing. "Her messages were most edifying, building faith to such a high peak that it seemed only natural for people to believe for what they desired. Calvary Temple joins me in extending a hearty invitation". Next section: "the Thomas Welch healing revival now in progress at Calvary Temple, 123 N. Lake St., Los Angeles, California, Rev. LeRoy M. Kopp, Pastor.

All of these events occurred during a time when the "Latter Rain Message" was promoted by many of Branham's close associates and posed a threat to the existence of his stage persona. This was a time when Branham's "Message" was transitioning from humble beginnings to include claims of striking people down from the platform for questioning his supernatural authority. It was a time when his "Message" was creating an army of "prophets" and "evangelists". The group formed "Joel's Army",[634] using Branham's "Manifest Sons of God" doctrine. [635]

Clearly, it was a time of transition from William Branham's former stage personas that I never knew had existed. "The "Message" that I knew was being born. Little did I know that at the same time Branham's ministry was shifting into high gear, the "Americanization" project started by former Congressman William D. Upshaw and Roy E. Davis started preparing for its next phase. I was too distracted by the information I'd just stumbled onto linking Joseph Mattsson-Boze's "Latter Rain" affiliation to specific sermons preached by William Branham. Why had Mattsson-Boze chosen these particular sermons? Why were we never told about Branham's "Latter Rain" history? For that matter, who was this Joseph Mattsson-Boze from Chicago?

---

[634] Joel's Army Marches On. Accessed 2020, May 28 from https://equip.org/article/joels-army-marches-on.
"According to Branham, healing will be commonplace. 'Oh, waiting for the manifestations of the sons of God (Hallelujah), when God will make Hisself known, when they'll stop sickness, they'll stop cancer, they'll stop diseases.' In response to a question, Branham made reference to the coming of Joel's Army. 'Yes, Brother Copp, I am sure that you are referring to Joel's prophecy in the Old Testament, Joel 2:28, how that he prophesied that in the last days he would pour out his spirit upon all flesh, the sons and daughters would prophesy, the old man would dream dreams and the young men would see visions.'"
[635] Southern Poverty Law Center, Klanwatch Project, Militia Task Force. 2008. Intelligence Report: A Project of the Southern Poverty Law. "Through Cain came all the smart, educated people down to the antediluvian flood — the intellectuals, bible colleges," Branham wrote in the kind of anti- mainstream religion, anti-intellectual spirit that pervades the Joel's Army movement"

REV. LEROY KOPP:
Foursquare Tabernacle. 1933, Jul 28. Covina Argus
Misc. 1914, Oct 8. News. The Robinson Index
Thursday, August 24. 1922, Aug 23. Abilene Daily Reflector
Revival Series Opens in Lucas. 1934, Sep 24. News Journal
Faith vs. 1916, Mar 9. Judgment. Fairview Enterprise
Ex. 1951, Feb 19. Rep. Upshaw Discards Crutches After 59 Years. The Los Angeles Times
Rev. 1935, May 16. Kopp Opens Revival Campaign. Visalia Times Delta
Misc. 1917, Sep 13. News. The Robinson Index
Misc. 1936, Oct 22. News. Fairview Enterprise
West Van Nuys Mission. 1943, Oct 29. The Van Nuys News
Judgment Day Soon? The Horton Headlight Commercial. 1916, May 11
Hear Rev. 1947, Sep 6. LeRoy Kopp. Argus Leader
Misc. 1914, Nov 13. News. The Goodland Republic and Goodland News
Rev. 1946, May 4. LeRoy M. Kopp. The Minneapolis Star
New Hamlin Editor Starts News Reform. 1915, Dec 22. Hiawatha Daily World
Evangelist Plans Return for New Revival Meetings. 1951, Apr 28. The Los Angeles Times
Bethel Temple - Assembly of God. 1949, Jan 15. The Los Angeles Times
Calvary Tabernacle. 1947, May 10. The Los Angeles Times
Revival Series Opening Set. 1952, Jul 27. The Los Angeles Times
Rev. 1934, Aug 4. LeRoy Kopp to Continue Services. The Minneapolis Star
KGER. 1966, Nov 8. The Los Angeles Times
Golden Gate Auditorium. 1954, Dec 4. The San Francisco Examiner
Camp Meeting at Fairview. 1915, Aug 19. The Kansas Democrat
Kopps Feature U. 1921, Oct 20. B. Conference. The Morrill Weekly News
Rev. 1914, May 1. Mr. LeRoy Kopp Ill. Brown County World
Evangelist Plans Return for New Revival Meetings. 1951, Apr 28. The Los Angeles Times
Christian Israel Week. 1951, Aug 18. The Los Angeles Times
Held Good Conference. 1919, Nov 6. The Robinson Index
Radio Evangelist Speaks Tonight at West V. 1943, Oct 29. N. Mission. The Van Nuys News
Bethel Temple - Assembly of God. 1949, Jan 29. The Los Angeles Times
Foursquare Revival. 1931, May 8. The Wichita Citizen
Calvary Temple - City Wide. 1952, Apr 19. The Los Angeles Times
Calvary Temple Anniversary Due. 1949, Feb 26. The Los Angeles Times
Open at Woodlake. 1935, May 14. Visalia Times Delta.
Rev. 1935, May 29. Kopp Opens Services in City. Visalia Times Delta
Rev. 1922, Aug 22. Kopp to Nebraska. Abilene Daily Chronicle
Former Fairview Boy Heads Large Temple. 1948, Mar 18. Fairview Enterprise
Misc. 1940, Dec 26. News. Fairview Enterprise
Rev. 1915, Dec 27. LeRoy Kopp Quits Issuing Hamlin Paper. Hiawatha Daily World
Misc. 1921, Nov 10. News. Sabetha Herald
Radio Evangelist Speaks Tonight at West V. 1943, Oct 29. N. Mission. The Van Nuys News
Misc. 1934, Jul 28. News. Star Tribune
Misc. News Escaped Sanitarium. 1914, Jul 16. Fairview Enterprise
Mr. 1973, Feb 8. Vernon A. Kopp. Fairview Enterprise
Return to Sanitarium. 1914, Jul 16. The Morrill Weekly News
Hamlin Reporter is Sold. 1915, Dec 15. The Topeka State Journal

PAUL KOPP

First Baptist. 1944, May 27. The San Bernardino County Sun
Come to Church. 1944, Jun 3. The San Bernardino County Sun
Evangelism Head Dated at Baptist Church. 1948, Feb 6. The News Review
Baptists Secure Interim Pastor. 1943, Dec 26. The San Bernardino County Sun
First Baptist. 1943, Nov 27. The San Bernardino County Sun
First Baptist. 1944, Jan 8. The San Bernardino County Sun
First Baptist, Downtown Evangelistic. 1944, May 27. The San Bernardino County Sun
W. 1944, Dec 7. C. T. U. Members Meet Friday; All Invited. The San Bernardino County Sun
First Baptist. 1943, Apr 23. The San Francisco Examiner
First Baptist. 1944, Jan 1. The San Bernardino County Sun
Hamilton Square Baptist. 1942, Sep 12. The San Francisco Examiner
First Baptist. 27. The San Bernardino County Sun
First Baptist. 1944, Jan 8. The San Bernardino County Sun
First Baptist, Downtown Evangelistic. 1944, May 27. The San Bernardino County Sun
W. 1944, Dec 7. C. T. U. Members Meet Friday; All Invited. The San Bernardino County Sun
First Baptist. 1943, Apr 23. The San Francisco Examiner
First Baptist. 1944, Jan 1. The San Bernardino County Sun
Hamilton Square Baptist. 1942, Sep 12. The San Francisco Examiner

ROY DAVIS
Two Counts Are Dropped After Court Hearing. (1944, May 6). The San Bernardino County Sun
Orphanage Head Asks Reduction in $16,000 Bail. (1944, March 4). The San Bernardino County Sun
Habeas Corpus Petition Denied. (1944, April 29). The San Bernardino County Sun
Minister Charged. (1944, March 15). Nevada State Journal.
Minister, Wife Seek Damages – Rev., Mrs. Davis Ask for Sum of $25,000. (1945, February 18). The San Bernardino County Sun

ROY E. DAVIS - TIES TO THE KENNEDY ASSASSINATION
Caufield, Jeffrey H. (2015, September 29). General Walker and the Murder of President Kennedy – The Extensive New Evidence of a Radical-Right Conspiracy.

325

CHAPTER 32

WILLIAM BRANHAM AND JOSEPH MATTSSON-BOZE

"You see these little pockets going through the air, they call 'saucers,'... One of them will drop right down and this terrestrial body will take on a celestial body[636]"

As a child growing up in the "Message", I never thought to ask the many questions I wonder about now. During my early teenage years, there were many questions that I was afraid to ask. As an indoctrinated adult, there were many questions I purged from my mind and had forgotten how to ask. When I escaped and healed enough to think critically about the "Message", many of those questions resurfaced and combined with even bigger questions. By that time, many of the men and women who had those answers were long gone.

Why was 1953 the first year the "prophet" mentioned his "1933 prophecies" during a recorded sermon?[637] Why did he not mention the "1933 prophecy" of the "women's vote" until 1960,[638] and why did he

---

[636] Branham, William. 1965, Aug 22. Christ is Revealed in His Own Word

[637] Branham, William. 1953, Mar 26. Israel and the Church? "People, we're living in the end time. How many of you people heard years ago down here when they was going to have me arrested down here for preaching on that "mark of the beast"? When I said that Mussolini, when he first come in power twenty-some-odd years ago, I said, "If Mussolini ever goes towards Ethiopia, mark this down, there will never be peace till Jesus Christ comes." And I said, "There'll be three great isms, Communism, Fascism, and Nazism." And I said, "They'll wind up in one ism, and that one ism will dominate the world and will burn the Vatican City." You remember me saying that years and years and years ago. And just exactly that way!"

[638] Branham, William. 1960, Nov 13. Condemnation by Representation. "It shall also...has been an evil thing done in this country, they have permitted women to vote. This is a woman's nation, and she will pollute this

mention it at all, since women had been voting since 1920?"[639] Why did he say the "women's vote prophecy" was fulfilled with John F. Kennedy[640] until JFK's was assassinated and then stop saying it? Why would the prophecy appear to change after the assassination?[641] Why did he say during the 1956 election that it was the "turning point for America?[642] What did the ministers on the platform with the "prophet" think about these "prophecies" as they watched details of the "prophecies" shift and change over time? If the meetings were as miraculous as he claimed, why did most of them never join the "Message" cult following?

While Roy Davis, William Upshaw, the Reverends Kopp, F. F. Bosworth and others worked to promote Branham after the divisions in Pentecostalism that were caused by the "Latter Rain", Joseph Mattsson-Boze and other "Latter Rain" leaders did the same. With Mattsson-Boze's connections, networking to promote the "prophet" was an easy task. Even so, he knew that he would need to go beyond "Latter Rain Message" circles. Joseph Mattsson-Boze was a very vocal supporter of "Latter Rain"; helping Branham's public image helped his own public image and built his customer base for the "Herald of Faith". If the Latter Rain Movement's catalyst was William Branham, exposing critical flaws in Branham's claims would have exposed his own. Therefore, Joseph Mattsson-Boze and his "Herald of Faith" team coordinated with William Branham and his "Voice of Healing" team.

I had some photographs of William Branham and Joseph Mattsson-Boze, and found a few photographs taken at William Branham's home. The angles of some of the photographs seemed odd, as if both teams had

---

nation as Eve did Eden." Now you see why I'm hammering the way I do? I got THUS SAITH THE LORD. "In her voting, she will elect the wrong person."

[639] 19th Amendment. Accessed 2020, May 18 from https://www.history.com/topics/womens-history/19th-amendment-1

[640] Branham, William. 1962, Oct 13. The Influence of Another. "No more than twenty years ago, right from this same building, It told of President Kennedy coming in. It told exactly what would take place, that the women and so forth would put this fellow in, and exactly what he would be. And we knowed it all along, and told just exactly what would happen. And here it is today. And here is that conference coming up, the federation of church, and all coming together. Why, it ought to put us in action! That's right. Uh-huh. 166 Word by word, as He spoke, has been fulfilled right by us."

[641] Branham, William. 1964, Jan 12. Shalom. "And all these other things, like machines and automobiles, and—and how everything has come right down exactly what He said, until a woman ruling this nation, which, perhaps, is the church. And then the end come."

[642] Branham, William. 1956, Mar 4. Making a Way. "I—I'm predicting that this year America will receive Christ or reject Christ. See? I believe this will be the turning point, that America will go in. We'll have a revival in this day, or we won't have a revival. And I believe that this is the year that America will make its decision."

their own photographers, and were capturing different angles at the same time. Joseph Mattsson-Boze looked at the camera in one shot, while others looked at another photographer.

Shortly after William D. Upshaw posed as a wheelchair invalid seeking healing in Rev. Kopp's church, Joseph Mattsson-Boze escalated his efforts to connect William Branham with other minsters who might host big revival meetings. Mattsson-Boze attempted to persuade Billy Graham to allow Branham to join in the Billy Graham Campaigns.[643] I was surprised at how respectful the "prophet" was towards Billy Graham during this period of time.[644] In the version of William Branham's stage persona and the "Message" I discovered during the "Latter Rain" years, Billy Graham could bring salvation to thousands of people. In later versions of Branham's stage persona and "Message", however, he spoke strongly against Billy Graham, denominations, and trinitarianism. He referred to them as "blinded" [645] reprobates who could never receive his "Message" and become part of the "Bride of Jesus Christ". Branham even used the similar spelling between his last name and Graham to promote his "Manifest Sons of God" theology[646] — Branham implied that he was the "Son of Man" being manifested while Graham was preparing "Sodom" for divine judgment.

Lining the events up chronologically, it started to appear as though it were a very well-orchestrated plan. It seemed unlikely that all of these men, all of these connections, and all of these unusual events would coincidentally happen to be linked together.

When I first began studying the "Latter Rain Message", I was surprised how many familiar names and faces that I encountered.

[643] Branham, William. 1952, Feb 24. Believing God. "Billy Graham was asked, recently. Mattsson-Boze today is up there taking my book to Billy Graham, on an interview. But, and they're wanting me to follow him, there at Washington now, in that big auditorium."

[644] Branham, William. 1951, Sep 30. Expectation. "Bless this great city; send them a revival, Lord. Send Thy servants in here from different parts of the nations where they're ministering now and give this great city a shaking for God. When Thy servants come in, Billy Graham and them, Lord, pour out Your Spirit upon them. Literally thousands will be saved and turned to Christ."

[645] Branham, William. 1965, Nov 27. Trying To Do God A Service Without It Being God's Will. "I can see Billy Graham, he's got every denomination in the country with him … So the denomination will never receive it, neither can they receive it. And they're just as blinded to it as the Jews when they hung Jesus on the cross."

[646] Branham, William. 1964, Apr 3. Jehovah Jireh. "And Graham is six letters, and six is man's number, man's day; man was created, in—in Genesis 1:26, on the sixth day. But seven is God's number; seventh day, God rested. Not six, showing this G-r-a-h-a-m would be to the church that's in the world; but, A-b-r-a-h-a-m, Abraham is seven letters. Say, 'There's nothing in numbers.' … Notice, the sixth is a messenger to be sent to the world. And, notice, seventh is God's number. And notice at this time of the appearing now, or the revealing of the Son."

Joseph Mattsson-Boze was a leader in the movement,[647] taking the "Latter Rain" version of the "Message" to all parts of the world. He was the pastor of the Philadelphia Church in Chicago, working with A. W. Rasmussen. During the early 1940's, Mattsson-Boze toured the country as a Swedish American revivalist.[648] Until the "Latter Rain" split Pentecostalism, he was affiliated with the Assemblies of God sect that Bosworth helped to establish. As the "prophet" promoted other "divine healers"[649] in his "Voice of Healing Publication", Mattsson-Boze would sponsor them through his Philadelphia Church.[650] Ministers such as Levi Pethrus who sponsored the "prophet's" meetings in Stockholm[651] were part of both the "Latter Rain" and I.A.O.G.[652]

I found it interesting that Boze also took Rev. Freeman to Stockholm, which led to an arrest and court battle.[653] This was a big event in the ministry, yet none of the sermons of Branham (we had access to hear) mentioned this at all. The versions of the sermons that we did have rarely mentioned Branham's promotion of Rev Freeman, his ministry, or the "miracles" in Freeman's meetings. In fact, the version we had sounded like he was *not* in support of Freemen's healing abilities.[654] Joseph Mattsson-Boze collaborated with other "Latter Rain" leaders in the United States, such as Myrtle Beall[655] who was the leader of the "Latter Rain" Bethesda Missionary Temple in Detroit, Michigan.[656]

[647] Thackery, Archibald. Joseph Mattsson-Boze, a thoroughgoing revivalist. 2008, Dec 24. Accessed 2020, May 18 from https://lrm1948.blogspot.com/2008/12/joseph-mattsson-boze-thoroughgoing.html
[648] A Million Bibles Distributed Here. 1944, Apr 1. The San Francisco Examiner
[649] Example: Deaf. Dumb and Blind Healed at Selinas in Freeman Meetings. 1948, July. The Voice of Healing.
[650] Philadelphia Church. 1949, Sep 17. Chicago Tribune. "Healing Campaign continues through September 25, at the Coliseum, 15th and Wabash, Rev. William Freeman afternoons."
[651] Branham, William. 1951, Apr 13. The Works That I Do Bear Witness Of Me. "Brother Lewi Pethrus from Stockholm, Sweden. It's the head of the Filadelfian Church, the greatest Pentecostal church in the world. And I had a meeting there for him and, when I was at Stockholm."
[652] Philadelphia Church. 1951, Mar 24. Chicago Tribune. "SPRING CONVENTION AND ANNIV. SERV. REV. LEVI PETHRUS of Sweden. Guest speaker."
[653] 5th Annual Spring Convention. 1950, Apr 15. Edmonton Journal. "The arrest of Rev. Freeman and Rev. J. Mattsson-Boze on their way to church in Stockholm, Sweden. The furor raised against them by the Swedish press and radio. The court hearing.
[654] Branham, William. 1950, Jan 15. Believest Thou This? "A man come to me here not long ago. He said, 'Brother Branham, I been to Freeman, I been to Roberts, I—I been to Ogilvie, I been to all of them. They can't do me no good. I come to you.'"
[655] Philadelphia Church. 1950, Apr 22. Chicago Tribune. "Mrs. M. D. Beall, Rev. J. L. Beall, and Rev. A. E. Frink of Detroit, Mich.
[656] Thackery, Archibald. 2013, Oct 1. Mom Beall and Bethesda. Accessed 2020, May 16 from https://lrm1948.blogspot.com/2013/10/mom-beall-and-bethesda.html

It was just across the river from Windsor, where Branham would begin claiming a man was struck down by God for questioning.

Joseph Mattsson-Boze's church often advertised topics that aligned with Ku Klux Klan agenda, such as anti-Catholicism.[657] He also promoted subject matter contained in the Voice of Healing newsletter that Branham edited, themes of war and impending doom.[658] I was surprised as I looked over the ministers that Joseph Mattsson-Boze connected to William Branham[659] to see that Joseph Mattsson-Boze promoted them along with William Branham in his "Herald of Faith".

I thought back to the times that William Branham mentioned his "supernatural" gifts being printed in "Herald of Faith".[660] I always thought this was vindication of their accuracy. But could I really use the word "vindication", knowing that it was an advertising scheme? As I looked at the advertisements for "signs", "miracles", "wonders" by those connected to Joseph Mattsson-Boze,[661] it was difficult not to compare it to the advertising technique of the circus. There were big tents, big attractions, and big surprises. William Branham promoted big names in the "Voice of Healing."[662] They all claimed to "raise the dead", "heal the sick", "speak the prophecies".[663] Each minister attempted to create a sermon more interesting than the next.

Over time, they transitioned from normal "spiritual" attractions to science fiction. One minister closely connected to William Branham began to claim that Unidentified Flying Objects were a sign from God in his revival advertisements.

---

[657] Philadelphia Church. 1950, Nov 25. Chicago Tribune. "The Biblical Significance of the Removal of the Vatican from Rome to America"

[658] Philadelphia Church. 1950, Oct 28. Chicago Tribune. "Russia's Coming Defeat in the Next War According to Bible Prophecy".

[659] Philadelphia Church. 1950, Oct 28. Chicago Tribune. "Rev. Nunes will tell his life story"

[660] Branham, William. 1960, Nov 25. Conference. "I was on my way to Sunday school, and when I was getting my Bible, a vision came before me; and I was stopped in the floor. And here was what it said. It's on yellow paper. Will be printed in the 'Herald of Faith' right away, because most all of it is fulfilled."

[661] Bible Days Are Here Again. 1954, Jan 27. Medford Mail Tribune. "Signs Miracles Wonders. ... Bethel Temple ... Philadelphia Church - Chicago, Ill. Rev. Matteson Boze, Pastor. Dallas Revival Center — Dallas Texas, Rev. Jack Coe, Pastor.

[662] Rev. William Branham in Chicago. 1961, Jun. Herald of Faith. "Rev. Branham and some of the ministers who took part in the Campaign"

[663] City Wide Revival with Rev. O. L. Jaggars. 1954, May 22. Chicago Tribune. "How to Raise the Dead at a Respectable Funeral"

330

How Flying Saucers Are Kidnapping Human Beings from The Earth
1- Documented proof that Flying Saucers are real
2- Little Men in Flying Saucers are real
3- Flying Saucers are Kidnapping Human Beings.
A nationally famous sermon preached before audiences of thousands [664]

At first, I thought our "prophet" would never have preached sermons about "UFOs" and "Flying Saucers" — even if he did preach fear about earthquakes,[665] atomic and hydrogen bombs.[666] But the deeper I dug, the more surprised I became. William Branham preached about flying saucers over 40 times from 1953 to 1965.[667] In fact, he used the subject of "flying saucers" when he transitioned to later versions of the "Message" and claimed that the "Rapture" would involve a flying saucer.

> *You see these little pockets going through the air, they call "saucers," so forth. People so…That, well, we better leave that alone. "Hear all these people come up missing?" you say. Don't hear from them; they're standing there, and they're not there. That's the way the Rapture is going to be. One of them will drop right down, and this terrestrial body will take on a celestial body*[668]

[664] City Wide Revival with Rev. O. L. Jaggars. 1954, May 22. Chicago Tribune.
[665] Branham, William. 1965, Feb 19. This Day This Scripture Is Fulfilled. "I told Mr. Wood; is present tonight. And, I guess, eight or ten of the men, or fifteen, that was there at that time when it took place; the next morning, where the Lord came down in a whirlwind and ripped the mountain out around us, and cut the tops of the trees loose, and made three blasts, and said, "Judgment is headed towards the West Coast." 168 Two days after that, Alaska almost sunk beneath the earth. And since then, up-and-down the Coast, the belches of God's judgment against that spiritual screen. There is a iron curtain, there is a bamboo curtain, and there is a sin curtain."
[666] Branham, William. 1957, Apr 21. And Their Eyes Were Opened and They Knew Him. "One of these days there won't be even an ash left in Jeffersonville, there won't be one left in Charlestown, won't be one left in Louisville. This world is ripe for judgment. They have got a hydrogen bomb now that Russia can shoot from Moscow, land it on Fourth Street, and take every one of these powder plants around here, and sink it seventy-five feet under the ground, with one bomb. One bomb; fifteen miles square, it'll go to a hundred and fifty feet in the ground. The hand is on the trigger. The clock is ticking away. It's later than you think. Why wait till that time?"
[667] The Table. Accessed 2020, May 18 from https://table.branham.org
[668] Branham, William. 1960, Nov 25. Conference.

William Branham and his campaign team began to use these sci-fi themes as focal points for articles in the "Voice of Healing" publication.[669] In the issue of "Voice of Healing" advertising William Upshaw's "healing", for instance, there were "spiritual" cloud formations and articles that claimed that the word "uranium" fulfilled Luke 21:26-27. *"Atomic bomb sign of the end".* The issue advertised William Upshaw's alleged healing (without the wheelchair claim) in the middle of an article explaining the "signs" in the skies.

> *The word "heaven" is translated from the Greek "Ouranus", root word for Uranium, the element from which atomic bombs are made. The words of Jesus could well indicate that just before the Coming of Christ, the "power of uranium shall be shaken."*[670]

Whatever the cause, UFO or not, meetings organized and promoted by Joseph Mattsson-Boze drew massive crowds. Boze and F. R. Lummer, founder of "Herald of Faith" had a powerful platform to advertise. And by the time of William Branham's famous "Chicago Campaign",[671] the attractions and promotions had all but fully reversed the damage done by the "Latter Rain" split in Pentecostalism.

Of the research I uncovered during the "Latter Rain" days of the "Message", the biggest surprise came from meetings in Hagerstown, MD. Rev. Jim Jones, leader of Peoples Temple, had joined the "Message"![672] Like Branham and many others, Joseph Mattsson-Boze helped launch and promote Jones' career. Shortly after the formation of Peoples Temple in Indianapolis, Indiana; Jones took his place in the lineup of "Divine Healers" in the movement.

William Branham assisted in the launch of Jones' career, advertising Jones as a host pastor in the "Voice of Healing" magazine delivered to his subscribers nation-wide. Meetings were to be held at the Cadle Tabernacle, where Branham was already a familiar face. Soon,

---

[669] Page 1. 1952, Oct. The Voice of Healing. "What is the Mystery of the Flying Saucers? Are they of Supernatural Origin?"
[670] The Atomic Bomb Sign of the End. 1951, Sept. The Voice of Healing.
[671] The Chicago Campaign. Accessed 2020, May 28 from *https://branham.org/videos/ChicagoCampaign*
[672] Eastern Fellowship Convention. 1956, Apr 21. The Daily Mail.

Branham, Rasmussen, Boze, Osborn, Hicks, Bosworth, and others in the movement[673] would be familiar names in Peoples Temple. Joseph Mattsson-Boze and William Branham would work with Peoples Temple from 1956 through 1957.[674]

All of this was overwhelming. I wanted to know more about the "Americanization" project started by former Congressman William Upshaw and Roy Davis, but I also wanted to know more about Jim Jones and Peoples Temple. We were certainly never told that the infamous Rev. Jim Jones was a member of the "Message"! It was time to learn more about Jim Jones, and why he joined the religion of my family.

[673] Peoples Temple. 1957, Jun 1. The Indianapolis News. "Rev. William Branham will be ministering Tuesday through Friday afternoon and evening 2:30 and 7:30 p.m. Service to be conducted at Cadle Tabernacle. Morning Services 0 a.m. in Peoples Temple. A few of the ministering brethren include T. L. Osborne, Tommy Hicks, the renowned Bosworth and many others. 8,000 Laymen and 700 ministers were in attendance last year at our Christian Fellowship Convention Inc.
[674] The "Full Gospel" Origins of Peoples Temple. Accessed 2020, May 18 from https://jonestown.sdsu.edu/?page_id=92702

REV JOSEPH MATTSSON-BOZE

COLLECTION 0004: Papers of Joseph Mattsson-Boze, 1932-1988. 2018

Marantha Temple. 1953, Apr 11. The Brooklyn Daily Eagle

Philadelphia. 1949, May 14. Chicago Tribune

Eastern Fellowship Convention. 1956, Apr 21. The Morning Herald with Jim Jones of Peoples Temple

Bible Days are Here Again. 1954, Jan 27. Medford Mail Tribune

Chicago Minister at Philadelphia Church. 1937, Apr 10. Star Tribune

Hope Temple. 1963, Jul 6. The Minneapolis Star

Philadelphia. 1950, Nov 25. Chicago Tribune

15 Great Days of Spiritual Refreshing. 1959, Jun 27. Democrat and Chronicle

Rev. 1961, June. William Branham in Chicago. Herald Of Faith

Do Not Fail to Hear. 1943, Sep 4. The Dispatch

Missionary Says Africa Won't Go Red. 1961, Apr 15. The Greenville News

Faith Temple Church. 1973, Nov 10. The Greenville News

Philadelphia. 1951, Mar 24. Chicago Tribune

2 Return from Fellowship Meeting. 1958, Aug 1. Palladium Item

A Million Bibles Distributed Here. 1944, Apr 1. The San Francisco Examiner

Wm. 1954, Jul 17. Branham. Chicago Tribune

3 Great Days! The Corpus Christi Caller Times. 1959, Jun 2

Revival. 1960, Jul 23. Muncie Evening Press

Swedish Tenor Will Sing in Moline Church Monday. 1943, May 22. The Rock Island Argus

BH Tabernacle Hosting Fire-Day Convention. 1970, Apr 13. The News Palladium

First Christian Assembly. 1960, Mar 26. The Courier News

Welcome to our Services. 1943, May 15. The Dispatch

Bethel Tabernacle Pastor, Family Honored. 1943, Aug 10. The Dispatch

Faith Temple Plans Dedication Sunday. 1966, Dec 8. The Greenville News

Hear Joseph Mattsson-Boze. 1970, Sep 26. The News Palladium

Philadelphia. 1949, Sep 17. Chicago Tribune

Tonight Hear Rev. 1967, Jan 25. Mattsson Boze. The Monitor

Obituaries: J. 1989, Jan 31. D. Mattsson-Boze. The Monitor

PTL Club. 1978, Jan 29. Detroit Free Press

City Wide Revival. 1954, May 22. Jaggers Chicago Tribune Sat. UFOs

Minister to Speak. 1971, Oct 9. The Courier News

EINOR WAERMO. 1945, Apr 6. Oakland Tribune

World Missions Banquet Tonight!!! The News Palladium. 1967, Jan 7

Philadelphia. 1953, Dec 26. Chicago Tribune

Hear Einar Waermo. 1944, Apr 8. The San Francisco Examiner

Revival. 1960, Jul 23. The Star Press

Minister Says He Is Able to Work Miracles. 1950, Jan 25. The Sedalia Democrat

Rev. 1974, Mar 7. Ruel G. Braswell. The Terre Haute Tribune

Minister to Speak. 1971, Oct 9. The Courier News

ATTENTION! FULL GOSPEL BELIEVERS. 1960, Jul 9. The Indianapolis News

Philadelphia. 1950, Oct 28. Chicago Tribune

Opening Services Set for Marantha Temple. 1951, Mar 5. The Brooklyn Daily Eagle

3 Great Days of Special Services. 1959, May 30. The Corpus Christi Caller Times

5th Annual Spring Convention. 1950, Apr 15. Edmonton Journal

International Divine Healing Services. 1949, May 7. The Pantagraph

Church Name Changed. 1942, Nov 7. The Rock Island Argus

World Outreach Convention. 1973, Nov 8. The Greenville News
Philadelphia. 1950, Apr 22. Chicago Tribune
TONIGHT HEAR REV. 1967, Jan 25. MATTSSON BOZE. The Monitor
A. W. RASMUSSEN:
Accessed 2019, May 1 from. 3-The Sharon Orphanage Connection
http://abc-history.blogspot.com/2008/02/before-i-was-born-my-father-ramon-haas.html
History. Accessed 2019, May 1 from www.iaogi.org/styled-5/index.html
Rasmussen, A. W. 1973. The Last Chapter.
Faupel, William D. Windows from the North - Canadian Contributions to the Pentecostal
    Movement.
Assemblies of God International Fellowship. Accessed 2017, May 30 from
    http://Encyclopedia.com
IAOGI. Accessed 2017, May 30 from *http://areyoureadyministries.com/id5.html*
Accessed 2017, May 30 from the wayback machine https://web.archive.
    org/web/20160428051535/http://pc-onclark. org/history_1940_1944
The Brooklyn Daily Eagle. 1941, Nov 8. Minister's Bride.
Chicago Tribune. 1951, May 12. Philadelphia Church.
The Minneapolis Star. 1942, Oct 10. Philadelphia Church.
New Castle News. 1972, Jun 3. Rev. Rasmussen will speak in Tabernacle.
The Decatur Daily Review. 1977, May 7. Midwest Bible College Introduced.
York Daily Record. 1974, Jun 22. Guest Speaker.
Chicago Tribune. 1950, Aug 26. Philadelphia Church.
The La Crosse Tribune. 1974, Aug 14. Minister to Speak.
Chicago Tribune. 1951, Feb 24. Philadelphia Church.
Democrat and Chronicle. 1944, Apr 29. Missionary Day Highlight of Convention.
The Minneapolis Star. 1938, May 21. Philadelphia Church.
The Berkshire Eagle. 1963, Aug 16. Full Gospel Church Names Speaker for Campgrounds.
Chicago Tribune. 1950, Sep 9. Philadelphia Church.
Edmonton Journal. 1950, Feb 4. Edmonton Gospel Temple.
The Pantagraph. 1977, Apr 20. Midwest Bible College to Open in Former School.
Chicago Tribune. 1950, Dec 30. Philadelphia Church.
The Minneapolis Star. 1943, Mar 20. Philadelphia Church.
Chicago Tribune. 1950, Nov 25. Philadelphia Church.
Chicago Tribune. 1951, Dec 29. Philadelphia Church.
Democrat and Chronicle. 1959, Jun 27. 15 Great Days of Spiritual Refreshing.
Chicago Tribune. 1950, Dec 2. Philadelphia Church.
Chicago Tribune. 1950, Sep 30. Philadelphia Church.
Chicago Tribune. 1951, Nov 17. Philadelphia Church.
Alton Evening Telegraph. 1970, Sep 26. International Convention.
Chicago Tribune. 1951, Sep 29. Philadelphia Church.
The Daily Chronicle. 1954, Mar 19. Fellowship Chapel Announces Grand Opening.
The Brooklyn Daily Eagle. 1941, Nov 5. Pastor and Family Leave for Chicago.
Chicago Tribune. 1950, Dec 16. Philadelphia Church.
Chicago Tribune. 1949, Oct 1. Assembly of God.
Arizona Republic. 1943, May 29. Reorganized Latter Day Saints.
The Courier News. 1961, Jul 29. Christian Assembly.
Star Tribune. 1966, Jun 23. Full Gospel Meeting Set.
The Dispatch. 1942, Feb 14. Philadelphia Pentecostal Church.
The Minneapolis Star. 1943, Mar 20. Misc. News.
Chicago Tribune. 1951, Nov 10. Philadelphia Church.

Chicago Tribune. 1951, Jan 13. Philadelphia Church.
Chicago Tribune. 1950, Jul 29. Philadelphia Church.
The Brooklyn Daily Eagle. 1940, Jul 18. Famous Evangelist Tent Meeting Speaker.
The Canadian Mantle. 2018, Mar. The Latter Rain Movement of '48
Chicago Tribune. 1950, Feb 11. Philadelphia Church.
York Daily Record. 1972, Oct 6. Dover area class selects officers.
The Brooklyn Daily Eagle. 1951, Mar 3. Marantha Temple Services.
The Minneapolis Star. 1944, Jan 15. Hear Rev. A. W. Rasmussen.
The Minneapolis Star. 1944, Jan 22. Philadelphia Church.
Chicago Tribune. 1950, Dec 23. Philadelphia Church.
The Pantagraph. 1971, Oct 16. Dirksen Library Plans Unveiled.
The Indianapolis Star. 1975, May 31. Rev. Rasmussen Will Speak at Church Services.
Chicago Tribune. 1951, Jun 9. Philadelphia Church.
Chicago Tribune. 1951, Dec 8. Philadelphia Church.
Chicago Tribune. 1951, Feb 17. Philadelphia Church.
The Courier News. 1939, Apr 24. Club News.
The Chillicothe Constitution Tribune. 1956, May 26. Music Festival to Begin Belin U. Week.
Edmonton Journal. 1950, Apr 1. Edmonton Gospel Temple.
The Brooklyn Daily Eagle. 1941, Apr 26. Revival Continues in 5th Week.
New Castle News. 1978, May 27. Preachers sees 'dawn of new age'
The Brooklyn Daily Eagle. 1941, Jun 7. Hear Evangelist Lloyd L. Smith.
Florida Today. 1977, Nov 19. World Outreach for Christ Inc.
Chicago Tribune. 1950, Mar 25. Philadelphia Church.
Chicago Tribune. 1898, Nov 27. Misc. News.
Chicago Tribune. 1951, Mar 17. Philadelphia Church.
Chicago Tribune. 1951, Apr 28. Philadelphia Church.
The Daily Telegram. 1966, Jul 22. Deliverance Convention.
The Winona Daily News. 1974, Aug 16. To Attend Meet.
The Daily Leader. 1977, May 5. Bible College to Open In Bloomington.
Statesman Journal. 1970, Jul 17. Northwest Regional Convention of the Independent Assemblies of
    God, Int.
Chicago Tribune. 1951, Jun 2. Philadelphia Church.
The Minneapolis Star. 1952, Aug 16. 5th Avenue Temple Church.
Chicago Tribune. 1952, Feb 2. Philadelphia Church.
Democrat and Chronicle. 1944, May 6. Pentecostal.
Chicago Tribune. 1951, Nov 24. Philadelphia Church.
Chicago Tribune. 1950, Nov 11. Philadelphia Church.
The Brooklyn Daily Eagle. 1951, Mar 3. "Miracles are Happening"
Chicago Tribune. 1951, Mar 10. Philadelphia Church.
Chicago Tribune. 1886, Apr 17. Michigan-Purchase of an Evening.
Chicago Tribune. 1950, Sep 2. Philadelphia Church.
Chicago Tribune. 1952, Feb 16. Philadelphia Church.
The Brooklyn Daily Eagle. 1941, Jun 6. Sees Nazi Victory Over Norwegians A Hollow Triumph.
Chicago Tribune. 1950, Oct 28. Philadelphia Church.
Chicago Tribune. 1949, Jul 23. Philadelphia Church.
Chicago Tribune. 1951, Nov 3. Philadelphia Church.
The Brooklyn Daily Eagle. 1951, Mar 5. Opening Services Set for Marantha Temple.
Chicago Tribune. 1953, Apr 4. Philadelphia Church.
The Brooklyn Daily Eagle. 1941, Jun 28. Pentecostal Assembly Holds Revival Meetings.
Chicago Tribune. 1951, Sep 15. Philadelphia Church.

The Minneapolis Star. 1943, Mar 6. Philadelphia Church.
Chicago Tribune. 1949, Sep 24. Assembly of God.
Chicago Tribune. 1950, Dec 9. Philadelphia Church.
Chicago Tribune. 1951, Dec 15. Philadelphia Church.
Chicago Tribune. 1951, Dec 22. Philadelphia Church.
Democrat and Chronicle. 1944, Mar 18. Pentecostal Host Plans Convention.
Statesman Journal. 1970, Jul 15. Assemblies of God Will Meet Today.
Chicago Tribune. 1951, Feb 3. Philadelphia Church.
Edmonton Journal. 1945, Jun 2. Edmonton Gospel Temple.
Statesman Journal. 1970, Jul 16. Northwest Regional Convention of the Independent Assemblies of God, Int.
The Brooklyn Daily Eagle. 1941, Jul 26. Don't Fail to Hear.
The Brooklyn Daily Eagle. 1941, Dec 10. Salem Pentecostal Church Gets New Assistant Pastor.
The Courier News. 1936, Sep 28. Poultry and Supplies.
The Pantagraph. 1977, May 10. Midwest Bible College to Open in Former School.
Chicago Tribune. 1951, Apr 7. Philadelphia Church.
Arizona Republic. 1943, Jun 5. Miscellaneous.
The Woodstock Sentinel. 1923, Nov 29. Chapter Masons Entertained by Knights Templar.

WILLIAM BRANHAM'S STATEMENTS ABOUT JOSEPH MATTSSON-BOZE

Branham, William. 1953, August 30. Why I Am A Holy Roller
Branham, William. 1955, October 06. The Power of God
Branham, William. 1956, April 03. Shepherd of the Sheepfold.
Branham, William. 1956, June 17. Revelation, Book of Symbols.
Branham, William. 1956, October 01. The Ministry Explained.
Branham, William. 1957, August 07. Hear Ye Him.
Branham, William. 1957, August 09. Blind Bartimaeus.
Branham, William. 1957, August 11. Expectations and Leadings of the Spirit.
Branham, William. 1957, August 11. The Greatest Gift in the Bible.
Branham, William. 1957, July 25. Hear Ye Him.
Branham, William. 1957, July 28. Thirsting for Live
Branham, William. 1957, March 23. God in His Word.
Branham, William. 1957, May 16. We Would See Jesus.
Branham, William. 1958, September 27. Why We Are Not A Denomination.
Branham, William. 1959, June 10. As I Thought on my Way.
Branham, William. 1960, August 02. El Shaddai.
Branham, William. 1960, June 06. To Whom Would We Go.
Branham, William. 1961, January 23. Be Not Afraid It Is I.
Branham, William. 1961, May 20. From That Time.
Branham, William. 1962, July 22. Show Us the Father and It Will Suffice Us.
Branham, William. 1962, July 28. God Has Provided a Way.
Branham, William. 1963, January 18. Spirit of Truth.

WILLIAM BRANHAM AND EARLY TIES TO LATTER RAIN

Accessed 2019, May 1 from 3-The Sharon Orphanage Connection http://abc-history.blogspot.com/2008/02/before-i-was-born-my-father-ramon-haas.html
Bowman, Robert M. Jr. Word-Faith Movement. Accessed 2019, May 1 from https://www.watchman.org/profiles/pdf/wordfaithprofile.pdf
Word-Faith Heresy is Blinding. Accessed 2019, May 1 from https://www.delreychurch.com/blog/post/word-faith-heresy-is-blinding

Kovak, Ivan P. 2018. The Falsehoods of Christianity: Volume Two: (A Layman's Perspective),
    Volume 2 (Branham as one of Marilyn Hickey's "Word of Faith" favorites)
Kozar, Steven. 2017, Jan 9. The Word of Faith Cornucopia of False Doctrine. Accessed 2019, May
    1 from http://www.piratechristian.com/messedupchurch/2016/12/the-word-of-faith-
    cornucopia-of-false-doctrine
An Examination of Kingdom Theology - Part 1/3. Accessed 2019, Apr 20 from
http://www.apologeticsindex.org/l08.html
The New Order of the Latter Rain. Accessed 2019, Apr 20 from
http://www.spiritwatch.org/firelatter2.htm
The Latter Rain Movement of '48. Accessed 2019, Apr 20 from
https://lrm1948.blogspot.com/2018/01/the-north-battleford-story.html

CHAPTER 33

WILLIAM BRANHAM AND PEOPLES TEMPLE

"Happy to see, today, is our host pastor, Brother James Jones, from Indianapolis, back there[675]*"*

After leaving the belief system of the "Message", it's always awkward when encountering people who have also left that same belief system. Many former members that I've encountered are hesitant to speak about it, some of them expressing what they call "real pain" even thinking about the memories. Others are very excited to hear about our experiences, and to share theirs. Those willing to share their experiences often laugh at some of the things that we used to believe, after realizing just how strange it all seems now.

One couple that I encountered was in the Branham Tabernacle during the meeting William Branham claimed that "God" wrote on the wall — a moment referred to in the "Message" as the "Handwriting on the wall". They remembered being surprised when later hearing about this claim, when it was such a "normal" meeting. According to them, everyone showed up early to get a seat, sat through a long, long sermon, walked outside, and discussed where they were going out to eat. They didn't remember hearing anybody talking about anything unusual that happened during the service, which one would certainly expect should

---

[675] Branham, William. 1956, Oct 2. Father, the Hour Has Come

God Himself write on the wall in his own handwriting. I can remember them joking, saying, "*I guess going out to eat was more important than the 'handwriting'*"! That same couple informed me that when the book, *Raven: The Untold Story of the Rev. Jim Jones and His People* was published, it caused quite a stir in Jeffersonville. According to them, my grandfather and other leaders of the church protested to keep it out of the library. This, they said, made them even more curious and interested to read it. It wasn't long until they, too, left the "Message".

After learning that William Branham and his close associates helped launch Jim Jones' career in the Cadle Tabernacle in Indianapolis, I also wanted to know more. At the time, I knew very little about Jim Jones, and wasn't even aware that Jones was a minister in the "Message".[676] I remember how shocked I was when I read Jones' own handwriting, pleading with one of his Peoples Temple members to stay in the "Message". It was time to learn more about Peoples Temple, and the best place to start was the Laurel Street Tabernacle, where Jim Jones first heard about the "Message".

...

When ground broke for the new Laurel Street Tabernacle on the corner of Laurel and Prospect Streets on April 10, 1949, the people of Indianapolis, Indiana could have never known the impact this little building would have upon the world. Just a little over 4,000 square feet and seating 200, the new Assemblies of God church would soon be filled to overflowing as it took center stage for Full Gospel and Pentecostal Holiness revivals during the early 1950s. Assemblies of God District Secretary T. F. Zimmerman[677] traveled from the denomination's headquarters in Springfield, Missouri to preach the morning services while District Superintendent Roy E. Wead[678] offered the dedicatory address in the church led by the Rev. John L. Price. Jack

---

[676] Handwritten Notes of Jim Jones. Accessed 2020, May 28 from https://jonestown.sdsu.edu/?page_id=13782.
"God sent you to People's Temple and you must not release yourself. I know there are things about the Message that you may not see but it is God. As long as we love Christ we have unity and understanding to compensate for all the little things you & I might disagree on. Earl you will be making a serious mistake if you leave our Temple that God has ordained and declared you to be a part of."
[677] 1951, Apr 1. Assemblies of God Meeting. St. Louis Post Dispatch
[678] Laurel Street Church to be Dedicated.

Beam, who could later become a pillar for Jim Jones in Peoples Temple was on the board.[679] The Rev. Lester Sumerall, Assemblies of God missionary[680] and evangelist[681] from South Bend, Indiana, came to hold a series of nightly meetings in celebration.[682]

The church began in 1913 as just a small Sunday School class led by the Rev. D. B. Rickard. Within just two years, the class grew into a church body, and the original tabernacle was built across the street from the dedication. The church had continued to grow under the leadership of Rickard until 1922, when the torch was passed to the Rev. John L. Price.[683] Price was an Indianapolis native and WWII military veteran who served at the Assembly of God churches in the Hampton and Newport News, Virginia areas during his time stationed at Fort Monroe.[684] He was also very active in the Assemblies of God denomination, speaking at the annual conventions at Rev. Zimmerman's church in South Bend, Indiana,[685] the Glad Tidings Tabernacle in Munster, Indiana,[686] and other area revivals. Under his leadership, the church would continue to flourish and become a recognized name in the revival circuits, and Price would become a familiar face among the Assemblies of God leaders. Within just three years of the dedication ceremony, Price would represent Laurel Street Church at the two-week celebration of the grand opening of Richmond's new Assemblies of God Evangelistic Center at the First Assembly of God Church on National Road.[687]

With regards to the creation of Peoples Temple, the year of the Laurel Street Tabernacle's groundbreaking could not have been more symbolic. 1949 was a year of division and conflict within the Assemblies of God denomination, and leaders of the Assemblies would be forced to make very difficult decisions. 1950, when the church was

---

[679] 2013, Feb 17. Transcription of Marceline Jones. Accessed 2019, May 27 from
https://jonestown.sdsu.edu/?page_id=13157
[680] 1953, May 22. 'Spirits' Hold Grip on Girl. Windsor Star. "Rev. Lester Summerall of the Assembly of God Bission [sic] ... cooperated with the missionary"
[681] 1954, Apr 27. Westside Gospel Tabernacle. Indianapolis News. *"Hear Rev. Lester Summerall, world traveler, evangelist, and writer"*
[682] Laurel Street Church to be Dedicated.
[683] Laurel Street Church to be Dedicated.
[684] 1956, Sept 17. Rev. John L. Price. Daily Press.
[685] 1936, Oct. 1. Convention Set for Tabernacle. South Bend Tribune.
[686] 1932, Oct 1. Glad Tidings Tabernacle. The Times (Munster)
[687] 1952, Apr 11. Grand Opening of Richmond's New Evangelistic Center. Palladium Item.

dedicated, was the first year those decisions were enforced. The Post WWII Healing Revival was quickly spreading, and, with it spread a series of new, extra-biblical doctrines[688] that would play a critical role in the splitting of churches and the creation of new leaders. Though in their infancy, this set of doctrines was being accepted and promoted by numerous ministers and evangelists under the title "Latter Rain", which referred to an ancient prophecy in the book of Joel in the Christian Bible. Leaders of the movement taught that the Christian Church must restore and equip a "five-fold ministry"[689] which included modern-day apostles, prophets, evangelists, pastors, and teachers. Then, while appointing key individuals to these roles, the movement presented the idea that mainstream Christianity had become apostate and needed purging. Participants were asked to decide for themselves which side of the "spiritual war" they would take, and that those who joined the "five-fold ministries" would purge the wickedness and judge the apostate.[690]

Leaders of the Assemblies of God watched, horrified, while men and women they considered to be unqualified took leadership roles throughout the organization. They realized that this new theology was divisive. Due to the teaching that denominational churches had grown corrupt, those who joined the new movement were forced to consider those who remained *in* denominational churches as apostates. Assemblies of God leaders met in Seattle, Washington in September 1949 to determine how best to handle the situation, and after deliberation, concluded that the "New Order of the Latter Rain" was founded upon Christian extremism with the sole purpose of destroying fellowship among like-minded Christian believers.[691]

---

[688] Sharrock, Russell. 2006. Covenant Theology: A Critical Analysis of Current Pentecostal Covenant Theology. "These extra-biblical manifestations have become a de-facto evidence of a new level of spirituality and/or a new anointing."

[689] Vision for the Five-Fold Ministry. Accessed 2020, May 18 from https://www.latter-rain.net/vision-for-the-five-fold-ministry/

[690] Sharrock. "Tillian summarizes the Latter Rain or Dominion teaching stating: * The Church must be restored and equipped to rule by the five-fold ministries. * It must come to perfection and complete visible unity. * Out of the purified church will come a spiritual elite corps, a Corporate Christ who possess the Spirit without measure. * They will purge the earth of all wickedness and rebellion. * They will judge the apostate Church. * They will redeem all creation, and restore the earth. * They will eventually overcome death itself in a counterfeit of the Rapture. * The Church will thus inherit the earth, and rule over it from the Throne of Christ."

[691] 1949, Sept 9-14. Minutes and Constitution with Bylaws: Assemblies of God, the Twenty-third General Council. *"That we disapprove of those extreme teachings and practices, which, being unfounded Scripturally, serve only to break fellowship of like precious faith and tend to confusion and division among the members of the Body of Christ, and be it hereby known that this 23rd General Council disapproves of the so-Called "New Order of the Latter Rain"*

The Rev. John L. Price of the Laurel Street Tabernacle in Indianapolis was no stranger to the Latter Rain Revival. Former "faith healer" and revivalist F. F. Bosworth, who had joined Branham's campaign, frequented Indianapolis and the surrounding cities [692] and was a familiar face at the Cadle Tabernacle where Branham and Jim Jones would hold the first of their joint nation-wide healing revivals.[693] [694] Bosworth, who was instrumental in the creation of the Assemblies of God[695] and who claimed to be an authority on "divine healing", had written a book entitled "Christ the Healer"[696]. Price often preached on the same subject with sermons having the same title.[697]

Jim Jones, who was a Methodist pastor in Somerset, Indiana at the time, was also no stranger to the revival. He had taken interest in the evangelists promoted by Branham's Voice of Healing publication and was already making connections in the "Latter Rain" movement. He was called out as a "prophet" during a revival meeting in Columbus, Indiana, just north of Branham's church in Jeffersonville, and took his place among those in the "five-fold ministry." Later, he traveled with his wife, Marceline, to a "Latter Rain" revival at the Bethesda Temple in Detroit, Michigan, where he was so eager to speak that the Rev. Myrtle Beall invited him to the platform.[698] Beall, whose Assemblies of God church had chosen to side with the "Latter Rain" half of the division, was forced to withdraw from the Assemblies of God.[699]

[692] Example: 1924, Nov 10. Sermon Opening Evangelistic Drive is Heard By 3,000: The Rev. F. F. Bosworth Inaugurates Campaign at Cadle Tabernacle.
[693] 1956, Jan 21. Peoples Temple Full Gospel. The Indianapolis Star. *"The Temple will be host to William Branham soon."*
[694] Jones, Jim. 1956, Apr. The Open Door. "NATION WIDE MINISTERS CONVENTION: Special Speaker William Branham. Date June 11-15 Indianapolis Indiana Location Cadle Tabernacle"
[695] Liardon, Roberts. The Life of F.F. Bosworth by Roberts Liardon. *Accessed 2019, May 27 from* https://www.hopefaithprayer.com/word-of-faith/life-bosworth/ *"As the Pentecostal wave moved through the country, Assemblies of God congregations began to spring up. In 1910, Bosworth established the First Assembly of God church in Dallas, and people flocked there from miles around to hear him preach."*
[696] Bosworth, Fred Francis. 1924. Christ the Healer.
[697] 1951, May 12. Assemblies of God: Laurel Street Tabernacle. The Indianapolis News.
[698] 2013, Feb 17. Transcript of Marceline Jones. *Accessed 2019, May 27 from* https://jonestown.sdsu.edu/?page_id=13157 *"A short time after that we decided that we would go to a convention in Detroit ...to the Bethesda Temple."*
[699] Paul's Charge to Timothy. *Accessed 2019, May 27 from* http://scatteredchristians.org/PentecostalWomen.html *"MYRTLE BEALL (1896-1979) began preaching in the 1930s and later founded and pastored the 3,000-seat Bethesda Missionary Temple in Detroit, Michigan, which was dedicated in 1949. She was forced to withdraw from the Assemblies of God after accepting the post-World War II New Order of the Latter Rain movement which had originated at Sharon Schools in North Battleford, Saskatchewan, Canada. It claimed to be the latter rain miracle outpouring which was expected to precede Christ's coming. Allegedly God has raising up prophets and apostles to lead this miracle outpouring, and "the prophetic word" was emphasized, whereby the secrets of men's hearts were revealed. Beall's Bethesda*

In 1951, Jones was offered a large sum of money to hold a series of revivals in Los Angeles, California for the Rev. Orval Lee Jaggers. Jaggers was both an editor for Branham's publication[700] and closely affiliated with LeRoy Kopp of Calvary Temple[701]. Like Branham[702] [703], Jaggers taught unusual doctrines concerning the Zodiac's relationship to Christianity and teachings on Unidentified Flying Objects. Also, like Branham[704], Jaggers' extra-biblical doctrines resulted in the formation of a destructive cult.[705] It should come as no surprise that the subject of UFOs would be repeated by Jones in the Jonestown commune.[706]

Just outside of Richmond, Indiana in 1953, William Branham and Ern Baxter held a series of revivals in Connersville, Indiana at the Roberts Park Amphitheater. Two services were held daily from May 31 through June 10, one at 2:00 pm and another at 7:30 pm. The ministers invited the public under the guise of a "Plain Old Fashioned Revival".[707]

Missionary Temple became a very influential center for the New Order of the Latter Rain."

[700] 1951, Jan. Associate Editors. The Voice of Healing. (Listed as O. L. Jaggers).

[701] Rev. Dr. Orval Lee Jaggers. Accessed 2019, May 27 from
http://www.universalworldchurch.org/wiki/Rev._Dr._Orval_Lee_Jaggers

[702] Branham, William. 1953, Apr 3. The Cruelty Of Sin, And The Penalty That It Cost To Rid Sin From Our Lives. *"What's He doing? He is writing His first Bible. The first Bible was ever written, was written in the skies, the Zodiac. It starts out with the virgin, that's how He come first. It ends up with Leo the lion, the second Coming. And He is writing His first Bible. 44 The second Bible was written, was written by Enoch, and put in the pyramid."*

[703] Branham, William. 1955, May 22. The Ark. *He is in the world today, showing signs and wonders, and raising up people, great things taking place, "Showing signs in the heaven above, and on earth." Signs! Signs of flying saucers through the air, where even the Pentagon and all don't know what to think of it, "Signs in the heaven above." "And on earth," the healing of the sick, the raising of the dead, the opening of the blinded eyes, the casting out of evil spirits, the Gospel being preached, signs before His Coming!*

[704] The Message. *Accessed 2019, May 27 from http://old.freedomofmind.com/Info/infoDet.php?id=883. "The Message," otherwise referred to as "Branhamism," "Branhamites," "Bride Churches," "Evening Light Churches," or "Spoken Word" are collectively describing the worldwide cult following of William Marrion Branham from Jeffersonville, Indiana. With the exception of the more extremist sects, most consider Voice of God Recordings in Jeffersonville Indiana to be the cult headquarters. "The Message," is a Pentecostal-style doomsday cult which believed (until 1978) that the year 1977 was the time of Armageddon. The cult leader held joint campaigns with Jim Jones of Jonestown, Guyana, and some believe the events leading to 1978 massacre are related to his influence by William Branham."*

[705] The Universal World Church (Hawaii Fellowship). Accessed 2019, May 27 from
http://www.letusreason.org/Cults2.htm
. Hawaii fellowship of the Universal World Church is connected to the Church that was started by O. L. Jaggers who was influenced by the latter rain movement of the late 40's. He with along with a host of other now famous people such as Oral Roberts AA. Allen, David Nunn W. V. Grant, William Branham read a book that had a tremendous influence on their ministries as revival preachers. This book was Franklin Halls book Atomic power with God through fasting and prayer. Hall mixed Biblical concepts with occult methodologies. He stated that if believers did not fast their prayers would be hindered but if the pagans fasted god would answer their prayers. Hall thought without fasting prayer was ineffectual. He also had the belief that the Zodiac was Gods revelation to man finding Gospel pictures throughout. His belief in astrology was confirmed through occult teachings which included that UFO's were a revelation of Gods power.

[706] Q663 Transcript. Accessed 2019, May 27 from https://jonestown.sdsu.edu/?page_id=62344. *The UFOs – that means unidentifying [unidentified] flying objects – from some other planet in outer space apparently came over in groups of usually four or 16. Sixteen, let's hope sixteen's a good number for a change. They came over regularly at intervals all day long (pause) for days. They came right over the air base, as if doing surveillance.*

344

Branham and Baxter had recently held a similar series of revivals in New York, where Branham taught the "Latter Rain" message and British Israelism.[708] Not long after the Connersville revival, Jones changed the name of his Somerset Methodist Church to "Christian Assembly", and began advertising "Full Gospel Preaching" in the Sunday newspapers.[709] Within months, Jones became a familiar face in the local Indianapolis Pentecostal community, and was invited to preach for the first time at the Laurel Street Tabernacle. The Rev. Price had announced that he would soon be retiring, and Jones was a potential candidate to replace him.[710]

Armed with the intriguing "Latter Rain" doctrine, members of the church overlooked Jones' participation in the "New Order of the Latter Rain" and ignored the warnings included in the resolution from the Assemblies of God Council. Based simply upon the number of times Jones shared the pulpit at the Laurel Street Tabernacle during his participation with "Latter Rain", one could assume that Price and his congregation were considering a split from the main branch of the Assemblies of God. The church fully adopted Jones as an associate pastor and began advertising "Rev. James Jones" beside "Rev. J. L. Price" in their Sunday advertisements. It also changed the title to "New" Laurel Street Tabernacle and began advertising thousands of "miracles"[711] as was typical among ministers participating in the healing revival. They also introduced the slogan "Deliverance Center for All People". Price and Jones began holding "Miracle Services" advertising *"1,000 Miracles in 2 Months"*, making waves throughout the Assemblies of God community – especially among those who were aware of Jones' affiliation with the "Latter Rain". Price began claiming that his sermons were "the prophetic Word under anointed preaching",

[707] 1953, Mar 5. Plain Old-Fashioned Revival. Palladium-Item.

[708] Branham, William. 1950, Apr 5. Expectation. *"That's New York. See? "Preach the Gospel to every creature. These signs shall follow them that believe." He promised it. And then He promised the former rain and the latter rain. And we're living now, have been for years, under the latter rain. 23 And just before God cut off relationship with the Jews, He put nine spiritual gifts into the Church. And just before the Gentile's age is over, He's restoring back in the Church those nine spiritual gifts, giving the Gentile church its last call before turning again to Israel."*

[709] 1953, Nov 21. Christian Assembly. The Indianapolis News.

[710] Hall, John R. Gone from the Promised Land: Jonestown in American Cultural History. "in September 1954, Jones received an invitation to preach at the Tabernacle, the very time when the congregation's board was searching out a successor to the retiring minister, John Price.

[711] 1955, Jan 1. New Laurel Street Tabernacle. The Indianapolis Star.

signifying his acceptance of the position of "prophet" in the "five-fold ministry".

Not long after, sweeping changes came to the Laurel Street Tabernacle. It was announced that the Rev. W. L. Thornton would be replacing John L. Price as head pastor of the Laurel Street Tabernacle, and that he would be leading an "expansion and reorganization program". He had served for two years as the director of the youth organization of the main branch of the Assemblies of God after serving for three years as an evangelist in the Indiana area.[712] Thornton was strongly affiliated with the non-"Latter Rain" sect of the Assemblies of God, attending international conventions at the headquarters in Springfield, Missouri.[713]

Whether as a result of Thornton's impending takeover of the church and its direction or as the primary cause of it, Jones had created his own business entity registered in the State of Indiana as "Wings of Deliverance, Incorporated" on April 4, 1955. Jones himself had no theological degree and would have been ineligible for leading an Assemblies of God church for multiple reasons. That did not diminish his impact on the church, however, and his being replaced created divisions in the Laurel Street Tabernacle. Several members sided with Jones during the church split[714] and met briefly under the "Wings of Deliverance" name. Either symbolically claiming that his motivation was geared towards helping the people of the church or pure coincidence, the group started meeting under the name, "Peoples Temple". Eventually it transitioned to the title, "Peoples Temple Full Gospel".

Within weeks, Jones' "Latter Rain" and "Voice of Healing" community came to his aid. In January 1956, William Branham agreed to preach at Peoples Temple.[715] In February, "Latter Rain" evangelist and close business associate of William Branham, the Rev. Joseph Mattsson-Boze of the Philadelphia Church in Chicago, offered Jones an

---

[712] 1955, Jul 16. New Pastor Leads Church Expansion. Indianapolis Star.
[713] 1952, Apr 4. Thornton Goes to Convention. Linton Daily Citizen.
[714] Hamlett, Ryan. 2014, Feb 25. The Devil in the Old Northside. *Accessed 2019, May 27 from https://historicindianapolis.com/the-devil-in-the-old-northside-2/ "After leaving Somerset, Jones spent a short while as an associate minister at Laurel Street Tabernacle near Fountain Square, where he gathered the first few members of what would become the People's Temple."*
[715] 1956, Jan 21. Peoples Temple Full Gospel. Indianapolis Star.

honorary Certificate of Ordination into the Independent Assemblies of God[716] – the "Latter Rain" side of the division in the Assemblies – and joined Jones in series of revival meetings.[717]

In a handwritten note found on the back of the Certificate of Ordination, Jones accepted his membership into the Independent Assemblies of God as he expressed a very clear amount of distaste for his recent experience at the Laurel Street Tabernacle. He wrote:

> *Note. This ordination was given voluntarily by Joseph Mattsson-Boze Executive & Official of Independent Assemblies. No creed or autocratic jurisdiction as to teachings of church organization only requirement is that ministers practice the Love of Christ and live honorable and practice every aspect of integrity in his pastoral and [unintelligible] relationships. This was given as an honorary recognition without my request for our good work as an independent church in Indianapolis, Ind. I naturally accept their ordination in that it requires no endorsement of a limited creed dogmatic ritual or narrow religious restrictive fellowship.[718]*

The Peoples Temple was officially born, and Jones had officially taken his place in the "Latter Rain" revival. Nationally, he was gaining recognition. Locally, however, Jones was dealing with the fallout from the recent church split. Once again, his "Latter Rain" and "Voice of Healing" community came to his aid. Jones began advertising that Peoples Temple would be host to William Branham in a "Brotherhood-Healing Crusade" at the Cadle Tabernacle from June 11th to the 15th, 1956. Ministers and delegates from several states would be attending the revival, with up to one thousand ministers expected. Among them was a "who's who" lineup of ministers involved with both the "Latter Rain" and the "Voice of Healing" revivals. The featured speakers included Joseph Mattsson-Boze, "Latter Rain" evangelist and publisher

---

[716] Certificate of Ordination and Note, Independent Assemblies of God. Accessed 2019, May 27 from https://jonestown.sdsu.edu/?page_id=13774
[717] 1956, Apr 21. Eastern Fellowship Convention. The Daily Mail.
[718] Ordination Certificate of Jim Jones into Independent Assemblies of God. Accessed 2020, May 28 from https://jonestown.sdsu.edu/?page_id=13774

of the Herald of Faith; Rev. A. W. Rasmussen, leader of the Latter Rain and head of the Independent Assemblies of God; Dr. David Du Plessis, the head of the World Pentecostal Fellowship and William Branham, who many considered to be the leader of the faith healing revival, a close associate to each of the other speakers.[719]

Peoples Temple would host the convention once more in 1957, announcing Branham as the featured minister in both afternoon and evening services held again at the Cadle Tabernacle, and with "Voice of Healing" editors and revivalists in the morning at Peoples Temple. The Rev. Tommy L. Osborn, editor for Voice of Healing[720], evangelist Tommy Hicks[721], and F. F. Bosworth were the featured ministers.[722]

Jones not only worked as a "healing evangelist" in William Branham's Message following, he also pastored his Peoples Temple church with the same doctrine and title. When one Earl Jackson, a Temple parishioner, attempted to escape, Jones pleaded with him to return to the "Message".

> *Personal Bro[ther] Jackson, My beloved brother in Christ, concern for you kept me up praying the entire night! I [am] going to speak sincerely and frankly! God sent you to People's Temple and you must not release yourself. **I know there are things about the Message that you may not see but it is God.** As long as we love Christ we have unity and understanding to compensate for all the little things you & I might disagree on. Earl you will be making a serious mistake if you leave our Temple that God has ordained and declared you to be a part of. Don't go out to see the proof of what I just said. Hear me as a voice crying to you from the depths of love & fondness for you. "Stand still and see the salvation of the Lord." Don't go back on the light! I know you wouldn't intentionally but if you leave the place that Christ has set you in[,] much sorrow and heartache will be the result. God impressed my mind strongly in every prayer in the early hours before dawn that you would be*

---

[719] 1956, Jun 9. Peoples Temple Will Be Host to the Great William Branham Brotherhood-Healing Crusade
[720] Associate Editors. 1951, Dec. Voice of Healing. (Listed as T.L. Osborne)
[721] Address Directory. 1951, Dec. Voice of Healing.
[722] Peoples Temple. 1957, Jun 1. Indianapolis Star.

making a terrible mistake to leave. Please hear my counsel which I give with a heart full of love for you![723]

Learning that William Branham joined Jim Jones and Peoples Temple at the launch of Jones' career as a "faith healer" and "Latter Rain" evangelist in 1956 was sobering. We had been taught that William Branham had the "gift of discernment" and that he could peer into the very soul of the people he worked with on the platform and in private interviews. Learning that William Branham held private interviews[724] with members of Peoples Temple and did not warn them of the tragedy that would come raised many questions for me. Learning that William Branham and Joseph Mattsson-Boze continued to work with Jones in Indianapolis through 1957 also raised more questions. It was surprising to learn that Joseph Mattsson-Boze and Jim Jones worked closely with each other at a time when Mattsson-Boze worked closely with William Branham, but when I learned that Jim Jones was the host of Branham's own healing campaigns outside of the state of Indiana it was almost overwhelming. How many of the 1956 and 1957 meetings were hosted by Jim Jones? How many of the *"[Blank Spot(s) on Tape]"* in William Branham's sermon transcripts were a result of Branham's collaboration with Jim Jones?

---

[723] Handwritten Notes of Jim Jones. Accessed 2020, May 18 from *https://jonestown.sdsu.edu/?page_id=13782*
[724] Example during Peoples Temple Meetings: Branham, William. 1956, Jun 11. Hear Ye Him. "On the private interviews this afternoon, in a room, a young woman, I'd say middle aged, come in, been a teacher for years."

PEOPLES TEMPLE

Assemblies of God Meeting. 1951, Apr 1. St. Louis Post Dispatch

Laurel Street Church to be Dedicated. 1950, Dec 8. Indianapolis News

Transcription of Marceline Jones. 2013, Feb 17. Accessed 2019, May 27 from
    https://jonestown.sdsu.edu/?page_id=13157

'Spirits' Hold Grip on Girl. 1953, May 22. Windsor Star.

Westside Gospel Tabernacle. 1954, Apr 27. Indianapolis News. "Hear Rev. Lester Summerall,
    world traveler, evangelist, and writer"

Rev. John L. Price. 1956, Sept 17. Daily Press.

Convention Set for Tabernacle. 1936, Oct. South Bend Tribute.

Glad Tidings Tabernacle. 1932, Oct 1. The Times Munster

Grand Opening of Richmond's New Evangelistic Center. 1952, Apr 11. Palladium Item.

Sharrock, Russell. 2006. COVENANT THEOLOGY: A Critical Analysis of Current Pentecostal
    Covenant Theology

Sharrock. 1949, Sept 9-14. Minutes and Constitution with Bylaws: Assemblies of God, the Twenty-
    third General Council.

Hinchcliff, A. M. 1999. Sons and Sonship. North Battleford, SK: Sharon Children's Homes and
    Schools.

Death Takes Well Known Village Man. 1951, Mar 2. Desert Sun.

Oppenheimer, Jerry. 2017. The Kardashians: An American Drama.

Branham, William. 1947, Nov 2. The Angel of God.

Burkun, Michael. 1997. Religion and the Racist Right: The Origins of the Christian Identity
    Movement.

Branham, William. 1945. I Was Not Disobedient to The Heavenly Vision.

Branham, William. 1948, Mar 4. The Angel of God.

Branham, William. 1951, May 7. Expectations.

Branham, William. 1954, Aug 10. Prayer Line.

The New Order of the Latter Rain: Their history and legacy. Accessed 2019, May 27 from
    http://www.letusreason.org/Latrain7.htm.

Ern Baxter. Accessed 2019, May 27 *from https://csmpublishing.org/about/leadership/ern-baxter/*

Gardner, Velmer. 1954, July. Seven Spiritual Signs That Jesus Will Come in Our Time. The Voice
    of Healing.

Cloud, David. 2013, Aug 21. William Branham's Bogus Healings. Accessed 2019, May 27 from
    https://www.wayoflife.org/reports/william_branhams_bogus_healings.html.

Peoples Temple Full Gospel. 1956, Jan 21. The Indianapolis Star.

Jones, Jim. 1956, Apr. The Open Door.

Liardon, Roberts. The Life of F.F. Bosworth by Roberts Liardon. Accessed 2019, May 27 from
    https://www.hopefaithprayer.com/word-of-faith/life-bosworth/

Bosworth, Fred Francis. 1924. Christ the Healer.

Assemblies of God: Laurel Street Tabernacle. 1951, May 12. The Indianapolis News.

Transcript of Marceline Jones. 2013, Feb 17. Accessed 2019, May 27 from
    https://jonestown.sdsu.edu/?page_id=13157

Paul's Charge to Timothy. Accessed 2019, May 27 from
    http://scatteredchristians.org/PentecostalWomen.html

Associate Editors. 1951, Jan. The Voice of Healing. Listed as O. L. Jaggers.

Rev. Dr. Orval Lee Jaggers. Accessed 2019, May 27 from
    http://www.universalworldchurch.org/wiki/Rev._Dr._Orval_Lee_Jaggers

Branham, William. 1953, Apr 3. The Cruelty of Sin, and the Penalty That It Cost To Rid Sin From
    Our Lives.

Branham, William. 1955, May 22. The Ark.

The Message. Accessed 2019, May 27 from
  http://old.freedomofmind.com/Info/infoDet.php?id=883

The Universal World Church (Hawaii Fellowship). Accessed 2019, May 27 from
  http://www.letusreason.org/Cults2.htm

Q663 Transcript. Accessed 2019, May 27 from *https://jonestown.sdsu.edu/?page_id=62344.*

Plain Old-Fashioned Revival. 1953, Mar 5. Palladium-Item.

Branham, William. 1950, Apr 5. Expectation.

Christian Assembly. 1953, Nov 21. The Indianapolis News.

Hall, John R. Gone from the Promised Land: Jonestown in American Cultural History.

New Laurel Street Tabernacle. 1955, Jan 1. The Indianapolis Star.

New Pastor Leads Church Expansion. 1955, Jul 16. Indianapolis Star.

Thornton Goes to Convention. 1952, Apr 4. Linton Daily Citizen.

Hamlett, Ryan. 2014, Feb 25. The Devil in the Old Northside. Accessed 2019, May 27 from
  https://historicindianapolis.com/the-devil-in-the-old-northside-2/

Peoples Temple Full Gospel. 1956, Jan 21. Indianapolis Star.

Certificate of Ordination and Note, Independent Assemblies of God. Accessed 2019, May 27 from
  https://jonestown.sdsu.edu/?page_id=13774

Eastern Fellowship Convention. 1956, Apr 21. The Daily Mail.

Associate Editors. 1951, Dec. Voice of Healing. Listed as T. L. Osborne

Address Directory. 1951, Dec. Voice of Healing.

Peoples Temple. 1957, Jun 1. Indianapolis Star.

*Special thanks for the research made available by Fielding McGehee on Alternative Considerations
  of Jonestown & Peoples Temple (jonestown.sdsu.edu) concerning Jim Jones, Peoples Temple,
  the connection to William Branham, Latter Rain, and the Healing Revival.*

*Also special thanks to Archibald Thackeray for his research made available on The Latter Rain
  Movement of '48 (rm1948.blogspot.com)*

CHAPTER 34

WILLIAM BRANHAM AND THE THIRD WAVE

"And a Voice said to me, 'I'll meet you in there. That'll be the Third Pull[725]"

When people think of Louisville, KY, they think about bourbon and horse racing. The locals think about the Louisville Cardinals Basketball, and dream of one day having an NBA team. Even though I spent much of my childhood away from Louisville, I'm still fascinated by its rich history — history that has long been forgotten by many people. Louisville has done very well to preserve as much of that history as possible, and it's evident just by walking down the city streets. Historical markers have been placed throughout the city, and tourists can stop and read the historical information as they look at the surroundings to picture what it must have looked like in days gone by. History from several different eras has been captured, and history trail maps are available for those who wish to take a journey through time.

When people think about Louisville, they seldom think about it being part of the battleground for Civil Rights, yet Louisville was one of the cities to remain segregated long after the 1954 Supreme Court ruling against segregation of schools.[726] Fourth Street in downtown Louisville

---

[725] Branham, William. 1956, Jan 1. Why Are People So Tossed About?
[726] Living the Story: The Civil Rights Movement in Kentucky. Accessed 2019, Sept 15 from https://www.ket.org/education/resources/living-story-civil-rights-movement-kentucky/

is now peaceful, and a popular weekend hangout for many people. Visitors can grab a bite to eat in the Hard Rock Cafe, near the massive marquee of a guitar outside, or simply sit in one of the many restaurants with outdoor seating to listen to the featured live music. But at one time, Fourth Street in downtown Louisville was very active with protests and demonstrations by those seeking freedom. Even Martin Luther King, Jr. visited Louisville in his battle for Civil Rights and equality. It was significant enough to merit a "Civil Rights Trail", a historical journey through the Civil Rights milestones in Louisville. It is a reminder for visitors to open back the curtains of time and see why freedom should not be taken for granted.

The protests in Louisville were so successful that an unsympathetic mayor was thrown out of office.[727] And the first "public accommodation law" in the South was passed in Louisville, Kentucky. When people think of Civil Rights Battlegrounds, they often think of Alabama or Mississippi. They think of places like Arkansas, where city and state officials battled the Federal government.

In the "Message", we were even further disconnected. When we thought about William Branham's many visits to battleground cities, we only thought about the "prophet", his "healing" revivals, or "getting the 'Message' out". We were told stories about William Branham at these locations but were never really told about the political turmoil of the era at the time he frequented them. Many of us overlooked the very heated statements that William Branham made against Civil Rights leaders or protests. Worse, many people in the 'Message" were not well enough informed to know why this mattered. That is not surprising, since William Branham also spoke harshly against education and the educated.

Northern Kentucky and Southern Indiana in the 1950s, like many parts of the country, were segregated: people with black skin were treated differently than people with white skin. People with dark skin were labeled "colored" and forced to use separate facilities from those used by people with white skin. In 1954, Andrew Wade attempted to move into an all-white neighborhood in Louisville, Kentucky. The

[727] Louisville Downtown Civil Rights Trail Markers Project. Accessed 2020, May 28 from http://louisville.edu/artsandsciences/dce/civil-rights-markers/

family was met with violence.[728] An angry mob shot bullets through the window and burned a cross in their lawn. On June 27, 1954, the home was bombed, and the family retreated into segregation. Though its popularity had decreased since its heyday in the 1920's, the Ku Klux Klan still posed a threat to African Americans. But after the 1954 Supreme Court ruling in Brown vs. The Board of Education of Topeka, Kansas, the door had been opened to large-scale desegregation of school systems.

African Americans began protesting against racial discrimination all across the country, especially in states that did not honor the Supreme Court decision. Protests were common in streets of Louisville, Kentucky, which was just across the Ohio River from William Branham's hometown of Jeffersonville. This was the case in major cities across the country. It gave rise to other white supremacy groups, such as the National States Rights Party (N.S.R.P.), a terroristic white supremacy group later involved with bombings in Birmingham, Alabama. I was surprised to learn that during the heat of the battle for Civil Rights during the 1950's, the N.S.R.P. national newsletter was published in Jeffersonville, Indiana.[729]

Long before joining William Branham's "Message", Jim Jones advocated for racial equality.[730] He spent hours preaching on the streets in the segregated black communities in and near Indianapolis, Indiana. Even against opposition posed by local religious leaders, Jones welcomed all races into his church community. This did not end with the group's migration to California and beyond; Peoples Temple and African Americans stood side-by-side long after leaving Indianapolis. And in the late 1950's, Peoples Temple was well-known for helping the less fortunate in African American communities.[731] This passion to help the needy was not limited to local communities, either. Jones established funds to help families adopt less-fortunate children from other countries and urged congregants to adopt.[732] His own family was

---

[728] Remembering the Wades, the Bradens and the Struggle for Racial Integration in Louisville. Accessed 2020, May 18 from https://wfpl.org/remembering-wades-bradens-struggle-racial-integration-louisville
[729] Subject: Birmingham, Alabama Sixteenth Street Baptist Church Bombing/September 15, 1963 Part 6 of 11. Federal Bureau of Investigation.
[730] Race and the Peoples Temple. Accessed 2019, Sept 15 from
https://www.pbs.org/wgbh/americanexperience/features/jonestown-race/
[731] Church Helps. 1959, Sep 5. Indianapolis News.

no exception. Jim and Marceline Jones had adopted a variety of children from Korean American, African American, and Native American descent. He had been publicly recognized for his work with the South Side of Indianapolis since the early 1950s, donating every available hour to helping underprivileged children.[733] He sought out to establish new meaning to the word "brotherhood".

When he joined forces with William Branham to organize a massive "healing" revival, Jones called it the "Brotherhood" - Healing Crusade.[734] He wanted an open door *"to all mankind",* and advertised the meetings with that title.[735] But he was in for a big surprise when working with William Branham and his associates. Branham's many connections to white supremacy would have not aligned with Jones' motive and direction.

During the Wednesday night service with Jim Jones in 1956, William Branham warmed up the audience by telling a story about an African American slave. At the end of the story, and in front of Jones' African American parishioners, William Branham used an offensive ethnic slur: "darky".[736] He also stated that a white man and a "colored" woman "have no dealings", comparing segregation to ancient Samaritans as depicted in the New Testament.[737]

White supremacy groups of the 1950s were strongly against interracial marriage,[738] and often used examples of illegitimate children born to "colored" women. William Branham was no exception to this rule. Branham frequently spoke against interracial marriage. And in the Friday night service with Jones, Branham gave the same sort of example.

---

[732] Korean Waifs' Adoption Called 'Lesson' in Religion. 1960, Feb 25. The Indianapolis News.

[733] Student Minister Sponsors Drive to Aid South Side Area Juveniles. 1953, Feb 28. Jones Somerset Transition the Indianapolis Star.

[734] Peoples Temple. 1956, Jun 2. The Indianapolis News. (Advertising William Branham)

[735] Jones, Jim. 1956. The Open Door.

[736] Branham, William. 1956, Jun 13. Jehovah Jireh. "He said, "If Christ has made you free, Mose, then I'll go down and sign the proclamation, and I'll set you free to preach the Gospel." He signed it that morning, and set the old darky free."

[737] Branham, William. 1956, Jun 13. Jehovah Jireh. "'Why,' she said, 'it's not customary for you Jews to ask we Samaritans such. We have no dealings.'"

[738] Oh, Reginald. Interracial Marriage in the Shadows of Jim Crow: Racial Segregation as a System of Racial and Gender Subordination. Accessed 2020, May 18 from https://lawreview.law.ucdavis.edu/issues/39/3/defining-voices-critical-race-feminism. "As a system of legal subordination, racial segregation concerns the regulation of gender relations as much as it concerns the regulation of race relations."

Having spent time in public school in the South, I was familiar with racial slurs and insulting language. When Branham used phrases like "Aunt Jemima" and "Auntie" towards African American women, it bothered me. But I never thought about his stories of African Americans with "venereal diseases" could be used as a political tool.

Do what He tells you to do. So I just kept on walking. And after while I looked laying across the gate, and there was a typical old Aunt Jemima, with a man's shirt tied around her head. She was... tears running down her cheeks. And I passed by. She said, "Good morning, Parson." And I said, "Good morning, Auntie," walked on by. I said, "Well, how... She said, 'Parson.'" I turned back, I said, "Pardon me, a minute, Auntie." I said, "You called me a parson." She said, "Yes, sir." And I said, "How did you know I was a parson?" She said, "I knowed you was coming." And I said, "You knew I was coming?" Said, "Yes, sir." And she said, "I've been standing here since four o'clock." I looked on her. I said, "Well, bless your heart." She was wet on the back yet. Said, "Yes, sir, I've been standing here." Said, "Did you ever read the story about the Shunammite woman?" And I said, "Yes, ma'am." Said, "I's that kind of woman." She said, "And I promised the Lord, if He'd give me a baby, I'd raise it for Him." And said, "He give me a fine boy." And she said, "Parson, I raised that boy, but when he got to be a man," said, "a young man, he got with some wrong company. And he done wrong." And said, "He got a bad disease, a venereal disease."

I never thought about the fact that William Branham called Civil Rights leaders "communistic", just as other white supremacists did, or how he mixed themes of anti-interracial marriage with non-supportive statements against integration. When speaking of integrating schools, Branham said, *"they don't need those things"* and, *"a 'colored' man is satisfied in the state he is in"*.[739] In 1956, while Martin Luther King, Jr was organizing support for Rosa Parks after she had refused to give up

---

[739] Branham, William. 1963, Jun 28. O Lord Once More.

her seat so a white man could take it, William Branham introduced his "Christian forfeits their rights" doctrine.[740] This doctrine would open the door to Branham openly blaming the "colored race" for the election of John F. Kennedy.[741]

In 1957, Branham and Jones parted ways. According to Jones, Branham said, *"I don't believe a thing in that Bible, hardly",*[742] and Branham apparently advised Jones on how to preach sermons that sell to crowds to keep his ministry going.[743] I'd seen that quote early in my research before finding all of the many questionable activities in Branham's campaign, and discounted it as Jones blowing off steam to his own audience. After all I'd uncovered, however, I was not so sure that Jones was wrong about this. Regardless, the two men separated, and the campaign strategy employed by Joseph Mattsson-Boze and William Branham came to an abrupt end.

Meanwhile, Branham's mentor Roy Davis, whom Branham continued to promote, claimed leadership of 50,000 white supremacists in the South.[744] Davis organized secret meetings in key locations to prevent integration in the school systems. According to Davis, members of the Dallas police force were included in his membership number. If this were true, Davis had government officials in Dallas under his control. Dallas was under federal court order to integrate but had refused to do so. Davis was a member of the Oak Cliff White Citizens

---

[740] Branham, William. 1956, Sep 17. The Lamb and the Dove. "I hope you understand what I mean. Sheep lay still. Now, a real sheep, a sheep forfeits its rights, and that's what I was trying to get at yesterday when I was speaking of the way some of our Christian sisters are dressing and going on, and our brothers the way they're carrying on."

[741] Branham, William. 1960, Nov 13. Condemnation by Representation. "One of the greatest mistakes that the colored race ever made, was down in Louisiana and over in there, when they voted for Kennedy, the other night, put him in. They actually spit on that dress of Abraham Lincoln, where the blood of the Republican party that freed them, and voted a Catholic."

[742] Annotated Transcript Q612. Accessed 2020, May 18 from *https://jonestown.sdsu.edu/?page_id=62945*

743 Annotated Transcript Q612. Accessed 2020, May 18 from *https://jonestown.sdsu.edu/?page_id=62945* " Some are listening. They won't tell you the truth, because the black book is the easiest gravy train that they've ever been on. Yet Allen [A.A. Allen, Pentecostal evangelist] came to me, Oral Roberts [Pentecostal evangelist] spoke this, Billy Graham came right to us – Ijames [Archie Ijames], Jack [Jack Arnold Beam], and me – in Claypool Hotel, said I don't believe a thing in that Bible hardly. But he said, it's the way to make a living. Billy Graham, who I prophesied his death, Billy Branham rather, said his head would be— I said he'd lose his head. His head was cut off in Texas. [Editorial note: The reference is to William Branham, an evangelical preacher and acquaintance of Jim Jones during the Temple's Indianapolis days. Branham died in an automobile accident on Christmas Eve 1965 in Texas, but was not decapitated.] He said you can't preach the truth about the Bible, you will be in trouble. I said, I choose to treat th— preach the truth. He said, well, I'll be around, while you will be in trouble. Well, I'm still here, and his head is cut off from his body."

[744] Retired Preacher Claims Bid to Top Dallas Klan Post. 1958, Mar 28. Lubbock Morning Avalanche.

Council,[745] and held public debates in protest of integration, and those protests were very effective.[746] White supremacy claimed the upper hand when the school system declared they would remain segregated. Dallas was but one city, however, and Davis' was fighting a war — not a single battle. If the "Americanization" project were to succeed, Davis must have similar victories in key cities and states across the nation. Davis now had Ku Klux Klan presence in multiple states. By 1959, news media and government officials realized that the Ku Klux Klan was re-organizing for a Third Wave, and from the look of things, war was indeed brewing.[747] Some smaller white supremacy groups began fighting each other for power while others combined for strength in numbers. They stood in unity against desegregation.

Davis began openly challenging Arkansas Klan leader George Edwards to gain control of his sect of the Ku Klux Klan.

> *Dear sir:*
>
> *On several occasions, privately in the presence of a small handful of men in the Odd Fellows Hall on the Texas side of Texarkana, you made certain statements and dangerous charges against the undersigned. You later followed up with threats against the undersigned. I have nothing to say about your threats, as I believe a man can take a corn cob and lightening bug and chase you out of Arkansas. But I am interested in the cause (?) you so nobly misrepresent, and I want the people of Arkansas to have the benefit of your alleged information about the Original KKK.*
>
> *Therefore, I challenge you AGAIN for a public debate to be held in the following cities, Texarkana, Little Rock, Fordyce, Magnolia, and Pine Bluff, challenging and daring you to meet me in this contemplated debate, to bring all your ADL*

---

[745] Pro, Con, Put Before Board Meet. 1958, Jun 26. Dallas Morning News. "R. E. Davis, president of the Oak Cliff White Citizens Council"

[746] Dallas Schools Will Remain Segregated. 1958, Jun 26. Sedalia Democrat. "The Rev. R. E. Davis, who said he was president of a local White Citizens Council, said if the board carries out integration it would be 'aiding and abetting the Supreme Court in destroying every vestige of constitutional law and order — shaking the very pillars of the Republic"

[747] Klan. 1959, Jun 7. Arkansas Gazette.

*stuff, reading it before the public, and to give me an opportunity
to reply.*

*If what you say concerning me and the National
Organization are true, then I should be in the penitentiary. If
untrue, I assure you will be. Now put up or shut up, Mr.
Edwards... What say you concerning the debate?? Why do you
continue to get people (only a small handful) in your
clandestined [sic] organization, telling them that you represent
the second largest group in the United States, when you KNOW
this is false? Or are you distinguishing yourself as the
President of the Ananias Club of Arkansas???*

*Or, are you so disturbed over the fact that Klansmen in
Arkansas are continuing to repudiate you and your false claim?
Is someone paying you to wreck, and tear down, and slander
real Klansmen? Is anyone doing this? I want an answer, the
people want an answer. Will you give us that answer????*
Yours truly,
R.E. Davis
NATIONAL IMPERIAL DRAGON
KNIGHTS OF THE ORIGINAL KU KLUX KLAN
3311 Glenhaven St.
Dallas, 11, Texas[748]

At the end of the letter, Davis signed as the National Imperial
Dragon, which was the highest rank of his sect. He then gave it to the
news media,[749] exposing Edwards' secret rank and position. His hand
now forced, Edwards stepped forward and eventually lost control of his
sect. Then, from Texas to Florida, Davis began organizing meetings for
a united stand against desegregation and in support of white supremacy.
He was so brazen that he went unmasked — though he used his 1920's
alias "Lon" — and declared that he was planning a national recruitment
drive. Reporters counted people coming from 43 counties in Florida,

---

[748] Davis, Roy. 1960. An Open Letter to George F. Edwards, Leader of a Band of Banished Klansmen in the State
of Arkansas.
[749] Texarkana Lawyer Reveals Leadership of Klan Faction. 1959, May 31. Arkansas Gazette. "Edwards
statement came two days after R. E. Davis of Dallas made a public statement that he was national imperial
dragon, Knights of the Original Ku Klux Klan, U.S.A. Davis charged the Association of Arkansas Klans was
made up of banished Klansmen and said it was headed by a Texarkana lawyer."

some from Georgia, and some from South Carolina. They were standing firmly against integrated schools.[750]

As laws passed in each State to enforce integration and racial equality, William Branham voiced his opinion against those siding with equality. He called the laws "ridiculous"[751] and continued to use interracial marriage as his motivation.[752] Branham gave alleged "examples" of African Americans he said were against integration of schools. And to those integrating, he said, *"the people do wrong by doing that".*[753] Branham introduced doctrines against education itself, and claimed that Africans had "no business" for reading, writing, and arithmetic.[754] He also introduced doctrines against hybrid food, furthered the doctrine by comparing it to the animal kingdom, and after turning his listeners against "hybreeding", began to apply the doctrine to ethnicity.[755] No longer was the "Message" promoting a Biblical, single bloodline originating from Adam,[756] as William Branham did using

---

[750] Klansmen Call For Members. 1959, Aug 24. Cincinnati Enquirer.

[751] Branham, William. 1957, Oct 6. Questions and Answers on Hebrews #3. "The people here now in these segregations and laws and things they're passing, I think it's ridiculous. I really do. Listen, just let those people alone, they know what they want. God made a man a colored man, and he's happy about it. Absolutely! If God made me a colored man, I'd be happy about it"

[752] Branham, William. 1957, Oct 6. Questions And Answers On Hebrews #3. "I think I might express this while I'm on it. The people here now in these segregations and laws and things they're passing, I think it's ridiculous. I really do. Listen, just let those people alone, they know what they want. God made a man a colored man, and he's happy about it. Absolutely! If God made me a colored man, I'd be happy; if He made me a white man, I'm happy; if He made me a yellow man, I'd be happy. God made us in our colors, and He made us the way He wanted us, and we're all His children. Absolutely! And they oughtn't to fuss and carry on like that. That's wrong to do that. They shouldn't do it. God made us…the way we want it. And the colored man, he don't want to get out there and break up his—his generation or his color, and mix it in the white and everything like that. I don't blame him. I don't. The colored man has things that the white man don't even possess. Absolutely! That's exactly right. And God never intended them to be that way."

[753] Branham, William. 1957, Oct 6. Questions and Answers on Hebrews #3. "I think the lady down there at Shreveport made one of the best—best comments I ever heard in my life. She made a comment, and they put it in the paper. She walked up, she said, "The way these things are going in here, in this segregation, I don't want my children going to school over at that white school." Said, "They won't get the attention they'd have if they had a colored teacher." That woman's a smart woman. She knowed what she was talking about, they get a better education. That's exactly right. So I think the people do wrong by doing that."

[754] Branham, William. 1961, Apr 11. "Today they want to make an educational school out of it: reading, writing and arithmetic. When I got to Africa amongst my colored brethren, what did they know? Reading, writing, and arithmetic, they had no business for that. That's the reason when they seen a real true moving, God come into the midst of the people, thirty thousand accepted Christ at one altar call: Durban, South "

[755] Branham, William. 1961, Apr 11. "If I was a colored man, or a brown man, or a yellow man, or a red man, I would be just as happy about it. Yes, sir. I sure would. That's the way that my Maker wanted me and that's the way I am. Right. Why does man want to tamper with anything for? When man gets into it, he ruins it. Let it alone the way God made it. Let a man be what he is; by the grace of God let him be."

[756] Branham, William. 1955, Feb 22. Jehovah Jireh. "Whether we are white, brown, yellow, black, it doesn't make a bit of difference to Him. We all come from one person, Adam."

previous versions of his stage persona. Branham's "Message" started claiming that multiple bloodlines exist, which should not be "hybrid".

In 1954, before the Ku Klux Klan began to rise for its Third Wave, this was not the case. Until Roy Davis began to organize his sect, Branham claimed that all bloodlines were alike. Even during the 1956 sermons with Joseph Mattsson-Boze and Jim Jones, William Branham claimed that skin tone came from sun exposure — not from a separate bloodline.[757] Was this why Jim Jones abandoned William Branham? Did Jim Jones learn about William Branham's deep connections to white supremacy? Was the "Message" movement rooted in a worse evil than that of Peoples Temple?

Little did I realize at the time that the "Message" was being weaponized. Not simply as a tool for swaying religious opinion; the "Message" recordings of William Branham were being used for neuro-linguistic programming.[758] Brainwashing. Branham and those involved were attempting to sway politics using the stage persona that had been created. The "Americanization" project was preparing for its final stage.

---

[757] Branham, William. 1956, Sept 30. Witnesses. "Here is a colored woman, a white man, the only difference, we're both human beings, the same blood. God made of all nations one blood. The only difference is the country she was raised in, the country I was raised in, an Anglo-Saxon, and her an African down where the sun's hot and up where it's not. We're different color of our skin. We're both human beings bought by the Blood of Christ."

[758] St. Petersburg court declares books by U.S. missionary Branham extremist. Accessed 2020, May 24 from *rapsinews.com/judicial_news/20200521/305831637.html.* "Brochures authored by XX century U.S. missionary William Branham have been defined as extremist literature … In April of 2017, an examination by experts of St. Petersburg State University revealed that the texts contained "technics of neuro-linguistic programming" aimed to set up the spectre of an enemy and insult the feelings of certain religious believers and priests. The results of the expert examination served as the basis of the claim, according to the statement."

LOUISVILLE CIVIL RIGHTS:
A Self-Guided Tour of Louisville's Civil Rights History. Accessed 2019, Sept 15 from
    https://louisville.edu/braden/oral-history-tours-exhibits/civil-rights-driving-tour
Explore Louisville's Civil Rights History - US Civil Rights Trail. Accessed 2019, Sept 15 from
    https://civilrightstrail.com/destination/louisville/
Louisville Downtown Civil Rights Trail. Accessed 2019, Sept 15 from
    https://civilrightstrail.com/attraction/louisville-civil-rights-trail/
Living the Story: The Civil Rights Movement in Kentucky. Accessed 2019, Sept 15 from
    https://www.kct.org/education/resources/living-story-civil-rights-movement-kentucky/
Wade, Andrew * Notable Kentucky African Americans Database. Accessed 2019, Sept 15 from
    https://nkaa.uky.edu/nkaa/items/show/300003773

JIM JONES
Reiterman, Tim. Jacobs, John. 1982. Raven: The Untold Story of the Rev. Jim Jones and His
    People.
Race and the Peoples Temple. Accessed 2019, Sept 15 from
    https://www.pbs.org/wgbh/americanexperience/features/jonestown-race/
The Civil Rights Movement in Mendocino County, California. Accessed 2019, Sept 15 from
    https://jonestown.sdsu.edu/?page_id=33222
Student Minister Sponsors Drive to Aid South Side Area Juveniles. 1953, Feb 28. The Indianapolis
    Star.
Peoples Temple. 1956, Jun 2. The Indianapolis News. (Advertising William Branham)
Jones, Jim. 1956. The Open Door
Korean Waifs' Adoption Called 'Lesson' in Religion. 1960, Feb 25. The Indianapolis News.

ROY E. DAVIS
Minister May Take Over Klan. 1958, Mar 28. Corsicana Daily.
Retired Preacher Claims Bid to Top Dallas Klan Post. 1958, Mar 28. Lubbock Morning Avalanche.
Dallas Klan. 1958, Mar 28. Lubbock Morning Avalanche.
Texarkana Lawyer Reveals Leadership of Klan Faction. 1959, May 31. Arkansas Gazette.
Klan Groups are Banished. 1959, May 29. Arkansas Gazette.
Klansmen Call for Members. 1959, Aug 24. The Cincinnati Enquirer.
Davis, Roy. 1960. An Open Letter to George F. Edwards, Leader of a Band of Banished Klansmen
    in the State of Arkansas.

WILLIAM BRANHAM
Branham, William. 1956, Jun 13. Jehovah-Jireh (With Jim Jones)
Branham, William. 1956, Jun 15. An Exodus (With Jim Jones)
Branham, William. 1956, July 26. Love
Branham, William. 1963, Jun 28. O Lord, Just Once More
Branham, William. 1956, Jul 28. Making the Valley Full of Ditches
Branham, William. 1960, Nov 13. Condemnation by Representation
Branham, William. 1961, Apr 11. But It Wasn't So from the Beginning
Branham, William. 1954, May 16. Questions and Answers (Law Having a Shadow)
Branham, William. 1956, Sept 30. Witnesses

362

CHAPTER 35

WILLIAM BRANHAM AND THE KENNEDY PROPHECY

"One of the greatest mistakes that the colored race ever made, was down in Louisiana and over in there, when they voted for Kennedy, the other night, put him in[759]"

Shreveport, Louisiana sits between the Cross Lake and Red River in northern Louisiana. It is home to riverboat and hotel casinos, science and historical museums, art galleries, and a variety of entertainment choices. Though I had never visited Shreveport, it felt as if the city were dear to me in a way that I could not explain. I had heard its name many, many times on recordings of William Branham throughout the years, and had often browsed photos of Shreveport attractions that I intended to visit one day. Shreveport, Louisiana, is the location chosen to print William Branham's "The Voice of Healing" publication. When Branham first began publishing the newsletter, he did so from Shreveport. Shreveport was the city chosen for several key sermons in the 'Message"; often new doctrines, new ideas and promotions originated from Shreveport. This should come as no surprise, since Jack Moore, pastor of Life Tabernacle and a fundamental part of Branham's campaign team, was in Shreveport, Louisiana.[760]

---

[759] Branham, William. 1960, Nov 13. Condemnation by Representation.
[760] Healing and the Joseph Anointing. 2020, May 18. Accessed from
https://healingandrevival.com/BioJMoore.htm

At the time Branham created the early versions of his stage persona, Shreveport would have looked much different than it does today. The differences are not just from an architectural standpoint, but also from an historical one. Like Louisville, Shreveport, Louisiana has a fascinating history and some of that history was made during the battle for Civil Rights. Whether directly or indirectly, some of those historical events came as a result of William Branham and the men working with him.

I never knew most of this history until long after leaving the "Message". I never knew just how significant Shreveport was to the "Message". In the same way, I never knew how significant Shreveport was to the Civil Rights Movement. When I first moved to Jeffersonville, a "Message" believer told me that they attended Branham's meetings in Shreveport. "I saw 'God' on the platform", the man said. *"Jesus Christ Himself returned to the earth through William Branham. A man could not have done the things we witnessed"*, he said "That was not a man – that was God in a man!"

For William Branham and his history, I slowly began to realize that Shreveport was not just significant because of the advertising and the sermons, there were other aspects of Shreveport to consider. Many pathways converge at Shreveport: pathways of people who created the "prophet", people who promoted the "prophet", people the prophet promoted, and people who believed the doctrines created by the "prophet". Even "prophecies" were added to Branham's stage persona that were linked to Shreveport in one way or another.[761]

When I learned that Shreveport was significant to the battle for Civil Rights, I wanted to see how that timeline fit with the "prophet's" timeline. In the years leading up to Jim Jones' separation from William Branham's "Message", the battle stage was being set. 1957 would be the last year that Jim Jones, Joseph Mattsson-Boze, and William Branham teamed up for the "Brotherhood-Healing Crusade" in Indianapolis, Indiana. For the last crusade, T. L. Osborn, Tommy Hicks, and F. F. Bosworth headlined while William Branham held daily meetings at the Peoples Temple event.[762] In 1958, however, Jones

---

[761] Branham, William. 1956, Sep 30. Witnesses. "When I was in Shreveport, Louisiana, the Lord woke me up one night and showed me a vision."

began to abandon his Full Gospel leanings for what would eventually become an affiliation with the Disciples of Christ denomination.

Now that I knew of the conflicts of interest between Branham and Jones on the issues of Civil Rights, it was hard not to think about Jim Jones' motivation in leaving the "Message". White supremacists gave "race mixing" labels of "Communist" or "Un-American". Ironically, Jones — a strong Civil Rights — supporter, began to identify as Communist.[763] William Branham, in opposition to integration, continued to label Civil Rights leaders "Communistic", and this included the freedom fighters in Shreveport, Louisiana.[764] In one breath, he would claim to support equal rights.[765] Then in another, he would label those seeking freedom as "communist" or reprobate. Those in William Branham's meetings were suddenly faced with a flurry of "communist" labels. Martin Luther King, Jr. was "communist".[766] White children in school advocating for equal opportunity were communists.[767] A white men who married a "colored" girl was "communist".[768] Though William Branham had not yet publicly identified with Roy E. Davis'

---

[762] 1957, Jun 1. Peoples Temple. The Indianapolis News

[763] Q235 Transcript. Accessed 2020, May 18 from http://jonestown.sdsu.edu/?page_id=27388. "We would like to look for critical reviews, at one insider's view of the Communist Party USA. In order for fascism to be avoided, there has to be a strong communist party, a strong socialist movement, and free, independent strong trade union [unions], none of which exist in USA, and that is why to avoid your utter destruction, materially most of you, and murder of the rest, I brought you here to regroup, recoup, rehabilitate and gain strength, and militancy, and a proper education in Marxist-Leninism, which you had never picked up, even though I was avowedly, openly Marxist-Leninist and atheist, you have never picked it up, for the most part, in the United States, except for a handful"

[764] Branham, William. 1964, Aug 30. Questions and Answers #4. "Down there that day in Shreveport when that uprise come, and them…and there was all them young colored inspired out there, communistic"

[765] Branham, William. 1964, Aug 30. Questions and Answers #4. "That's why I different with the Afrikaans message; they didn't even believe those people had a soul. That's what got me disliked there. I said, "That man's a man as same as I am. He's got the rights to the same privilege that I have. His skin don't mean no difference to me, or no other man that's borned again of the Spirit of God."

[766] Branham, William. 1964, Apr 18. A Paradox. "Like I said, this Martin Luther King is leading his people to a crucifixion. It's communistic.

[767] Branham, William. 1964, Aug 30. Questions and Answers #4. "But look, it isn't them real genuine borned again Christian colored people that's causing all of this trouble. You want to condemn them for that, what about some of our renegade white kids? See? Now, what sauce for the goose is for the gander. Well, our white kids cause twice as much trouble as they have. That's exactly right. Where's it at? In our colleges and things like that. Some of our higher-educated people is causing those things. See? 174 Well, what is it? Now, to show you that it's communism and not them colored people, that's how communism has always come in to take over."

[768] Branham, William. 1964, Aug 30. Questions and Answers #4. "I seen some real pretty colored girl, intelligent, nice-looking kid, just as pretty as any woman you'd want to see…What does she want to marry a white man and have mulatto children? What would an intelligent colored girl want with such a thing as that? Is because that something…that communist…And how would a—a fine…a—a—a colored man want to marry a white woman and have mulatto children?"

and the Third Wave of the Ku Klux Klan, he was saying exactly what Roy Davis and other white supremacists wanted him to say.

Due to the scars earned during the 1920s when William D. Upshaw helped the Ku Klux Klan narrowly escaped extinction, the K.K.K. and other white supremacy groups faced heavy scrutiny by the United States Government. This scrutiny dramatically increased as the battle for Civil Rights grew heated and hate crimes were committed all across the South. The Klan's power of persuasion was limited to drumming up support under concealment. William Branham, however, did not face such scrutiny. Anything said during a sermon — no matter how many people were persuaded — was protected under the law of "freedom of speech". Branham spoke out against Civil Rights, and at least from public appearance, did so without the watchful eye of the United States Government getting involved. (Though the question could be raised about Branham's tax investigation,[769] since the United States Government had in the past used tax law to circumvent problems making criminal charges "stick"). When William Branham spoke, he spoke before large audiences. Unsuspecting crowds, many unaware that political agenda had entered religious context, began associating Branham's anti-Civil-Rights views with religion. Others, who only attended sermons in which Branham avoided those views or spoke the opposite, would have never known that William Branham had any political agenda.

The nation was primed for the Klan's "third pull" towards white power. In July 1958, in Knoxville, Tennessee, the National States Rights Party was born.[770] It was the result of a merger of the United White Party and States Rights Party. Though it was formed in Knoxville, its headquarters and mailing address was in Jeffersonville, Indiana,[771] William Branham's small hometown of less than four thousand people. The N.S.R.P. produced "The Thunderbolt"

[769] Branham, William. 1960, Mar 4. Thirsting for Life. "I'm in a tax dispute myself, of the money that I spent in these meeting. The government said, 'It ought to be mine alone. I ought to pay taxes on all that'"
[770] Newton, Michael. 2017. The National States Rights Party: A History.
[771] National States Rights Party. Federal Bureau of Investigation. Accessed 2019, Sep 23 from https://vault.fbi.gov/National%20States%20Rights%20Party/National%20States%20Rights%20Party%20Part%201%20of%201%20. "The National States Rights Party was formed in July, 1958, at Knocksville, Tennessee, as the result of a merger of the United White Party and representatives of the States Rights Party. The mailing address was Post Office Box 261, Jeffersonville, Indiana."

publication, a white supremacy newspaper used for spreading anti-integration propaganda. The N.S.R.P. sought out to become a new political party that was a rival to the Democratic and Republication parties. It claimed that the major political parties had betrayed the "White Christian Civilization".

I was surprised the first time I stumbled onto archives of the publication. Many of William Branham's statements from sermons that I remembered could be found in the articles. Like Branham, The Thunderbolt spoke violently against interracial marriage. Like Branham, it violently opposed Martin Luther King, Jr, and blamed King for the violence rather than blaming the terroristic supremacy groups or individuals supporting them. I could almost hear the "prophet's" voice as I read it "Martin Luther King would lead his people to a massacre!" Democrat and Republican parties are "filthy". The "colored people" seeking freedom were "communistic". The "colored people" have better schools, "what difference does it make anyhow?"[772] But as many times as we heard those sermons, every Wednesday evening, twice on Sunday, and often in-between, we never caught it. It was difficult to catch; for in almost the same breath that he blasted those seeking freedom and desegregation of public schools, William Branham claimed to support integration. We had completely overlooked the political agenda.

In 1960, all the white supremacy groups united against the Kennedy-Johnson Presidential Campaign.[773] Roy Davis wrote letters to the Dallas Morning News, stirring up white supremacists to vote against John F. Kennedy. The National States Rights Party published articles and staged protests against Kennedy. Kennedy supported Civil Rights and was a threat to their very existence. In November of 1960, William Branham introduced his claim that he had had a "1933" prophecy concerning women voting (though he had never mentioned this "prophecy" before). According to this new addition to his lineup of

---

[772] Branham, William. 1963, Jul 21. He Cares. "The question down there is "segregation of school." Now, I was there at the first uprise, and I heard it, and I—I know from what I speak of. The colored people has fine schools, sometimes much better than the other schools. And, for instance, in Shreveport they got finer schools than the white school is. But it's the idea of somebody inspiring them that they should go and mix themselves together. Which, I think that it'd be all right, but as long as the people are protesting it, those southern people, then what difference does it make anyhow?"

[773] Krochmal, Maximilian. 2011. Labor, Civil Rights, and the Struggle for Democracy in Mid-Twentieth Century Texas.

"1933 prophecies", Branham claimed that by allowing women to vote, Americans would cause the destruction of the United States. "Condemnation by Representation" was the first time this "prophecy" was mentioned, and it slowly became integrated into his "seven" prophecies he claimed to have had in 1933. Interestingly, 1960 was also the year that William Branham introduced a "converted gangster"[774] into the stage act, a killer-now-Christian who followed him around the country, "hitchhiking" to attend meetings around the United States.[775]

The next year, white supremacy groups declared all-out war against John F. Kennedy. Roy Davis opened Klan membership drives in Shreveport,[776] the former city of Branham's campaign headquarters. Davis claimed that his objective was for "states' rights", a nod to the NSRP and their intentions. In what would become a nationally publicized event, Davis posed in the Ku Klux Klan uniform for all to see. Reporters claimed that Shreveport was a "favorite visiting spot for the nation's top Klan man", and publicly named Roy E. Davis as the National Imperial Wizard of the Original Knights of the Ku Klux Klan.

According to the newspapers, the Ku Klux Klan had been targeting Shreveport and northern Louisiana for several months, and Davis was preparing for "war". Davis said, *"A hot war for white supremacy is inevitable" "'Negros' are 'turning the white man's government into a mongrel government'".*[777] I couldn't help but think about William Branham himself making the same claim. Branham said, *"One of the greatest mistakes that the colored race ever made was down in Louisiana and over in there, when they voted for Kennedy, the other night, put him in".*[778] While Davis was targeting northern Louisiana with clandestine membership drives, William Branham targeted the area using public speeches in the form of "sermons"[779] and distribution of audio recordings. To further gain publicity, Davis invited reporters to

---

[774] Branham, William. 1960, Mar 10. Elijah and the Meal Offering. "Brother Pat Tyler, which is a converted gangster; Brother Williams setting right there"

[775] Branham, William. 1960, Mar 10. Elijah and the Meal Offering. "Pat Tyler, another bosom friend of mine sitting over here. Brother Pat, stand up. You all might know Pat Tyler. Thank you, Brother Pat. God bless you. He was an outlaw, a gunman, killer. God saved him and made a saint out of him. Hitchhiking across the country, to follow the meetings and things."

[776] 1961, Feb 10. Ku Klux Klan Active in Shreveport Area. The Times (Shreveport)

[777] Ku Klux Klan Active in Shreveport Area. 1961, Feb 10. The Times (Shreveport).

[778] Branham, William. 1960, Nov 13. Condemnation by Representation.

[779] Example: 60-1127e The Queen of the South. 61-0117 The Messiah.

the membership drives,[780] and used Branham's slogan in fliers posted throughout the city: *Yesterday, Today, and Forever.*[781] The battle intensified as crosses were burned in the front lawns of the opposition. Davis was arrested, fingerprinted, and questioned.[782] But this was only the beginning of the war, there were far bigger battles to come.

In the same sermon that William Branham announced his new "women's vote" prophecy and began to focus his political agenda against John F. Kennedy, during the time of Roy E. Davis' Klan membership drive in Shreveport; William Branham announced that he, too, was headed to Shreveport, Louisiana. He was still promoting Roy Davis, at home and across the nation with public nods to him in his sermons but now he was headed right to the battlefield, in Shreveport, Louisiana.

I had heard Branham's "slave story" many, many times, but without the historical context, I never noticed the political motivation. He said, "They should realize their position, not fussing, fighting" And then began to associate that directive to slavery.

> *They don't realize that a son and a daughter of God should act like a son and daughter of God. They should realize their position, not fussing, fighting, stewing, carry on, and hold grudges.*
>
> *Here sometime ago in the south here, they used to sell the colored for slaves. And they'd sell them on the lots just like you would cars, used cars, get a bill of sale with them... Never was right. Then when... One day there was a broker came by and wanted to buy some slaves on a plantation. And they'd buy the big men and breed them to big women, and make heavier slaves to pull their carts, and plows, and things, and do their work. And one day a broker came by and he said, "How many slaves you got?" Said, "I got a hundred, or two." Said, "Take a look at them."*

---

[780] 1961, Feb 17. Blindfolded Newsmen Taken to Shreveport Klan Meeting. Arkansas Gazette.
[781] Ku Klux Klan Labels. 1961, Jan 20. The Times. (Image of Klansman on horse with slogan, 'Yesterday, Today, and Forever')
[782] Being Fingerprinted. 1961, Apr 7. The Times.

He noticed all of them; they was away from their homelands, and they'd had to whip them, and everything, to make them obey, and 'cause they were sad. They knowed they'd never be back home no more; they'd have to die here in a strange land; and they never would be back home no more.

But they noticed one young man, they didn't have to whip him. Boy, he had his chest out, his chin up. He's always on the go. That broker said, "I'd like to buy that slave." He said, "But he's not for sale." Said, "Why isn't he for sale?" Said, "Is he the boss over the rest of them?" Said, "No, he's a slave." Said, "Do you feed him different than you feed the rest of them?" Said, "They all eat in the galley together." Said, "What makes him so much difference than the rest of the slaves?" And the owner said, "I wondered that for a long time, but one day I found out. Over in the homeland where he came from in Africa, his father is a king over the tribe. And though he's an alien, and away from his homeland, he still conducts himself as a king's son."[783]

I had never noticed how this story could have been used as a political strategy. I knew very little about the political landscape of the time. I heard what he wanted white males to hear. But what did African Americans in the heat of this battle hear? Did they try to "realize their position?" Or were African Americans offended by the many things that I never caught William Branham saying in his sermons?

---

[783] Branham, William. 1960, Nov 27. The Queen of the South.

NATIONAL STATES RIGHTS PARTY:
Newton, Michael. 2017. The National States Rights Party: A History.
Mulloy, D. J. 2018. Enemies of the State: The Radical Right in America from FDR
The Present-Day Ku Klux Klan Movement. 1968. United States Congress.
National States Rights Party. Federal Bureau of Investigation. Accessed 2019, Sep 23 from
   https://vault.fbi.gov/National%20States%20Rights%20Party/National%20States%20Rights%
   20Party%20Part%201%20of%201%20
National States Rights Party - Item 014. Accessed 2019, Sep 23 from
   http://jfk.hood.edu/Collection/Weisberg%20Subject%20Index%20Files/N%20Disk/National%
   20States%20Rights%20Party/Item%20014.pdf
National States Rights Party - Item 028. Accessed 2019, Sep 23 from
   http://jfk.hood.edu/Collection/Weisberg%20Subject%20Index%20Files/N%20Disk/National%
   20States%20Rights%20Party/Item%20028.pdf
National States Rights Party. Archive.org. Accessed 2019, Sep 23 from
   https://archive.org/stream/NationalStatesRightsPartyFBI/NSRP-NYC-6_djvu.txt
National States Rights Party - The Black Vault. Accessed 2019, Sep 23 from
   https://documents.theblackvault.com/documents/fbifiles/national_states_rights_party_part01.
   pdf

ROY E. DAVIS:
124-90123-10054. 1962. JFK Assassination System Identification Collection. Federal Bureau of
   Investigation
1960, Oct 10. Letters from the Readers. Dallas Morning News.
1961, Feb 17. Blindfolded Newsmen Taken to Shreveport Klan Meeting. Arkansas Gazette.
1961, Feb 11. Klan Opens Member Drive in Northwestern Louisiana. Arkansas Gazette.
1961, Apr 7. Dallas Resident Questioned Over KKK Activities.
1961, Feb 11. KKK's Membership Very Small in Texas. Dallas Morning News.
1961, Feb 10. Ku Klux Klan Active in Shreveport Area. The Times (Shreveport)
1961, Feb 9. Cross Burned in Front of Rep Brooks Home. The Times (Shreveport)
1961, Feb 10. Ku Klux Klan Active in Shreveport, Area. The Times (Shreveport)
1961, Feb 10. Won't Tolerate KKK, Mayor Fant Declares. The Times (Shreveport)
1961, Feb 11. U.S. Attorney Studies Burning Here. The Times (Shreveport)
1961, Jan 20. Ku Klux Klan Stickers Put on Windows. The Times (Shreveport)
1961, Jan 20. Yesterday, Today, and Forever. The Times (Shreveport)
1961, Apr 7. Klan Leader Picked Up, Warned by Police Here. The Times (Shreveport)
1961, Feb 21. Parish, City Officials Criticize Revived Klan Movement Here. The Times

WILLIAM BRANHAM'S POLITICALLY MOTIVATED STATEMENTS
Branham, William. 1964, Aug 30. Questions and Answers #4
Branham, William. 1964, Apr 18. A Paradox
Branham, William. 1965, Aug 18. And Knoweth It Not
Branham, William. 1963, Jul 21. He Cares, Do You Care?
Branham, William. 1960, Nov 13. Condemnation by Representation
Branham, William. 1960, Dec 5. The Ephesian Church Age.
Branham, William. 1960, Dec 11. The Laodicean Church Age.
Branham, William. 1960, Nov 27. The Queen of the South.

CHAPTER 36

WILLIAM BRANHAM'S FAMILY MOVES TO TUCSON

"He had plenty of schools he could go to[784]"

The year 1963 was pivotal for the "Message". A large part of what "Message" believers are trained to believe originated during or after 1963.[785] Branham claimed to have "opened" the Seven Seals described in the Book of Revelation in the year 1963. In 1963, he claimed to have been visited by Seven Angels.[786] He preached "The Token", a very popular sermon among his followers in 1963. "Conduct, Order, and Doctrine of the Church", Branham's instructions for leaders in his cult following (also called "Church Order") was preached in 1963.

I will never forget when my family moved back to Jeffersonville in the mid 1990's. In a casual conversation with another "Message" believer, I quoted the "prophet" to make a point. Jokingly, he asked, "was that before 1963 or after 1963, brother?" Some sects of the "Message" believe that Branham's 1963-1965 sermons to be "inspired" while they place far less emphasis on the sermons before 1963. Before the sermons were re-branded and re-sold in MP3 format, some families I

---

[784] Branham, William. 1962, Oct 14. The Stature of a Perfect Man.
[785] Branham, William. 1963, Mar 24. Questions and Answers on the Seals. "And now with faith, believing, with this promise laying before us, with the Seals of the Bible being opened to us, that God keeps His Word!"
[786] Branham, William. 1963, Mar 24. The Seventh Seal. "Did anybody think of that, of those seven Angels being This, being the Message that was coming forth, them Angels bringing me back here for That? See?"

knew only owned the sermons that were preached after 1962. Either the hundreds of cassette tapes took up too much space or the families couldn't afford to purchase the entire collection. They simply were not as important to some people.

...

When Roy E. Davis warned America that war was inevitable, his words could not have been more prophetic. The Klan leader had been stirring up anger and hatred from Texas to Florida and everywhere between. His arrest and fingerprinting, however, created new risks for those connected to him. Davis had a lengthy trail of criminal activity; from Texas to Georgia, Tennessee to Kentucky, Indiana to Arkansas, to California, and back to Texas, where the circle began to start once more.

In declassified F.B.I. documents, it becomes clear that Roy Davis was already being tracked by the Federal Government. And when John F. Kennedy was elected president, this would have made Roy Davis a classified public enemy of the State. Kennedy was elected with a promise to the oppressed African American community: He would create equal opportunity for all mankind "by the stroke of the President's pen".[787] With Kennedy's election began an inquiry into all terroristic white supremacy groups. Davis' Original Knights of the Ku Klux Klan was no exception. The O.K.K.K. was systematically posing a threat to the United States economy[788] while using physical violence to silence supporters of Civil Rights — all while touting itself as an "anti-communist Christian association". Though it is heavily redacted and many names are hidden, the focal point of the FBI's investigation is clear: The "Imperial Grand Dragon" (Roy Davis) had organized his forces to create pressure against anyone or anything that promoted equality.

Even interracial television programs were targeted by the Klan's strategy of coercion towards white supremacy.[789] I thought back to the

---

[787] Blight, David W. Scharfstein, Allison. King's Forgotten Manifesto. Accessed 2020, May 18 from https://www.nytimes.com/2012/05/17/opinion/kings-forgotten-manifesto.html
[788] United States v. Original Knights of the Ku Klux Klan, 250 F. Supp. 330 (E.D. La. 1965)
[789] [789] United States v. Original Knights of the Ku Klux Klan, 250 F. Supp. 330 (E.D. La. 1965). No 105-1057.
"after the meeting, the Imperial Dragon indicated that members of his organization were writing letters to "peacefully influence" television stations in the South to refuse to air television programs deemed objectionable

statements that William Branham made in his public sermons against these television programs. Looking at it through the lens of white supremacy and discrimination, however, his statements sounded entirely different. Branham spoke against I Love Lucy, an interracial comedy.[790] Civil Rights supporter Elvis Presley was depicted in 1960 movie "Flaming Star", which made a political statement about mixing race and racial equality. During multiple sermons, William Branham spoke harshly against Elvis Presley — not only his person, but even his first name. The use of the name "Elvis" for a baby born to a family in the "Message" was not permitted.[791]

Meanwhile, support for Civil Rights was also quickly growing in the South. With the support of President John F. Kennedy, Civil Rights leaders now had the protection of military police. January 1, 1963, marked the 100-year-anniversary of the Emancipation Proclamation freeing African American slaves. Martin Luther King, Jr. started a campaign asking President Kennedy for a second emancipation proclamation on the anniversary of the first.

Shortly before the anniversary, in September of 1962, protests erupted at Ole Miss in Jackson, Mississippi. White supremacists began protesting the enrollment of James Meredith, a black US military veteran. [792] White supremacists were activated on campus, protesting the presence of an African American in the university. Those protests turned violent. It became dangerous for African Americans to live in Jackson, simply for having a different color of skin. Convoys of military troops were sent into Jackson to restore law and order, and scenes from the school looked just like scenes of war. White supremacists had become militarized.

William Branham publicly blasted the African Americans for this event, speaking through both sides of his mouth. He said he supported freedom but said the "colored" people were *"selling their birthrights"*.[793]

---

to the Klan"

[790] Branham, William. 1955, Mar 11. "Brother, by their fruits, you'll know them. Who—what was that? Lucy, something about Lucy, or something like "I Love Lucy." Some of them programs like that. I don't watch her nonsense. I read my Bible; I love to serve the Lord."

[791] Branham, William. 1965, Dec 6. Modern Events Are Made Clear By Prophecy. 'That's the reason I say don't, never call your child 'Ricky,' or 'Elvis,' or something. Elvis means 'cat,' Ricky's a 'rat.'"

[792] James Meredith at Ole Miss - 1962 Riot. Accessed 2019, Sep 28 from https://www.history.com/topics/black-history/ole-miss-integration

[793] Branham, William. 1962, Oct 14. Stature of a Perfect Man. "But I tell you one thing, that boy wasn't down

Branham said he supported James Meredith but took the side of segregation. According to Branham, *"he had plenty of schools he could go to"*.

When Martin Luther King Jr. pressed Washington for a second "emancipation", he ignited the fuse that would explode into war. As the days grew nearer to the 100-year-anniversary, lines were drawn in the sand. One hundred years had passed since slavery was abolished, yet the nation was still divided by racial segregation. Churches in the North prepared for January 1st by uniting in support of equality. Catholic and Protestant churches alike joined together against segregation.[794]

Meanwhile, white supremacists in the South were preparing for the inevitable militant response from Washington. One hundred and sixty-six United States marshals were injured in the riots at Ole Miss, which sent a clear message to Washington: "War is coming."

William Branham himself prepared by taking his children out of school in Indiana and transplanting them to Tucson, Arizona, far out of harm's way. Two days before the anniversary of slavery ending, Branham announced the move in a sermon to his Jeffersonville congregation. But he also announced that wasn't planning to stay with his family; he said that his plans were to become mobile.[795]

Roy Davis' sect of the Klan prepared by stockpiling weapons of war under the name "Louisiana Rifle Association" in Shreveport, [796] Louisiana, but the FBI was not aware of the connection until August of 1963. Roy Davis and his associates were now armed for war against the government.

---

in there just because that, their schools. That boy is a citizen. He's American. This is freedom for all. The color of a man shouldn't change his difference. We all… "God," said, "of one man, made all blood, all nations." We're all one. But, that boy, he was a soldier. He's a veteran. He fought for what's right. He had a right to go to school. That's right. But he had plenty of schools he could go to. 387 It's what the thing is. If you get behind it, it's this present-day denominational stuff up there, that's inspiring that. Why? They're swinging those colored votes from Republican to Democrat, and they're selling their birthrights by it."

794 Creeds Unite, Call Conference in Fight Against Segregation. 1962, Dec 1. Star Gazette. "For the first time on the American scene, nationwide organizations of Roman Catholics, Orthodox, Protestants and Jews are linking forces for concerted action on racial problems. To launch the combined approach, they've called a 'National Conference on Religion and Race' next Jan. 14-17 in Chicago."

795 Branham, William. 1962, Dec 30. Is This the Sign of the End, Sir? "Now, as far as I know, let me tell you. As far as I know, I'll be leaving in the next two or three days, Wednesday morning, to…for Tucson. I'll not go to Tucson to preach. I'm not going there to preach. I'm going to Tucson, to establish my family in school, and then become a wanderer."

796 Original Knights of the Ku Klux Klan (Louisiana), aka Louisiana Rifle Association. 1964, Mar 12. Federal Bureau of Investigation.

Learning about the events leading up to Branham's migration to Tucson raised many questions for me. We were told that it was a "spiritual move", yet it seemed more like a strategic one. Looking at the family photos, it almost seemed as though the family decided to leave the "Message". William Branham preached firmly against shorts, yet his son was wearing them. Exposed shoulders and knees were forbidden for women, yet his daughters dressed according to the current fashion.

Now that I knew about the Ku Klux Klan's stockpile of weapons, it was hard not to think about the "prophet's" own collection. He claimed to be a simple "hunter" but had more rifles than any man that I knew.[797] Many of them were hunting rifles — as if he needed that many — but he also had handguns, many of them. When he was alive, very few of his followers had the privilege of seeing inside his luxurious 1964 "den", and only his close associates knew about the large number of weapons he owned and carried. He had stockpiles of weapons in cases, and weapons for concealed carry; everything from hunting rifles to military-grade weapons. He could have gone on a hundred hunting trips and not had time to get familiar with all his weapons.

In today's version of the cult following, Branham's "den" and his weapon cache are considered to be a monument in the "Message", but when he transplanted his family to Tucson, his followers had no idea about the number of weapons that he owned and carried.

I knew that I would never answer the question as to why the "prophet" had so many weapons. So instead, I began to focus back to his statement made just before the turn of the new year: "I'm going to Tucson, to establish my family in school, and then become a wanderer". There were a lot of sermons preached in 1963, the year many consider pivotal in Civil Rights history. Most of them were in Tucson, Phoenix, or Jeffersonville, but these were only the locations of the speeches we had access to hear. They accounted for his revival series and Sunday services in his home and affiliated churches. If Branham did start traveling as he claimed, either the sermons were not available, or the trip was not for religious reasons.

---

[797] Brother Branham's Den in Tucson. Accessed 2020, May 18 from http://tucsontabernacle.org/photo-gallery/tucson-arizona/brother-branham-s-den-in-tucson/

Looking over the index of transcripts including dates and locations, I found sermons preached in Tucson, Phoenix, and a few nearby cities. There were also sermons preached in Jeffersonville, and in Chicago to the "Latter Rain" crowd. Except for a revival series in New York, Branham didn't really "wander" that much. I began to wonder why he needed to travel back-and-forth from Tucson to Jeffersonville, especially when his sermons were recorded and also broadcast between churches by telephone.[798] But then I started to think about the gaps of time between services, and his statements to the crowd before leaving to "wander". During some of these gaps, he claimed to witness "supernatural" events. I wondered, "Did Branham travel to the places that he *claimed* he did when he preached those sermons?"

---

[798] Branham, William. 1964, Jun 14. The Unveiling of God. "Now, I believe, if I understand, they got a telephone hookup somewhere, that this Message is going into Phoenix and to—and to different parts, by telephone. And so now we trust that if that's so...I don't know; just told that before coming in. And—and all the people out there are really enjoying good health and—and the Glory of the Lord upon them."

BATTLE OF OXFORD (OLE MISS RIOT OF 1962)

Meredith, James. 2019. Three Years in Mississippi.

Goudsouzian, Aram. 2014. Down to the Crossroads: Civil Rights, Black Power, and the Meredith March.

Doyle, William. 2003. An American Insurrection: James Meredith and the Battle of Oxford, Mississippi, 1962

Barrett, Russell. 1965. Integration at Ole Miss

Lambert, Frank. 2009. The Battle of Ole Miss: Civil Rights v. States' Rights

Integrating Ole Miss: A Transformative, Deadly Riot. Accessed 2019, Sep 28 from
   https://www.npr.org/2012/10/01/161573289/integrating-ole-miss-a-transformative-deadly-riot

James Meredith at Ole Miss - 1962 Riot. Accessed 2019, Sep 28 from
   Integration">https://www.history.com/topics/black-history/ole-miss-integration

ROY E. DAVIS:

124-90123-10054. 1962. JFK Assassination System Identification Collection. Federal Bureau of Investigation

1960, Oct 10. Letters From the Readers. Dallas Morning News.

1961, Feb 17. Blindfolded Newsmen Taken to Shreveport Klan Meeting. Arkansas Gazette.

1961, Feb 11. Klan Opens Member Drive in Northwestern Louisiana. Arkansas Gazette.

1961, Apr 7. Dallas Resident Questioned Over KKK Activities.

1961, Feb 11. KKK's Membership Very Small in Texas. Dallas Morning News.

1961, Feb 10. Ku Klux Klan Active in Shreveport Area. The Times (Shreveport)

1961, Feb 9. Cross Burned in Front of Rep Brooks Home. The Times (Shreveport)

1961, Feb 10. Ku Klux Klan Active in Shreveport, Area. The Times (Shreveport)

1961, Feb 10. Won't Tolerate KKK, Mayor Fant Declares. The Times (Shreveport)

1961, Feb 11. U.S. Attorney Studies Burning Here. The Times (Shreveport)

1961, Jan 20. Ku Klux Klan Stickers Put on Windows. The Times (Shreveport)

1961, Jan 20. Yesterday, Today, and Forever. The Times (Shreveport)

1961, Apr 7. Klan Leader Picked Up, Warned by Police Here. The Times (Shreveport)

1961, Feb 21. Parish, City Officials Criticize Revived Klan Movement Here. The Times

ORIGINAL KNIGHTS OF THE KU KLUX KLAN:

105-71809 - Original Knights of The Ku Klux Klan (Louisiana), aka Louisiana Rifle Association. 1964, Mar 12. Federal Bureau of Investigation.

105-70801 - Original Knights of The Ku Klux Klan - Louisiana (1964-65). 1964, Mar 12. Federal Bureau of Investigation.

Caufield, Jeffrey H. General Walker and the Murder of President Kennedy: The Extensive New Evidence of a Radical-Right Conspiracy.

124-90123. JFK Assassination System. Federal Bureau of Investigation.

124-10183, Original Knights of The Ku Klux Klan (OKKKK). Federal Bureau of Investigation.

124-10214. The Original Knights of The Ku Klux Klan, Aka The Original Ku Klux Klan, Formerly Known as U. S. Klans, Knights of the Ku Klux Klan, Inc., (Texas) IS - Klan. Federal Bureau of Investigation.

MARTIN LUTHER KING JR.

'Fly-In' Planned to Hit Airport Race Barriers. 1961, Jun 6. Los Angeles Times.

Civil Rights Movement History 1962. Accessed 2019, Sep 28 from
   https://www.crmvet.org/tim/timhis62.htm

Major King Events Chronology: 1929-1968. Accessed 2019, Sep 28 from
  https://kinginstitute.stanford.edu/king-resources/major-king-events-chronology-1929-1968
Dr. Martin Luther King's 1962 Address. Accessed 2019, Sept 28 from *https://www.press.org/mlk*
Listen to newly discovered 1962 MLK Jr. Speech. USA Today. Accessed 2019, Sep 28 from
  https://www.usatoday.com/story/news/nation/2014/01/20/found-martin-luther-king-jr-speech/4663937/
1962 | Historic photos show Civil Rights icon Martin Luther King. Accessed 2019, Sep 28 from
  https://www.deseretnews.com/top/2237/24/1962-Historic-photos-show-civil-rights-icon-Martin-Luther-King-Jr-at-work-at-play.html

WILLIAM BRANHAM - ABOUT MARTIN LUTHER KING JR
Branham, William. 1963, Jun 28. O Lord Just Once More.
Branham, William. 1963, Jun 30. The Third Exodus
Branham, William. 1963, Jul 7. The Indictment
Branham, William. 1964, Apr 18. A Paradox
Branham, William. 1964, Aug 30. Questions and Answers

WILLIAM BRANHAM - MIGRATION TO TUCSON
Branham, William. 1962, Dec 30. Is This The Sign of the End, Sir?
Branham, William. 1963, Jan 20. Just Once More Time, Lord
Branham, William. 1963, Jun 26. Why?
Branham, William. 1963, Jun 28. A Greater Than Solomon is Here
Branham, William. 1964, Jul 26. Recognizing Your Day and its Message
Branham, William. 1965, Apr 26. Proving His Word

WILLIAM BRANHAM - POLITICALLY MOTIVATED STATEMENTS
Branham, William. 1964, Aug 30. Questions and Answers #4
Branham, William. 1964, Apr 18. A Paradox
Branham, William. 1965, Aug 18. And Knoweth It Not
Branham, William. 1963, Jul 21. He Cares, Do You Care?
Branham, William. 1960, Nov 13. Condemnation by Representation
Branham, William. 1960, Dec 5. The Ephesian Church Age.
Branham, William. 1960, Dec 11. The Laodicean Church Age.
Branham, William. 1960, Nov 27. The Queen of the South.

WILLIAM BRANHAM - I LOVE LUCY
Branham, William. 1955, Mar 11. The Seal of the Antichrist
Branham, William. 1956, Aug 1. The Arrow of God's Deliverance Shot from a Bow
Branham, William. 1957, Oct 6. Questions and Answers on Hebrews #3

WILLIAM BRANHAM - ELVIS
Branham, William. 1963, Jan 20. The Voice of God in This Last Days

379

CHAPTER 37

WILLIAM BRANHAM AND THE MYSTERIOUS 'CLOUD' OF 1963

'The humane society give me what they call an Oscar, or whatever you want to call it, for saving a life[799]*"*

The events leading up to 1963 were starting to paint a very disturbing picture in my mind. William Branham's mentor, Roy E. Davis, was declaring war against Civil Rights. The propaganda campaigns from William Branham's sermons worked either alongside or in cooperation with the white supremacy groups against John F Kennedy for his support of Civil Rights. Kennedy was sending a military presence to the South as white supremacy groups turned violent. The FBI was conducting an investigation into Roy Davis after learning that the Original Knights of the Ku Klux Klan were arming themselves under the alias "Louisiana Rifle Association". White supremacy groups were rising against freedom seekers like James Meredith, who simply wanted to attend a public university and have equal opportunity.

Hearing Branham repeating the things that the white supremacy groups were saying about these men turned my stomach. Seeing statements in publications produced by hate groups, statements exactly like William Branham's sermons contained about freedom fighters such as Martin Luther King being "communist" was awful. Listening to him

---

[799] Branham, William. 1965, Jul 25. What Is the Attraction on the Mountain?

publicly shame African Americans was more than I could stand, now that I understood the context and the climate of our country in those days.

When I learned that he announced plans to take his children out of school just two days before Martin Luther King's request for a Second Emancipation, after Roy Davis declared that he was preparing for war, and that he had no intentions to stay with them, but was planning to "become a wanderer", I couldn't stop thinking about the "Americanization" project and Roy Davis' plans for a Third Wave of the Ku Klux Klan. Did William Branham move his family out of harm's way on purpose? Was he planning to part ways with Roy Davis? Did he decide to become a "wanderer" to go into hiding from Davis and his militant sect of the Ku Klux Klan? Or did he plan to join them?

If he did separate from Roy Davis, it would have been significant. Davis ordained Branham into the Pentecostal faith and trained him in the "faith healing" ministry. It was in Roy Davis' Pentecostal church where Branham met his first wife, Hope. Branham had stood by Davis' side, even after his criminal activities and Ku Klux Klan affiliation were exposed in Jeffersonville, Indiana. He assumed leadership over Roy Davis' congregation and joined with elders of Roy Davis' Pentecostal church when Davis was extradited to Arkansas.

After Roy Davis and William Upshaw were involved with the orphanage scandal, Branham drew even closer to them, using Upshaw to pose as a "wheelchair invalid" in his "healing" meetings. Branham dropped the name "Roy Davis" over a hundred times, in meetings from California to Florida and up into Canada. And that was just in the transcripts that we were allowed to see — there is no way of telling how many times William Branham promoted Roy Davis prior to 1947 or in the sermons that were "lost".

Roy Davis was a name we grew up hearing often in the "Message". This "Doctor Davis", as William Branham called him, was a part of our religion, even though we had no idea what he represented. Until I learned the details surrounding the situation leading to the "prophet's" move to Tucson, I would never have even considered the two men

381

parting ways. The thought of the "prophet" going into hiding as a "wanderer" would never have crossed my mind.

At first, it seemed as though that were the case. William Branham started describing a conflict in opinion over doctrine between Davis and himself. And I thought for sure that Davis' nationally publicized exposure as the Imperial Wizard of the Ku Klux Klan would have caused Branham to sever ties. Even after discovering Branham's awful statements against African Americans, I thought surely the two men must have separated. Later, when I learned that William Branham knew the Imperial Wizard's travel schedule as late as 1964[800] — that of a man whose schedule even the Federal Government did not know — I was absolutely shocked! *"He's down here in Florida somewhere they told me"*. Not only was he aware of Davis' location, he expected Davis to attend some of his meetings. Branham held multiple meetings, in multiple states. The places that Branham "wandered" were places Davis knew intimately. He preached near the "Davis Mountains".[801] Another meeting was in Fort Worth,[802] one of Roy E. Davis' political strongholds. Was more going on during William Branham's frequent trips from Tucson to Jeffersonville than we knew about?

I thought back to some disturbing information that I had stumbled onto in 2011. A former "Message" member had pointed out a stop in Houston, Texas, on March 4, 1963.[803] This date is so problematic to "Message" theology that it has been the subject of debate for decades. William Branham's daughter, Rebecca, published an entire newsletter to explain how this date was possible, because according to the timeline, it simply could not have happened as William Branham claimed in his sermons.[804]

William Branham claimed to be away from the public, hunting, on February 28, 1963, during a strange cloud event in Arizona.[805] To his

---

[800] Branham, William. 1964, Apr 16. And When Their Eyes Were Opened. "Old Dr. Davis is sitting here, look; which, I don't know whether he is or not. I think he's down here in Florida, somewhere, *they told me*. Dr. Davis, if you're here, he was the one ordained me in the Missionary Baptist church."

[801] Branham, William. 1964, Mar 13. The Voice of the Sign. "Cause, he lives here in Texas, is out here from Davis Mountains."

[802] Branham, William. 1964, Mar 8. The Token. "I hope my old teacher is sitting here today. Doctor Roy E. Davis, many of you knows him, right here at Fort Worth"

[803] Rivera Nathan. 2012. A Logical Refutation of William Branham's Message

[804] The Road to Sunset. Accessed 2020, May 18 from http://en.believethesign.com/index.php/Road_to_Sunset

[805] Branham, William. 1963, Jun 23. Standing in the Gap. "How many saw, "A mysterious cloud in the sky"?

Tucson peers, he was away hunting, and then leaving for Jeffersonville. To his Jeffersonville crowd, he had just come from Tucson, and claimed to be standing just below the cloud, hunting. The problem? He was allegedly hunting javelina, but hunting season for javelina was not until March 1-10, 1963.[806]

Even more troubling, Branham gave several locations that he claimed to be standing under the cloud. The one we remembered most in the "Message" was Rattlesnake Mesa, and "Message" believers make their pilgrimage to the "hallowed site" each year, calling it "Sunset Mountain" since the "prophet" claimed that his hunting trip took place on "Sunset Mountain".[807] He claimed that "Sunset Mountain" is where he stood under the mysterious cloud formation.

It's very confusing, because after Branham was given a detailed description of the cloud, he claimed to be Northeast of Flagstaff or Prescott. I began to wonder why William Branham was so insistent upon being there. What was he doing in Houston that was important enough to be deceptive?

I first discovered this information in the book, *A Logical Refutation of Branham's Message*. I was shocked the first time I learned that Branham's *"exact location"* spanned over 320 km, and that when "Message" believers were given the "proof" of the cloud, they were only given the initial query — not the full report.

The mysterious cloud that floated across northern Arizona on February 28, 1963, was important to the "Message". Many "Message" believers — including I myself — were shown the articles in Life and Science magazines that covered the information concerning the cloud. The preliminary report given by James E. McDonald was passed around the cult following as if it were written especially for us. His report was the second half of a two-part "confirmation" that William Branham was in Arizona at the time he claimed to be. Because McDonald's report described the cloud over Flagstaff, the "prophet" changed his story to claim that he had been at that location during the cloud event.

You see the hands. And now the Life magazine picked it up. And I have the—the article here this morning, in the Life magazine here, to show. Now here It is, the same time I was there. See the pyramid of the Cloud? I was standing just below this. "

[806] T-12. 1963 Javelina Hunt Regulations, Arizona Game & Fish Department.
[807] Rattlesnake Mesa. Accessed 2020, May 18 from
http://en.believethesign.com/index.php?title=Rattlesnake_Mesa

While William Branham claimed to be present for a "supernatural event", McDonald was observing the cloud from a scientific perspective. This would have been extremely risky for Branham, if not for the summary of McDonald's preliminary investigation. At the time of the preliminary report, McDonald had no idea what caused the cloud. That was all that Branham needed to distract his listeners from the question as to his actual whereabouts. "Were they angels?" "Did they visit the 'prophet'?" His listeners were so intently focused upon whether or not the "cloud" was made by angels that none of his listeners questioned the timing of hunting season, the distance from his alleged hunting location or even whether or not William Branham was in the State of Arizona at the time.

The focus wasn't the location — it was the "mystery". The focus was placed upon the cloud and the scientist, not Branham's own location. They never noticed that Branham originally claimed to be near the southern border of Arizona, over three hundred miles from the path of the cloud, or that he claimed his hunting trip — and cloud experience — came after his trip to Houston. They never thought about the fact that if his Houston meeting was March 4th while the cloud event happened February 28th. He could not have went hunting after the Houston trip and stood beneath the cloud!

It was painful for me to see information that made me completely reject something that I'd believed since I was a small child. Details buried in the report created by James McDonald simply didn't align with Branham's version of the story. We were never told that there was a second cloud, or that witnesses captured photos of the cloud's path across the state — instead of "angels" piercing through the sky heading to outer space as Branham had claimed. We were never told that James McDonald continued his research after the preliminary report, and that he had multiple hypotheses explaining the cause of the formation.

Like any scientist, McDonald created a list of items to investigate, and then followed up on each item in the list. If he continued his research, and "Message" leaders in Arizona were so interested in using it to confirm the "supernatural", then what was his conclusion? And why was it not discussed in the "Message"? If the "prophet" really went from Arizona to Texas, to Arizona, then to Indiana because of a "little

384

boy saved from the electric chair", who was the "little boy" and what did he do?

There were more unanswered questions in the details than in the cloud story itself. By now, with everything I'd uncovered about William Branham's private life, I could easily see why he would want us to focus on a cloud rather than the timeline of his whereabouts. I myself was far more interested in the timeline.

...

When the "halo" photograph of William Branham under the Houston Coliseum lights was captured, William Branham and The Voice of Healing did not have rights to use the photo. The photographers who captured the photo held the copyright. And as late as December 1950, they refused to allow Branham to use the photo in book sales.[808] The photographers were Theodore Kipperman and James Ayers.[809]

When Branham was in Houston in the spring of 1963, he was protesting the execution of Ayers' nephew.[810] January 14, 1963, Leslie Douglas Ashley and Caroline Lima were sentenced to death in Houston, Texas.[811] Their executions were to be carried out on February 28th, the very day of the cloud event. For Texans in the early 1960's, the case would have seemed very unusual. Leslie Douglas Ashley was a "female impersonator" and the events leading up to the murder were sexual in nature. His accomplice, Caroline, was a prostitute. Both dressed as female prostitutes, and the duo entered into a weekend of sex with real estate tycoon Fred Tomes.[812] After murdering Mr. Tomes and burning his remains, they fled to New York where they were finally captured.[813]

---

[808] Cause of Delay of the Branham Life Story. 1950, Dec. The Voice of Healing. "We regret the unexpected delay in the Branham Life Story. Brother Branham had received permission to use the copyrighted picture taken in the San Houston Coliseum. This he planned to use on the cover. However, at the last minute this permission was denied, so an extra six weeks were required by the Doubleday publishers to prepare a new cover"

[809] Branham, William. 1951, Jul 18. The Angel of the Lord. "Mr. Kipperman, and Mr. Ayers, of the Douglas Studios, in Houston, Texas 51-0718"

[810] Branham, William. 1963, Apr 28. Look. "little Ayers. That man that taken the picture of the Angel of the Lord, who, that night over there at Houston, and criticized me and said everything in the world about me. Throwed his arms around me, hugged me, said, "Just think, Brother Branham, the very man that I said was hyp-...practicing hypnosis, has come to save my son from the electric chair."

[811] Houston Pair Given Death, Mother Calls DA 'Murderer'. 1963, Jan 14. Amarillo Globe Times.

[812] Doomed Texas Pair Get Stay of Execution. 1963, Mar 30. Tucson Daily Citizen.

William Branham bragged about helping stay the execution, but he never gave the details of how he did it. He claimed that he had talked the governor of Texas into a pardon,[814] but that appears to have been exaggeration. Execution was halted March 30, 1963, due to an insanity plea.[815] Leslie Douglas Ashley began claiming that he was the "Biblical prophet Elijah", just as Branham suggested he was himself. I wondered, "Did William Branham save Leslie Douglas Ashley by teaching him how to act out the part of his stage persona?"

After learning the nature of the crimes committed by the "boy" that William Branham claimed to have "saved", I began to wonder why Branham got involved. I wondered what Mr. Ayers said to Branham to convince him to associate his name to the very negative publicity of this case. It would be career suicide for any religious figure to try and defend Ashley. Was Branham convinced to assist the photographers because of the photo that Branham "authenticated" using George J. Lacy? Is this how he gained publishing rights?

I found a court hearing for a case involving James Ayers and Theodore Kipperman, the two men who took the photo. Ayers had been convicted of counterfeiting, Kipperman was involved, and tried to appeal in January of 1952.[816] He was investigated by the Federal Bureau of Investigation for forging the signature of Mrs. O. W. Tidwell. The jury found substantial evidence against the claims made by Ayers and Kipperman, and appeal was denied. When Branham "saved" Ashley, whether by apparently convincing him to be the next "Elijah" or not, a religious entity was formed. James Ayers, the counterfeiter, and Leslie Douglas Ashley created a religious organization named The Ashley-Ayers Evangelistic Association.[817] A new "prophet 'Elijah'" was created!

Leslie's mother, Sylvia Kipperman Ayers, was on the board of directors. The strategy was effective. Ashley was deemed criminally

[813] Murder Suspects Wisecrack, Giggle on Dallas Stopover. 1961, Mar 11. Dallas Morning News.
[814] Branham, William. 1963, Apr 28. Look. "I talked there before them all. And what did the governor do? Pardoned it."
[815] Doomed Texas Pair Get Stay of Execution. 1963, Mar 30. Tucson Daily Citizen. "evidence of insanity was suppressed in the trial and at a sanity hearing for the 25-year-old Ashley who likes to call himself the Biblical prophet Elijah."
[816] Ayers v. United States No. 13590. 1952, Jan 31. United States Court of Appeals Fifth Circuit.
[817] Articles of Incorporation of Ashley-Ayres Evangelistic Association, Inc. 1964, May 29.

insane and was then committed to an institution. That did not hold him however, and he broke free. When he escaped, he was named in the FBI's Top 10 Most Wanted List.[818] Agents were told to be on the lookout for Ashley, who could be posing as either a man or a woman. They described him as extremely effeminate in speech, and stated that he frequently dressed in women's clothing. According to the reports, they were looking for someone who associated closely with homosexuals and prostitutes, while carrying a Bible and quoting from it.

On April 24, 1965, Ashley was arrested by the F.B.I. He was working as a side-show act in a carnival in Atlanta, Georgia.[819] Federal agents sent Ashley back to Houston, where he faced a new trial. After serving a 15-year-sentence, Ashley changed his last name and gender, and became "Leslie Elaine Perez". Under this name, Ashley ran for a Harris County Democratic position as a transsexual candidate. Over time, Leslie Perez transitioned from a FBI's most wanted criminal into a respected political activist. By 1994, she was featured in a four-page spread in The Advocate. She regularly donated her time and money to helping liberal Democratic candidates run for election and was recognized for her "indefatigable support of Bill Clinton". She also spearheaded efforts to help the homeless, fight crime, and educate the public about the AIDs virus. With her mother Sylvia, she distributed condoms and safe-sex literature to the streets of Houston.[820]

When William Branham described "saving a life" for Leslie Douglas Ashley, this outcome is not what I had pictured. The governor didn't "pardon it" as Branham had claimed, and he didn't win an "Oscar" from the "humane society".[821] Learning the details about the "prophet's" Houston trip had me even more curious. By now, I was seeing a distinct pattern of claiming "supernatural" events while giving misleading or inaccurate details in his stories — and it appeared to be intentional. Details changed far too frequently.

While it was clear the actual cloud event did not fit within the alleged timing of events that he gave in his sermons, I was still curious

[818] Leslie Douglas Ashley One of the 10 Most Wanted Men. 1965, Apr 8. Daily Sikeston.
[819] Carnival Workers' Tip Brings Arrest. 1965, Apr 24. Lubbock Avalanche.
[820] The three faces of Leslie Perez. 1994, Aug 23. The Advocate.
[821] Branham, William. 1965, Jul 25. What is the Attraction on the Mountain? "The humane society give me what they call an Oscar, or whatever you want to call it, for saving a life."

as to why "Message" leaders in Arizona were not telling us what happened with McDonald's investigation. The West Coast had since 1959 been preparing a missile defense system in anticipation of Russian invasion. The inter-continental ballistic missile tests resulted in blasts or cloud phenomenon so frequently that the Air Force had to explain the results to the public.[822] Details of the testing often made the Tucson newspaper, sometimes on the front page. This was especially the case after President Kennedy announced his inspection of the defense system.[823]

Vandenberg AFB announced nuclear testing in April of 1962, [824]and citizens of Arizona grew concerned that nuclear fallout from the detonations would threaten their environment. Almost every month, sometimes every week, details of Vandenberg's test program were published in the Tucson newspapers. "Message" leaders in Arizona would have been very familiar with these tests. As many as 750 missiles were being approved in other West-Coast facilities,[825] but the number being installed and tested in Vandenberg was classified to the public. The United States was entering the arms race, and most of the testing was carried out at Vandenberg. By January of 1963, the Titan II was nearly operational.[826]

To say that all the testing had Southern California and Arizona on edge would be a tremendous understatement. Jet fighter testing, mysterious explosions, and top-secret testing of weapons of mass destruction kept the people of Arizona on their toes. Some of the blasts were close to home, making people wonder if the Russians had already invaded.

When William Branham described hearing a "blast" to the people in Jeffersonville, Indiana, it would have had an altogether different meaning to the people in Tucson. Tucsonans were quite familiar with unexpected blasts.[827] Also, when William Branham spoke of the "scientist" who "investigated" the cloud,[828] any "Message" believers in

[822] Example: Titan Shot Fails, Atlas Postponed. 1962, Feb 24. Arizona Republic. "it soared skyward after a blast."
[823] Record Crowds Applaud Kennedy On Coast Tour. 1962, Mar 24. Arizona Daily Star.
[824] U.S. Ready To Resume Nuclear Testing in Air. 1962, Apr 24. Yuma Daily Sun.
[825] Missile Fired in Hurry. 1962, Sep 29. Arizona Daily Star.
[826] Titan II Test Firing Succeeds. 1963, Jan 11. Arizona Republic.
[827] Mystery Blast Again Awakens Tucsonians. 1962, Feb 6. Tucson Daily Citizen.

Tucson would have known that Branham was referring to University of Arizona's Dr. James E. McDonald. They would have also known that he was *still* investigating the cloud,[829] and that his initial query was not a final report. In fact, his confirmation that the cloud was not naturally formed would have been even more exciting to Branham's followers.[830] "Message" believers in Tucson would have wondered if McDonald would eventually conclude that the formation was "supernatural" instead of "unnatural". They would have also been curious to see how Washington responded.

The Department of Defense was purposely vague in their descriptions of the timeline for top-secret testing, and in some cases they were denying events that could raise the curiosity of the Russians. Vandenberg AFB did admit on March 30th that a routine launch occurred.[831] Almost daily, articles were published describing McDonald's investigation. He and other colleagues worked together to triangulate the altitude and path of the cloud and found that it was at an unbelievable altitude of 45 kilometers from the ground.

Citizens in Arizona began sketching faces into the photos of the cloud. One woman sketched Jackie Kennedy's face. Others began to imagine shapes of fish, or a hangman's noose.[832] "Message" believers superimposed the cloud over paintings of Jesus Christ, and some of them believed that this was the image actually seen over the skies in Arizona. What they did not know at the time was that McDonald was not investigating the unnatural formation for "normal" scientific reasons. McDonald was trying to prove that the cloud was the result of

---

[828] Branham, William. 1963, Jun 23. Standing in the Gap. "Now, this scientist here is trying to—to get all the information about the picture, that he can, about the people who has the picture. He is studying it. 83 Now, he says here that it would be impossible for it to be a cloud, because moisture doesn't go over about, I'd say, about six or eight miles high, something like that. When we go overseas we usually fly nineteen thousand feet, and we're above the storms then. But this cloud, according to this article here of this scientist, is twenty-six miles high.

[829] Still Pursuing 'Cloud'. 1963, Apr 3. Arizona Daily Sun.

[830] More on Cloud. 1963, Apr 3. Arizona Daily Sun.

[831] U.S. Missile Interception Test Success. 1963, Apr 5. Traverse City Record. "The Defense department announced yesterday the Army's Nike-Zeus anti-missile missile 'recently' intercepted the Air Force Titan missile over the southwest Pacific. ... The Defense department did not say when the intercept occurred. But the Air Force announced on March 30 that there had been routine training launch of a Titan missile from Vandenberg Air Force Base Calif."

[832] That Cloud. 1963, Apr 6. Arizona Daily Sun. "One woman obligingly sketched Jackie Kennedy's face inside her rendition"

other-worldly flying aircraft, and that the United States had been visited by other-worldly beings.[833]

McDonald was not well-respected among his peers, especially with regards to claims made during his investigations. While William Branham was claiming "supernatural vindication" by using James McDonald's initial query, His listeners in Arizona would have been reading reports of McDonald's "scientific" claim that aliens from outer space were invading the United States. McDonald was preparing research to present his theory on UFOs to the United States government. The February 28, 1963 cloud was but one of many examples that McDonald intended to use as "proof" that UFOs were alien technology.[834] As a result, he was the target of ridicule in Arizona.

But while "Message" leaders in Tucson failed to mention McDonald's public speeches and discussions on UFOs to followers of the Branham movement, there was a more disturbing piece of information being concealed: The February 28th cloud research was abandoned after Vandenberg declassified the missile launch dates. When the Vandenberg AFB published the launch history, and both an Atlas D and TAT/Agenda D missile were confirmed to have launched on February 28, 1963,[835] McDonald abandoned this particular set of clouds. They were then "identified flying objects".

McDonald's investigation of the cloud would pale in comparison to the investigation about to come. When President John F. Kennedy was assassinated, a large-scale inquiry into white supremacy groups was launched. Shortly after Lee Harvey Oswald stated that he was a "patsy", Oswald was shot and killed by Jack Ruby. As a result, Roy Davis, and everyone connected to him, were part of the investigation. This investigation most certainly would have included the Rev. William Marrion (Marvin) Branham.

---

[833] Study Indicates UFOs From Outer Space. 1966, Oct 6. Tucson Daily Citizen.
[834] McDonald's Study Indicates UFOs Come from Outer Space. 1966, Oct 6. Tucson Daily Citizen.
[835] Vandenberg AFB Launch History.

JAMES MCDONALD

UFO Expert to Address Newman Forum. 1967, Nov 15. Albuquerque Journal
UFOs Not from Outer Space, Probers Claim. 1969, Jan 7. Colorado Springs Gazette Telegraph
Flying Saucers Worry UN Secretary. 1967, Jun 27. Eau Claire Leader
Misc. 1966, Oct 8. News. Tucson Daily Citizen
Saucers: Probe from Outer Space? The San Bernardino County Sun. 1967, May 2
UFO Buff Found Dead Near Tucson. 1971, Jun 14. Casa Grande Dispatch
Yarborough's Report. 1963, Mar 29. The Hondo Anvil Herald
UFO Talk Scheduled at Forum Tucson Daily Citizen. 1967, Oct 5
Study Indicates UFOs From Outer Space. 1966, Oct 6. Tucson Daily Citizen
AF, City to Meet on Titan Locations. 1960, May 26. Tucson Daily Citizen
Council Assures Air Force Tucson Wants Titans, Won't Question Sites. 1960, May 24. Tucson
     Daily Citizen
Scientists Still Up In Air About Flying Saucers. 1968, Sep 14. The Indiana Gazette
Mystery Blast Again Awakens Tucsonians. 1962, Feb 6. Tucson Daily Citizen
Still Pursuing 'Cloud'. 1963, Apr 3. Arizona Daily Sun
U. 1963, Apr 5. S. Missile Interception Test Success. Traverse City Record Eagle
Rare Cloud. 1963, May 9. The Fresno Bee The Republican
Tucson Tonight Tomorrow. 1967, May 15. Tucson Daily Citizen
More on Cloud. 1963, Apr 3. Arizona Daily Sun
UFOs Not from Outer Space, Prober's Claim. 1969, Jan 7. Colorado Springs Gazette Telegraph
Flagstaff Cloud Too High for Own Good. 1963, Apr 6. Arizona Daily Sun
UFO Sightings Nothing New. 1967, Dec 18. Alton Evening Telegraph
Letters to the Editor. 1966, Mar 30. Tucson Daily Citizen
Arizona Physicist Charges Air Force Whitewash on UFOs. 1967, Mar 3. Albuquerque Journal
Camouflage Over UFOs. 1968, Nov 25. The Kansas City Times
Did Anyone See UFO? Tucson Daily Citizen. 1968, Oct 8
UFO Mystery Unsolved. 1969, Mar 19. Lubbock Avalanche-Journal
Anthropology Students from California Touring Northland. 1963, Apr 9. Arizona Daily Sun
Letter from Dr. 1964, May 7. James E. McDonald. The Deming Headlight

CLOUD RESEARCH

... And a High Cloud Ring of Mystery. 1963, May. Life Magazine.
Rivera, Nathan. 2011. A Logical Refutation of Branham's Message
JFK Says Free Men Will Isolate Cuba. 1963, Mar 19. Arizona Daily Star
Missile Testing is Necessary. 1964, Mar 13. Arizona Daily Star
Mighty Titan II Missile Blows Up in First Test Out of Silo. 1963, Feb 17. Arizona Daily Star
Titan II Test Firing Succeeds. 1963, Jan 11. Arizona Republic
Air Force Launches Atlas at Vandenberg. 1963, Feb 28. Tucson Daily Citizen
Armed Atlas May Zoom 3,000 Miles. 1962, May 18. Tucson Daily Citizen
Missile Warhead Tested. 1963, Apr 27. Arizona Republic
Did You See It? Arizona Republic. 1963, Mar 4
U. 1963, Jun 6. S. Told Truth Best Weapon. Arizona Daily Star
Accidental Explosion of Titan II Produces Shocking, Awesome Sight. 1963, Feb 18. Tucson Daily
     Citizen
Atlas Flies 7,000 Miles. 1963, Aug 1. Arizona Republic
Missile Soars 5,000 Miles in Half-Hour. 1963, Nov 14. Arizona Republic
Rare 'Nacreous' Clouds Seen in Tucson. 1963, Mar 1. Arizona Daily Star

U. 1963, Apr 25. S. Flight Tests Atlas E Missile. Arizona Republic
JFK To Visit Vandenberg Test Sites. 1962, Mar 13. Tucson Daily Citizen
Titan II Missile Blows Up. 1963, Feb 17. Arizona Republic
100th Launching of Agena Made. 1963, Jul 15. Arizona Daily Star
Minuteman ICBM Missile Misses Again. 1963, Jan 8. The Yuma Daily Sun
Air Force Atlas D Flies 7,000 Miles. 1962, Jul 13. Arizona Republic
THOR's Thrust. 1963, May 9. Arizona Republic
Atlas Test Launch Conducted by SAC. 1963, Sep 12. Arizona Republic
State Airman Helps Launch Titan Missile. 1963, Nov 14. Tucson Daily Citizen
'Cloud' Photos Wanted. 1963, Mar 7. Arizona Daily Sun
Army Hails Missile Feat. 1963, Apr 5. Arizona Republic
Sentry Satellites Put in Fixed Orbit. 1963, Oct 18. Arizona Republic
THOR's Thrust. 1963, May 9. Arizona Republic
Atlas Passes Test. 1963, Mar 22. Arizona Daily Sun
Atlas F Blasts Off. 1962, Nov 15. Arizona Republic
Record Crowds Applaud Kennedy On Coast Tour. 1962, Mar 24. Arizona Daily Star
Advanced Atlas Test Termed Successful. 1963, Mar 22. Arizona Daily Star
THOR's Thrust. 1963, May 9. Arizona Republic
Atlas Test Launch Conducted by SAC. 1963, Sep 12. Arizona Republic
State Airman Helps Launch Titan Missile. 1963, Nov 14. Tucson Daily Citizen
'Cloud' Photos Wanted. 1963, Mar 7. Arizona Daily Sun
Army Hails Missile Feat. 1963, Apr 5. Arizona Republic
Sentry Satellites Put in Fixed Orbit. 1963, Oct 18. Arizona Republic
THOR's Thrust. 1963, May 9. Arizona Republic
Atlas Passes Test. 1963, Mar 22. Arizona Daily Sun
Atlas F Blasts Off. 1962, Nov 15. Arizona Republic
Record Crowds Applaud Kennedy On Coast Tour. 1962, Mar 24. Arizona Daily Star
Advanced Atlas Test Termed Successful. 1963, Mar 22. Arizona Daily Star
Nike-Zeus Intercepts ICBM in Pacific Test. 1962, Dec 23. Arizona Republic
Missile Killer Intercepts Atlas High Over Pacific. 1962, Dec 13. Arizona Daily Star
Minuteman Destroyed in Combat-Type Test. 1962, Sep 29. Arizona Daily Star
Air Force Tests Flights Atlas E on Target. 1963, Jun 5. Arizona Republic
Atlas Test Launch Conducted by SAC. 1963, Sep 12. Arizona Republic
Titan Shot Fails, Atlas Postponed. 1962, Feb 24. Arizona Republic
Missile Warheads Sought Which Can Pierce Defense Systems. 1963, Nov 10. Arizona Daily Star
Vandenberg Satellite Lights Up Skies Here. 1963, Apr 6. Tucson Daily Citizen
Alouette Beeps Back Signals on Space Noise. 1962, Sep 30. Arizona Republic
Advanced Atlas ICBM Travels 4,000 Miles. 1962, Nov 15. Arizona Daily Star
'That Cloud' Caught by Camera Lens. 1963, Mar 2. Arizona Daily Sun
Ionosphere Probe Highly Successful. 1963, Jul 31. Arizona Republic
Ranger-4 Zooms toward Moon. 1962, Apr 24. The Yuma Daily Sun

WILLIAM BRANHAM CLOUD STATEMENTS
Branham, William. 1962, Dec 23. The Reproach for The Cause of The Word.
Branham, William. 1962, Dec 30. Is This the Sign of The End sir?
Branham, William. 1963, Mar 4. An Absolute.
Branham, William. 1963, Jun 23. Standing in The Gap.
Branham, William. 1965, Jul 25. What Is the Attraction on the Mountain?
Branham, William. 1965, Nov 27. Trying to Do God A Service Without It Being God's Will.
Branham, William. 1963, Mar 18. The First Seal.

Branham, William. 1963, Mar 24. The Seventh Seal.
Branham, William. 1963, Jun 1. Come Follow Me.
Branham, William. 1963, Jun 30. Is Your Life Worthy of the Gospel?
Branham, William. 1963, Nov 28. Testimony.
Branham, William. 1964, Dec 27. Who Do You Say This Is.

CHAPTER 38

WILLIAM BRANHAM AND THE ASSASSINATION OF JOHN F. KENNEDY

"Form an image unto the beast... We see all this. The very Catholic president... It ain't Kennedy, far as I know he's a man like I am or anybody else. It's not that. It wasn't Ahab. Ahab was a pretty good fellow. It was that Jezebel behind him[836]"

Learning that William Branham was in Texas while claiming to be in Arizona was the key that unlocked several doors, and finally started to finish out the edges of the puzzle that I had started to piece together so long ago. It was interesting to learn what William Branham was doing in Houston, and to learn the backgrounds of the men that Branham was working with. After hearing Branham's politically charged statements against African Americans, however, my curiosity grew to wonder why Branham would alter the dates of his own timeline during one of the most critical milestones in the Civil Rights Movement.

By 1963, the battle for Civil Rights was quickly spreading, and Dallas/Fort Worth was soon to become the epicenter. William Branham's mentor, Roy E. Davis, had a political stronghold in the area. Davis was a member of the Oak Cliff White Citizens Council in Dallas, a group that was very outspoken in their protests against President

---

[836] Branham, William. 1962, Apr 7. The Signs of His Coming.

Kennedy and desegregation of the school systems. As head of the Ku Klux Klan in Texas, Davis himself was also very outspoken. He publicly stated that he would *"rather die or be put in prison than to allow 'Negro' children to be integrated with white children in the Dallas white schools".*[837]

The F.B.I. was already monitoring the White Citizens Council, recognizing the imminent threat. Almost 90% of the African American population of Texas was on the eastern side near Dallas, and when Dallas was ordered to integrate on January 27, 1958, white supremacists revolted.[838] In June of 1958, as the battle against integration was exploding, Davis was elected president of the white supremacy council to lead the opposition. Interestingly, this was the same time Branham held campaigns in the Dallas/Fort Worth area. It was also one of the campaigns in which William Branham told his "slave" story describing African Americans as "aliens".[839]

By 1963, during the time that William Branham was in Texas (later claiming to be in Arizona), Dallas was on the verge of all-out war between racists and freedom seekers. African American freedom seekers in Dallas began protesting Dallas' refusal to obey Federal law and desegregate the schools. Dallas white citizen councils declared the laws to be "treason" and declared the President to be guilty of committing treason when he enacted them.[840] An FBI investigation found that the pamphlets were produced by the Dallas Indignant White Citizens Council of which Roy Davis was also a member, and which formed in 1963 shortly after William Branham's trip to Texas.[841] This group of men would later be arrested at the Dallas Trade Mart for suspicion of conspiracy.

---

[837] Original Knights of the Ku Klux Klan Louisiana (1964-65) File #105-71801. "T-3 advised that one of the other main speakers was a Reverend R. E. Davis who gave a very strong anti-desegregation speech. T-3 advised that Reverend R. E. Davis stated he would rather die or be put in prison than allow negro children to be integrated with white children in the Dallas white schools."

[838] Office Memorandum to director, FBI from SAC, Dallas. Citizens Councils Internal Security. 1957, Oct 23.

[839] Branham, William. 1958, Jun 11. Thirsting for Life. "And though he's an alien, and amongst strangers, yet he conducts himself as a king's son. oh if it would make a negro, who snowed that his father was a king and he was an alien"

[840] Wanted for Treason. 1963. Dallas Indignant White Citizens Council.

[841] Assassination of President Kennedy. 00-2-34030. "On December 6, 1963, Intelligence Unit Corporal Robert Westfall, Dallas Police Department, furnished names and background on Gene Andre Quinn and Bobby Saville Joiner as being possible suspects responsible for the origin of the 'Wanted for Treason' leaflets."

Shortly after the council was formed, William Branham began claiming that President Kennedy was violating the constitution.[842] He claimed that when Kennedy activated the National Guard to give equal opportunity to African Americans, the declaration to enforce desegregation "broke the constitution". William Branham began making aloud the same statements that Davis and his men were printing and in so doing, he publicly supported the Indignant White Citizen's Council against President Kennedy[843] — even if he did not mention them by name. Branham then went on to compare Martin Luther King, Jr. to Hitler,[844] and claimed that President Kennedy's support of equal rights was a denial of freedom of religion. This, he said, was the "antichrist".[845] This floored me. I had never realized that William Branham claimed that President Kennedy was the antichrist for supporting Civil Rights. I personally supported Civil Rights!

Immediately after making that statement, William Branham compared Kennedy to the Pharaoh of Egypt and declared *"the exodus is at hand"*. Those who sided with Kennedy were to be *"Excommunicated from the Word"*. I started noticing the many times William Branham spoke about John F. Kennedy. For religious sermons, these were very politically charged statements! They started during the time Kennedy was running for office, shortly after Davis became Imperial Grand Dragon of the Original Knights of the Ku Klux Klan. Branham's political statements became heated as the battle for Civil Rights

---

[842] Branham, William. 1963, Jun 30. The Third Exodus. "Then when it come back to this fellow we got up here, that knows not Joseph, freedom. Pulling for those colored votes, and not knowing it was a republican party that freed them, in the first place. Selling out their birthrights, to such a thing as that, to lead them into a death trap, to show that every man-made system has got to fall. Exactly right. And Mr. Kennedy nationalized that guard, and send those men right back into the face of their own fathers standing there under the constitution. That broke the constitution again. 136 Said, "We'll not fight. No, sir." And said, "I hope the nation can find out that we're not living anymore under a democracy, but under military dictatorship." 63-0630M

[843] The "Wanted For Treason" leaflet stated, "5. He has illegally invaded a sovereign State with federal troops."

[844] Branham, William. 1963, Jun 30. The Third Exodus. "One thing, I pray that Brother Martin Luther King will certainly soon wake up. He loves his people; there's no doubt. But if he just only see where his inspiration. What good would it do if you went to school, a million of you laying yonder, dead? Wouldn't just be, go to school, just the same? Now, for—for hunger, if it was for something another, slaves, the man would be a martyr to give his life for such a cause, a worthy cause, and that would be a worthy cause. But just to go to school, I—I don't see it. See? I don't think the Holy Spirit is agreeing with him, at all, on that. It's got the people all worked up, in a bunch of ballyhoo, you see. 143 Just—just like Hitler did, over in Germany, led them right into a death trap."

[845] Branham, William. 1963, Jun 30. The Third Exodus. "The natural man, the antichrist, is growing now. Through politics, he's already got to the White House. In religion, he's got all the people so scrupled up, till actually they'd fall right for it. And the denominational leaders, practically every church that there is in the nation, is already in the confederation of churches. Raamses is growing. And they're all uniting together, and that's what they'll have. And what does it do? It makes a power, a beast just like the first one."

396

intensified, and they became especially more aggressive as the battle moved to Texas.

William Branham was right about one thing: a "showdown" was coming. President Kennedy announced his trip to Dallas, and the white supremacy groups began to rally their efforts in protest. By the time he arrived, anger and hatred had been stirred up to the point of violence. As the presidential motorcade made its way through the crowds, the President was greeted by both love and hatred. Protestors flew Confederate flags and signs promoting white supremacy. African Americans pushed through the crowds to shake hands with the man who could grant them freedom. Shortly after, while riding through the Dealey Plaza, the President was shot by Lee Harvey Oswald. Two days later, Oswald was killed by Jack Ruby.

Every answer to the questions behind the assassination plot disappeared with Oswald's death. As the information produced by a massive federal investigation was reviewed, the door was opened to a much larger investigation into conspiracy. Oswald and Ruby appeared to be pawns in a much larger game. The United States Secret Service opened an investigation into the Dallas white supremacy groups.

Working with the Dallas Police Department, they traced the "Wanted for Treason" leaflets to Bobby Joiner, of the White Citizens Council, and Roy Davis. Witnesses claimed that the purchaser of the printers Joiner and Davis used looked like Lee Harvey Oswald in a wig.[846] The printing presses for the "Wanted for Treason" leaflet were traced to printing equipment borrowed by Roy Davis from Earl Thornton. The Dallas Police investigator — of the same police force in which Davis claimed to have planted Klan members — said that he knew Davis personally. He told the Secret Service that Davis was not involved, and that he was no longer the Imperial Grand Dragon of the Ku Klux Klan.[847]

Davis had successfully re-birthed the old Klan from 1915, spread it across the nation, and then disconnected himself. The group then

---

[846] Assassination of President Kennedy. 00-2-34030. "He still thought the purchaser looked more like Oswald's photo, except that he had dark curly hair."

[847] Assassination of President Kennedy. 00-2-34030. "On December 9, 1963, Inv. Brumley, Intelligence Unit, Dallas Police Department, discussed this case with the reporting agent, and he through that Earl Thornton, Klansman, and former associate of Rev. Roy Davis, might be suspect in this case. Thornton offered to allow Davis to use his printing equipment when Davis was in business as Grand Dragon of the Ku Klux Klan. Brumley, who knows Davis personally, doubted however that Davis printed these leaflets."

splintered, forming multiple separate Klan organizations. Government reports had difficulty linking them all together and had to describe connections appended to documents. It even confused the agents, and documents had to be updated with the correct organization name.

The sect Davis created was significant enough to gain the attention of the Director of the FBI. Interviews producing information concerning the Original Knights of the Ku Klux Klan were to be reported to the Director himself.[848] The pressure from Washington was intensifying. The hot debate in the 1964 Congress was the Civil Rights Bill, which would increase the Federal Government's power to enforce equality. The Ku Klux Klan, and everyone associated with the Klan, quickly became the center of attention.

In 1964, everyone involved with white supremacy groups began to scramble to cover their tracks. In the version of the "Message" that I grew up in, we gave several "verse titles" to the "prophet". He was the "prophet of Malachi 4",[849] which was a secret code for, "He is the prophet 'Elijah'". He was "Revelation 10:7", secret code for "the 'messenger' for our 'age'". But most troubling, he was "Luke 17:30", the "Son of Man". Or more specifically, the "Son of Man" being revealed, in secret, to his cult following.

This was problematic when we encountered knowledgeable Christians. To most Christians, the "Son of Man" is Jesus Christ. *"The Son of Man has authority on earth to forgive sins"* (Luke 5:24). I never noticed that William Branham had started this doctrine in 1964, just as the United States Government began investigating white supremacy groups. William Branham's self-promotion "Son of man being revealed doctrine" began in November of 1964.[850] I thought back to how the "prophet" claimed to have "saved" Leslie Douglas Ashley, and how that "salvation" turned out to be through an insanity plea after Ashley claimed to be the return of "Elijah the prophet." Branham already claimed to be "Elijah", while also claiming to be "sane". To use the same strategy, Branham would have had to take things to a whole new

[848] Example: From Director, FBI to SAC New Orleans. Original Knights of the Ku Klux Klan Racial Matters. 1964, Sept 18.
[849] The Fulfillment of Malachi 4:5. Accessed 2020, May 18 from
http://en.believethesign.com/index.php/The_Fulfillment_of_Malachi_4:5
[850] Branham, William. 1965, Nov 27. Trying to Do God A Service Without It Being God's Will. "Luke 17:30, is, the Son of man is to reveal Himself among His people. Not a man, God! But it'll come through a prophet."

level. Was William Branham preparing for an insanity plea by claiming to be Jesus Christ?

When white supremacy leaders are interrogated before the House of Representatives their statements are documented and made available to the public.[851] This was fortunate for my sake, with regards to finding the final pieces to my puzzle. When the committee prepared their interrogation questions for the Original Knights of the Ku Klux Klan, they questioned John D. Swenson. The committee recognized Roy E. Davis as the man who organized the rebirth of the original Ku Klux Klan. Roy Davis had appointed Swenson, and Swenson appointed Royal Young to lead the group as it grew and splintered. Davis also appointed Young to his position of Imperial Dragon. The investigation exposed the fact that Roy Davis had re-activated the Klan under William Simmons' 1915 secret oath.[852] I had stumbled onto a goldmine! The problem? When the records were subpoenaed, the Original Knights of the Ku Klux Klan burned all records,[853] including membership records, to conceal all traces back to the men involved.

Through the money exchanged, Federal Agents were able to identify entities created by the Ku Klux Klan that were used as false fronts to mask their agenda.[854] Leaders of the Original Knights of the Ku Klux Klan were getting paid through the Louisiana Rifle Association. Checks, signed by Ku Klux Klan leaders,[855] uncovered some of the hidden secrets. They were cashed in Shreveport, Louisiana, and in February of 1964, when Branham started his "Son of Man" doctrine, began distributing rifles for a "wrecking crew". This was the Klan's term for those appointed to execute violent orders.

---

[851] Activities of Ku Klux Klan Organizations in the United States; Parts 1-5. Index to Hearings Before the Committee on Un-American Activities, House of Representatives, Eighty-Ninth Congress, First and Second Sessions.

[852] Transcript: Activities of Ku Klux Klan Organizations. "Mr. Swenson, it is the result of the committee's investigation that Roy E. Davis, in reactivating a Klan group in 1960, is a member of the 1915 Ku Klux Klan organization, adopted for his organization that which was used by the Knights of the Ku Klux Klan under William Joseph Simmons".

[853] Transcript: Activities of Ku Klux Klan Organizations. "he said he burned the records to keep them from falling into the hands of the enemy."

[854] Transcript: Activities of Ku Klux Klan Organizations. "So the record might establish that the Louisiana Rifle Association was, in fact, the cover name of the Original Knights of the Ku Klux Klan"

[855] Transcript: Activities of Ku Klux Klan Organizations. "I hand you two envelopes, one containing canceled checks drawn against the account of the Monroe Hunting and Fishing Club, payable to the Louisiana Rifle Association, endorsed by the Louisiana Rifle Association, and another envelope containing checks against the account of the Monroe Hunting and Fishing Club, payable to cash, and endorsed by J. D. Swenson."

I noticed something very disconcerting about the timing of the hearing. The hearings began January 4, 1966, just days after William Branham was killed in Texas. Was there more to his death than we were told? Was Branham preparing to testify on behalf of the State?

On December 24, 1965, William Branham died in Friona, Texas.[856] An oncoming vehicle hit the driver's side of Branham's car, crushing him. He was taken to the Northwest Texas Hospital, where he died from injuries suffered in the collision. While his wife, Meda, was in critical condition, his body was sent back to Jeffersonville, Indiana for funeral preparation. His body was held from the grave until Easter of 1966.[857] The burial, held at the Eastern Cemetery in Jeffersonville, was scheduled for April 11th.

The details surrounding his death, before and after, were troubling to those close to William Branham. After President Kennedy's death, William Branham began to fear being shot with an infrared scope,[858] and mentioned it in sermons. In a letter seemingly threatening to expose the details if not paid, William Branham's daughter Sarah also made disturbing statements. According to his daughter, William Branham was about to expose the names of people "doing wrong", including cult members and even family. She claimed that he was very upset the day of the crash and argued with Meda about exposing "many things and names".[859] According to Sarah, her father had amassed $3,113,676 plus $130,645 in stocks.[860] Sarah, having inside knowledge, sent some of the

---

[856] Texas Crash Fatal to Local Pastor. 1965, Dec 25. Tucson Daily Citizen.

[857] Evangelist's Burial Rites Set for Today. 1966, Apr 11. Anderson Daily Bulletin.

[858] Branham, William. 1963, Nov 28. Testimony. "Talk about President Kennedy being shot? I've had to be guarded many times from being shot with an infrared scope, and maybe at three or four hundred yards away, at nighttime. They can see just the same as they can in the daytime, through that spotter scope at night. And I've been in Catholic countries where radicals and everything, down in Mexico there where they sent back there, and send word, telegram messages wrote by everything, "We'll get you tonight," and so forth like that, going in and out, and looking for me. And perhaps I will get it sometime. That's all right. But I got Something that will take care of me when that time comes, see."

[859] Branham, Sarah. 1989, July. Take It With You. Accessed 2020, May 28 from *http://the-messenger-of-god.blogspot.com/2011/09/*. "I remember that my father was very troubled before we left Tucson for the Jeffersonville meetings where he was to preach "The trail of the serpent" and expose names of the people of this message that were doing wrong including family members."

[860] Branham, Sarah. 1989, July. Take It With You. Accessed 2020, May 28 from *http://the-messenger-of-god.blogspot.com/2011/09/*. "Just recently a noted lawyer in New York looked into the matter and showed me different bank statements which are still in my possession. One shows the amount in cash of 3,113,676 plus stocks 130,645 plus other things. This money was left untouched since the departure of my father. According to the notary document it is fixed for 25 years. I am asking myself what will be done with the large sum of money accumulated by now after the 26th of October, 1990. After the accident things changed dramatically. Suddenly Billy Paul was in possession of lots of money. He built a custom home with all gold fixtures and custom furniture. My mother was very upset."

information in a letter to expose men involved, and she mentioned some of the large transactions made between leaders of Branham's cult.[861] According to Sarah, things were not as they seemed within the religion her father created and at the end of the letter, she threatened to have the "law" clean it up. But the most troubling statement, for me, was at the beginning of the letter. Meda Branham asked Sarah to *"take it with you to the grave"* after approaching her and asking how much she remembered from before the accident.[862]

Hundreds of people from across the country traveled to Jeffersonville, Indiana, for Branham's funeral. Rumors were spread that he would rise from the grave[863] on Easter, just like Jesus Christ, the "Son of Man". Some noticed that the face of the body looked nothing like the man being buried. Even as his casket was lowered into the ground, the hopeful watched, waiting for the resurrection. But the skies did not part with rays of sunshine and hope. Instead, it rained. And as the day passed, so did all hope of the "Son of Man" Branham rising from the grave.

A pyramid tomb marks the spot where his body will forever remain. It has been a long, long journey since that first day when I entered the Clark County Courthouse and began my research. I will never forget how overwhelmed I felt as I dug, page-by-page, through volumes of courthouse records, or how shocked I was that all of the records survived the 1937 flood. There was so much information available, completely overturning many of the fallacies that I was trained to believe.

And yet, with all the answers I'd found to questions I had about the "Message", each answer raised even more questions that may never be answered. There were so many areas of research still to be explored, so many interesting details yet to uncover. I could never look at the "Message" the same way, especially now that I knew the dark secrets

---

[861] Branham, Sarah. 1989, July. Accessed 2020, May 28 from *http://the-messenger-of-god.blogspot.com/2011/09/*. Take It With You. "All insiders know about the 65,000 dollars Brother Sidney Jackson gave to Rev. Pearry Green who promised to take him as a co-pastor and accommodate him in Tucson."
[862] Branham, Sarah. 1989, July. Accessed 2020, May 28 from *http://the-messenger-of-god.blogspot.com/2011/09/*. Take It With You. "I don't know how many times my mother told me: "Take it with you to the grave." What she meant by that I have to tell you now. It seems that I cannot live with it no more and I am sure I couldn't die with it. I'm getting so nervous even thinking about it, simply cannot bare it any longer. In the way I look at it, it is indirectly connected with my father's accident."
[863] Some Members of Sect Think Minister To Rise From Dead. 1966, Apr 11. Kokomo Tribune.

behind about its political themes. Each event had two sides: the public appearance, and what went on behind the scenes. I could not "unsee" that which I had already seen.

We knew only what leaders of the "Message" wanted us to see. But there was much, much more to see. There is much more background information to the stories we were taught and for the men who taught them. Each story paints such a different picture than the one that had been painted in our minds. There are so many more details missing about the events which have been lost to time, never to be found. My journey out of the "Message" had ended, but a much, much bigger journey was only beginning.

ROY E. DAVIS

Dallas Klan. 1958, Mar 28. Lubbock Morning Avalanche.

Texarkana Lawyer Reveals Leadership of Klan Faction. 1959, May 31. Arkansas Gazette.

Klan Groups are Banished. 1959, May 29. Arkansas Gazette.

Klansmen Call for Members. 1959, Aug 24. The Cincinnati Enquirer.

Davis, Roy. 1960. An Open Letter to George F. Edwards, Leader of a Band of Banished Klansmen in the State of Arkansas.

ROY E DAVIS - CONNECTIONS TO KENNEDY ASSASSINATION EVENT

Caufield, Jeffrey H. (2015, September 29). General Walker and the Murder of President Kennedy – The Extensive New Evidence of a Radical-Right Conspiracy.

00-2-34030. Assassination of President Kennedy. 1963, Nov 12. United States Secret Service.

124-900123-10054. JFK Assassination. 1962, Mar 5. Federal Bureau of Investigation

105-71801. Original Knights of The Ku Klux Klan. 1963, Nov 15. Federal Bureau of Investigation

Activities of Ku Klux Klan Organizations in the United States; Parts 1-5. 2018, Mar 2. Committee on Un-American Activities.

ROY E DAVIS - ORIGINAL KNIGHTS OF THE KU KLUX KLAN:

105-71809 - Original Knights of The Ku Klux Klan (Louisiana), aka Louisiana Rifle Association. 1964, Mar 12. Federal Bureau of Investigation.

105-70801 - Original Knights of The Ku Klux Klan - Louisiana (1964-65). 1964, Mar 12. Federal Bureau of Investigation.

124-90123. JFK Assassination System. Federal Bureau of Investigation.

124-10183, Original Knights of The Ku Klux Klan (OKKKK). Federal Bureau of Investigation.

124-10214. The Original Knights of The Ku Klux Klan, Aka the Original Ku Klux Klan, Formerly Known as U. S. Klans, Knights of the Ku Klux Klan, Inc., (Texas) IS - Klan. Federal Bureau of Investigation.

WILLIAM BRANHAM DEATH AND FUNERAL:

De Corado, Sarah (Branham). 1989, July. Take It with You. Accessed 2019, Nov 11 from https://earlychurchus.org/articles

Evangelist's Burial Rites Set for Today. 1966, Apr 11. Anderson Daily Bulletin

Tucson Minister Dies of Injuries. 1965, Dec 15. Arizona Republic

Brother Billy's Resurrection. 1966, Apr 13. Hobbs Daily News

Prophet's Burial Monday; Followers Congregate. 1966, Apr 10. Independent Press Telegram

Preacher Killed Dec. 19 Buried Today; Sect Thinks He Will Rise. 1966, Apr 11. Rushville Republican

Funeral Causes Traffic Jam at Jeffersonville. 1965, Dec 2. Rushville Republican

Faith Founder is Buried Four Months After death. 1966, Apr 11. The Fresno Bee

Evangelist William Branham was Buried. 1966, Apr 14. The Kan Republican

Founder of a Faith Buried. 1966, Apr 1. The Kansas City Times

Jeffersonville swamped for burial of sect leader. 1966, Apr 11.

Some Members of Sect Think Minister to Rise from Dead. 1966, Apr 11. Kokomo Tribune

Texas Crash Fatal to Local Pastor. 1965, Dec 25.

ADDITIONAL RESOURCES

ROY E. DAVIS TIMELINE

1890 - Roy Elonza Davis born April 28, 1890 in Omaha, Morris County, TX

1894 - February 18. Emma Sabina Davis (Dowdy) born. This was Roy Davis Sr. first wife he married in Texas.

1909 - June 14. Roy Davis was a stenographer and ticket clerk for the Southwestern Railroad in El Paso, Texas

1910 - November 12. Roy Davis travels to the Sierra Madre for big game hunting.

1911 - January 19. Roy Davis appointed chief of the Rock Island paying card department in El Paso, Texas.

1912 - September 19. Roy Davis charged with forgery in El Paso, Texas by judge E. B. McClintock, and was turned over to the grand jury on $500 bond.

1913 – August 6. Allie Lee Davis (Garrison) born August 6, 1913.

1915 - February 8. "Birth of a Nation" silent film released promoting the Ku Klux Klan as a heroic and Christian organization.

1915 - August 17. Leo Frank lynching in Georgia ignites the racial issues in the South.

1915 - August. Second Ku Klux Klan formed on Stone Mountain, GA. William Joseph Simmons declares himself the Imperial Wizard of the Invisible Empire. Roy Davis claims to have written the group's constitution and bylaws.

1916 - January 10. Roy E. Davis swindles the First State Bank of Boonsville.

1916 - March 10. Sheriff Lee Mann travels to Tipton, OK to find Roy Davis after a man by the same name was arrested. Mann issues a warrant in the states of Texas, Oklahoma, and Kansas.

1916 - March 10. Davis runs away to Georgia with a woman from Fort Worth.

1916 - Unknown month and day. Roy Davis (under alias Lon Davis) was given $25 to purchase an organ for the Fairview Baptist Church in Pickens County, Georgia. When the organ was never delivered, Roy claimed that he had purchased a different one for $35 to be delivered in its place. Davis left the community and the organ was never delivered.

1917 – Mrs. Chitwood (Formerly Miss Starett) in Georgia recognizes Roy Davis as he was using alias "Lon Davis." She writes Sheriff Mann and is offered $50 reward.

1917 - May 19. Roy E. Davis flees to Spartanburg, SC, and is arrested for the First State Bank of Boonsville, Texas swindling charge. Sheriff Mann of Wise County, TX came to Franklin County, Georgia to transfer him back to Texas.

1917 - June 29. Roy Davis goes to prison over bank swindle in Decatur, TX

1917 - Unknown month and day. Roy Davis gets new trial and the jury agrees to suspend his sentence for good behavior.

1919 - January 15. Lon Davis in Adairsville, GA debates W.H. Bird of Fort Payne, AL Church of Christ on church principals and doctrines.

1919 - Unknown month and day. Roy Davis indicted for the 1916 organ fraud from the Fairview Baptist Church, accused by W. J. James of Pickens County Georgia. When the case came to trial, Davis' attorney approached James and offered money if the trial was dismissed.

1920 - Summer. Roy Davis, under the alias "Lon Davis," becomes pastor of the Acworth Baptist church.

1921 - April 14. Rev. Lon Davis (editor) advertises his "The Progress" newspaper in Acworth, GA. Anti-Catholic rhetoric. Copies of the issue were sold for $1.00.

1921 - June. Roy Davis, under the alias Lon Davis, holds a Ku Klux Klan meeting at the Acworth Baptist Church.

1921 - July 7. Deacons of the Acworth Baptist Church, organized by Deacon H. M. Williams, vote to disbar Davis from the church after making his defense before the congregation.

1921 - July. H. M. Williams receives threatening letter from the Ku Klux Klan.

1921 - July 15. Roy Davis ousted by Acworth, GA Church after his being exposed as having swindled a bank in Texas, living a dual life, wife and child abandonment, and holding Ku Klux Klan meetings in the church.

1921 - August 2. Roy Davis preaching revival meetings in Shults, OK with a subject "What is your life in the home," promoting the idea that the Sabbath should become a legal holiday and that Americans today were desecrating the Sabbath.

1921 - August 3. Roy Davis purchases a new Ford automobile and it was announced in the McCurtain Gazette of Idabel, OK that he was a pastor in the town.

1921 - November 16. Roy Davis, wife, and daughter traveled to and returned from Detroit, Texas to Idabel OK.

1921 - Unknown month and day. Ex-Sheriff Lee Mann who arrested Roy Davis receives a threatening letter from the Ku Klux Klan in Georgia over his arrest of Davis.

1921 - September. United States Government proposed a full probe of the Ku Klux Klan over its secrecy and terroristic nature. Congressman William D. Upshaw stopped the probe through litigation. During the proceedings, it was made known that Upshaw was both a Klan member and personal friend to William Joseph Simmons.

1922 – May 30. Rev. Roy E. Davis unable to secure Convention Hall in Atlanta to lecture in the interest of the Ku Klux Klan

1922 – July 14. Dr. Roy E. Davis, "high Klan official" spoke at Malone Theatre speaking about the interests of the Ku Klux Klan. Mentioned "Closer relationship of pure Americanism". A large number of guests allegedly signed up to become members of the Ku Klux Klan

1922 - July 22. Dr. R.E. Davis K.K.K. lecturer in Poplar Bluff, MO, challenges Capt. C.D. Unsell to a debate on the virtues of the KKK. Appears to be a KKK membership drive. Davis gives address to interested people "K.K.K. City, Poplar Bluff American".

1922 - August 1. Roy E. Davis (Klan lecturer living in Atlanta GA) in Blytheville, Arkansas gives a debate speech at a baseball field (big turn-out by locals). He promotes K.K.K. virtues.

1923 - January 11. Roy Davis, as an official spokesman of the Ku Klux Klan, holding meetings with William Joseph Simmons meetings was denied use of an auditorium in Albany, GA

1923 - January 13. Roy Davis held Klan rally and claimed that the Invisible Empire was not anti-negro, anti-Catholic, or anti-Jewish.

1923 - February 17. Roy Davis opens The Brickbat in Meigs, GA to publish the principles of the Ku Klux Klan.

1923 - May 28. Roy E. Davis (editor of Brickbat) lambastes a grand jury ruling in Valdosta, GA on releasing 2 men attacking a fellow Klan member, J. McDonald. The 2 men got into a fight with McDonald when they asked where Roy E. Davis was. The sheriff stepped in and put guards around McDonald and Davis as protection.

1923 - May 29. Roy Davis is charged with fraud for the 1916 organ purchase for the Fairview Baptist Church

1923 - June 27. Roy Davis criminal libel as brickbat editor

1923 - June 30. Roy Davis fired from GA farmer's union after being exposed as having lived dual life in Texas and Georgia.

1923 – July 14. Rev. Roy Davis fired as Head of Georgia Farmer's Union for living a dual life.

1923 - August 17. Roy (aka Lonnie Davis) in Wichita Falls, TX is flogged with a wet rope by 5 unmasked men. Lonnie's brother Z.W. Davis says Lonnie is hospital and asks acting Texas Governor T.W. Davidson to investigate. Article states that Lonnie Davis is believed to be the same as the former president of the GA Farmer's Union and K.K.K. organizer in Valdosta, Meigs and Fitzgerald, GA. No reason given of the flogging, maybe more mischief or perhaps KKK members in Texas doling out a punishment.

1924 - February 29. Roy Davis addresses large crowd in Chattanooga, TN, on behalf of the Knights of The Flaming Sword. In his speech, Davis admits that he has been banished from the Ku Klux Klan. He spoke very harshly against Hiram W. Evans and claimed Evans' reorganization of the Klan was operated by Jews and foreigners.

1924 - October 5. Chattanooga, TN, Dr. R.E. Davis (former ambassador of the Knights of the Ku Klux Klan at Washington) is now the organizer of the Knights of The Flaming Sword. News article describes the Flaming Sword group as Anti-Klan. Knights of The Flaming Sword is Col. William Simmons's Klan group. Davis described Texas Klan members being converted to the Flaming Sword.

1925 - January 18. Dr. Roy E. Davis (Royal Ambassador of the Knights of The Flaming Sword) calls on members of the same group to quit. Cites the Flaming Sword is "dedicated to one proposition of accumulating millions for private individuals". In other words, it's a money scam.

1925 - January 23. Roy Davis defends Knights of the Flaming Sword after it was being accused of being a "money making order". Davis compares William Joseph Simmons to "Moses" of the Old Testament. Davis orders the group to disarm.

1925 - May 29. Tennessee Knights of The Flaming Sword turns against William Joseph Simmons. Roy Davis, former Royal Ambassador for the group is listed as living in Etowah, Tennessee. Davis orders the group to disband.

1925 - July 31. Nazarene church revival in Perry, OK

1927 - April 21. Nazarene church revival in Perry, OK

1928 - September 1. Nazarene church revival in Perry, OK

1929 - April 20. Parishioner in Roy Davis church divorces her husband. Husband blames Roy Davis.

1930 - February 5. Roy Davis sends a letter to the editor of the Louisville Courier Journal describing his church and protesting the government's strategy to enforce prohibition. Davis said that his church often had drunk men and Women sitting in each other's laps during service.

1930 - February 8. Local Baptist ministers write the Louisville Courier Journal to denounce Davis' views on alcohol and to declare him not aligned with Baptist policy.

1930 - March 20. Roy Davis accused of fraud in Louisville by Mrs. Minnie Burgin and was held on $300 bond.

1930 - March 22. Assistant Prosecutor William Bomar recommends fraud charges against Davis be dismissed.

1930 - October 10. Davis arrested for violation of the Mann Act after having taken Allie Lee Garrison (age 17) from Tennessee to Louisville for debauchery.

1930 - October 11. Roy E. Davis evangelist and singer is jailed on Mann Act charges in Louisville, KY. 40-year-old Davis brought 17-year-old Allie Lee Garrison (to be his wife later) across state lines from Chattanooga, TN. He was arrested in Jeffersonville, IN at a church revival meeting. Mann Act is a Federal offense and Davis was arraigned by a U.S. commissioner. The Mann Act or White Slavery Act of 1910 is a violation of bringing Women across state lines for prostitution or for sex.

1930 - October 12. Davis charged with violation of the Mann Act. Sixty Women showed up at court to protest

1930 - October 12. Davis hold joint revival with Ralph Rader. Davis claims to be a "former spiritualist" who is exposing other spiritualists.

1930 - October 14. Davis indicted by grand jury violation Mann act

1930 - November 3. Davis serves 10 days jail time after contempt of court when sixty Women disrupt his trial.

1931 - April 17. Roy Davis, Dan Davis, and Wilburn Lee Davis hold revival in Jeffersonville, Indiana.

1931 - April 18. Jeffersonville Evening News announces that Roy Davis was pushing the paper to print one-sided articles.

1931 - September 15. Davis charged with defrauding Miss Lelia Cain but was released on $11,000 bond.

1931 - September 25. Davis extradited from Jeffersonville to Louisville for defrauding Miss Lelia Cain. Jeffersonville newspaper states that Davis was choir director for Ralph Rader's services until Rader terminated him.

1931 - December 31. Davis places advertisement in the Louisville Courier Journal to purchase a printing press.

1932 - July 6. Davis' First Pentecostal Baptist Church of Jeffersonville enters the Southern Indiana Church Baseball League and defeats Henryville, Indiana 8 to 3.

1933 - May 23. Roy E. Davis Jr. and Sr. sell Adams Street, Louisville KY church property to L. Rothermel Kirwan.

1933 - William D. Upshaw holds meetings in Louisville, KY to promote prohibition.

1933 - February 4. Hope Brumbach (William's fiancé) leads devotional meeting in the Pentecostal Baptist Church.

1933 - February 18. William Branham described in newspaper advertisement as an elder of the Davis' Pentecostal Baptist Church.

1933 - February 25. Hope Brumbach (William's fiancé) leads the youth ministry in the Pentecostal Baptist Church.

1934 - March 30. Roy Davis sues several parties in Jeffersonville (including churches, their members, and cemeteries) for the estate of Laura Belle Eaken.

1935 - July 19. Roy Davis steals a piano and a pulpit from Reverend Walter Ulrey, head of the New Albany, Indiana and Louisville, KY Volunteers of America.

1935 - August 13. Roy Davis sued by Rev. Ulrey. 250 people came to the trial.

1938 - Unknown month and day. Roy E. Davis arrested in Hot Springs, AR for disturbing the peace. Ordered to leave town.

1939 - January 13. Rev. Roy E. Davis is ordered extradited from Louisville, KY to Hot Springs, AR on charges of removing a car from a Mrs. Gay in Hot Springs (crossing state lines in stolen vehicle). Davis jumped bond in Jeffersonville, IN on same charge, till they caught him in Louisville. Claims Mrs. Gay gave him permission to take the car out of Arkansas. Also claimed "those in control" in Hot Springs sought his return in because of his participation in a murder investigation. Roy states "I won't live if I go back (Hot Springs), I believe I'll be ambushed". No reason given for that statement, perhaps a KKK deal?

1943 - September 15. Ussher-Davis Foundation opened in San Bernardino. Actress Elizabeth Ussher, Roy Davis, and William D. Upshaw primary board members. Other members include Fred M. Barton, former head of a boys' school in Oklahoma, and George Pearson of Upland, CA.

1944 - February 21. after Davis' arrest in the Ussher-Davis Orphanage scam, the Riverside Press (CA) states the FBI records show that Davis had a long record. Police Chief Eugene Mueller says Davis was arrested in Louisville, KY in 1930 on charges of obtaining money under false pretenses. No disposition of that case was mentioned. In 1938, Davis was again arrested in Hot Springs for disturbing the peace, but the prosecution was dismissed. Davis was then ordered to leave town. In 1939, he was taken into custody on the mortgaged property (Mrs. Gay's car) offense. No disposition of that case mentioned.

1944 - February 22. Complaints filed against Roy Davis by J. T. Williamson, former superintendent of the Ussher-Davis Foundation, and Lena Robertson for failure to pay wages. Roy Davis, his wife Allie, and George W. Mooney were arrested.

1944 - February 26. Roy Davis accused of mail tampering and theft of money donated by Mrs. Caroline McLeod to her son.

1944 - February 28. Roy Davis charged for grand theft. Bail was set at $11,000 and Davis was held at the Upland jail. Davis was unable to post bond.

1944 - March 4. Roy Davis issued plea for reduction of $16,000 bail. Judge Charles L. Allison granted a writ of habeas corpus.

1944 - March 15. Roy Davis charged for petty theft and illegal possession of a firearm as a convicted felon.

1944 - April 18. Roy Davis went on trial before Federal Judge Pierson M. Hall for impersonating an F. B. I. agent. Davis claimed that he experienced "divine revelation" telling him to obtain $85,00 from Miss Elizabeth Ussher, which she gave after he convinced her that he was an agent for the Federal Bureau of Investigation. Assistant U. S. Attorney Llewellyn J. Moses presented the case as prosecuting attorney.

1944 - April 20. Roy Davis testified by written letter that a "vision" came to him while he was eating a peach, in which he saw the orphanage. Miss Elizabeth Ussher remembered his story, but testified that it was an orange, not a peach, that brought the vision.

1944 - April 27. Roy Davis petitioned for another writ of habeas corpus, filed by Attorneys Julius J. Novack and Joseph T. Ciano.

1944 - May 6. Two petty theft charges were dismissed after one of the witnesses disappeared, and bail was reduced to $2500. Chief Criminal District Attorney Theo G. Krumm said that the Rev. Mr. Davis was convicted of a felony in the crime of swindling in Texas in 1918. Davis was held on gun charges.

1949 - June 15. Dan Davis, Roy's Brother, dies in Louisville. Dan was named as the former head of the East Market Street Mission. He was for 10 years a Pentecostal minister.

1950 - March, 16. Roy Davis hold revival at Assembly of God Church in Grandbury Texas. David listed as a "Baptist preacher filled with the Holy Ghost".

1950 - October. Roy Davis gives a testimony for the Voice of Healing publication. Voice of Healing was created by Gordon Lindsay to promote the ministry of William Branham. In the article, Davis declares himself to be William Branham's first pastor, who introduced Branham to the Pentecostal faith. He preached Branham's ordination sermon, signed his ordination certificate, and heard Branham preach his first sermon. Davis claimed he was the first to watch Branham pray for the sick. Roy referred to William Branham as his "Timothy," referring to the Biblical helper under Apostle Paul's mentorship. Davis states that he was a member of the Ft Worth, Texas Chamber of Commerce and Executive Committee. He claims that he was born in Fort Worth and named his business manager as J. F. Owens. Davis lists his address as 3404 So. Main Street, Ft. Worth, Texas.

1951 - April 13. In Phoenix, AZ, William Branham refers to and confirms the Voice of Healing article

1951 - June 4. In Connersville, Indiana, William Branham confirms being ordained by Roy Davis. He claimed that William D. Upshaw (who had been walking on crutches for decades) entered his prayer line in a wheelchair, and that Roy Davis was the one who sent Upshaw into the meeting.

1953 - September 7. In Chicago, IL, William Branham describes being in a revival meeting with Davis. According to Branham, Davis walked up to the platform and challenged the speaker by asking them to take sulfuric acid. Branham claimed that he had a statement describing the event sealed by a notary public.

1953 - November 30. In West Palm Beach, FL, William Branham describes Roy Davis' introduction of William D. Upshaw, and claimed that Upshaw was for sixty-six years an invalid in a wheelchair confined to crutches and a bed.

1955 - February 27. In Phoenix, AZ, William Branham describes Roy E. Davis as a Doctor [of Divinity] out of Dallas Texas. He describes being ordained as an elder at Davis' church in Jeffersonville, IN.

1955 - October 7. R.E. Davis Sr. advertises his sermon or lecture on "From Darkness to Light" at the Mt. Ashburn Church of Christ in Dallas. The church was located at 712 Parkview Ave. at the corner of Lindsley street.

1955 - October 13. a new Church of Christ is opened at the Odd Fellow's Hall located on 611 1/2 East 10th street in Oak Cliff (Dallas). R.E. Davis Sr., evangelist and debater will be the minister for the opening service.

1956 - July 11. the Odd Fellows on 611 1/2 East 10th street in Oak Cliff (Dallas) announced their elected officers. Dallas District Attorney Henry C. Wade gives the big speech. R.E. Davis is elected chaplain.

1956 - December 15. In Parkersburg, WV, William Branham describes William D. Upshaw as being confined to his wheelchair for sixty-six years. According to Branham, Upshaw was a Vice President of the Southern Baptist Convention. Branham describes an "Aunt Jemima" disrupting the meeting with a big scream, "knocking ushers right and left" as she came to the platform.

1957 - January 20. In Jeffersonville, IN, William Branham mentions a phrase Davis commonly used: Like pouring peas on a dry cowhide"

1957 - January 25. In Lima, OH, William Branham described Roy Davis as a preacher of "Divine Healing." (The same type of ministry Branham himself claimed to have.)

1957 - March 6. R.E. Davis Sr. writes a letter to the editor in the Dallas Morning News. He praises Dallas District Attorney Henry C. Wade, tells people to quit meddling in Wade's business. Note: Henry Wade gave a speech to the Odd Fellows.

1957 - March 6. In Phoenix, AZ, William Branham describes Doctor [of Divinity] Roy Davis as his teacher. Branham claimed that Davis was a lawyer before his conversion and "took everything from a legal standpoint in the Bible." He describes Davis sticking his finger up his mouth during the service if he disagreed with Branham's statements. Branham claimed Davis described several of his cases when he was practicing law.

1957 - April 7. In Jeffersonville, IN, William Branham described William D. Upshaw as having a broken back forced to be moved around in a wheelchair for sixty-six when Roy Davis sent him to see Branham.

1957 - July 27. In Tacoma, WA, William Branham describes being ordained in the Missionary Baptist Church. He describes Davis as a minister from Big Springs,

Texas. He claimed that Davis' church in Jeffersonville was not of the Pentecostal faith as Davis claimed, but sovereign Baptist.

1957 - September 8. In Jeffersonville, IN, William Branham describes Roy Davis' printing press in Jeffersonville, and the "paper" that Davis printed. Branham claims that the press and paper was burned with fire while it was printing copies. Branham claimed that this was in response to Davis calling him a "puppet." Then he compared Davis to the Bible as the fulfillment of the parable of the man sewing seed dressed in white.

1957 - December 29. In Jeffersonville, IN, William Branham describes conversing with Davis after his alleged angelic visitation (1945).

1958 - February 21. Roy Davis Sr. gives speech at the Danish Room in the Adolphus Hotel in downtown Dallas to the Oak Cliff White Citizens Council about the impending School Integration issue. Stated "he would rather die or be put in prison then allow Negro children be integrated with White children in Dallas White Schools".

1958 - March 25. In Middletown, OH, William Branham describes conversing with Davis after his alleged angelic visitation (1945).

1958 - May 18. Roy Davis signs petition circulated by Rev. Carey Daniel (President of White Citizens Council of America) along with 330 other Dallas Clergy. Petitions states: "I believe forced Integration is wrong and I am opposed to the mixing of White and Negro children in our public schools".

1958 - May 21. In Bangor, ME, William Branham described being ordained in Roy Davis' church. Branham describes Davis sending Upshaw to his meeting for healing.

1958 - Jun. According to an FBI document (confidential informant) states the Roy E. Davis Sr. Grand Dragon, broke away from the U.S. Klans, Knights of the Ku Klux Klan organization and formed the Original Knights Of The Ku Klux Klan. Eldon Lee Edwards, Grand Wizard (Atlanta, GA) visits Dallas and convinces Klan members there to rejoin the U.S. Klans, Knights of the Ku Klux Klan. Dallas Klan members were disgruntled with Davis over mishandling funds. Note: Davis had a cross burning at his home in Dallas in 1958 and had to call the Dallas Police out. Most likely it was these disgruntled Dallas Klan members. The U.S. Klans, Knights of the Ku Klux Klan was Eldon Lee Edwards consolidation Klan effort made up of various chapters of KKK in the south. Edwards died in 1960.

1958 - June 20. Roy Davis Sr. is elected President of the Oak Cliff White Citizens Council (OCWCC) as per FBI document. In another FBI document it is noted that the "vehement" members of the Texas White Citizens Council left that group to join OCWCC, because the Texas White Citizens Council was made up with a bunch of lawyers that only wanted to sign petitions. Other members include Addie Barlow Frazier (Dixie Leber).

1958 - June 25. Rev. R.E. Davis shows up at a Dallas School Board meeting along with 2 other members of the OCWCC, Addie Barlow Frazier (Dixie Leber) and Lloyd S. Riddle. Also, in attendance was Earl Thornton (Klan member, JBS, owner of Thornton Electric). They discussed Integration and segregation. Two black men also showed up, a Prophet M.D Willet (preacher from Little Rock, AR) and local Dallas NAACP rep, Edwin C. Washington. Washington is booed by the white segregationists.

1958 - August 26. According to an FBI document, Roy E. Davis makes a trip to Little Rock, Arkansas and gives some membership papers unknowingly to an FBI KKK informant for safekeeping. Appears Davis was perhaps making another membership drive for his Original Knights of The Ku Klux Klan. Names revealed were Dallas men, one of them was M.H. Brumley. Brumley was a Dallas Police Intelligence detective and most likely a plant by the DPD to gain information on the Dallas KKK. Dallas Police Jesse Curry mentioned he used his cops at times to join these extremist groups for Intel reasons.

1959 - March 28. Roy E. Davis is interviewed by UP reporter in Dallas. Davis declares himself as a retired Baptist preacher and Imperial Klan Dragon of the KKK in Texas, Oklahoma and Arkansas (most likely the Original Knights of The Ku Klux Klan, as reporter was not aware of KKK groups or terminology). Davis exaggerates the Dallas County Klan membership at 40-45,000 strong (see February 11, 1961). Also, he tells reporter that some of his Klan members are State legislators, primarily from East Texas. Davis also says he has policemen, lawyers and ministers in his Klan group. Davis also claims membership in Houston area around 1,000 strong. He tells reporter that he instructed his Klan members not to be involved with the Little Rock, Arkansas crisis (school Integration). States: The Little Rock crisis was probably brought about by Communists. We believe the doctrines of the NAACP are opposed to the concept of Americanism and are Communist inspired in several instances". Davis is clearly lying to this reporter on his membership and exaggerating his position for PR purposes.

1959 - April 9. In Los Angeles, CA, Lily Upshaw, William D. Upshaw's widow, attends one of William Branham's meetings. Branham described Roy Davis sending Upshaw to Branham for healing.

1959 - April 19. In Los Angeles, CA, William Branham describes meeting his first wife Hope Brumbach (leader of the youth ministry in Davis' church in Jeffersonville), and describes their first visit to Davis' Missionary [Pentecostal] Baptist Church. Though he was an elder and ordained in it, Branham claimed that he never joined Davis's church. He claimed that Davis ordained him, and he became the minister of his own tabernacle.

1959 - May 20. Roy E. Davis, National Imperial Dragon of the Ku Klux Klan in a UPI dispatch from Dallas said the Klan were not responsible for a bunch of posters that were posted in and around the city of Texarkana. Evidently the posters had death threats on them. He told the UPI reporter that he had been in the Klan for 43 years (back to 1916) and condemns the posters.

1959 - May 28. in Texarkana, TX, Roy E. Davis identified himself as the Imperial Dragon of the National Original Knights of The Ku Klux Klan. He said recruiting posters found in Texarkana were not from his group, but from an Arkansas group of wannabe Klan members headed up by a Texarkana attorney (George F. Edwards).

413

Davis said Edwards was ejected by him. The Arkansas group also consisted of Minutemen.

1959 - May 30. George F. Edwards is interviewed in Texarkana concerning his KKK group. Edwards responds to Roy E. Davis' charge of the Association of Arkansas Klans was made up of banished Klansmen with Edwards in charge. The Texarkana Gazette called for all lawyers to banish any lawyer associated with the KKK. Edwards admits new interest in his group due to the posters in Texarkana.

1959 - June 7. the Arkansas Gazette does a story on the Klan. It cites a revival of the KKK in 1955, due mostly to the Supreme Court "Brown vs. Board of Education" school Integration. The article goes through the various KKK groups in 1959, and names U.S. Klans, Knights of the Ku Klux Klan (Eldon Lee Edwards, Atlanta, GA) as having a nationwide membership from 12-15,000. The article cites the Rylie, TX unit as being affiliated with U.S. Klans, Knights of the Ku Klux Klan. From there it cites Roy E. Davis as being a member of that Rylie, TX U.S. Klans, Knights of the Ku Klux Klan. However, the article states that Roy E. Davis was expelled from that group.

1959 - June 9. in Little Rock, Arkansas, A.C. Hightower declares himself as the Grand Dragon of the newly chartered (1 week old) U.S. Klans, Knights of the Ku Klux Klan in Arkansas. This is Eldon Lee Edward's united Klan (Atlanta, GA). Arkansas is very leary of the Klan and fought to keep it out. Even Arkansas Governor Fabus, an ardent racist who fought the Little Rock Central High School Integration efforts, publicly bad-mouthed them. Hightower states Roy E. Davis was banished from the Klan (most likely U.S. Klans, Knights of the Ku Klux Klan). The article goes on to explain the other Arkansas Klan group out of Texarkana is Association of Arkansas Klans with its only member, George F. Edwards (Davis' nemesis).

1959 - July 7. In Cleveland, TN, William Branham described being ordained by Doctor [of Divinity] Roy E. Davis.

1959 - Unknown month and day. Roy E. Davis writes a scorching letter to his KKK nemesis in Texarkana, lawyer George F. Edwards. Davis heard through some of his Klan members meeting at the Odd Fellows in Texarkana (Texas side) about Edwards bad-mouthing him. He challenges Edwards to a debate and asks him to bring his "ADL" literature (Jewish Anti-Deformation League). He signs the letter R.E. Davis, National Imperial Dragon, Knights of the Original Ku Klux Klan.

1959 - Unknown month and day. Letter sent to "Patriots and Klansmen of Arkansas" warning them to beware of Davis' enemies George F. Edwards (Texarkana lawyer), Eldon Lee Edwards (Grand Wizard of the US Klans in Atlanta), and the ADL. The letter was sent on behalf of the "Original Ku Klux Klan."

1959 - August 24. 200 gather to hear Florida's leader of the Ku Klux Klan. Imperial Wizard "Lon" Davis unmasked himself before the crowd.

1960 - October 10. R.E. Davis writes letter to editor in Dallas Morning News titled "Back Turned on South". Davis states he always supported the Democratic party but will not support the Kennedy-Johnson presidential ticket. Praises the Morning News for endorsement or support of Vice-President Nixon.

414

1960 - December 11. In Jeffersonville, IN, Branham describes being baptized by Roy E. Davis under the Oneness Pentecostal baptism of "the Name of the Lord Jesus Christ" when he was a child.

1961 - January 1. In Jeffersonville, IN, William Branham describes Roy Davis singing "Steal Away and Pray with Jesus."

1961 - April 7. Roy E. Davis arrested in Shreveport, LA, for Klan activities. It was learned that several in his Klan organization had criminal record, and the police had a copy of Davis' long arrest record.

1961 - February 10. the Arkansas Gazette (Little Rock) states a big Klan membership drive was underway in Northwestern Louisiana. The paper reports R.E. Davis, self-styled National Imperial Wizard of the Original Knights of The Ku Klux Klan had been in Louisiana for 6 months and several days in Shreveport. Davis states that the Shreveport area had 1,000 men strong and 3 more charters were to be issued. Davis went on to explain that he will be organizing a Woman's Unit called the White Karmellia next week. Davis says the Klan's aims are "were to fight for states' rights, constitutional government and White Supremacy". Davis also said, "Negroes were turning the White Man's government into a Mongrel government". He went on to say the Klan would not let them do it, regardless of what this statement may imply". The Times (Shreveport) newspaper featured Roy E. Davis wearing a white Klan robe. Davis said that "he is the only Klansman who can boast having all the degrees of the Klan conferred on him. He said that he helped write the constitution, by-laws, and ritual of the original Klan when it was revived in 1915."

1961 - February 11. R.E. Davis Sr. is interviewed by Dallas Morning News on Klan in Texas. Davis claims Klan membership in Texas is small. Davis denies he did any membership drives in Louisiana (LIE) and was not connected with the Overton Brooks cross burning incident in Shreveport. Davis also states he does not condone lawlessness. Also, he said the Klan would do every legal thing possible to fight school Integration.

1961 - February 16. Newsmen were blind-folded and taken to a Klan meeting in a wooden area near Shreveport, LA. Roy Davis was not present, but claims there were 5 chapters of his Original Knights of The Ku Klux Klan in Northwest Louisiana.

1961 - April 13. In Bloomington, IL, William Branham describes Roy Davis sending Congressman Upshaw into his meeting in Los Angeles California. Branham claimed that he saw a vision of the former congressman being healed.

1961 - April 7. R.E. Davis is questioned in Shreveport, LA over the Democrat Louisiana Representative Overton Brooks home cross burning incident on February 8, 1961. Suspected Original Knights of The Ku Klux Klan members were involved. Imperial Wizard Davis states he suspected Shreveport members of his KKK did it. Davis claims there are 35 chapters of his Original Knights of The Ku Klux Klan in Louisiana with big ones in New Orleans and Baton Rouge. It appears that Davis is not in control of his Klan group.

1961 - April 25. In Chicago, IL, William Branham claimed that he left Roy Davis' Baptist Church to become Pentecostal. Though Davis introduced him into his "first

Pentecostal assembly," Branham claimed that he knew nothing about the Pentecostals until he saw a vision and left Davis' church.

1961 - June 1. In Jeffersonville, IN, William Branham describes Roy Davis' church in Jeffersonville being burnt to the ground. He claimed that afterward, the people were "scattered sheep without a shepherd."

1962 - March. Roy E. Davis is identified as one of the picketers at the Dallas Theater Center in Highland Park (Dallas). Dallas Police said Roy Davis and Charles Powell Sr. (JBS member) were responsible for the protest. The picketers were protesting the plays showing there as Communist inspired. A mysterious committee wrote Paul Ragiordosky (Dallas Theater Center President) some condemnation letters about communist playwrights and actors. Ragiordosky turned the letters over to the FBI and the FBI contacted Dallas Police. The FBI revealed the Dallas Police identified Davis while monitoring the protest. The FBI also revealed the U.S. Klans, Knights of the Ku Klux Klan (Eldon Lee Edward's Klan Atlanta, GA) through an informant that this group charted it's U.S. Klans, Knights of the Ku Klux Klan Realm of Texas Klavern in Rylie (suburb of Dallas) on December 12, 1957. They used the cover group name of Soldiers of the Flaming Sword as not to call attention to them as a KKK group (obvious old Roy Davis KKK name). Roy Davis left this group in June of 1958 and started his Original Knights of The Ku Klux Klan. In 1959, the U.S. Klans, Knights of the Ku Klux Klan was falling apart and without a Texas Klan leader. Grady S. Frazier (not sure if related or married to Dixie Leber) was trying to lead and reorganize the group. Grady S. Frazier ran a Texaco Service Station in Dallas.

1962 - November 11. In Jeffersonville, IN, William Branham describes being ordained by Roy Davis. He claims that he separated from Davis over doctrinal teaching.

1963 - July 21. In Jeffersonville, IN, William Branham describes Roy Davis as a personal friend who baptized him. He compared Davis' baptizing him to John baptizing Jesus.

1963 - August 3. In Chicago, IL, William Branham described Davis ordaining and baptizing him. Again, Branham compared Davis' baptizing him to John baptizing Jesus.

1963 - November 14. In New York, NY, William Branham described Davis ordaining and baptizing him. Again, Branham compared Davis' baptizing him to John baptizing Jesus. Immediately afterwards, a woman begins to speak in tongues.

1963 - November 30. In Shreveport, LA, William Branham described Roy Davis ordaining him and sending William D. Upshaw for healing. Branham claimed that he never heard of Upshaw.

1964 - February 9. In Bakersfield, CA, William Branham describes being ordained by Roy Davis in Davis' Missionary [Pentecostal] Baptist Church.

1964 - March 8. In Dallas, TX, William Branham is expecting Roy Davis to be in attendance at the meeting. He describes Davis as his teacher, and the one who baptized him into the Pentecostal faith at Davis' Missionary [Pentecostal] Baptist Church. Branham describes Davis as being from Fort Worth, TX.

1964 - March. Original Knights of The Ku Klux Klan records burned.

1964 - April 12. In Birmingham, AL, William Branham described being ordained by Doctor [of Divinity] Roy E. Davis from Fort Worth Texas. At the end of the sermon, Branham holds a mock court trial, and paints a picture of calling William D. Upshaw as his witness. He claims Upshaw told him that he was the head speaker for the Southern Baptist Convention, and that Doctor [of Divinity] Roy E. Davis sent Upshaw to the meeting.

1964 - April 27. In Tucson, AZ, William Branham described being ordained as a minister by Doctor [of Divinity] Roy E. Davis at age 17. (1925 or 1926). Branham claimed that Davis' church burned down at the time he was the assistant pastor, and that Davis moved to the mountains near Van Horn, TX.

1964 - August 30. In Jeffersonville, IN, William Branham recognized "Brother Fleeman" who was a member of Roy Davis' congregation. Branham asks if he remembers Kenneth Adcock, and describes a picture he has of them together with Doctor [of Divinity] Roy E. Davis. He also asks "Brother Fleeman" if he remembers F. F. Bosworth.

1965 - February 18. In Jeffersonville, IN, William Branham described preaching on the same grounds where Roy Davis was a pastor. Branham described being an elder in Davis' church.

1965 - May 18. The Federal Bureau of Investigation claimed that Mississippi residents made every effort to "frustrate" agents investigating the murder of three Civil Rights workers. The F. B. I. was investigating the murders of Michael Schwerner, Andrew Goodman, and James Chaney who disappeared after being held on a traffic violation. It was announced that the main Klan organization in Louisiana was led by Wizard Roy E. Davis.

1965 - June 26. Original Knights of The Ku Klux Klan investigated for arms deal by the Internal Revenue Service. Roy E. Davis listed as leader of the organization whose headquarters in Jonesboro, LA.

1965 - October 20. Leadership of the Original Knights of The Ku Klux Klan in Bogalusa, LA was passed from Royal Virgil Young Sr. (a former railroad engineer) to Roy E. Davis of Jonesboro, LA. The group reported 1000 members.

1966 - Roy E. Davis Sr. dies August 12, 1966. He is buried at Restland Memorial Park cemetery in Dallas.

1967 - December 11. The Present-Day Ku Klux Klan Movement Report is presented to the Ninetieth Congress First Session by the Committee on Un-American Activities. The report describes Roy Davis reactivating the Ku Klux Klan in Louisiana in 1960 after the state having no effective activity for several decades. Davis held the title of Imperial Wizard of the Original Ku Klux Klan

2004 - Allie Lee Davis died November 7, 2004. She is buried next to Roy Davis Sr. at Restland Memorial Park cemetery in Dallas.

MORE BOOKS BY JOHN COLLINS

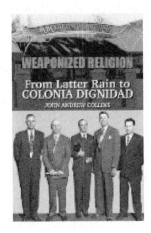

The Latter Rain Movement of the late 1940s and 1950s created a new breed of Pentecostalism that dramatically impacted Christianity in the United States as well as many other countries around the world. Initially viewed as a movement by God, a number of well-respected men and women participated in the movement during its early years. Over time, however, many of those same men and women came to realize that there were wolves among the sheep. Political ideologies not aligned with sound biblical theology crept into the movement, causing the group to explode into several splinter groups. New sects were created, and while some of them reformed, others became very destructive and militant. Such is the case with Paul Schäfer Schneider, leader of the Colonia Dignidad compound in Chile. When Schäfer's Pentecostal community was raided by government officials, it was discovered that the men and women dressed in the style of Pentecostal-holiness fashion had been manufacturing, selling, and using weapons — including sarin gas — all from what appeared to be a humble religious community. Schäfer was the leader of a splinter group of "The Message", the cult following of William Marrion Branham, aka William Marvin Branham, from Jeffersonville, Indiana.

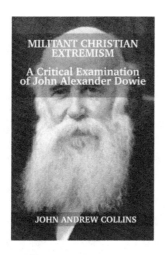

Thoroughly Documented Expose of an Early Charismatic Charlatan. I have spent the last 6 years studying Pentecostalism and started asking, who were the real pioneers of the modern-day signs and wonders movement. John Alexander Dowie truly is the grandfather of the American movement and sets the stage for every charlatan after. This book shows just how extreme, dishonest, and dangerous John Alexander Dowie was and why the movement following him continued to practice such manipulative tactics, such as Dowie's students John G Lake and Frank Sanford. Excellently written.
- Ralph E Brickley Jr

Outstanding research of a shadowy figure. I really love and appreciate this book! When I was involved in Pentecostal circles, for the most part they presented a sanitized version of Dowie's history. It seemed to me he was presented as a revered figure. Somebody to be emulated. As mentioned in the description of this book Dowie influenced directly or indirectly so many of the Pentecostal leaders and founders of the early 20th Century. (See the description for the names) And in turn I might add other luminaries who followed such as Hagin, Copeland, Price, and a slew of others. As well as so many televangelists of today.
- Steven Johnson

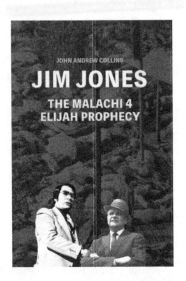

A Must Read for Charismatics. Very engaging from the very beginning! A must read if you are a Charismatic or Pentecostal. Really sheds light on why there is so much corruption and sin in the current Charismatic Movement, i.e., Todd Bentley, John Crowder, Jason Westerfield, Benny Hinn, David Tomberlain, etc. It's those who have and obey His commandments who will inherit the kingdom, not "miracle" workers who only say "Lord, Lord!"
- John Taylor

It was very insightful. Eye-opening to some of our American church Pentecostal history. I have bought multiple copies of this book. I think its content is so important. it warns us about the dangers of extra-biblical teaching and the following of personalities. In my opinion, it should be read by every Pentecostal- charismatic believer. We need to face the real history, of our movements, whether good or bad, I highly recommend this book! Couldn't put it down!
- Brian Pond

Made in the USA
Coppell, TX
31 December 2023

27092927R00246